T0375319

LADY LIBERTY

LADY LIBERTY

THE ANCIENT GODDESS OF AMERICA

Richard N. Rhoades
MA. DIV.

Lady Liberty
The Ancient Goddess of America

iUniverse books may be ordered through booksellers or by contacting:

iUniverse
1663 Liberty Drive
Bloomington, IN 47403
www.iuniverse.com
1-800-Authors (1-800-288-4677)

ISBN: 978-1-4759-7485-0 (sc)
ISBN: 978-1-4759-7487-4 (hc)
ISBN: 978-1-4759-7486-7 (e)

Print information available on the last page.

iUniverse rev. date: 12/14/2015

Photos and Art Illustrations
Art Illustrations were done by Sharon Higgins, Southwestern Artist who lives in Albuquerque, New Mexico: pages, 24 (2), 25, 27, 28 (2), 29, 48, 49, 56, 63, 70, 75, 76 (1), 77, 78, 84, 165, 166, 167, 170, 171, 176 (3), 177, 181, 203 (2), 206, 219, 265.
American Library, Paris: pages, 207, 214.
American Numismatic Society: page, 38.
Art Resources: page, 115.
Grand Orient de Paris: pages, 178, 181.
Holman Bible Atlas, Thomas Brisco © 1998, Broadman & Holman Publishers: page, 4.
Library of Congress:
Pages, 61, 134, 192, 195, 222.
Mairie de Paris: page, 116.
New York Public Library: pages, 190, 194.
National Park Service, Statue of Liberty National Monument: pages, 160, 164, 192, 193, 205, 208, 216, 220, 226, 237.
Wikimedia Commons: pages, 7, 54, 55, 56, 57, 64, 65, 66, 67, 71, 73, 179, 188, 189, 202, 229, 233, 236, 237, 259, 284, 285, 334, 342.

Scripture quotations marked AKJV are from the Authorized King James Version of the Bible.

Scripture quotations marked JPS are from the Tanakh, published by The Jewish Publication Society.

Scripture quotations marked NASV are from the New American Standard Bible © 1960, 1962, 1963, 1968, 1971, 1972, 1973, 1975, 1977, 1995 by the Lockman Foundation. Used by permission.

Contents

Other Works by

Richard N. Rhoades

★

FAITH

Of The Ages

The Hebraic Roots

Of The Christian Faith

★

The Babylon Code

Is AMERICA In Prophecy?

★ www.ladylibertybooks.net

To the Lord God Adonai; then to my mother Thelma Rhoades, whose love and belief in me never wavered; then to my wife Judith Rhoades, whose love and advice has been a great source of comfort and council; and then to that vast army of American Patriots who, regardless of the personal cost, dedicated their lives to the preservation of the great moral and spiritual values on which this nation was founded.

Acknowledgements

Dᴜʀɪɴɢ ᴛʜᴇ ᴛᴇɴ ʏᴇᴀʀs of researching and writing for this work there were many who assisted me and need to be acknowledged. First and foremost is my wife Judith, whose love and encouragement has been like a solid rock. Marion Lynch of Albuquerque, New Mexico, advised me in the initial manuscript writing. Sharon Higgins, the gifted Southwestern Artist, who lives in Albuquerque, unselfishly gave of her time and talent to provide the many art illustrations. Gale Anderson, of Las Cruces, New Mexico, advised me on the editing of the manuscript. Rick Lastrapes, who lives in Albuquerque, graciously gave of his time to proof-read the manuscript and offer helpful suggestions.

Then there are the many researchers, authors and publishers, who have recorded and published their works for posterity. Without their tireless dedication, research, and publication of their works this book would never have been possible.

I am also indebted to the many libraries across this great country. Staff members, such as those working in the National Park Service of the Statue of Liberty National Monument, the Library of Congress, the New York Public Library, Atlanta Public Library, Albuquerque, Roswell, and Las Cruces libraries in New Mexico, Sacramento, Marysville and Yuba City libraries in California, as well as libraries in Paris, France, such as the American Library and Mairie de Paris Library, were extremely helpful in providing photos, articles and relevant data for this book.

I dare not forget the Joseph Good, founder of *Hatikva Ministries,* who first introduced me to this subject while teaching on *God's*

Learning Channel, located in Midland, Texas. Nor should I fail to mention Al and Tommie Cooper, who were instrumental in bringing this subject to my attention through their Southwest TV broadcasts. Had they not been faithful to their callings this book would have never been written.

Finally, I want to thank the Lord God Adonai. Had He not provided the inspiration, direction and guidance during the past seventeen years the completion of this book would have been an impossible task.

Preface

O<small>N</small> O<small>CTOBER</small> 28, 1886, a new era began in America's quest for liberty. On that wet and foggy morning in New York City almost one million people gathered in the streets and along the harbor to watch 20,000 military, government, and civilian marchers as they paraded in celebration of America's new icon, *Liberty Enlightening the World*. On that historic day the twenty year old dream of the French Professor Edouard-Rene Lefebvre Laboulaye (1811-1883) and the celebrated French sculptor Frederic Auguste Bartholdi (1834-1904) became a reality.

Once again the leaders of both France and America came together in a united cause. Only this time it was to dedicate the gigantic statue named *Liberty Enlightening the World* now standing atop its own pedestal on Bedloe's Island in New York Harbor. As the ceremony began dignitaries took their bows and made their speeches. Finally, with a wave of the hand and a tug on a rope a huge French flag slid off the statue's massive head, revealing *Liberty Enlightening the World* in all her glory. The crowds cheered, ships in the harbor blew their horns, and the military gave America's new Goddess of Liberty a twenty-one gun salute.

For the elite of Freemasonry the dedication of *Liberty Enlightening the World* was much more than the dedication of a gigantic statue. It was the dedication of a hallowed Masonic shrine of the Great Goddess of antiquity.

For Bartholdi, who was a lover of the great statutory works of antiquity, the dedication of *Liberty Enlightening the World,* in New York Harbor, was much more than the realization of a long-awaited dream. It was a historic symbol that linked together the people of the New World with ancient civilizations, which had built and erected statues of this same female deity thousands of years earlier at the gateways of their own cities.

For most Americans, *Liberty Enlightening the World* was simply a gigantic statue that was given as a gift to America from the people of France. It's true that the French people did contribute financially to the Liberty project. It's true that the French government did play an important role in the formal transfer and safe conduct of Bartholdi's gigantic statue to New York Harbor. But as you shall soon see, the real movers behind the conception, building, and erection of America's treasured icon, *Liberty Enlightening the World* (the statue's original French Masonic name), on Bedloe's Island (now Liberty Island), belonged to the secret society of Freemasons, on both sides of the Atlantic.

The Secret Society of Freemasonry

According to the elite of Freemasonry, the building and erection of *Liberty Enlightening the World* was the most significant event since King Solomon's building of the Temple. Equally significant, Masonry's elite claim that Masons are the descendants of Hiram, King of Tyre, who was initiated into the "Ancient Mysteries," and assisted King Solomon in the building of the Temple.[1]

Masonic tradition holds that one day three rebel craftsmen from Hiram's crew tried to force Hiram to reveal the password of the master builder's degree. He refused. One worker with a gauge struck him in the throat. A second worker, struck him in the breast with a square. Hiram was killed by a third worker, who had a maul.

Within Masonry, Hiram is regarded as a martyr, who was the great example of protecting secrets. Albert G. Mackey, a Thirty-third Degree Mason and former Secretary General of the Supreme Council for the Southern Jurisdiction of the United States, describes Hiram as "a cunning man, endued with understanding (2 Chron. 2:13) . . . filled with wisdom and understanding, and cunning to work all works in brass" (1 Kings 7:13-14).[1]

According to Mackey, Hiram was, most likely, acquainted with the Dionysian fraternity in Tyre, a society of the "Ancient Mysteries". As a result of Hiram's affiliation with the sect, he was able to communicate those "Ancient Mysteries" to the Jewish builders of the Temple.[2]

Thus the name "Hiramites" is a name bestowed upon Freemasons to indicate their line of descent from Hiram, especially those of the Twenty-first Degree.[3]

For the vast majority of Freemasons the secret society of Freemasonry is merely an Order made-up of like-minded men and women whose primary purpose is to make a significant contribution to their community and country. But to the elite of Freemasonry, the symbols, rites, and blood oaths are meant to conceal the "Ancient Mysteries" and "inner doctrines" of the Craft, to which the rank and file are never made known.

In an organization that has a graduated system of thirty-three degrees, seventy-five percent of adherents never advance beyond the Third Degree. Between the Fourth and Thirty-third Degrees are those considered to be of the "right mind," who have influence in society, right up to the presidents of the United States. And, unlike other degrees, in the Scottish Rite, the Thirty-third Degree cannot be earned; it can only be bestowed by the Supreme Council.

Thus in Scottish Rite Freemasonry the Council controls who becomes a member of the "inner circle". In this, the elite of Freemasonry attempt to attract the most influential members of society with an "outer doctrine," while concealing the hidden secrets of an "inner doctrine" reserved for the "inner circle".

For the elite of the elite, however, the Thirty-third Degree is still not the top of the Order. Because there are the Illuminati levels above that (and even the Thirty-third Degree itself is unofficially divided into two streams, one knowing far more than the other). These levels are not mentioned in any Freemason's guidebook. It is believed by many that the people who belong to this select group are the agents of the New World Order.

Even the leaders of Freemasonry admit that the majority of people who join the Order *do not* know what Masonry really teaches. Manly P. Hall, a Thirty-third Degree Mason, who is often cited as "one of the foremost authorities on esoteric philosophy," and when he died *The Scottish Rite Journal* referred to him as "Masonry's Greatest Philosopher," says in his book entitled *Lectures on Ancient Philosophy:*

> Freemasonry is a fraternity within a fraternity . . . an outer organization concealing an inner brotherhood of the elect . . . .
>
> . . . it is necessary to establish the existence of these two separate yet independent orders, the one visible and the other invisible.
>
> The visible society is a splendid camaraderie of "free and accepted" men enjoined to devote themselves to ethical, educational, fraternal, patriotic, and humanitarian concerns.
>
> The invisible society is a secret and most august fraternity whose members are dedicated to the service of a mysterious arcanum arcandrum (defined as a secret; a mystery).
>
> Those brethren who have essayed to write the history of their craft have not included in their disquisitions (a formal treatise) **the story of that truly secret inner society which is to the body Freemasonic what the heart is to the human body.**
>
> In each generation only a few are accepted into the inner sanctuary of the Work . . . .
>
> . . . the great initiate-philosophers of Freemasonry are . . . masters of that secret doctrine which forms the invisible foundation of every great theological and rational institution.[4] (Emphasis added.)

In the late 1800s, Albert Pike was Masonry's leading philosopher and remains to this present date the most revered Mason of all time. His body is interred at the House of the Temple in Washington, D.C., and his statue stands close by. Until 1947, Pike's book *Morals and Dogma of the Ancient and Accepted Scottish Rite of Freemasonry* was given to every Scottish Rite Freemason who reached the Fourteenth Degree, and it is still recommended on all Masonic reading lists. Interestingly, Pike admits to Masonry's aim to deceive Initiates who join the Order, saying:

> Masonry, like all the Religions, all the Mysterys, Hermeticism and Alchemy, **conceals its secrets from all except the Adepts and Sages, or the Elect, and uses false explanations and misinterpretations of its symbols to mislead those who deserve only to be misled;** to conceal the Truth, which it calls Light, from them, and to draw them away from it.[5] (Emphasis added.)

Continuing on, Commander Pike says:

> The Blue Degrees (the first three degrees of Masonry) are but the outer court or portico of the Temple. Part of the symbols are displayed there to the Initiate, **but he is intentionally misled by false interpretations.** It is not intended that he shall understand them; but it is intended that he shall imagine he understands them. Their true explanation is reserved for the Adapts, the Princes of Masonry.[6] (Emphasis added.)

Here we see from the Supreme Commander's own words that the vast majority of those who become Freemasons *do not* know what Freemasonry really teaches. For this reason, most Freemasons vehemently deny any occult attachments or hidden agenda to their fraternity.

Therefore, it is not this writer's intention to vilify the vast majority of well-meaning Freemasons. But it is our intention to show that the rituals, symbolism, philosophy, and religion of Freemasonry is rooted in the "Mysteries" of the ancient Chaldeans, which can be traced all the way back to the first deified queen of Babylon, Semiramis.

Moreover, it can also be established that the modern day Masonic revival and exaltation of the Goddess of Liberty is directly linked to the ancient cult worship of this great pagan female deity, whom the faithful followers of Yahweh knew as "Wickedness" and the "Mother of Harlots".

About this Book

As a youth I grew-up believing that the *Statue of Liberty* and America were one in the same. Like most Americans, I believed that the *Statue of Liberty* was the very embodiment of everything America represented; that without the *Statue of Liberty* there could be no free and just America.

All this began to change, on January 12, 1996, when I sat in a TV studio at *God's Learning Channel,* in Midland, Texas, founded by Al and Tommie Cooper. That day, as I sat listening to Joseph Good teach my understanding of what I had grown up believing about the *Statue of Liberty* changed. Joseph made an astounding claim, saying: "The *Statue of Liberty* is in the Book of Zechariah."

As I listened to what Joseph was teaching, questions raced through my mind: "Could it be true? Is the *Statue of Liberty* really in the Scriptures? If true, what does it mean?" I had to find the answers to those questions.

At the time, what I believed would be a simple research study developed into a ten year project of fact gathering. To my amazement, during that ten year period I accumulated reams of data on the exaltation of a great pagan female deity, who was worshiped by the "Mystery" cults of both the ancient and new worlds. Even more amazing was my discovery that our great national icon, *Liberty Enlightening the World/The Statue of Liberty,* is linked to the ancient cult worship of this same great pagan female deity.

My quest for the truth began in the public libraries. In fact, much of what you will read in the pages of this book can be found in your own public library, including the statue's Masonic influence. Most books written on the *Statue of Liberty* are highly informative as to the historical data. But few give any conclusions as to its pagan origins. And none examine those pagan origins in the light of Scripture.

Contrary to the misconception of many, it is only when we take historical data and examine it in the light of Scripture that we discover the real origins of Bartholdi's Great Goddess statue *Liberty Enlightening the World.* Historians chronicle history, but Scripture defines it. And make no mistake, the "Mystery" cult's exaltation of the Great Goddess of antiquity, represented by Bartholdi's giant statue now standing in New York Harbor, is a major theme in the Scriptures.

From a historical perspective, the data presented in this book will establish the following: 1) that the woman addressed in the Book of Zachariah (5:5-11) and the Apocalypse, Revelation 17 & 18, is a pagan female deity, who was exalted and worshiped among the peoples of the ancient world under many different names and titles; 2) that with the conquest of Western Asia by Macedonia, and later Rome, the licentious religion of this female deity was adopted by the Greeks and Romans, and flourished not only in Rome proper but throughout the empire, especially among the Gauls (now France); 3) that during the American Revolutionary War, of 1776, this same female deity was exalted by the revolutionary American Freemasons as *Columbia,* the Goddess who breaks the chains of tyranny and sets men free; 4) that during the French Revolution, of 1789, this same female deity was exalted by the revolutionary French Freemasons as "the Goddess of Reason"; 5) that at the beginning of the Second French Republic, in 1848, this same female deity was personified as the New French Republic's "Goddess of Enlightenment" by the French Freemasons; 6) that Freemasonry symbolism heavily influenced the French sculptor Bartholdi and the design of his statue *Liberty Enlightening the World;* and 7) that the exaltation of Bartholdi's statue is not only historically linked to the third century Roman Goddess *Libertas* but can be traced all the way back to the ancient Sabine's worship of a female deity known as the "goddess of *liberty,*" which existed before the founding of Rome, in 753 or 752 B.C.E.

From a biblical perspective, the following can be established: 1) that a revival of the Great Goddess and her cult following is predicted to take place in a latter day country code-named "the land of Shinar"; 2) that her shrine predicted to be built, erected, and placed upon her own pedestal is that of a historic deified woman; 3) that the primary character of this pagan female deity is moral unrighteousness, especially as it regards fraud, dishonest weights and measures; 4) that the two women described by Zechariah are two great empires, which played a major role in carrying her cult worship from Western Asia to the peoples of the north peninsula (now Europe); 5) that the *Woman* addressed in Revelation 17 & 18 is the same *Woman* addressed in Zechariah 5:8-11; 6) that this great female deity was known among the faithful worshipers of Yahweh as "Wickedness" (Zech. 5:8) and "the Mother of Harlots" (Rev. 17:5); 7) that a worldwide revival of the exaltation of this pagan female deity is destined to take place in a latter day country code-named "the land of Shinar"/"Babylon"; 8) that like the ancient land of Shinar this great latter day country will be identified as the land of this same pagan female deity; and 9) that both Zechariah and the Hebrew writer of the Apocalypse link the future destruction of this great latter country to the exaltation of this same pagan female deity.

Hopefully, this book will answer some of your questions about the origins and real meaning of the *Statue of Liberty.* Please feel free to research the data presented in this book, as much of it can be found in your own public library.

To Our Jewish Friends

In reading this book you will find some Christian doctrine. But that's OK. The Jewish people have dealt with Christian doctrine for two thousand years and today's Judaic Faith remains as strong as ever.

What you will find in this book is a highly vivid and forceful message from the ancient Hebrew prophets about the exaltation of a great pagan female goddess in a latter day country code-named "the land of Shinar" ('Babylon'), written in the context of the last days. The names "Shinar" and "Babylon" carries us back to a much older time and power, of which the Jewish people of that day were well acquainted.

For this reason, a major portion of this book was written with the Jewish people in mind, especially American Jews.

Therefore it is our hope that Jewish people, especially American Jews, will take note of this great latter day message of the Hebrew prophets. Because we believe it was given by God to such a People and time as this.

Richard Rhoades

PART I

Ancient Foundations
Of The
Great Goddess

1

ANCIENT LAND OF SHINAR

In the biblical account of the land of Shinar the narrative begins with the descendants of Noah, who after the Flood began to spread across the earth. At that particular time the Bible says:

> ". . . the whole earth used the same language and the same words. It came about as they journeyed east, that they found a plain in the land of Shinar and settled there. They said one to another, 'Come, let us make bricks and burn *them* throughly.' And they used brick for stone, and they used tar for mortar. They said, 'Come, let us build for ourselves a city, and a tower whose top *will reach* into heaven, and let us make for ourselves a name, otherwise we will be scattered abroad over the face of the whole earth'" (Gen. 11:1-4; NASV).

The "land of Shinar" is the name given to the Babylonian plain between the Tigris and Euphrates rivers. It is the very part of Western Asia that was first settled after the Great Flood. Scholars agree that when the people, who were called Sumerians, settled the land of Shinar, meaning "between the rivers," they developed a high degree of civilization. Establishing villages scattered across the plain these early settlers developed an intricate network of irrigation canals and dikes that allowed them to grow fruits, grains, and vegetables and transport them to market, enabling them to develop a prosperous economy and sustain an ever-growing population. In addition, they were heavily engaged in fishing and raising cattle, and mastered the skills of weaving, pottery making, carpentry, and masonry. From these exploits emerged a new and more complex society. Villages became cities comprised of a social, political, and judicial system that was based on a city-state model.[1]

A highly inventive people, the early settlers were the first to use the arch and wheel. They also understood the complex technology of alloying tin and copper to make bronze and then fashioning it into usable tools. In mathematics, they originated a system of numerical notations, based on 10's and 6's, which persist to this day in the way we tell time and in the division of the circle into 360 Degrees.[2]

Their most crowning achievement was the development of writing, called cuneiform, using wedge-shaped marks pressed onto clay tablets. This was the beginning of written history. Surviving clay tablets have left modern civilization a remarkable collection of early Sumerian literature, such as epic tales, hymns, myths, and the earliest known law code. They even wrote a heroic poem, the Epic of Gilgamesh, which came close to the biblical account of the judgment of God on sinful man in the story of the Great Flood, which covered the earth long before it was recorded in the Hebrew Scriptures by Moses.[3]

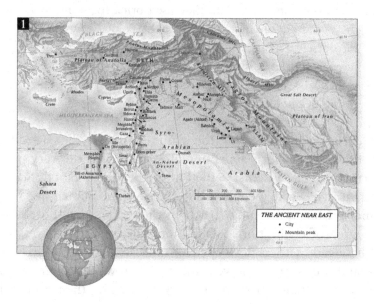

The above map shows the land of Shinar, which included the southern and parts of northern Mesopotamia. It was in this region that the Euphrates and Tigris rivers deposited rich fertile soil that produced an abundance of fruits, vegetables and grains. Here cities were built of mud-brick that were dominated by step-pyramids called *ziggurats* that honored their gods.

In the biblical narrative the Hebrew name "Shinar," as a geographical name, appears alongside the great cities of Mesopotamia: Babel, Erech, Accad, and Calneh (Gen. 10:10). In the *Septuagint* (Greek translation of the Hebrew Scriptures), the name "Shinar" is translated "Babylonia" (e.g. Isa. 11:11 and Zech. 5:11). Addressing this ancient understanding, the scholars of the *Jewish Encyclopedia* state:

> In the Bible, Babylon and the country of Babylonia are not always clearly distinguished, in most cases the same word (Babylon) being used for both. In some passages the land of Babylon is called Shinar; while in the post-exilic literature it is called the land of the Chaldeans . . . . In the historical books, Babylonia is frequently referred to (there are no fewer than thirty-one allusions in the Book of Kings) though the lack of a clear distinction between the city and the country is something puzzling . . . . The Greek name Mesopotamia, which arose after Alexander's time, means identically the same.[4]

Tower of Babel

Although there is nothing in the biblical narrative to indicate that the Tower of Babel was a temple tower or *ziggurat,* scholars agree that the 'tower' referred to in Genesis 11 is a *ziggurat* or Mesopotamian temple tower.[5] The word *ziggurat* means "to raise up, to elevate," and was the central feature of the great temples and shrines built in every important Mesopotamian city. The scholars of *Unger's Bible Dictionary* inform us that these step-pyramid *ziggurats* were consecrated to the guardian deity and protector of the city.[6] The scholars of *The Illustrated Bible Dictionary* write:

'The Tower of Babel,' an expression not found in the OT, is commonly used to describe the tower (migdol) intended to be a very high landmark associated with the city and its worshipers. It is generally assumed that, like the city, the tower was incomplete (Gen. 11:8), and that it was a staged temple tower or multi-storied *ziggurat* first developed in Babylonia in the early 3rd millennium BC from the low temenos or platform supporting a shrine set up near the main city temples (as at Erech and Uqair).[7]

As to the actual significance and size of the tower, which prompted Yahweh's divine intervention, the narrative of Genesis 11 is silent. There are some clues, however, from discovered ruins of a *ziggurat* believed to be a duplicate of the tower, or perhaps the remains of the tower itself. The scholars of the *Encyclopedia Judaica* write:

The particular *ziggurat* described in the biblical narrative was formerly identified with the tower of Ezida, the temple of the god Nebo in Borsippa; a city southwest of Babylon. However, the discovery at the end of the 19th century of Esagila, the great temple of Marduk in Babylon, has led most scholars to agree that it is the tower of this temple which inspired the writer of Genesis 11. This *ziggurat,* which was called "E-temen-an-ki"; "house of the foundations of heaven and earth"; rose to a height of about 300 feet square . . . . It is interesting to note that the Babylonians believed Esagila was built by the gods, thus making the statement in Genesis 11:5 ". . . which the sons of men built," particularly meaningful, since it may be understood as a polemic against this belief. This tower, which was the object of such pride among the Babylonians, was the product of strictly human endeavor which can quickly and easily be destroyed with the Divine Will.[8]

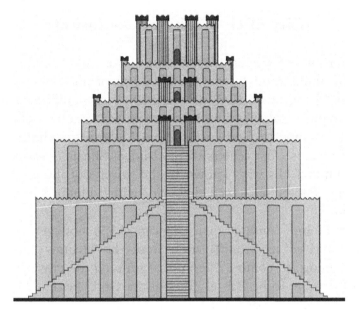

**Reconstruction of the Etemenauki,
which was 91 meters (300 ft.) in height.**

As to the immense size of the actual Tower of Babel, the Scottish historian Cunningham Geikie writes:

> It is at Borsippa, more than twelve miles in a straight line from the huge mound known as Babel that we find the most interesting trace of the earliest stages of Babylon, in the vast heap that has immemorially become the name of Birs Nimrod, or the Tower of Nimrod.
>
> This great ruin, a bare hill of yellow sand and bricks near the left bank of the Euphrates reaches a height of 198 feet; a vast mass of brickwork jutting from the mound to a further height . . . 235 feet in all. If measurements given by ancient authorities are correct, the building must have indeed been immense, for the Great Pyramid itself is only 750 feet square at its base, and rises to a height of only 480 feet; whereas this tower from a square base of over 600 feet rose 120 feet higher.[9]

City of God/City of Confusion

The name of the city Babel (*bab,* "gate" and *el* "God") was originally understood by the first builders of ancient civilization to mean "the gate of God" (Gen.10:10). The significance of the ancient name "Babel" cannot be overstated. Because the name "Babel" ('gateway to God') tells us much about the character and purpose of those first settlers of the land of Shinar (Babylonia); to make God and His ways known to the peoples of the earth. Thus the name "Bab-el" endowed their city with additional honor and importance.[10]

After Elohim confused their language (11:9), however, the name "Babel" derived its pronunciation from the Hebrew root word *balal,* meaning "to confuse". From that time on the city which was originally meant to be Bab-el, "the gate of God," became known as Babal—"the city of confusion".

Both Christian and Jewish scholars agree that the Tower of Babel narrative is a turning point in history, in that it signals the end of the era of universal monotheism which had existed since the beginning of time. One scholar writes: "Since the divine election of Abraham and his descendants immediately follows, it must be tactily assumed that the incident led to the introduction of idolatry into the world."[11]

Land of Cush

In the biblical narrative we find that Cush, the son of Ham (Gen. 10:6), settled in the region of Mesopotamia, which is also called "the land of Cush". The first mention of the land of Cush ('Mesopotamia/Babylonia') says:

> Now a river flowed out of Eden to water the garden; and from there it divided and became four rivers. The name of the first is Pishon; it flows around the whole land of Havilah, where there is gold. The gold of that land is good; the bdellium and the onyx stone are there. The name of the second river is Gihon; it flows around

the whole land of Cush. The name of the third river is Tigris; it flows east of Assyria. And the fourth river is the Euphrates (Gen. 2:10-14; NASV).

Some scholars believe that the Pishon and Gihon could be translated as "gusher" and "bubbler".[12] One authority suggests that they might be the long forgotten names of minor tributaries to the Tigris and Euphrates. It is further suggested that these four streams once converged near the head of the Persian Gulf to create a lush plain that in later memory remained the symbol of an earthly paradise.[13] Other scholars see a striking comparison between the biblical narrative of Noah and the great Flood recounted in the early Mesopotamian work of the Babylonian Gilgamesh epic.

In the Babylonian epic the gods decided to send a deluge to still the intolerable clamor of men which is disturbing their sleep. But first, one of them chooses a man named Utnapishtim to survive the catastrophe and gives him instructions to build a boat in which to ride out the flood. He takes aboard his family and the beasts of the field and wild creatures. "With the first glow of dawn," the Gilgamesh chronicler writes, "a black cloud rose up from the horizon." Soon all is submerged in a storm so fierce that even the gods are frightened. On the seventh day, as the tempest subsides, Utnapishtim lands on a mountaintop and sends out, in succession, a dove, a swallow, and a raven to find dry land; and when he emerges from his vessel, the Babylonian hero—like Noah—offers a sacrifice for his deliverance. The mountain on which Utnapishtim landed has been placed in northern Iraq, only 300 miles southeast of Turkey's Mount Ararat.[14]

Geological surveys of Mesopotamia indicate that, sometime in the distant past, waters of the Persian Gulf submerged sizable coastal areas. If this sudden rise of the sea level was caused by torrential rains and the breaking up of the waters beneath the earth there can be little doubt that the great Flood would have been commemorated in history and legend by these first races of men who settled in the land of Shinar ('Babylonia').

Cush the Confounder

In the Genesis account, the Cush chronology is a list of Cush's five sons; Seba, Havilah, Sabtah, Raamah, and Sabtechah (v. 7). Then, in the following verse are the words:"And Cush begat Nimrod" (v. 8).

According to the ancient historian Jacob Bryant (1715-1804), who is considered by many to be the greatest Christian scholar of all time, tells us that Ham was revered as the chief deity, the Sun, by the Chaldeans ('Babylonians'), and by most peoples in the east.[15] Equally significant, among the peoples of the ancient world Cush was regarded as the god of *chaos* and *confusion*.

The nineteenth century Scottish theologian Alexander Hislop informs us that Cush gained his notoriety as the father of idolatry, saying:

> As the tower-building was the first act of open rebellion after the flood, Cush, as Bel, was the ringleader of it . . . that Cush was known to Pagan antiquity under the very character of Bel, "The Confounder," a statement of Ovid clearly proves. The statement to which I refer is that in which Janus (Cush) "the god of gods," from whom all the other gods had their origin, is made to say of himself: "the ancients . . . called me Chaos." Now, first, this shows that Chaos was known not merely as a *state* of confusion, but as the "*god* of Confusion." But, secondly, who that is all acquainted with the laws of Chaldaic pronunciation, does not know that Chaos is just one of the established forms of the name of Chus or Cush?[16]

Here we see that the land of Cush, also known as the land of Shinar ('Babylonia'), gained its renown as a "land of rebellion" from Cush, who is regarded by the ancient writers of antiquity as "the father of idolatry". Affirming the above comment of Ovid, the sixth century Latin historian Gregorius Turonensis attributes to Cush what is said more generally to be attributed to his son, Nimrod; "that Cush had a pre-eminent share in leading mankind away from the true worship of God."[17]

Nimrod

In the Genesis account of Noah's descendants is the account of Nimrod's arrival on the scene of history, stating: "Now Cush became the father of Nimrod; he became a mighty one on the earth. He was a mighty hunter before the Lord" (Gen. 10:8-9; NASV).

In Jewish thought the Hebrew word for "before" *paneh,* means "to turn away" with respect "to a human face" or "the surface of the body." Scholars agree that since the face can be an obvious indicator of human emotion, it is also used "in conjunction of anger," as in Isaiah 4:5; Psalm 21:9; and Jeremiah 3:12.

Thus the phrase "(Nimrod) was a mighty hunter *before* the Lord" also has a strong inference of meaning "against" the Lord. This same meaning is affirmed in the *Septuagint,* where Nimrod is called a mighty hunter "against" the Lord. Affirming the *Septuagint* rendering of *paneh,* the scholars of the *Jewish Encyclopedia* tell us that Nimrod was "he who made all the people rebellious against God."[18]

Josephus tells us that it was Nimrod who led the people to build the city called Babylon and the Tower of Babel, saying:

> Now it was Nimrod who excited them to such an affront and contempt of God . . . . He also gradually changed the government into tyranny, seeing no other way of turning men from the fear of God . . . and they built a tower, neither sparing any pains, nor being in any degree negligent about the work; and, by reason of the multitude of hands employed in it, it grew very high . . . . The place where they built the tower is now called Babylon (Josephus, *Jewish Antiquities,* Book I, 4:2, 3).

The third century Roman historian Justin states that Nimrod strengthened the greatness of his acquired dominion over the first races of men by waging a campaign of continued possession "having subdued, therefore, his neighbors; when, by accession of force, being still furthered strengthened, he went forth against other tribes, and every new victory paved the way for another, he subdued all the peoples of the East."[19]

The noted Bible commentator Matthew Henry maintains that when Nimrod's tower project was thwarted by the Lord—the confusion of their language, so that they could not understand one another's speech—"'out of that land he went forth into Assyria and built Ninevah.' To him is ascribed the foundation of the great Babylonian empire and also the building of the cities which were afterwards combined together under the general name of Ninevah. He therefore becomes also the founder of Assyria, and this country is called by the prophet Micah (5:6) 'the land of Nimrod.'"[20]

Cunningham Geikie points out that although there is no established record to verify Nimrod's aim of world domination he, nevertheless, believes that history concurs the following:

* That Nimrod was without doubt the major military leader for the world of his time.

* That he was the founder of a "great empire" that absorbed the whole of West Asia, and one who was "the Caesar or Napoleon of the first races of men."

* That Nimrod was worshiped as a god some time by his people; "There is at least little doubt that the great king was deified after his death if not before it," says Geikie.[21]

The Great Emancipator

The Scriptures indicate that during the beginning of Israel's conquest of the land of Canaan, about 1400 B.C.E., there was an abundance of wild beasts that threatened the inhabitants of the land (Ex. 23:29-30). Thus there can be little doubt that the same threat existed among the first races of men in the land of Shinar, about 3200 B.C.E., at the time of Nimrod.

Tradition holds that Nimrod's skill in hunting down wild animals that threatened people, combined with his ability to build and organize, placed him in a unique position; that of a "Deliverer". Most scholars agree, however, that Nimrod was not content with merely protecting people from the fear of wild beasts. Instead, he went about to set people free from the fear of the Lord, which resulted in his being given the title "Emancipator," or "Deliverer".[22]

According to the writings of antiquity there was a man who lived at the time of Nimrod, named Phoroneus. In three different accounts, we are told that Phoroneus lived about the time when men used one speech; when the confusion of tongues began; and when mankind was scattered abroad.[23]

The second century C.E. (AD) Greek historian Pausanias records that this man was the first that gathered mankind into communities.[24] The first century B.C.E. (BC) Roman historian Gaius Hyginus wrote that he was the first of mortals that reigned.[25] And the fifth century Christian writer Lutatius Placidus states that he was the first that offered idolatrous sacrifices.[26] "This character," says Hislop, "can agree with none but that of Nimrod."[27]

Interestingly enough, the name Phoroneus is derived from the word *Pharo,* which means "to cast off, to make naked, to apostatize, to set free."[28] Ancient writers conclude that the name Phoroneus "The Apostate" was most likely given to him by the descendants of Noah, who continued to hold to Noah's primitive faith. While the name Phoroneus "The Emancipator" was most likely given to Nimrod by his followers.[29]

Josephus writes:

> Now it was Nimrod who excited them to such an affront and contempt of God. He was the grandson of Ham, the son of Noah, a bold man, and of great strength of hand. He persuaded them not to ascribe it (happiness) to God, as if it was through his means they were happy, but to believe that it was their own courage which procured that happiness. He also gradually changed the government into tyranny, seeing no other way of turning men from the fear of God, but to bring them into a constant dependence on his power. (Josephus, *Jewish Antiquities,* Book I, 4:2, 3).

Ancient "Mystery" Cults

According to tradition the growing interest in the "Mystery" cults were linked to Nimrod's violent death. Ancient historians maintain that Nimrod's end came suddenly, and was cloaked in mysterious circumstances. Some maintain that Nimrod's sudden death was an act of tribunal judgment.

The Roman historian Gaius Hyginus states that Ninus (Nimrod) met with a violent death similar to that of Pentheus, Lycurgus, and Orpheus, who were said to have been "torn in pieces".[30]

Chaldean legend holds that Nimrod's death came by the command of a "certain king".[31] Some believe that this "certain king" was the patriarch Shem. Alexander Hislop writes: "If Shem (the younger son of Noah and a faithful follower of Yahweh) was at that time alive, as beyond question he was, who so likely as he?"[32]

According to Egyptian tradition the death of Nimrod came, not by open violence, but by a seventy-two man tribunal that condemned him to die and be "cut in pieces," as a warning to others who might follow in his footsteps.[33]

The act of cutting a dead body as a warning to other violators of the sacred Covenant is also cited in the cutting of the dead body of a certain Levite's concubine in pieces (Judges 19:29), and sending one of the parts to each of the twelve tribes of Israel.

A similar action was performed when King Saul killed an ox and sent its dismembered parts to the twelve tribes, saying: "Whoever does not come out after Saul and after Samuel, so shall it be done to his oxen" (1 Sam. 11:7).

Some scholars believe that it was Shem who persuaded the tribal elders to make such a terrible example of the apostate Nimrod by cutting up separate members of his body and sending them to each of the chief cities where his cult following had been established. Alexander Hislop writes:

> . . . it will be readily perceived that, in these
> circumstances, if idolatry was to continue—if, above all,
> it was to take a step in advance, it was indispensable that
> it should operate in secret. The terror of an execution,
> inflicted on one so mighty as Nimrod, made it needful

that, for some time to come at least, extreme caution should be used. In these circumstances then, began, there can hardly be doubt, that system of "Mystery", which having Babylon for its center, has spread over the world.[34]

"Mystery" Cult Rites

Although the "Mysteries" were carefully protected and kept secret, there is evidence that the initiation rites Nimrod had instituted were dramatic productions designed to create awe and terror in the minds of the Initiates. It is said that in these initiation rites, under the seal of secrecy and the sanction of an oath, men were gradually led back to the idolatry that had been publically suppressed, while new rites were added that made it more blasphemous than before.[35]

The priests of the secret-initiation rites were the mind-control wizards of their day. It is said that after the candidates had passed through the confessional and sworn the required oaths, they were brought to "the highest pitch of excitement, that after having surrendered themselves implicitly to the priests, they might be prepared to receive anything."[36] The British historian John Gardner Wilkerson (1797-1875) writes:

> Strange and amazing objects presented themselves. Sometimes the place they were in seemed to shake around them; sometimes it appeared bright and resplendent with light and radiant fire, and then again covered with black darkness, sometimes thunder and lightning, sometimes frightful noises and bellowings, sometimes terrible apparitions astonished the trembling spectators. Then at last the great god, the central object of their worship, Orisis, Tammuz, Nimrod, or Adonis was revealed to them in a way most fitted to soothe their feelings and engage their blind affections.[37]

Eusebe Salverte maintains that the initiation rites of the cults of the "Ancient Mysteries" as observed by the Greeks can be traced all the way back to the Babylonians, saying:

> All the Greeks, from Delphi to Thermopyle, were initiated in the Mysteries of the temple of Delphi. Their silence in regard to everything they were commanded to keep secret was secured both by fear of the penalties threatened to a perjured revelation, and by the general confession exacted of the aspirants after initiation—a confession which caused *them* greater dread of the indiscretion of the priest, than gave *him* reason to dread *their* indiscretion.[38]

The Chaldeans taught that it was by the works and merits of those initiated into the "Mysteries" that they must be *justified* and accepted by God.[39] It was only through the Initiate's adherence to the "Mysteries" by which his sin could be removed. The ancient historian Ouvaroff writes:

> Accordingly the Mysteries were termed Teletae, 'perfections,' because they were supposed to induce a perfectness of life. Those who were purified by them were styled Telumenoi and Tetelesmenoi, that is, 'brought . . . to perfection,' which depended on the exertions of the individual.[40]

It is worthy to note that within the ancient literature of Greece, Egypt, Phoenicia, and Rome, regardless of the differences that existed between the peoples of these countries, in all *essential* respects, the "Mysteries" of the cults and secret societies who practiced them were basically the same.

Thus we should not be surprised that the various allied Masonic fraternities, such as the Mystic Shrine' Eastern Star; Knights Templar; Daughters of the Nile; Rainbow for Girls; Order of DeMolay for Boys; Ancient and Accepted Scottish Rite of Freemasonry; York Rite; Oriental Shrine of North America; Order of the Golden Key; Ancient Toltec Rite; Masonic Relief Association of the U.S.A. and

Canada and Holy Arch Knight Templar Priests, all claim that their origins are rooted in the "Mystery" cults of antiquity.

Affirming Masonry's claim to the ancient origins of Freemasonry, Commander Albert Pike writes:

> With her traditions reaching back to the earliest times, and her symbols dating farther back than even the monumental history of Egypt extends . . . it was in the cradle of the human race, when no human foot had trodden the soil of Assyria and Egypt.[41]

Semiramis

Apparently, the sudden and violent death of Nimrod, who was at the height of his popularity, shocked the peoples of that day. When the news of Nimrod's death spread throughout Babylonia, it is said that his devotees felt as though the greatest benefactor of mankind was gone; the "gaiety of nations eclipsed. Loud was the wail that everywhere ascended to heaven among the apostates from the primeval faith for so dire a catastrophe."[42]

With the death of Nimrod there arose a new ruler of Babylon. Instead of a man, it would be a woman. Her name was Semiramis, the wife of Nimrod, who finished building the fortifications of Babylon,[43] and later became the object of universal worship.

Scholars agree that there is ample evidence to support this claim. For instance, the ancient historian Ovid states that the reason the statue of Rhea or Cybele is universally represented with a crowned tower on her head was "because she first erected them in cities."[44]

The British archeologist Henry Layard maintains that Rhea or Cybele, the "tower-crown" goddess, was just the female counterpart of "the deity presiding over bulwarks fortresses."[45] Jacob Bryant writes:

> Under the name of the 'Mother of the gods,' the goddess queen of Babylon became an object of almost universal worship. "The Mother of the gods," says Clericus, "was worshiped by the Persians, the Syrians, and

all the kings of Europe and Asia, with the most profound veneration." Tacitus gives evidence that the Babylonian goddess was worshiped in the heart of Germany, and Caesar, when he invaded Britain, found that the priests of this same goddess, known by the name of Druids, had been there before him.[46]

George Rawlinson, the distinguished historian and professor of ancient history at Oxford University, says:

> Beltis, the wife of Bel-Nimrod . . . . She is far more than the mere female power of Bel-Nimrod, being in fact a separate and very important deity. Her common title is "the Great Goddess." In Chaldean her name was Mulita or Enuta—both words signifying "the Lady," in Assyria she was Bilta or Bilta-Nipruta, the feminine forms of Bil and Bil-Nipru. Her favorite title was "the Mother of the Gods," or the "Mother of the Great Gods;" whence it is tolerably clear that she was the "Dea Syria" worshiped at Herapolis under the Arian appellation of Mabog. Though commonly represented as "the wife of Nin," and in one place "the wife of Assur."
> . . . She seems thus to have united the attributes of the Juno, the Ceres or Demeter, the Bellona and even the Diana of the Classical Nations: for she was at once the Queen of Heaven . . . . In these later capacities she appears to have given rise to some of the Greek traditions with respect to Semiramis, who was made to contract an incestuous marriage with her own son Ninyas . . . .[47]

Interestingly enough, the name "Semiramis" is a later Hellenized form of the Summerian name "Sommur-amat," or "gift of the sea". The initial element "sammur," when translated into Hebrew becomes "Shinar," which in the Hebrew Scriptures becomes synonymous with the land of Babylon, or Babylonia.

Hope of the World

Ancient writers chronicle her beauty, which was also attributed to her Greek and Roman counterparts, the Greek goddess of love Aphrodite, and the beautiful but licentious Roman goddess Venus. So great was her beauty, it is said that her devotees regarded her as the embodiment of everything attractive in the female form and the perfection of female beauty.[48]

On one occasion, it is said that the sudden appearance of Semiramis among her subjects quelled an uprising, and the memory of her drew such admiration among her devotees that they erected a statue in her honor.[49] The late fourth or early fifth century Egyptian historian Nonnus, wrote and spoke of her as "the hope of the whole world."[50] Alexander Hislop writes:

> . . . the Ephesian Diana . . . was represented with all the attributes of the Mother of the gods, and, *as* the Mother of the gods, she wore a turreted crown, such as no one can contemplate without being forcibly reminded of the tower of Babel. Now this tower-bearing goddess Diana is by an ancient scholiast (sic) expressly identified with Semiramis . . . . A scholiast (sic) on the *Periergesis* of Dionysius, says Layard (*Nineveh and its Remains,* vol. ii, p. 480, Note), makes Semiramis the same as the goddess Artemis or Despoina. Now, Artemis was Diana, and the title of Despoina given to her, shows that it was in the character of the Ephesian Diana she was identified with Semiramis; for Despoina is the Greek for Demina, "The Lady," the peculiar title of Rhea or Cybele, the tower-goddess, in ancient Rome.—Ovid, *Fasti,* lib. iv. 340.[51]

According to most ancient accounts, Semiramis has been described as having *golden* or *yellow hair* and *blue eyes.* For instance, in Greece she was worshiped as the *yellow-haired* Ceres. In the northern parts of the Roman Empire she was worshiped as the *yellow-haired* Europa (Ovid, *Fasti*). In Homer's *Illiad* the goddess Minerva is called "the *blue-eyed* Minerva." The huntress Artemis/

Diana, who is identified with the moon, is addressed by Anacreon as the "*yellow-haired* daughter of Jupiter." Dione, the Mother of Venus, is described by Theocritus as "*yellow-haired.*" Venus herself is often called "Aurea Venus," the "*golden Venus*" (Homer's *Illiad*). The Indian goddess Lakshmi, "Mother of the Universe," is described as having "a *golden* complexion" (Asiatic Researchers). Ariadne, the wife of Bacchus (Nimrod), was called "the *yellow-haired* Ariadne" (Hesoid, *Theogonia*).[52]

Apparently, Semiramis was not only beautiful: she was driven by an obsession with the "Mysteries" of the occult. After Nimrod's death, it is said that she instigated a false religion that was adopted and propagated by a hierarchy of priests and priestesses, to whom were assigned the task of indoctrinating Chaldean (the sophisticated and elite of Babylonia) Initiates into the various degrees of "illumination".

Alexander Hislop informs us that the Chaldean Mysteries can be traced to the days of Semiramis, who lived only a few centuries after the flood, and who is known to have impressed upon the people of that day the occult beliefs of her own depraved and polluted mind.[53]

Titles of the Great Goddess

As queen of Babylon ('Babylonia'), Semiramis' beauty and ambition were surpassed only by her many different titles. According to the writers of antiquity the titles by which she was known best are as follows:

* **Goddess of Fortifications:** although it is said that Nimrod surrounded Babylon with a wall, it was Semiramis who gained the glory of finishing the fortifications of Babylon. Thus like Nimrod, Semiramis was known as the "goddess of fortifications".[54]

* **Woman:** in almost all nations, there was a great goddess regarded as the "Habitation of God," and

was known under the name of Ashta or Isha, "the Woman".[55]

★ **The Lady:** as the great male divinity of Babylon, Nimrod was called "Baal" or "Belus," which means "Lord," and as the great female deity of Babylon, Semiramis was called "Beltis." which in English means "Lady".[56]

★ **Goddess of Liberty:** as the Roman goddess of personal freedom, she was known among her devotees as *Libertas*.[57]

★ **Mother of the Gods:** under the name "Mother of the gods," the first deified queen of Babylon became an object of universal worship, eclipsing the worship of Nimrod.[58]

★ **Mother of Harlots:** as the great goddess of temple prostitution, among the first races of men, especially those who kept the primitive faith of the patriarchs, Semiramis was known as the "Mother of Harlots".[59]

★ **Lady of the land:** in the writings of the Assyrian King Assur-nacirapli (about 885 B.C.E.), one of the temples he rebuilt in Cahal was the temple of "the Lady of the land".[60]

★ **Virgin Mother:** as the self-proclaimed "Virgin of Prophecy," who miraculously gave birth to Tammuz, the re-incarnated Nimrod, Semiramis was worshiped in Asia as "Virgo Deipara," the *Virgin* Mother.[61]

★ **Madonna:** Nimrod was known as Baal or Lord, and Semiramis was the female equivalent "Baalti," meaning "My Lady" in English, "Mea Domina" in Latin, and "Madonna" in Italian.[62]

* **Queen of Heaven:** in Egypt she was the greatest
and most worshiped of all divinities. During and after
Egyptian bondage the Israelites worshiped her as the
"Queen of Heaven" (Jer. 7:18; 44:17-19, 25).[63]

Virgin of Prophecy

Scholars agree that long after the great Flood the peoples of the
ancient world still had a knowledge of the Edenic prophecy, which
promised that the "seed of the woman" would "bruise the serpent's
head," and in so doing would have his own heel bruised. The idea
of a Deliverer slaying the serpent can be found in many ancient
traditions: Apollo slaying the serpent Pytho; Hercules strangling
serpents while yet in his cradle; Horus piercing a snake's head with
a spear; Calyia, the malignant serpent slain by Vishnu in his avatar of
Krishna; and Thor bruising the head of the great serpent with his
mace, to name a few.

It was this common knowledge of the Edenic prophecy which
the people of that day knew implied the death of a Deliverer had
to happen before the curse could be removed. For Semiramis, it
was this common knowledge of the Edenic prophecy which she
would use to hold onto the power of her throne and establish a false
religion aimed at supporting her rule as queen of Babylon.

Since it was Nimrod the people wanted, it was Nimrod they
would get. Semiramis would proclaim herself to be the "Virgin of
Prophecy" and bring back Nimrod, as a god. In life her husband
had been honored as the great "Deliverer". In death, she would have
him worshiped as a god.

That Semiramis was sexually immoral there is ample evidence.
Alexander Hislop tells us that the child she brazenly presented to her
subjects was fair while Nimrod was black.[64] Some believe that she
may have become pregnant while Nimrod was away. Or, it may have
happened shortly after his death. Regardless of the circumstances,
the child she carried she claimed to be his. Some believe that she
may have lied to cover up her adultery as an immoral queen to save
her own life. The actual circumstances are unknown.

Tradition holds that Semiramis claimed to have been the object of a divine encounter; that Nimrod had "visited her in a flash of light"; and that the "seed" she bore in her womb was the reincarnation of the king himself.

Semiramis claimed that she was a virgin; that she had been the object of a marvelous miracle; that she was, in fact, the long awaited "Virgin of Prophecy"; and that the child she carried was the promised "Seed of the Woman," which would remove the curse from the world.

Apparently, the time was right for such a lie. "The scheme," says Hislop, "thus skillfully formed, took effect. Semiramis gained glory from her dead and deified husband; and in the course of time both of them, under the name Rhea and Nin, or 'Goddess-Mother and Son,' were worshiped with enthusiasm that was incredible, and their images were everywhere set up and adored."[65]

Thus it was, in the ancient land of Shinar ('Babylonia') the foundations were established for the cult worship of four historical figures: Cush, Nimrod, Semiramis, and Tammuz. Cush, the ring leader of the rebellion against Yahweh, was worshiped as Bel "the Confounder" and Merodach "the Great Rebel". Nimrod, the famous but rebellious king, who in death, was proclaimed by Semiramis to be the Sun-god, and was worshiped as the illuminator of the material world and *enlightener of the souls of men*. Semiramis, the beautiful but immoral queen, was worshiped by the peoples of the ancient world under the titles "Woman," "Goddess of Liberty," "the Lady," "Madonna," "Mother of God," and "Queen of Heaven," but among the faithful of Yahweh she was known as "Wickedness," "the Great Whore," and "Mother of Harlots". Tammuz, the bastard child of Semiramis, was proclaimed to be the reincarnation of Nimrod, and the god whose death and resurrection represents the annual cycle of fertility and vegetation.

2

GREAT GODDESS
OF THE NATIONS

ANCIENT WRITERS TELL US that the exaltation of Semiramis as the Virgin of Prophecy, and her child Tammuz, as the promised Seed of the Woman, gave new hope to all the peoples of the ancient world. Alexander Hislop writes: "The Babylonians in their *popular religion* supremely worshiped a goddess mother and son who was represented in pictures and images as an infant or child spread across the whole earth."[1]

The accompanying illustration of a clay image shows that the Babylonian peoples were devout worshipers of the Goddess, as Ishtar with child in her arms.

In India, the Mother Goddess and child were worshiped as Devaki and Crishna, pictured with rays of glory around their heads as the child nursed from its mother's breast.

**Ishtar and
Child**

**Devaki and
Crishna**

In Egypt, the mother and child were worshiped as Isis and Horus.

By the time Christianity appeared on the scene, paintings and statues of a mother with child in her arms had become such a part of the pagan culture it is said that many of the statues were simply renamed and worshiped as the Virgin Mary, with her baby Jesus in her arms.

Isis and Horus

In Tibet, China, and Japan, it is said that Jesuit missionaries were astonished when they discovered that the Goddess and child were worshiped as devoutly as the Madonna and child Jesus were worshiped in Rome.[2] Sing Moo, the Holy Mother of China, was portrayed with a child in her arms and a "nimbus" or radiant light, in the form of a circle or halo around her, exactly as if her image had been fashioned by Roman Catholic craftsmen.[3]

The Scandinavians called her Disa, who was also pictured with a child. The Etruscans called her Nutria, and among the Druids she was worshiped as the "Mother of God".[4] Ancient Germans knew her as the virgin Hertha, who held a child in her arms.[5]

In ancient Harrapan, the Mother Goddess was worshiped as Shakti and her child as Siva; and in Asia, among the Phrygians, she was worshiped under the name Cybele and her child as Deoius.[6]

As the Goddess Ishtar, the reincarnation of Semiramis, the Babylonians worshiped her as "the Goddess who rejoices over mankind." She was also called "the mistress of heaven and earth," "the Great Goddess," "the queen of all the gods," "the Goddess of war and battle," "the queen of victory," "she who arranges battles," "she who defends from attacks."[7]

One scholar of the *Unger's Bible Dictionary* informs us that Herodotus (the Greek Father of history) referred to the custom of the Babylonians, who "compelled every native female to attend the temple of the goddess once in her life to prostitute herself in honor of the goddess."[8]

The ancient Sumerians called her Nanna; the Greeks knew her as Aphrodite or Ceres the "Great Mother" with the babe at her breast; or as Irene, the "Goddess of Peace," with the boy Plutus in her arms; and her Roman devotees knew her as Venus and her child as Jupiter.[9] Among the Phoenicians, the Mother Goddess was known as the "Lady of the Sea".[10] "Regardless of her name or place," says one writer, "she was known as the wife of Baal, who bore fruit although she never conceived."

Cult Worship of the Great Goddess

Although the mother and child were often worshiped together, a strong cultus of the Goddess herself developed on its own. Alexander Hislop says, "while the mother derived her glory in the first instance from the divine character attributed to the child in the mother, in the long run, practically eclipsed her son."[11]

Due to the excavated ruins of ancient civilizations by men such as the American archeologist, William F. Albright (1891-1971) and the British archeologist Austen Henry Layard (1817-1894), scholars have been able to learn more about the character of the ancient Great Goddess, as exhibited by her devotees.

In the fifteenth century B.C.E., as the Canaanite Goddess, Ashtoreth, archeologists have found that she was worshiped as the Great Goddess of Tyre and called by the name *Qudshu*, "holiness". One scholar tells us that she was frequently represented as a nude woman bestride a lion with a lily in one hand and a serpent in the other, and called *Qudshu,* "the Holiness," meaning "the Holy one". In a perverted moral sense, she was a divine courtesan.[12] High places had chambers for male prostitutes who consecrated themselves to her and were called *gedshim,* "sodomites" (Deut. 23:18; 1 Kings 14:24; 15:12; 22:46) and sacred harlots called *gedeshot* (1 Kings 14:23-24; 2 Kings 23:7).[13]

As Asherah, this same Canaanite deity is depicted as the wife of Baal. In one fragment of the Baal Epic the Goddess appears in an incredibly bloody orgy of destruction. For some unknown reason she fiendishly butchers mankind, young as well as old, in a most horrible and wholesome fashion, wading ecstatically in human gore up to her knees—even up to her throat—all the while exulting sadistically. As the Goddess of sensual love, maternity, and fertility, licentious worship was conducted in her honor.[14]

In south Arabia her name was Athar, meaning "to be fertile". Here her cult following identified her with the Babylonian goddess Ishtar.[15] Recent uncovered archeological ruins have confirmed the existence of her cult following at numerous sites in Israel, producing lewd miniature statues of the Goddess dating from the second and first millennia B.C.E. As the Goddess Ashtoreth (her Hebrew name meaning "shame") she was worshiped as the patron Goddess of sex and war.[16]

In the Hebrew Scriptures we are told that Sidon was a center of worship for one of her cults (1 Kings 11:5, 33; 2 Kings 23:13); that her idolatrous worship polluted the people of Yahweh (Judges 2:13); and that even wise King Solomon succumbed to her sensual worship (1 Kings 11:5; 2 Kings 23:13).

Henry Layard documents the worship of the Goddess found on Assyrian artifacts, saying: "A very fine specimen, cut in agate, represents an Assyrian goddess, perhaps Astarte, or the moon, with ten stars, and with a dog seated before her. In front of her is the moon's crescent, and a priest in an attitude of adoration. A tree and a ram goat, both common to Assyrian symbols, complete the group."[17]

Astarte/Ishtar

As the "Queen of Heaven," the Great Goddess was often worshiped by both the ancient Israelites and pagan devotees. Layard writes:

27

She was "the Queen of Heaven," frequently alluded to in the sacred volumes (Jer. vii. 18, xliv. 17, etc.). Diodorus mentions the vases which were placed on tables before the divinities in the Babylonian temple, the prophet describes the drink offerings to her; and in the sculptures, the king is constantly represented with a cup in one hand, in the act of preforming some religious ceremony. The planet, which bore her name, was sacred to her; and in the Assyrian sculptures, a star is placed upon her head. She was called Beltis, because she was the female form of the great divinity,

Queen of Heaven

or Baal; the two, there is reason to conjecture, having been originally but one, and androgyne (sic). Her worship penetrated from Assyria into Asia Minor, where its Assyrian origin was recognized. In the rock-tablets of Pierium she is represented, as in those of Assyria, standing on a lion, and crowned with a tower, or mural coronet; which we learn from Lucian, was peculiar to the Semitic figure of the goddess.[18]

Artemis

In Ephesus the Goddess was known among the Greeks as "Artemis of the Ephesians". Her temple in Ephesus was one of the seven wonders of the ancient world, four times the size of the Parthenon at Athens. She was worshiped as the goddess of virginity, fertility, and motherhood. Thus she is depicted as a Goddess with many breasts. A tower-shaped crown, the symbol of the "Tower of Babel," adorned her head, identifying her with the Great Mother Goddess of Babylon, Semiramis. Once a year there was a festival held in her honor, to which all the peoples of Asia Minor, who could do so, came with wives and children, bringing costly offerings to Artimis and rich gifts for the priests.

In the Book of Acts, Luke tells us that it was a time when the silversmiths made great gain from making and selling small images of the Goddess (Acts 19:23-40). Quoting the words of the silversmith Demetrius, Luke writes: ". . . almost throughout all Asia, this Paul hath persuaded and turned away much people, saying that they be no gods which are made with hands . . ." (v. 26).

The scholars of the *International Standard Bible Encyclopedia* tell us that Artemis was a deity of Asiatic origin, the Mother Goddess of the earth, whose seat of worship was in Ephesus, the capital of the Roman province of Asia,[19] saying:

> She may, however, be identified with the Cybele of the Phrygians whose name she also bore, and with several other deities who were worshiped under different names in various parts of the Orient. In Cappadocia she was known as Ma; to the Syrians as Atargatis or Mylitta; among the Phonecians as Astarte, a name which appears among the Assyrians as Ishtar; the modern name Esther is derived from it. The same goddess seems to have been worshiped by the Hittites, for a female deity is sculptured on the rocks at Yazlli Kaya, near the Hittite city of Boghazkeul. It may be shown ultimately that the various goddesses of Syria and Asia Minor all owe their origin to the earlier Assyrian or Babylonian Ishtar, the goddess of love, whose chief attributes they possessed. The several forms and names under which she appears are due to the varying developments of different religions.[20]

As a Roman fertility Goddess she was also worshiped as Diana, who was invoked by women to aid conception and delivery. The most famous place of worship for the Roman goddess was the grove of Diana on the shores of Lake Nimi at Aricia, near Rome, which was a shrine common to the cities of the Latin League.

Diana with a torch.

The scholars of *The Encyclopedia of Religion* inform us that Diana was a Roman moon Goddess, whose name is derived from the root word *dyeu,* meaning "the shining one".[21] Some hold that the name "Diana" stems from the adjective *dius,* meaning "luminous" (Paulus-Festus, ed. Lindsay, 1913, p. 65 L.), while others trace it to the root word *diu,* "by day".[22]

The most important aspect of the Goddess was that she represented the light of night as opposed to the light of day. Cicero (*De natura deorum* 2. 68-69) wrote of her saying, "It is thought that Diana is identified with the moon; . . . she is called Diana because at night she provides, so to speak, the day."[23]

For some, Diana was known as "the bringer of light," which according to one ancient writer, demonstrated a quality of *lucifera* ('Lucifer'), as "the light bringer" (Martial, 10.70.7).[24]

At the time of the reign of the Roman Emperor Caligula (37-41 C.E.), it is said that on the great day of Diana's festival, August 13, which was regarded to be the brightest day of the month (Statius, *Silvae* 3.1. 59-60), when the full moon would follow daylight, women would join a procession and carry torches from Rome to the grove of Aricia near Lake Nemi: one "would bear the light of the goddess," as Propertius expressed it (2.32. 9-10).[25]

As a Roman Goddess, in 238, 58, and 45 B.C.E., at least three temples were built in Rome to exalt her as the Goddess Libertas.[26] As the Goddess of personal freedom she was represented as a matron wearing the Phrygian cap, symbolic of liberty.[27]

In ancient Rome, Libertas had state priests who presided over the public festivities and her exaltation. During these celebrations, cult images of the Goddess were displayed to her devotees, which included the *vindicta,* the *pileus,* the *sceptre,* and at her feet, a *cat* and a *broken vase.* The *vindicta* represented the staff with which a slave was tapped to grant freedom. The *pileus* (Phrygian cap) symbolized the status of free men. The *sceptre* represented her dominion over mankind. The *cat,* which had not been domesticated in Rome, symbolized man's natural instinct for freedom. And the *broken vase* represented the end of confinement as a slave.[28]

It is said that the following prayer was offered by her devotees to invoke the favor of the great Babylonian Goddess:

I beseech thee, Ishtar,
Queen of all cities, leader of all men
Thou art the light of the world,
Thou art the light of heaven . . .
Supreme is thy might, O lady,
exalted art thou above all gods . . .
At thy name
the earth and heavens shake,
and the gods they tremble . . .
Where thou glancest,
the dead come to life,
and the sick rise and walk;
the mind of the diseased is healed
when it looks upon thy face . . . . [29]

3

GREAT GODDESS
OF TWO CONTINENTS

IN 334 B.C.E., WHEN Alexander the Great led his army across
the Hellespont he was determined to drive the Persians out of Asia
Minor. At the battle of Issus, in November 334, although his men
were outnumbered three to one, Alexander defeated the army of
Darius III. After a surprising victory, it is said that Darius wrote a
letter to Alexander, offering one of his daughters for marriage, half
of the Persian Empire, and an alliance between the two empires.
Alexander wrote back to Darius, saying: "First, I defeated your
generals. Now I have defeated yourself and the army you led. In
the future, let any communication you wish to make with me be
addressed to the king of all Asia."[1]

Two years later, in 332, the Phoenician Empire, which had
existed for a millennium and more, was conquered by Alexander.
Scholars agree that one of the primary objectives of Alexander's
conquest of other peoples was to adopt the cultures and religions
of those he conquered, and make them a part of his own culture.
Merrill C. Tenny, former Dean of Wheaton College, says:

> The conquests of Alexander in the fourth century
> B.C. had established new contacts with the Far East
> and had facilitated the syncretism of Western organized
> religions with the Eastern mysticism. When the armies of

Alexander returned to Europe, they brought with them a new attitude and new teachings. Religion became increasingly the affair of the individual rather than of the state, and the gods of the Western pantheon were identified with the Eastern deities, who promised direct revelation to their devotees and who might be approached personally through mystic rites. Because of the erotic character of their worship they were called "mystery religions."[2]

About one hundred years later, in 197, Rome defeated the Macedonians at Thessaly and, afterwards, went on to conquer Western Asia by defeating Macedonia's chief ally, Antiochus III of Syria. At this time Alexander's empire was overrun and absorbed into the emerging Roman Empire.

Great Goddess of the Greeks

Among the many legends of the ancient Greeks, the legend of Europa was one of the most revered. Homer mentioned her only in passing. But in the classic works *Europa and the Bull,* attributed to Moschus and Syracuse, and the *Metamorphoses* of the Roman poet, Ovid, Europa was the immortal princess of Phonecia, who was seduced by the Father of the gods, Zeus, and taken to his birthplace on an island of the north peninsula (now Europe), Crete.

According to tradition, one morning the daughter of the king of Sidon had a dream in which two continents in female form laid claim to her. In the Greek legend, the great Mother Goddess that belonged to Asia by birth, would be claimed by the peoples of the white races and given the name Europa by Zeus.

While Europa and her girl companions were frolicking by the sea, Zeus was smitten with Europa and changed himself into a handsome white bull. He approached the girls so gently they ran to play with him. Zeus knelt down and Europa climbed on his back. Then the bull charged into the sea, and on the journey the princes and Zeus were accompanied by strange creatures: Nereids, Tritons, and Poseidon himself. Europa then begged Zeus not to desert her.

Zeus replied that he was taking her to Crete, his original home, and that her sons from this union would be grand kings who would rule all men. In time, Europa gave birth to Minos and Rhadamanthus, wise rulers who became judges in the netherworld after death. And Europa gave her name to a continent—Europe.[3]

The British historian Norman Davies tells us that in 1628 B.C.E., among the ancient Minoans, at Crete, the chief deity they worshiped was the great Earth Goddess, later known as Rhea, the great Mother of the gods. Her places of worship were set on mountaintops, in caves, and in temple-sanctuaries in palaces. Surviving sealstones portray naked women embracing sacred objects in ecstasy. Blood sacrifices of animals were surrounded by images of her cult, sexual orgies, and statuettes of fertility goddesses. In times of danger the sacrifice of animals was supplemented with the sacrificial offerings of children.[4]

According to Davies, the Hellens were the first to use the name "Europe," which was derived from the Greek Goddess named "Europa," as a name for their territory to the west of the Aegean Sea, making the continent of Europe distinct from the older lands in Asia Minor and the Orient.[5]

Imbedded deep in the legend of Europa was the Greek notion that Hellenism, even with its pagan mythology, worship of deities, human sacrifice, and slavery, was a land of liberty when compared to the Persian-ruled despotism of Western Asia.[6] Thus the notion that Greece (in the West) was a land of liberty, and Persia (in the East) a land of tyranny, became the cornerstone of tradition which linked Western Civilization with the Greek Mother Goddess of Europe—"Europa".

Great Goddess of the White Race

In adopting the Great Goddess of Asia and giving their homeland her name, "Europa," the Hellens not only established a distinct country, distinguishing the northern peninsula from the older lands of Asia, they made a clear distinction between the white race and the tawny people of Asia, as well as the black people of Africa.

Interestingly enough, *The Original Webster's Unabridged Dictionary* informs us that the term "Europe" means "white face, the land of white people as distinguished from Ethiopians, black-faced people, or tawny inhabitants of Asia or Africa."[7]

In Greek mythology, the Greek deities were always depicted in human form, as intelligent and with beautiful bodies.[8] Consequently, Greek belief in its own superiority was rooted in the concept of its Greek deities. Thus it was no coincidence that the Greek legend of the great Asian Goddess included the giving of her name "Europa," meaning "goddess of the white race," to the peoples of the northern continent (Europe).

Perhaps the most defining classical work reflecting this superior Greek attitude is the *Persae,* written by Aeschylus, about 525 B.C.E., who had himself fought at Marathon. In his *Persae,* Aeschylus stereotypes all Persians as "cringing, ostentatious, arrogant, cruel, effeminate, and lawless aliens."[9]

Norman Davies notes that there is a definite connection between the superior attitude of the Greeks and Western Civilization, which was adopted by the Romans, who passed on to Western Civilization the tradition of Europe, with all its attitude of superiority, priority, and belief in the right to dominate.[10]

Nowhere was this attitude of arrogance, superiority, and a belief in the right to dominate manifested in its most extreme form than among the German peoples, in the late-1930s to mid-1940s. During this period the Nazi Party, under the leadership of Adolf Hitler, inflamed the German people's feelings of superiority and the right to dominate others in a way that had not been seen since the days of Rome. This was especially true with the Jews. As a result, millions of Jews, men, women, children, and even babies, were killed unmercifully, and then declared to be "not human".

Great Goddess of the Romans

Like the Greeks, history concurs that the Romans often adopted the deities of the peoples they conquered. This was especially true of the great Asian Goddess. Alexander Hislop writes:

The literal Babylon was the beginner and supporter of tyranny and idolatry. The city and its whole empire were taken by the Persians under Cyrus; the Persians were subdued by the Macedonians and the Macedonians by the Romans; so that Rome succeeded to the power of the old Babylon. And it was her method to adopt the worship of false deities she had conquered; so that by her own act she became the heiress and successor of all the Babylonian idolatry, and of all that was introduced into it by the immediate successors of Babylon, and consequently of all the idolatry of the earth.[11]

Manly Hall tells us that when the Persian Mysteries of the great Asian Goddess were brought into southern Europe they quickly spread among the people. Her cult grew rapidly, especially among the Roman soldiery, and during the Roman wars of conquest her teachings were carried by the legionaries to nearly all parts of Europe.[12] This was especially true of the Roman provinces of Spain, Portugal, Germany, and France.

Norman Davies informs us that over the centuries the Romans came into contact with virtually all the gods of the Mediterranean, each of whose cults they added to their collection. This was especially true of the oriental mystery cults of Atargatis from Syria, Cybele, the Great Mother Goddess of Asia Minor, and Isis of Egypt,[13] all counterparts of the great deified queen of Babylon, Semiramis. Professor George Rawlinson writes:

To the Greeks and Romans Semiramis was the foremost of women, the greatest queen who had ever held a sceptre, the most extraordinary conqueror the East had ever produced. Beautiful as Helen or Cleopatra, brave as Tomyris, lustful as Messalina, she had the virtues and vices of a man rather than a woman, and performed deeds scarcely inferior to those of Cyrus or Alexander the Great.[14]

Scholars agree that the Great Goddess was worshiped in Rome as the "goddess of *liberty*". In *Smith's Classical Dictionary,* Servius is quoted as saying that she was worshiped by the Romans as the "goddess of *liberty*" because at Terracina (or Anxur) slaves were emancipated in her temple and because the freedmen of Rome are recorded on one occasion to have collected a sum of money for the purpose of offering it in her temple.[15]

So great was her adoration among the people of that day, she was often referred to as a "living Goddess". For instance, in a book by Adueluis, a Roman writer of the second century C.E. (AD), the Goddess is portrayed as explaining who she is, saying:

> I am Nature, the universal Mother, mistress of all elements, primordial child of time, sovereign of all things spiritual, queen of the dead, queen also of the immortals, the single manifestation of all gods and goddesses that are . . . . Though I am worshiped in many aspects, known by countless names and propitiated with all manner of different rites, yet the whole earth venerates me. The primeval Phyrigians call me PESSINUNTICA, mother of the gods, the Athenians . . . Cecropian ARTEMIS; for the islanders of Cyprus, I am Paphian APHRODITE; for the archers of Crete, I am DICTYNNA; for the trilingual Silicians, Stygian PROSPERINE, and for the Eleusians, their ancient MOTHER OF CORN. Some know me as JUNO, some as BELLONA of the Battles; others as HECATE, RHAMNUBI . . . but races of Aetheopians, whose lands the morning sun first shines upon and the Egyptians who excel in ancient learning and worship me with ceremonies proper to my godhead, call me by my true name, namely QUEEN ISIS.[16]

As the Great Goddess of personal freedom her image was struck on Roman coins.

Roman coin with sovereign Goddess Libertas.   **Roman coin with profile of Goddess Libertas.**

On the left is Libertas portrayed as the Goddess of freedom. In her right hand she bears the *pileus libertais* (cap of freedom). In her left hand is a sceptre, symbolizing her rule over mankind. On the right is a profile of the head of the Goddess, which is a classic representation of a first century Roman woman.

Thus it was that the Great Goddess of Asia was adopted by two great empires, Greece and Rome, and thereby became the Great Goddess of two continents, Asia and Europe. As you shall soon see, in the late eighteenth century her cult following was revived by the secret society of Freemasonry as the French "Goddess of Enlightenment" and America's Revolutionary Goddess "Lady Columbia," who was later replaced by her devotees as the Great Goddess of personal freedom—"Lady Liberty".

PART II

Modern Foundations
Of The
Great Goddess

4

FREEMASONRY
IN EARLY AMERICA

TRADITION HOLDS THAT SOME form of Freemasonry arrived in North America with the first settlers of the 1607 Jamestown colony. Although this may have been the case, there is no actual documentation to verify it. The first recorded Freemason to settle in colonial America was John Skene, who immigrated to North America in 1682, and is listed as a member of the Aberdeen Lodge in 1670.[1]

The first recorded American settler to become a Freemason was Jonathan Belcher, while on a visit to England, in 1704, was initiated into a Masonic Lodge.[2] The following year Belcher returned to America and became a prosperous merchant. In 1730, Belcher became governor of Massachusetts and New Hampshire. At that time Freemasonry was beginning to be establish within the colonies.

In 1733, Andrew Belcher, Belcher's son, became the Deputy Grand Master of Massachusetts's Provincial Grand Lodge and took an active role in promoting Freemasonry among the colonists.[3] Then, between 1733 and 1737, the Grand Lodge of England chartered the Provincial Grand Lodges in Massachusetts, New York, Pennsylvania, and South Carolina.

In 1733, St. John's Lodge of Boston, which met at the "Bunch of Grapes" tavern, was the first recorded officially chartered lodge in North America.[4]

In 1743, the Grand Lodge of England appointed a Boston merchant, Thomas Oxnard, to be the Provincial Grand Master of North America.[5] By the year 1750, two other lodges had been established in Boston under the supervision of the parent St. John's Lodge, which then warranted more than forty lodges among the colonies.[6]

In 1752, what was called an irregular lodge was established, without the official approval of the Grand Lodge of England, and began meeting at the "Green Dragon" tavern, also known as the "Freemasons Arms" and "Headquarters of the Revolution," where the Boston Tea Party was later planned.[7] Shortly afterwards, when the members of the St. John's Lodge began to complain about the irregular lodge, its members applied for official recognition not from the Grand Lodge of England but from the Grand Lodge of Scotland, which offered a higher degree.[8]

It wasn't until the British Masonic troops with their field lodges, chartered by both the Irish and Scottish Grand Lodge, began to arrive in America, in 1756, that the irregular lodge was given official standing under the name "St. Andrews".[9] Soon afterwards, St. Andrew's Lodge began to authorize its own lodges, claiming to be the Provincial Grand Lodge of America which operated under the authority of the Grand Lodge of Scotland.

Then, on August 28, 1769, St. Andrew's Lodge began conferring a special degree called the "Knight Templar Degree".[10] Although it is uncertain as to the origins of this special degree it is believed to have originated from the revolutionary Jacobites.[11]

Masonic Influence of British Field Lodges

At the same time civic Masonic lodges were being chartered among township colonies, Freemasonry was also being popularized among the colonies by British Army field lodges, which were conducted in a similar fashion to civil lodges. As the British Army moved from town to town so did their field lodges, resulting in the popularization of Freemasonry among the colonies on a much broader scale.

At that particular time, due to the British Army's popularization of Freemasonry, American commanders, as well as their troops, who became comrades-in-arms with the British, jumped at the opportunity to become fellow Freemasons. Men such as Israel Putman, Benedict Arnold, Joseph Frye, Hugh Mercer, John Nixon, David Wooster, and George Washington became full-fledged Initiates of the Craft.[12] As a result, Masonic lodges proliferated as the Craft grew in numbers and popularity. From that point on the secret society of Freemasonry became an accepted part of colonial culture and, very soon, was influencing every aspect of American life.

Masonry's Influence on the Founding Fathers

Although numerous books have been written on the lives of the Founding Fathers, there is little mentioned about their Masonic affiliations. Over the centuries, like an unspoken code of protocol, to address their affiliation with the secret society of Freemasonry has been viewed by the elite of society as neither being Christian or "politically correct". The French historian Vicomte Leon de Poncins says of this forbidden code of silence:

> Freemasonry is practically never mentioned in the Press, history books are silent about the power and influence of the Order, and governments and parliaments never dare debate such a dangerous subject. Reports of Masonic meetings and Congresses are not available to the public; Masonic magazines and publications are not placed in the Bibliotheque Nationale (French National Library) or the British Museum, although the law of the land demands it.[13]

Even today this same forbidden code of silence exists in America, especially as it regards the Masonic affiliations of the Founding Fathers. History concurs, however, that many of the Founding Fathers, while professing to be devout Christians, had one foot, and often both feet, planted firmly in the Freemason camp.

Today little, if anything, is ever said about the Founding Father's acceptance of Freemasonry's blood oaths, different levels of esoteric knowledge, and commendation of the Craft to the first peoples of the New Republic. Nevertheless, the record of Freemasonry's Founding Fathers reads like a virtual "Who's Who".

Benjamin Franklin

Among the New Republic's Founding Fathers none were more supportive of the Craft than Benjamin Franklin. On December 8, 1730, Franklin printed in his newspaper, *The Pennsylvania Gazette,* the first documented notice about Freemasonry in North America. His article began with the statement: "There are several lodges of Free Masons erected in this Province . . . ."

The following year, at the age of twenty-five, Franklin himself became a Freemason, in February 1731. Three years later, by the age of twenty-eight, Franklin was appointed Grand Master of Pennsylvania. That same year he printed the first Freemason book to be published in America, which was a reprint of James Anderson's *Constitutions of Freemasons*—the "Bible" for English Freemasonry.[14]

As a politician, Franklin was unequaled among his peers. He earned the title of "The First American" for his early campaigning for colonial unity, as an author and spokesman in London for several colonies, and then as the first United States Ambassador to France.

When Franklin went to France as an ambassador he was honored at the top Masonic lodge, the Lodge of Perfection, and his signature, written in his own hand, is in their record ledger close to that of Marquis de Lafayette.[15] In Franklin's latter years, while in France, about the age of seventy, he was inducted into the French Lodge of Nine Muses ('Nine Sisters'), and became its Master.[16]

While serving as America's ambassador to France, Franklin was well-known for his sexual indulgences with French women who played an important role in the country's male dominated secret societies of France. Some believe that it may well have been during Franklin's participation in sexual indulgences with the French Brotherhood that he contacted syphilis from which he eventually died.[17]

Thomas Jefferson

According to a 1951 edition of the *Holy Bible, Masonic Edition,* there is abundant evidence that Thomas Jefferson was a Mason.[18] Although Jefferson's allegiance to the Craft has been disputed by many, the following can be established:

* That Jefferson went to the Second Continental Congress with references to "nature's God" in his first draft of the Declaration of Independence, which was a traditional Deist concept taken from the atheistic work of the French Masonic philosopher Jean Jacques Rousseau (1712-1778).[19]

* That Jefferson became one of the greatest admirers of the revolution that destroyed the French nation, in 1789. In 1791, after returning to the New Republic as America's Minister to France, he described the devastation as "a beautiful revolution," and stated that he believed the revolution reflected the national will of the French people.[20]

* That Jefferson viewed Adam Weishaupt, whom the Freemason socialist Louis Blanc (1811-1882) called "the profoundest conspirator that ever existed,"[21] as merely "an enthusiastic philanthropist".[22]

* That Jefferson referred to Abbe Barruel's four volumes of work on exposing the radical doctrines of the Illuminati, first published in 1798, as "the ravings of a Bedlamite"[23] (a Bedlamite was a patient of the Bedlam hospital for lunatics in London).

* That Jefferson was identified with the Charlottesville Lodge No. 90, Charlottesville, Virginia, since his name appears on the minutes of the Lodge on September 20, 1817.[24] Poor records kept by Colonial Lodges, and

the destruction of records by fire and war, have made it
impossible to research the original Lodge records.

* That Jefferson was also a member of the Lodge of the
   Nine Muses in Paris and the Beenan Order (Order of
   the Bees) known in Bravaria as the Illuminati.[25]

It is also common knowledge that Thomas Jefferson was a great
admirer of Sir Francis Bacon (1561-1626). Lord Bacon was the
Supreme Leader of the Rosicrucian Society and authored a detailed
novel entitled *New Atlantis,* which was about the building of a
utopian society in the New World that was based upon the guiding
principles he believed were used to establish the legendary lost
civilization of "Atlantis".

Crediting Francis Bacon's efforts to keep the "Ancient
Mysteries" alive, Marie Bauer Hall says in her book entitled
Collections of Emblemes, Ancient and Moderne:

> He is the Founder of Free Masonry . . . the guiding
> light of the Rosicrucian Order, the members of which
> kept the torch of true universal knowledge, the Secret
> Doctrine of the ages, alive during the dark night of the
> Middle Ages.[26]

George Washington

On November 4, 1752, at the age of twenty, George Washington
was initiated into the First Degree of Scottish Rite Freemasonry in
the Fredericksburg Lodge No. 4, A.F. & A.M., in Fredericksburg,
Virginia. Although Washington rarely attended lodge meetings he
supported the Order most of his life. In a letter, he wrote to King
David's Lodge No. 1, in Newport, Rhode Island, on August 22,
1790, saying:

> Being persuaded a just application of the principles on
> which Free Masonry is founded, must be promotive
> of virtue and public prosperity, I shall always be glad to

advance the interests of this Society and be considered by them a deserving brother.[27]

On February 4, 1789, Washington was elected president of the United States and John Adams his vice-president. On April 30, Washington's inauguration ceremony was held and the oath of office was administered by Robert Livingston, Grand Master of New York's Grand Lodge.[28] The marshal of the day was General Jacob Morton, who also was a Freemason.[29] General Morgan Lewis, another Freemason, was Washington's escort.[30] Both Morton and Lewis later became Grand Masters of New York. The Bible Washington used to take his oath of office was that of St. John's Lodge No. 1 of New York.[31]

Among the first Justices appointed to the Supreme Court, the Court number was then six, two of these—William Cushing of Massachusetts and John Blair of Virginia—were Freemasons.[32] In the absence of Chief John Jay, Cushing acted as Chief Justice, and he administered the oath of office to President Washington at his second inauguration.[33] President Washington nominated two more Masons to the Supreme Court—William Paterson of New Jersey and Oliver Ellsworth of Connecticut,[34] making the majority of those appointed Freemasons. During Washington's two terms in office he nominated eleven Supreme Court Justices. Six of those eleven were Masons.[35]

Almost four years later, on September 18, 1793, when the cornerstone of the Capital building was officially laid The Grand Lodge of Maryland conducted the ceremony and Washington, who was a Master Mason (having completed the first three degrees of the Blue Lodge), was asked to preside over it.[36]

Among the many lodges attending the ceremony were the affiliated lodges of the Grand Lodge of Maryland, as well as Washington's own lodge from Alexandria, Virginia. Among the events of that day was a great procession of Masons. Then came a band, which was followed by Washington himself, accompanied with Masonic officers and members dressed in full Masonic regalia.[37]

When Washington reached the trench along the south-east corner of the Capital site, where the cornerstone was to be laid, he was handed a silver-plate commemorating the historical event, on which was inscribed the names of the various lodges in attendance. An artillery volley was fired. Washington then placed the plate on the cornerstone. Around it, he placed containers of corn, wine and oil, all symbolic of a standard Masonic "consecration" ceremony.

At that point everyone joined in a prayer and chanting, and another round of artillery was fired. Washington then walked to a Masonic three-stepped rostrum and gave a speech. When he finished more chanting followed, and a final round of artillery was fired.[38]

That Washington did indeed wear the Masonic regalia at the cornerstone ceremony, as well as participate in the Masonic ritual, there is ample evidence. Among the Brotherhood it is well-known that Washington had a least two Masonic aprons. In 1782, while in camp with his army at Newburgh, on the Hudson, directing an attack against the British, Washington was given a lambskin apron as a token of French admiration from a friend and Brother Mason, Elkanah Watson, who lived in Nantes, France.[39] A second Masonic apron was presented to Washington, in 1784, by the French General Lafayette, a Mason, whose wife had specially embroidered it for the General.[40]

According to Masonic historians it was the Lafayette apron that Washington wore at the cornerstone ceremony.

The design consisted of a number of Masonic symbols—the radiant eye, representing the invisible presence of "the Great Architect"; the Sun and Moon; the seven steps leading to the three primary symbols of Masonry, the open book, the compass and the square.

Between the two central columns are other symbols—the trowel, the ladder, the 1784 geometric representation of Euclid's theorem, etc. At the bottom of the distinctive square floor is a coffin from which a plant is beginning to sprout.[41]

Today, the silver trowel, the square and the level used by Washington for the cornerstone ceremony is held by the Potomac Lodge No. 5 of the District of Columbia. The apron and sash Washington wore is held by his lodge, Alexandria Lodge No. 22.

And on the left valve of the Senate doors of the Capital Building is a panel, designed in 1868, showing Washington standing next to the cornerstone holding a triangular trowel while wearing a Masonic apron. Surrounding Washington are several men dressed in Masonic regalia and holding two forms of the Masonic square.[42]

President George Washington, wearing the Masonic regalia at the laying of the cornerstone ceremony at the Capital site, in 1793.

In December 1799, Washington died. He was buried at his home at Mount Vernon, with full Masonic honors by his Alexandria Lodge No. 22, whose members were his pallbearers.

Other Notable Masons

Among the Founding Fathers, some of the better known Freemasons were Paul Revere, who made his famous midnight ride to warn of the British raid against Lexington and Concord. Paul Revere was a member of St. Andrew's Lodge, joining in 1760. In 1769, he became its Secretary and then its Master in 1770. And in 1775, Revere met at the Green Dragon Tavern with other Freemasons to plan the Boston Tea Party.[43]

Other notables include Patrick Henry, who made his famous speech at the Massachusetts Provincial Congress, in February 1775, and concluded by saying, "Give me liberty, or give me death."

Richard Henry Lee was a primary mover of the original resolution for independence and a signer of the Declaration of Independence. John Hancock, president of the Continental Congress of 1776, was a signer of the Declaration of Independence. Benjamin Rush was a member of Congress and a signer of the Declaration of Independence. Peyton Randolph was president of the First Continental Congress, a prominent attorney, and Provincial Grand Master of Virginia. Alexander Hamilton was the Secretary of Treasury, who was often called "The Banker of the Revolution." Robert Livingston and Roger Sherman, two of the five men appointed by Congress to draft a declaration of independence (both men were signers of the Declaration of Independence, and Livingston was the Grand Master of New York's Grand Lodge). Others included Joseph Hewes, William Hooper, Robert Pain, Richard Stockton, George Walton, William Whipple, William Ellery, just to name a few.

Signers of the Declaration of Independence

According to Manly Hall, of the fifty-six signers of the Declaration of Independence, fifty-three were Master Masons.[44] Henry C. Clausen, a Thirty-third Degree Sovereign Grand Commander of the Supreme Council of the Ancient and Accepted Scottish Rite of Freemasonry Southern Jurisdiction, U.S.A., maintains that fifty-six signers of the Declaration of Independence, on July 4th, 1776, were Freemasons.[45] And the researchers Michael Baigent and Richard Leigh tell us that only nine can be definitely identified as Freemasons, while ten others may have possibly been Masons.[46]

The Continental Army

Among General Washington's officers who were Masons, the 1951 *Masonic Edition* of the *Holy Bible* states that twenty-four of George Washington's major generals were Masons, as were thirty-three brigadier generals. The Masonic Commander Clausen maintains that inside Washington's army thirty-three Generals and six of his aides were Freemasons.[47] While the facts are uncertain, historians agree that during the War of Independence most of the officers and military personnel, on both the American and British sides, were either members of the Craft, or held to its ideals.

Masonry's Influence on the Presidency

According to one modern source, since the time of George Washington seventeen American Presidents have been Masons: George Washington, James Madison, James Monroe, Andrew Jackson, James Polk, James Buchanan, Andrew Johnson, James Garfield, William McKinley, Teddy Roosevelt, W. Howard Taft, Warren Harding, Franklin D. Roosevelt (FDR), Harry Truman, Lyndon Johnson, Gerald Ford, and Ronald Reagan.[48]

Contrary to Masonry's claim that James Madison was a Mason, however, Madison personally denied any participation in the Craft. In a letter of response to a concerned American who inquired about his reputed Masonic connections, Madison wrote back, saying, ". . . I never was a mason, and no one perhaps could be more a stranger to the principles, rites, and fruits of the Institution."[49]

It should also be noted that two years before Washington's death he responded to a letter written by the Reverend G. W. Snyder, who believed that Washington was a lodge Master. In a letter dated September 25, 1798, Washington replied, saying: "The fact is, I preside over none, nor have I been in one more than once or twice, within the last thirty years."[50]

Although John Adams was never a member of the Craft he, nevertheless, was firmly committed to the ideals Freemasonry represented. When Adams became president, in order to make the ideals of Freemasonry a fundamental part of the New Republic, he nominated the prominent Mason John Marshall as the first Chief Justice of the Supreme Court. Previously John Marshall was the Grand Master of Virginia (1793-1795).

Justice Marshall was eventually able to extricate himself from the Lodge and repudiated the Craft, saying, "The institution of Masonry ought to be abandoned as one capable of much evil, and incapable of producing any good which might be effected by safe and open means."[51]

America's more recent affiliate Masonic presidents include George H. W. Bush, a member of Skull & Bones; Bill Clinton of DeMolay; and George W. Bush, also a Skull & Bonesman.

To this present date America has been governed by Masonic presidents for well over one hundred years, or about half of America's existence as a sovereign nation.

Masonry's Influence on our Nation's Capital

While both Christian and Jews readily affirm the Judeo-Christian ethic upon which the United States of America was established there is little, if anything, ever mentioned about the incredible number of Masonic symbols and zodiacs which can be found engraved and sculptured in our nation's Capital, Washington, D.C. Although it is true that America was founded upon the Judeo-Christian ethic there is ample evidence that our nation's Capital is filled with the occult symbols of Freemasonry.

The "District of Columbia"

During the American Revolution the worship of the Great Goddess of antiquity was revived and celebrated by American Freemasons as "Columbia," the protector of the rebellion. For the elite of Masonry, it was Columbia who smashes the tyrants and breaks the chains of bondage.

Throughout the 1800s Masons, as well as much of the Colonial populace, viewed Columbia as the very *personification* of the New Republic. Paintings and pictures of the Goddess were prolific throughout the United States in the eighteenth and nineteenth centuries. As the *personification* of the New Republic the Goddess was often called "Lady Columbia" and "Miss Columbia".

In 1776, during the War of Independence, Columbia even appeared in the poetry of Phillis Wheatly (1753-1784), a black slave, who was the first published African American poetess. Expressing Colonial America's sentiments for the Goddess of the Revolution, Wheatly wrote:

One century scarce perform'd destined round.
When Gallic powers Columbia's fury found;
And so may you, whoever dares disgrace
The land of freedom's heaven—defended race!
For in their hopes Columbia's arm prevails.[52]

As the Great Goddess of the New Republic, on July 16, 1790, our nation's Capital was founded as the "District of Columbia". The following year, in 1791, within the District of Columbia our nation's new Capital City was named after George Washington. Today, America continues to honor both the Goddess Columbia and George Washington as "Washington, D.C.—the District of Columbia".

The "Goat Head" Pentagram

To the elite of Masonry, symbols are given supernatural powers at the moment of their creation. The ancient Egyptians also believed in this same supernatural power. Recent discoveries of archeologically have found thousands of ancient Egyptian symbols engraved on the walls of cities, tombs, and monuments, which represent supernatural powers and conveys hidden meanings.

One of the occult devotees' most important symbols is the pentagram. In the work entitled *Man, Magic and Myth: The Illustrated Encyclopedia of Mythology, Religion and the Unknown,* we are told that the star with five points is traditionally a "weapon of power and magic,"[53] as well as a symbol of Venus.[54]

Why is this symbolism an important aspect of the "Ancient Mysteries"? As earlier noted, among the peoples of the ancient world the Great Mother Goddess of all impurity and consecrated idolatry was identified with Venus ('the erotic star goddess').[55]

The most significant element of the pentagram is its positioning. With one of its points projecting upwards, it can be imagined as a man's body with arms and legs extended, symbolizing the dominance of the spirit over the four elements of matter. When the pentagram is inverted, the devil himself is positioned as the Goat Head of Mendes, which was known to the Knight Templars as "Baphomet".

Upright pentagram: **Inverted pentagram:**
spirit over matter.   **Goat head of Mendes.**

For those who understand occult symbolism an inverted pentagram, with two points projecting up-wards, is a symbol of evil because it overturns the proper order of things and demonstrates the triumph of matter over spirit. The two inverted upper points of the star are symbolic of the horns of the devil. The cabalist magician Eliphas Levi tells us that the inverted pentagram "is the goat of lust attacking the heavens with its horns, a sign execrated by initiates of a superior rank."[56]

In 1791, the French architect Pierre Charles l'Enfante, and his American associate, Andrew Ellicott, were commissioned to design the layout of the Capital. It is believed that both L'Enfante and Ellicott were Masons, as well as two of the three of the building commissioners, to whom they answered.[57] Although the design of the Capital is attributed to Charles l'Enfante it was actually the work of several men, all of whom were believed to be Masons.[58]

After Washington and Jefferson made modifications to the original prints submitted by L'Enfante, the revised prints of the layout of the Government Center, indicated by the below map, included a gigantic Masonic symbol that represented the hidden Luciferian religion of Masonry's elite. As you shall see, L'Enfante's celebrated plan of Washington, D.C., conforming to the cabalistic Baphomet, was designed so that the Goat Head's mouth is the White House.

Map of the city of Washington, D.C., 1792.

Today the best known occult pentagram design of an inverted five-pointed star is that of the layout of the White House in the nation's Capital, Washington, D.C. One only has to look at a map of the Government Center to see an obvious symbol of an occult pentagram. Dupont Circle, Logan Circle, and Scott Circle form the top three points of the Goat head of Mendes ('the Templers' god, *Baphomet*'). Washington Circle forms the extreme left-hand point of the Goat head. And the White House forms the fifth and bottom point of the inverted Goat head of Mendes.

The Washington Monument

On December 19, 1799, the day after the remains of George Washington were entombed at Mount Vernon, John Marshall, who was shortly afterward appointed as Chief Justice of the Supreme Court, stood in the House of Representatives and made a motion to build a monument in honor of George Washington. Five days later, on December 24, both Houses of Congress passed a resolution, declaring that a marble monument be erected in the Capital at the City of Washington to honor the late President. However, a lack of funds and disagreement over what type of memorial would best honor the late President prevented any progress on the proposed project.

It was not until 1836 that plans for a Washington Monument were put in action by the Washington Monument Society. That same year a Washington Monument design competition was sponsored by the Monument Society. Robert Mills, a Brother Mason, won the privately organized competition for the best Washington Monument design. Mills' design included a 600-foot-high square shaft rising from a Greco-Roman circular colonnade, wreathed with thirty-two columns, plus a porch.

Robert Mills' design of the Washington Monument.

Twelve years later, on July 4, 1848, under a clear sky with virtually every notable of the government in attendance, the cornerstone of the Washington Monument was set, accompanied with a Masonic ceremony officiated by the Grand Lodge of Masons of the District of Columbia. Among the guests on the platform were Mrs. Alexander Hamilton (then ninety-one years old), Mrs. Dolly Paine Madison, Mrs. John Quincy Adams, George Washington Parke Curtis, Martin Van Buren, Millard Fillmore, and many other distinguished guests. At the conclusion of the Masonic ceremony, the Grand Master said:

Washington Monument.

The several grand officers having reported that this structure has been erected by the square, the level, and the plumb, the cornerstone of which having been laid July 4, 1848, by the Grand Master of Masons of the District of Columbia, I now, as the Grand Master, do pronounce this obelisk to have been mechanically completed. (Full text of "The Dedication of the Washington National Monument.")

At that point the Masonic symbols of corn, wine, and oil were scattered and poured over the cornerstone, and a Masonic prayer was given to invoke a continuation of the Great Architect's blessings and prosperity upon the nation.

On February 21, 1885, over eight hundred people attended the dedication ceremony, and heard speeches by Ohio Senator John Sherman, William Willison Corcoran (of the Washington National Monument Society), Thomas Lincoln Casey of the Army Corps of Engineers, and U.S. President Chester Arthur.

After the speeches General William Tecumseh Sherman led the dignitaries and crowd to the east main entrance of the Capital building, where President Arthur reviewed passing troops.

For the elite of Freemasonry, the Washington Monument is the most important presidential monument in the United States. Because it is an obelisk set inside a circle.

The *Encyclopedia Americana* describes an obelisk as follows:

> . . a monument representing the sun in ancient Egyptian religions. It is a tapering monolithic shaft of stone, square in the cross section. The Egyptians were sun worshipers, regarding the great luminary as the creator of the universe, the maker of all gods above and below, and even as the author himself.
>
> The sun as Ra, the great god of the Egyptian religion, was represented upon monuments by the solar disc . . . . The two most striking and characteristic monuments which represented him on earth were the obelisk and the pyramid.
>
> The obelisk, symbol of light and life, represented his daily course, the pyramid, symbolic of darkness and death, the setting sun.[59]

Today there are only three major obelisks in the world, and two of them are in the United States. The first major obelisk was brought from Heliopolis, Egypt by the Roman Emperor Caligula, in 37-41 C.E., and erected on Vatican Hill, where it now stands in front of St. Peter's Square in Rome. The second major obelisk was brought to America in 1881 from Alexandria, Egypt, and was placed in Central Park in New York. The third major obelisk is the Washington Monument, built to honor our first Masonic President, George Washington.

Occultists believe that the spirit of the Sun-god "Ra" indwells the obelisk, and that the "Elect" must bow down before it twice to three times daily. Carl Claudy, a highly respected Masonic writer, explains the significance of the obelisk for Freemasons, saying:

> The initiate of old saw in the obelisk the very spirit of the god he worshiped . . . . From the dawn of religion the pillar, monolith or built up, has played an important part in the worship of the Unseen . . . . In Egypt, the obelisk stood for the very presence of the Sun God himself . . . . [60]

Designed, built, and dedicated by Freemasons, the Washington Monument was based upon an Egyptian obelisk that is filled with Masonic symbolism:

* It is built from 36,000 separate blocks of granite. The number 36 is an important number in Freemasonry, and is derived within Masonry by multiplying 3x12.

* Its capstone weighs exactly 3,300 pounds. The number 33 is another highly important number within Freemasonry.

* The Monument, which is 555 feet high, is hollow and contains 193 carved memorial stones, donated by various individuals, societies, states, and foreign governments, many of which are Masonic in origin. Masonic lodges throughout the world contributed 35 of these Memorial stones. These 35 stones were intermingled with the other Memorial stones, but the last several stones were placed at the 330 (33rd) foot level.

★ The total cost of the Washington Monument was reported to be $1,300,000 dollars, which emphasizes the important Masonic number 13. In occult numerology the number 13 means "Extreme Rebellion".

★ The Monument has 8 windows. In occult numerology the number 8 means "New Beginnings".

Had the elite of Masonry had their way, George Washington's remains would today be entombed under the Washington Monument. The Brotherhood appealed to the courts to have a receptacle for the remains of Washington be prepared so that it could be deposited under the Monument. Judge Augustine Washington denied the request, on the ground that they had been committed to the family vault at Mount Vernon in conformity with Washington's express wish. "It is his own will," said Judge Washington, "and that will is to (enforce) a law which I dare not disobey." (Text of "The Dedication of the Washington National Monument.")

Washington, D.C's. Zodiacs

In 1999, HarperCollins published a book written by David Ovason entitled *The Secret Architecture of Our Nation's Capital,* with a Foreword written by C. Fred Kleinkneche, a Thirty-third Degree Mason and Sovereign Grand Commander of The Supreme Council, the Thirty-third Degree (Mother Council of the World), Southern Jurisdiction of the United States.

According to the book's dust jacket, David Ovason has spent more than a decade researching the architecture and zodiacs of Washington, D.C., and maintains that our nation's Capital is filled with symbols of the occult.

In Ovason's book, he displays a series of no less than sixty-four photographs of shocking zodiacs, which are an integral part of Washington, D.C's. architecture. Ovason also documents the location of *twenty-three satanic zodiacs in the federal district alone!* Even the elite of astrology are overwhelmed by the significance of these many zodiacs in one district of one city.

Ovason also informs us that there are at least 1,000 zodiacal and planetary symbols in Washington, D.C.[61] In the Federal Reserve Board building alone there are two zodiacs that are situated on Saturn-like rings which run in horizontal planes to the earth, around the star-studded globe of a light fixture. A seated female image, which represents America and the Federal Reserve Board, holds in her left hand the "wand of office," while her right hand rests on the official seal of the Federal Reserve Board.

In the Dirksen Building on Constitution Avenue there are no less than twelve complete zodiacs incorporated into six arcane patterns. A total of thirty-eight zodiac images are displayed on each ceiling.

The Interstate Commerce Commission Building on Constitution Avenue is decorated with a sculpted naked woman with a sea horse, surrounded by dolphins. According to Ovason the detail is intended to represent the water signs of the zodiac—Cancer, Scorpio and Pisces.[62]

At the Department of Labor building another naked female image represents the fire signs of the zodiac—Aries, Leo and Sagittarius, while a nude male at the same location represents the earth signs of the zodiac—Taurus, Virgo and Capricorn.

Among the huge federal buildings within the Federal Triangle are a number of zodiacs on each building, represented by Virgoan and other zodiacal symbolism, such as: 1) The Mellon Foundation; 2) The Federal Trade Commission; 3) The National Archives; 4) The Department of Justice; 5) The Internal Revenue Building; 6) The Old Post Office; 7) The Federal Triangle Building with the Department Auditorium; 8) The Ronald Reagan Building; 9) the District Building; and 10) The Department of Commerce.[63]

In the Library of Congress, there are seven zodiacs which can be found at the following locations: 1) in the Great Hall; 2) on the spandrel above the main entrance; 3) on the walls of the corridors of the east front; 4) on the window recesses of the northeast room (formerly the map room); 5) on the clock over the entrance to the Main Reading Room; 6) in a mosaic detail of astronomy in the ceiling to the east of the Great Hall; and 7) in the ceiling dome of the southeast pavilion.

In the Arts and Industry Building of the Smithsonian Institution can be found a statue of the Goddess Columbia (located atop the structure) portrayed as the guardian of Science and Industry. According to Ovason, the image of the Goddess Columbia was meant to represent the District of Columbia as well as America.[64]

Pointing out the significance of all these zodiacs in the nation's Capital, the Sovereign Grand Commander Kleinkneche says in his Foreword: "these zodiacs were designed to point to the actual heavens—thus marrying the Capital City with the stars."

The Temple of Liberty

Another highly important Masonic symbol in the nation's Capital is the twenty foot statue atop the dome of Congress, which was originally called "Armed Liberty"—today "Lady Freedom". In 1863, it was completed by Thomas Crawford, a Mason, and was modeled after the Roman goddess *Libertas.* Interestingly, it was Jefferson Davis—the president of the Confederacy—who approved the final design of "Armed Liberty," in 1855.

Armed Liberty

Armed Liberty on Capital Dome.

For the elite of Masonry, Crawford's Armed Liberty statue, which stands atop the House of Congress clothed as a warrior, represents the ancient Roman Goddess who would fight for the rights, as well as the wishes, of her devotees through the legislation of her subjects, the elected members of Congress. It is also worthy to note that government documents in the archives of the Library of Congress record that in the early years of the New Republic the House of Congress was called *"The Temple of Liberty"*.[65]

The Capital's Federal Triangle

For the Masonic elite, the greatest monument of their Craft can be found in Washington, D.C., where the Masons built one giant code, making the entire city of Washington a tribute to America's Great Goddess. According to the researchers of *History International*, it was the French architect Pierre Charles l'Enfante who visualized the giant code when he designed his plans for the nation's Capital.[66]

The gigantic code, called "The Federal Triangle," is made up of the Washington Monument, the U.S. Capital Building, and the White House, which was designed to form a giant triangle. The significance of this triangle can be found in the stars above. Every year between August 10 and 15, just after sunset, three bright stars are aligned directly over the triangle: Arcturus, Regulus, and Spica.

The White House star is Arcturus, a golden-yellow star, which the Greeks called *"the Bear Watcher,"* and the Arabs call *Al Simak,* meaning "the one raised high".[67] Among the devotees of the occult, Arcturus is both a guardian and beneficial star, which confers high renown and prosperity. According to Ovason, just as the White House was the first of the three structures to be built, Arcturus is said to be among the first of the stars to be named.[68]

The Capital Building star is Regulus (Latin, meaning "little king, or ruler of a small kingdom"). To the elite of Masonry, Regulus is a star that represents ambition and power. Among the occultists, it has high ideals and a developed sense of independence.[69]

The Washington Monument star is Spica, which is the most powerful star in the Federal Triangle. Spica is a star that promises future growth, nourishment, and wealth.[70] Ovason suggests that

Spica may be the origin of the five-pointed star that adorns the American flag.

Above the Federal Triangle, hovering over Washington, D.C's. most important government buildings is the Constellation Virgo, the "Virgin Goddess" of antiquity, often referred to as "the Beautiful Virgin".

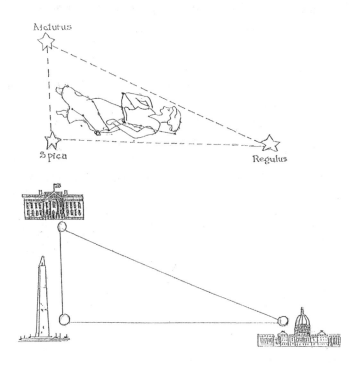

The Federal Triangle.

To the elite of Masonry, the orienting of the Washington Monument, the Capital Building, and the White House to the Constellation Virgo, was meant to seek divine benevolence from the Goddess on behalf of the government. Commander Pike once called for a painting of the Constellation featuring Virgo to be placed on the ceiling of every Freemason lodge.

During the nineteenth century Freemasons often reproduced images of the Virgin Goddess attended by a Master Mason under her zodiac sign. Among the 1,000 zodiacal and planetary symbols in Washington, D.C., the zodiac sign of the Goddess Virgo appears repeatedly throughout the city. There is even a bronze plaque of a rising Goddess Virgo attached to the statue of President James Garfield, a Mason.

Masonry's Influence on the Great Seal of the United States

On July 4, 1776, immediately following the signing of the Declaration of Independence, three members of the original five-man committee were chosen by Congress to draft the appropriate designs that would represent the new government on the Great Seal of the United States of America. This select group was comprised of three of the most important men of the New Republic, Benjamin Franklin, Thomas Jefferson and John Adams.[71]

First design of the Great Seal of the United States, 1776.

On the Obverse side (front), the design submitted to the new Congress portrayed a center shield heralding several symbols and flanked on both sides by the Goddess. On the right side the Goddess was portrayed as the Goddess Columbia, who was *personified* as the government of the New Republic, holding a staff topped by the Phrygian or Liberty cap, which by the eighteenth century was a symbol of revolt against the existing order and a call for a new order in which power was perceived to come from the people, not from God. On the left she was Lady Justice, *personified* as the government of the New Republic, without her blindfold, holding a pair of balance scales.

Above was the Eye of Providence, which represents the all-seeing, all-knowing, all-powerful Egyptian god Osiris (the god of nature and protector of civilization). The Eye of Providence defined exactly the "divine providence" upon whose protection the elite of Freemasonry firmly relied.

Below was the motto 'E PLURIBUS UNUM,' meaning "one out of many". Between the inner and outer borders were the inscription "SEAL OF THE UNITED STATES OF AMERICA," and the Roman numerals MDCCLXXVI (1776), which heralded the birth-year of the New Republic.

The Reverse side portrays Pharaoh, crowned and standing in a chariot, with his sword raised while in pursuit of the Israelites: rays from a pillar of fire guides Moses on the shore as he extends his arms to close the sea over the tyrant Pharaoh and his soldiers. A circumscribed motto read—"REBELLION TO TYRANTS IS OBEDIENCE TO GOD".

Second design of the Great Seal of the United States, 1780.

On March 25, 1780, Congress appointed a second committee to resolve the difficulties of the first design. This time the committee was comprised of John Scott of Virginia, James Lovell of Massachusetts, and William Harding of New Jersey.[72]

The front of their design portrayed a flaming shield in the center, with seven white and six red diagonal stripes on a field of blue, flanked on the right side by a soldier wearing the Phrygian or Liberty cap, and on the right was the Goddess, holding an olive branch in her left hand. Imprinted above the shield was a cloud of glory containing thirteen five-pointed stars. Below was a scroll bearing the motto "BELLO VEL PACI," meaning "Let there be war or peace".[73] An inscription between the inner and outer borders read "THE GREAT SEAL OF THE UNITED STATES OF AMERICA".

On the Reverse side was the Goddess portrayed as a sitting queen, holding a staff topped with a radiant Phrygian or Liberty cap. The word "SEMPER," meaning 'eternal' was inscribed above the Goddess, sitting as a royal queen personified as the New Republic. (On the accompanying illustration the word "SEMPER," meaning "eternal," has been crossed out and above is written "Virtute perennis," meaning "Everlasting because of virtue".) At the bottom were the Roman numerals MDCCLXXVI (1776).

Third design of the Great Seal of the United States, 1782.

On May 14, 1782, almost six years after the committee was first commissioned by Congress, three more men were selected, hoping this step would resolve the difficulties of the first two designs. This time Congress selected three men noted for their expertise in the field of heraldry and numismatics—Arthur Middleton and Edward Rutlege, both of South Carolina, and Elias Boudinot of New Jersey, who was later appointed as the third director of the United States Mint.[74]

Before the year's end the committee submitted its third design to Congress. On the Obverse side was a center shield, flanked by the crowned Goddess on the left, and an American soldier on the right. Imprinted above the shield for the first time was an eagle.

On the Reverse side was an unfinished thirteen step flat-platformed pyramid, with the Eye of Providence surrounded with rays of light and glory. Flanking the Eye of Providence were the Latin words "DEO FAVENTE". Below the thirteen step unfinished pyramid was the word "PERENNIS".

With this design emerged the eagle, the unfinished thirteen step pyramid, and the radiant Eye of Providence, which was almost entirely acceptable to Congress with a few adjustments in the art work and the replacement of the mottos.[75]

Fourth design of the Great Seal of the United States, 1782.

Expanding on the Third Design was the Secretary to the Congress Charles Thompson, who was well versed in the art of heraldry. Thompson took it upon himself to make a few changes on paper that caught the attention of William Barton, a Philadelphia attorney with a background in numismatics, who served as a consultant to the congressional board charged with the task of establishing the new U.S. mint and a national coinage system.[76] Thompson took the idea of the eagle and designed it to fill the entire area of the front field, as shown above. The eagle's talons held a bundle of thirteen arrows (the number 13 being highly significant within Freemasonry) and an olive branch, and a shield of red and white stripes crossed its breast.

William Barton took Thompson's eagle sketch and changed the stripes to thirteen red and white vertical stripes. Barton then added the motto "E PLURIBUS UNUM" and inserted a glory of thirteen five-pointed stars above the eagle's head.[77]

On June 20, 1782, the new Congress approved the Fourth Design to be the official seal of sovereignty for the New Republic. Mort Reed, one of the nation's foremost numismatists, says: "No one person is responsible for its completion because it contains at least two features from each previous suggestion, which rightfully makes it the work of Benjamin Franklin, Thomas Jefferson, John Adams, James Lovell, John Scott, William Houston, Arthur Middleton, Edward Ruteledge, Elias Boudinot, William Barton, and Charles Thompson."[78]

Moreover, there is ample evidence that all of these men had either strong ties to Masonry or were devoted Initiates of the Craft. The researcher Max Toth tells us that each of the three committees appointed by Congress were made up of "members holding various positions in Freemasonry."[79]

Following the approval and final adoption of the Fourth Design by Congress, in 1782, an engraving of the Obverse side, the one with the eagle, only was ordered into service. Orders for Reverse engravings, the one with the pyramid and Eye of Providence, were issued in 1782, 1789, 1841, 1883, 1884, and 1885.

The first time the Eye of Providence appeared on a U.S. Forty Dollar note was in 1778, in which the "Eye" was depicted looking down on thirteen stars, representing thirteen colonies. The unfinished pyramid made its first appearance on the Fifty Dollar bill composed of thirteen steps. Printed on it in large letters was the word "PERENNIS," which is translated "Everlasting," meaning "out of these thirteen steps, representing thirteen colonies, will emerge an 'everlasting nation'." Interestingly, it was Benjamin Franklin who designed and printed these Forty and Fifty Dollar bank notes.[80]

It wasn't until the Treasury Department issued the 1935 One Dollar bill that the occult symbols of the Reverse side of the Great Seal were again made public.[81] In a letter that has been recorded in several places, Henry Wallace, a Thirty-second Degree Mason and Vice President under FDR, put his recollections of the event on paper, saying:

The Latin phrase NOVUS ORDO SECLORUM impressed me as meaning the New Deal of the Ages.

Therefore I took the publication (a copy of a book entitled *The History Of The Seal Of The United States*) to President Roosevelt.

(He) was first struck with the representation of the 'All-seeing Eye,' a Masonic representation of the Great Architect of the Universe.

Roosevelt like myself was a 32nd degree Mason. He suggested that the Seal be put on the dollar bill rather than a coin and took the matter up with the Secretary of the Treasury.[82]

Reverse side of the One Dollar bill.

Addressing the mystic symbols of the Great Seal on the One Dollar bill, the noted author Texe Marrs writes:

> One of the more significant achievements of Roosevelt and Wallace was a revolutionary change in the design of the U.S. one-dollar bill. The all-seeing eye of Horus, the great Egyptian sun god, and the unfinished pyramid of the Illuminati were printed for the first time on the dollar bill, beginning in 1933. The Latin inscription *Novvus Ordo Seclorum,* or *New Secular World Order,* was inscribed on the one dollar currency note directly under the pyramid.
>
> Wallace, a New Age mystic and a follower of Nicholas Roerich, a major occultist of that era, was ecstatic with this because he realized that, now, millions of Americans and indeed, hundreds of millions of people throughout

the world were going to be conditioned day-in and day-out by an occultic symbol that, Wallace believed, had powerful magical powers and properties.[83]

Today the Obverse side of the Great Seal portrays an American eagle with outstretched wings and talons; above its head is a circle with thirteen silver buttons surrounding an illuminated field of thirteen five-pointed stars. On the eagle's breast is a shield with thirteen bars and stripes. In the eagle's right talon is an olive branch with thirteen leaves, and in its left, a bundle of thirteen arrows. In the eagle's beak is a ribbon inscribed with thirteen letters in E PLURIBUS UNUM on the ribbon.

The eagle has nine tail feathers and thirty-two or thirty-three feathers on each of the two wings.

Head of long-necked phoenix from the first Great Seal in 1782 until 1902.

The Great Seal's eagle holds a banner in its beak inscribed "E PLURIBUS UNUM". This phrase is popularly understood to signify the melting pot of many people into one nation, "out of many, one". To the elite of Freemasonry, however, Manly Hall says that *e pluribus unum* refers to the ancient Bacchic Rites—the rebirth of "one out of many" as "the flaming Sun".[84] Bacchus, a mythological deity who was killed by twelve Titans before the creation of mankind, is the E PLURIBUS UNUM, One from Many, a resurrection symbolized by the five-pointed star, or pentagram, representing "the human soul rising from bondage of the animal nature."[85] Hall writes:

> The pentagram is the true light, the Star of the Morning, marking the location of five mysterious centers of force, the awakening of which is the supreme secret of white magic.[86]

From 1782 until 1902, the design of the Obverse Great Seal was what appeared to be an eagle. The small tuft at the back of the head and the long-neck, however, indicates that the image of an eagle has been combined with that of the mythical phoenix, which has Masonic significance.

**First design
of the Obverse Great Seal,
1782.**

**Second design
of the Obverse Great Seal,
1841.**

**Third design
of the Obverse Great Seal,
1877.**

**Fourth design
of the Obverse Great Seal,
1885.**

Manly Hall tells us that in mysticism the eagle is a "symbol of initiation".[87] Rex Hutchens, a Thirty-second Degree Mason, says that among the Egyptians the eagle was a symbol of a "wise man" because the eagle's wings took him above the clouds into the "purer atmosphere and nearer to the source of light . . . the great Egyptian

Sun god Amun Ra . . . it is a symbol of the infinite Supreme Reason of Intelligence."[88]

Within the Craft, the nine tail feathers and either thirty-two or thirty-three feathers on each of the two wings of the eagle on the Great Seal also have Masonic significance. Some believe the nine tail feathers of the eagle represent the nine beings in the innermost circle of the "Great White Brotherhood," or the Illuminati. Others believe that the nine feathers represent the nine degrees in the York Rite of Freemasonry. The hidden secret of the thirty-two feathers on the right side are believed to represent the Thirty-second Degree inside the Scottish Rite of Freemasonry, and the thirty-three feathers on the left side are symbolic of the Thirty-third Degree.[89]

Addressing the unique symbolism of the Great Seal represented by the number 13, the noted author Ralph Epperson says in his book entitled *The New World Order:*

> It is quite certain that the student of history will argue that the number 13 used in all of these symbols simply refers to the thirteen states that ratified the Constitution. This would be a reasonable explanation, were it not for the fact that the Masons claim the number as one of their own. It appears as if they decided that it was time to form the United States when the number of states that could be united in the Union reached 13. As was just illustrated, the Masons consider the number to have Masonic significance. They apparently waited for just that time when there were exactly 13 states to form the Union, and not 12 or 14.[90]

According to the legend of the mythical phoenix, only one of these birds exists at any given time, and is said to nest in the distant parts of Arabia. After its 500 year life-span comes to an end, at death its body opens and a re-born phoenix emerges. Thus the mythology of the phoenix represents the rising from death.

To the elite of Freemasonry the image of a rising phoenix was understood to be symbolic of the ancient Atlantis legend reborn in America. Over the years, however, there has been an effort to tone down the mystic symbolism of the phoenix, which has been gradually substituted by the eagle.

Nevertheless, many representations of the phoenix still exist within the Capital. In the Old Senate Chamber of the U.S. Capital Building are images of the long-necked, crested phoenix. The shape of the beak, the long neck, the small tuft of feathers at the back of the head leaves little doubt that the original symbol of the New Republic was a phoenix, not an eagle.

The Reverse Great Seal is a thirteen-step pyramid. The unfinished pyramid is without a capstone. On top is the Eye of Providence enclosed in a radiant triangle, which in Masonic thought represents the Egyptian Sun-god Osiris. Heralding the significance of the "Eye," the Supreme Commander Albert Pike writes: ". . . the Blazing Star in our lodges has been regarded as an emblem of Omniscience, or the All-seeing Eye, which to the Egyptian Initiates was the emblem of Osiris, the Creator."[91]

Above the All-seeing Eye of Providence enclosed in a radiant triangle are the thirteen letters in "ANNUIT CORPTIS," meaning "Announcing the Birth of". Underneath the unfinished pyramid are the words "NOVUS ORDO SECLORUM," meaning "New Secular Order". It is from these words that Masons and advocates of a one world government derive the code-name "New World Order".

Reverse side of the Great Seal, 1909.

73

According to Henry Wallace, the above Reverse design of the Great Seal is the design which caught his attention, causing him to suggest to President Franklin Roosevelt to put the design on a coin, at which Roosevelt decided to put it on the back of the One Dollar bill—1935.

In 1950, C. William Smith wrote in the Masonic publication about "God's Plan in America," saying:

> God's plan is dedicated to the unification of all races, religions, and creeds. This plan, dedicated to the new order of things, is to make all things new—a new nation, a nonsectarian religion that has been called the religion of "The Great Light" . . . to unfold the New Age of the world—a "Novus Ordo Seclorum."[92]

In 1871, Commander Albert Pike revealed the identity of the "Great Light" in his work entitled *Morals and Dogma,* published by the Supreme Council of the Thirty-third Degree for the Southern Jurisdiction of the United States, saying:

> Lucifer, the Light-bearer! Strange and mysterious name to give to the Spirit of Darkness! Lucifer, the Son of the Morning! It is he who bears the Light, and with its splendors intolerable blinds feeble, sensual or selfish Souls? Doubt it not![93]

Later, on July 14, 1889, Commander Pike gave instructions to the generals of the twenty-three Supreme Councils of the World, saying:

> That which we must say to the crowd is—We worship a God, but it is the God that one adores without superstition.
>
> To you, Sovereign Grand Inspectors Generals (the name of the 33rd degree, the highest degree in Scottish Rite Masonry), we say this, that you may repeat it to the Brethren of the 32nd, 31st, and 30th degrees—the Masonic Religion should be, by all of us initiates of the highest

degrees, maintained in the purity of the Luciferian Doctrine . . . .

Yes, Lucifer is God . . . .

. . . the pure philosophical religion is the belief in Lucifer . . . Lucifer, God of Light and God of Good . . . .[94]

Heralding America's Goddess Image on U.S. Coins

Unable to secure the approval of Congress for the image of Columbia on the Great Seal, her devotees turned their attention to putting her image on U.S. coins. Mort Reed writes:

> The striking of one or more symbols on a coin is a devise which represents the virtues particular to a form of government.
> . . . While placing the likeness of any person on a coin may appear to be a matter of simple mechanics, in actuality a symbol on any coin represents that nation's political ambitions, and their deeds are judged accordingly. For that reason, a specific symbol must of necessity be proof of the fulfillment of the political promises made and kept in good faith.[95]

Libertas Americana

In 1782, Benjamin Franklin designed a commemorative Medal to honor American independence and called it "Libertas Americana". Franklin's design of the Goddess portrays her as serene and above the fray, with her hair flowing freely. From this point on America's benevolent Goddess of freedom would become the prototype for all future U.S. coins struck with her image.

A decade later, on April 2, 1792, the new Congress approved the first U.S. Coinage Act, which stated in part:

And be it further enacted, That upon the said coins respectively, there shall be the following devices and legends, namely: Upon one side of each of the said coins there shall be an impression emblematic of Liberty and the year of the coinage; and upon the reverse of each of the gold and silver coins, there shall be the figure or representation of an eagle with this inscription: 'United States of America,' and upon the reverse of each of the copper coins there shall be an inscription which shall express the denomination of the piece, namely cent, or half cent as the case may require.[96]

Thus it was that the new Congress authorized images of the Goddess to be struck U.S. coins. The following illustrations are but a few examples:

HALF-DOLLAR
(Heralding the Goddess of Liberty),
1801.

In the above Half-Dollar illustration the profile of Columbia is flanked by thirteen six-pointed stars (seven on the left side and six on the right, representing the thirteen colonies) divided by the word "LIBERTY". Notice that Columbia's hair flows down her neck and over her shoulders much like the image of Franklin's Libertas Americana.

ONE DOLLAR
(Heralding the Goddess of Peace),
1921-1935.

From 1921-1935, the One Dollar displays the Goddess Liberty for the first time as the Goddess of Peace, marking the termination of hostilities between the United States and Germany. With the lower part of her flowing hair, rays of light and glory radiate from her hair, intruding into the word "LIBERTY".

In 1916, President Woodrow Wilson (1913-1921) spoke at the inauguration of a new floodlighting system for the country's statue of the Goddess Liberty, saying in part:

> It was the hope of those who gave us this Statue and the hope of the American people in receiving it that the Goddess of Liberty and the Goddess of Peace were the same.
>
> The grandfather of my old friend the French Ambassador, and those who helped him make this gift possible, were citizens of a great sister republic established on the principle of the democratic form of government. Citizens of all democracies unite in their desire for peace. Grover Cleveland recognized that unity of purpose on this spot thirty years ago. He suggested that Liberty enlightening the world would extend her rays from these shores to every other nation.
>
> Today that symbolism should be broadened. To the message of liberty which America sends to all the world must be added her message of peace.

HALF-DOLLAR
(Heralding the Goddess *as* America),
1916–1947.

For the first time the Goddess was portrayed as dressed in a robe *personified* as the United States of America. Dressed in a garment representing the flag of the United States she walks toward a radiant sun. On her head she wears a Phrygian or Liberty cap and in her left arm bears branches of laurel and oak. Her right arm was outstretched and her right hand was open, as if offering peace. Several five-pointed stars (the Masonic five-pointed star represents "Reason" or "Intelligence"[97]) were visible in the upper cape-like portion of her dress. The sixth ray of sun (a Masonic symbol of the Great Architect[98]) is touching her flag striped robe.

SEEDS OF WORLD REVOLUTION

Following World War I, the British historian Nesta Webster (1876-1960) gave a lecture on the *Origin and Progress of World Revolution* to the officers of the Royal Artillery at Woolwich, England. By special request she repeated the lecture to the officers and non-commissioned officers of the Brigade of Guards in Whitehall, and then was asked to repeat it a third time to the officers of the Secret Service.

At their special request she wrote the book entitled *World Revolution: The Plot Against Civilization*. Winston Churchill was so convinced of her theory that in 1920 he wrote: "This conspiracy against civilization dates from the days of Weishaupt . . . as a modern historian Mrs. Webster has so aptly shown, it played a recognizable role on the French Revolution."[1]

In the early 1900s, when Nesta Webster was giving lectures on the social revolutions that took place during the French Revolution of 1848, the First World War, and the Bolshevick Revolution of 1917, and told her audience:

> The crisis of today is then no development of modern times, but a mere continuation of the immense movement that began in the middle of the eighteenth century. In a word, it is all one and the same revolution—the revolution that found its first expression in France of 1789. Both in its nature and its aims it differs entirely

from former revolutions which had for their origin some localized temporary cause. The revolution through which we are now passing is not local but universal . . . its causes must be sought not in popular discontent, but in a deep-laid conspiracy that uses the people to their own undoing.[2]

For many, both liberal and conservative, the term "conspiracy" is a word used only by the "uninformed," "uneducated," and "religious Right". For instance, the political analyst Rousas Roushdoony, in his book entitled *The Nature of the American System*, says of those who regard history in any sense as conspiratorial are "absurd, irrational and dangerously reactionary thinking, primitive, and naive—a form of belief in the devil."[3]

Zbigniew Brzezinski, former National Security Advisor for the former President Jimmy Carter, once wrote: "History is much more the product of chaos than of conspiracy . . . increasingly, policy makers are overwhelmed by events and information."[4] And the popular radio host Rush Limbaugh labels those who suggest a conspiratorial view of history as bonafide "kooks".

The problem with this analysis of a non-conspiratorial view of history is that it denies the facts of history, as well as the blatant admissions of the conspirators themselves. In fact, it denies the most elementary definition of the term "conspiracy" as defined in *The Original Webster's Unabridged Dictionary*, stating as follows:

A combination of men for an *evil* purpose; an *agreement,* between two or more persons, to commit some crime in concert; *particularly,* a combination to commit treason, or excite sedition or insurrection, against the government of a state; a plot; as a *conspiracy* against the life of a king, or a government.[5]

Robert Welch, the founder of the John Birch Society used to say: "There are only two schools of thought concerning views of history: those who believe in conspiracy and those who have never studied it." Even FDR, a lifelong politician, admitted: "In politics, nothing happens by accident. If it happens, it was planned that way."[6] Professor Antony Sutton adds:

> . . . the only reasonable explanation for recent history in the United States is that there exists a conspiracy to use political power for ends which are inconsistent with the Constitution. This is known by the official historians as "the devil theory of history," which again is a quick, cheap device for brushing facts under the rug. However, these critics ignore, for example, the Sherman Act, i.e., the anti-trust laws where conspiracy is the basic accepted theory. If there can be a conspiracy in the market place, then why not the political arena? Are politicians any purer than businessmen?[7]

Even according to the elite of Freemasonry, the quest to establish a One World Order has been the enduing dream of the "Mystery" cults for centuries. Manly Hall says in his book entitled *The Secret Destiny of America:*

> There exists in the world today, and has existed for thousands of years, a body of enlightened humans united in what might be termed, an Order of the Quest. It is composed of those whose intellectual and spiritual perceptions have revealed to them that civilization has a secret Destiny—secret, I say, because this high purpose is not realized by the many: the great masses of people still live along without any knowledge whatsoever that they are part of a Universal Motion.[8]

Ancient Origins of *Novus Ordo Seclorum*

While most historians agree that the philosophical aspect of the 1789 French Revolution originated with the radical ideas of the French philosopher Jean Jacques Rousseau, Nesta Webster tells us that this is only half-true, saying: ". . . if we were to seek the cause of revolution in mere philosophy it would be necessary to go a great deal further back than Rousseau—to the *Utopia* of Thomas More and even to Pythagoras and Plato."[9]

Thomas More

Scholars agree that it was Sir Thomas More (1478-1535), a lawyer, social philosopher and counselor to Henry VIII, who coined the word "utopia" when he gave the name to an imaginary island nation whose political system he described in the book entitled *Utopia,* published in 1516.

In *Utopia,* More contrasted the chaotic social life of European states of his own day with the ideal social order of *Utopia,* which has been the dream of Man since the expulsion from the Garden of Eden. Moreover, in More's *Utopia,* which is a communal ownership of land, private property does not exist, men and women are educated alike, and there is almost complete religious toleration.

For More, humanism is superior to a monarchy. Acknowledging their fundamental differences, More predicted that one day the two ideologies would eventually come into the reality of political conflict.[10]

Pathagoras

The *Encyclopedia Americana* tell us that Pythagoras, sometime around 530 B.C.E., founded a society of religious and ethical orientation that fostered strong bonds of friendship and a sense of elitism among its initiates through ritual, (and) esoteric symbolism.[11]

Hailed as an "ancient brother" by Freemasons, Albert Mackey, says that the "mysteries" of Pythagoras "were the most perfect approximation to the original science of Freemasonry which could be accomplished by a heathen philosopher . . . ."[12]

Plato

According to Manly Hall, Plato was not only an initiate himself in one of the many secret orders of his own day, he revealed many of the secret teachings to the people of his day (for which he was harshly criticized).[13]

In Plato's ideal society all monarchies and governments had to be abolished by whatever means necessary for the purpose of establishing new rulers, who would then be in a position to create a new society. For Plato, the ideal society would have a ruling class with a powerful army to keep it in power. The main tenants of Plato's ideal society can be summarized as follows:

★ Marriage and the family should be abolished so that all women would belong to all men and vise-versa.

★ All children should be taken by the State and raised by the State.

★ The ideal society should be made up of three classes: the ruling class, the military class, and the working class.

★ The ownership of private property should be abolished.

★ The ruling class should determine what is in the best interests of the working class.[14]

Ancient tablets record that the concept of the ideal society dominated by a ruling class did not originate with Plato. Rather, it began with the mythology of the early Babylonians. In the well-known Babylonian creation story, *Enuma elish,* which was composed not long before 1000 B.C.E. (but based on much older stories), the god Enki or Ea made man from one of the lesser gods, Kingu, for the purpose of working the earth to produce food and drink for the higher gods.[15]

According to Masonry's own account the origins of the ideal society began in ancient Babylonia, with the building of the Tower of Babel. The Masonic writer Author Edward Waite says in his book entitled *A New Encyclopedia of Freemasonry and of Cognate Instituted Mysteries:*

As regards Masonry, Babel of course represented Masonic enterprise and early expositors reaped full benefit from the fact. They remembered that the people who were of "one language and one speech" journeyed from the East towards the West, like those who have tried and proved as Master Masons. When they reached an abiding-place in the land of Shinar, it is affirmed that they dwelt therein as Noachidae, being the first characteristic name of Masons. It was here that they built their High Tower of Confusion . . . . Out of evil comes good, however, and (1) the confusion of tongues gave rise to "the ancient practice of Masons conversing without the use of speech."[16]

Waite goes on to say: "We know that the world of present values is in the melting-pot and that a New Order is to come . . . . The purpose of my Masonic life is concerned solely with a work in humility towards this end."[17]

Gnosticism

By the first century C.E. (AD), the cult of Gnosticism had become a prominent religion in the Mediterranean region, which taught that evil could only be understood by dualism—the doctrine of good and evil which coexist as divine principles; that Man was lowered to a certain state of being by successive emanations from the Creator; and that Man was saved by retracing the secretly revealed emanations until he arrived at the supreme principle of good.

In the dualism of the Gnostics, the doctrine of good and evil is represented by the two opposing heads of the eagle/ phoenix of the Thirty-second Degree Mason.

To the elite of Masonry, it is this dualism of good and evil which coexists as divine principles that mold and shape the individual.

Bible scholars agree that one of the Apostle Paul's primary purposes for writing his Epistle to the Colossians was to refute the heretical teachings of Gnostics, which consisted of ascetic ideas (Col. 2:20-23), and the worship of angels as intermediaries between God and man (Col. 2:18, 19). Supposedly, one could achieve perfection by progressing through a number of initiations and levels of wisdom in the spiritual mysteries.

Nesta Webster informs us that Gnostic rituals formed the basis of black magic, including the glorification of evil, which is an important part of the revolutionary movement. Webster writes: "The role of the Gnostics was to reduce perversion to a system by binding men together into sects working under the guise of *enlightenment* in order to obscure all recognized ideals of morality and religion."[18]

At the core of the Gnostic perversion was the belief that man is a god. Gnostics taught that since man is a god, he needs no special revelation other than the inner law of his own nature. And since that nature is divine, everything that springs from it is commendable. Consequently, those acts usually regarded in the Bible as sins are merely "mistakes," and not to be condemned.[19]

According to Gnostics, man could not reach heaven by leading a good moral life or through faith in God, but only through possession of *gnosis,* which he received through esoteric knowledge. In Gnostic thought it was impossible for the man who received *gnosis* to be corrupted by anything he might do; simply because he had evolved into a god.

Despite the denials of Masonry's elite there is ample evidence that the esoteric practices of Freemasonry go all the way back to the heretical teachings of the first century Gnostics. The noted occult authority Edith Star Miller explains Gnosticism's most visible link to Freemasonry, saying:

> Gnosticism, as the Mother of Freemasonry, has imposed its mark in the very center of the chief symbol of this association. The most conspicuous emblem which one notices on entering a Masonic temple, the one which figures on the seals, on the rituals, everywhere in

fact, appears in the middle of the interlaced square and compass, it is the five pointed star framing the letter G.

To the brothers frequenting the lodges admitting women as members, it is revealed that the mystic letter means Generation . . . . Finally, to those found worthy to penetrate into the sanctuary of Knights Kadosch, the enigmatic letter becomes the initial of the doctrine of the perfect initiates which is Gnosticism. (In the lower degrees, initiates are taught that it signifies Geometry, then God, then the Great Architect of the Universe.)

It is Gnosticism which is the real meaning of the G in the flamboyant star, for, after the grade of Kadosch the Freemasons dedicate themselves to the glorification of Gnosticism which is defined by Albert Pike as "the soul and marrow of Freemasonry."[20]

Jean Jacques Rousseau

Although the works of Jean Jacques Rousseau (1712-1788) never reached the common people to any significant extent, there is ample evidence that his works entitled *Contrat Social* and *Discours sur l'origine de l'ineglite parmi les hommes* contained the seeds of modern socialism in all its forms.[21]

According to Rousseau (1712-1778), a Mason, civilization is all wrong. Man, in his natural state, was free and happy. But under the paralyzing influence of social restraints placed there by civilization, especially by Christianity and Judaism, Man's freedom and happiness has been stifled. Thus for Rousseau, Man's only hope for obtaining true freedom and happiness lies in the casting off of those social restraints and returning to his first estate—the law of nature ('Humanism').

Adam Weishaupt

In the late 1700s, Adam Weishaupt (1748-1830), a German law professor, came on the scene and founded a new Order, which has been the most infamous of all the modern day secret societies. Born to Jewish parents on February 6, 1748, in Bavaria, Weishaupt's early training was with the Jesuits. Although Weishaupt later became a professor of Canon Law, at a Jesuit University of Ongolstadt, he never joined the Order. Instead, he came to hate the Jesuits and left them, vowing to destroy not only the Catholic Church but the Christianity it represented. Weishaupt then turned to the teachings of Rousseau and the anti-Christian Manicheans.

In 1771, Weishaupt was introduced to the ancient art of Egyptian occultism by a merchant named Kolmer, who was touring Europe in search of converts.[22] During the next five years Weishaupt worked on developing a plan that brought all these ideas together into one single organization, with the aim of applying them to the social reform teachings of his day. On May 1, 1776, Weishaupt launched his new Order called the "Illuminati".

Although Wesihaupt despised the Jesuits he structured his Illuminati Order much like that of the Jesuit Order. The Jesuit Barruel later wrote that Weishaupt admired the Jesuits, who were submitted to one authority and the same goal.[23] Like the Jesuits, Weishaupt's demand for absolute fidelity to the Order was a high priority. Nesta Webster writes:

> It was in the training of adepts that Weishaupt showed his profound subtlety. Proselytes were not to be admitted at once to the secret aims of Illuminism, but initiated step by step into the higher mysteries—and the greatest caution was to be exercised not to reveal to the novice doctrines that might be likely to revolt him. For this purpose the initiators must acquire the habit of "talking backwards and forwards" so as not to commit themselves. "One must speak," Weishaupt explained to the Superiors of the Order, "sometimes in one way, sometimes in another, so that our real purpose should remain impenetrable to our inferiors."[24]

To join Weishaupt's Order adapts had to believe that civilization was all wrong; that civilization was the agent responsible for causing Man to leave his natural state of freedom and happiness; and that in the process, civilization had caused Man to lose his original state of *liberty* and *equality*.

One of the greatest obstacles for achieving this goal was the ownership of property. For *equality* to exist, the doctrine of private property had to be abolished. To achieve this end the love of country and love of family had to give way to universal love so as to make the human race one happy family. Nationalism and patriotism had to be replaced with "Universal Brotherhood".[25]

Like Plato and Rousseau, Weishaupt believed that Man was inherently good. Since Man was inherently good, he had the capacity for self-government. For Weishaupt, the idea of self-government could be realized only when Man was delivered from the restraints imposed on him by civilization.[26] Since Man was inherently good he could live without restraints, controlling authorities, laws or civil codes. According to Weishaupt, Man only needed to be educated in a "just and steady morality". Of course, for Weishaupt, that "morality" was to be based upon the natural law of humanism.

Like Rousseau and Voltaire, Weishaupt also believed that religion was a major obstacle that kept Man from returning to his natural state of happiness, self-government, and freedom. All the ideas of the Hereafter, and all the fear of retribution for evil deeds had to be "rooted out" and replaced with the religion of Reason. "When at last Reason becomes the religion of Man, then the problem will be solved," said Weishaupt.[27]

Reduced to a simple formula the objectives of Weishaupt's Illuminati Manifesto can be summarized in the following five points:

1. Abolition of Monarchy and all ordered Government.

2. Abolition of all private property and inheritances.

3. Abolition of patriotism.

4. Abolition of the family, the institution of marriage and all morality, and the establishment of the communal education of children.

5. Abolition of all religion.[28]

For Weishaupt, the means by which these aims would be achieved was to spread *enlightenment*. And since Weishaupt believed in the inherent goodness of Man, "this would not be hard to accomplish," says Webster.[29]

Weishaupt's Perfect Cloak for Secrecy

At that particular time the teachings of Weishaupt's Illuminati were so radical to the general populace, the aristocracy and government authorities, he had to cloak them in secrecy. Professor John Robinson, the noted British historian and professor of Natural Philosophy at Edinburgh University, who was also a Mason and contemporary of Weishaupt, informs us that Weishaupt found the perfect cloak of secrecy for his Illuminati in the Order of Freemasonry.

Quoting part of a letter Weishaupt wrote to the Brotherhood, Professor Robinson writes in his book entitled *Proofs of a Conspiracy:* "The great strength of our Order lies in its concealment: let it never appear in any place in its own name but always covered by another name, and another occupation. None is fitter than the three lower degrees of Free Masonry, the public is accustomed to it, expect little from it, and therefore takes little notice of it."[30]

Another potent weapon in Weishaupt's arsenal of deception was the organized Church. Although Weishaupt hated Catholicism and the Christianity it represented he set out to use the Church to promote his radical ideas of social reform. Again, quoting Weishaupt's exact words from a letter written to his Brethren, Professor Robinson writes:

> Jesus of Nazareth, the Grand Master of our Order, appeared at a time when the world was in the utmost disorder, and among a people who for ages had groaned under the yoke of bondage. He taught them the lesson of reason. To be more effective, he took in the aid of Religion—of opinions which were current—and, in

a very clever manner, he combined his secret doctrines with the popular religion . . . . He concealed the precious meaning and consequences of his doctrines; but fully disclosed them to a chosen few. A chosen few received the doctrines in secret, and they have been handed down to us by the Free Masons.[31]

Of course, Weishaupt's analysis of Jesus is a complete fabrication of the biblical record. Quoting the very words of Jesus, John writes: "I have spoken openly to the world; I always taught in the synagogues and in the temple, where all the Jews come together; and I spoke nothing in secret" (Jhn. 18:20).

Nevertheless, for Weishaupt the organized Church was a perfect cloak to propagate the Illuminati's aims of world revolution. Professor Robinson says, "The happiness of mankind was, like Weishaupt's Christianity, a mere tool which Regents (the ruling council of the Illuminati Order) made a joke of."[32]

In the 1920s, Vicomte Leon de Poncins wrote a highly revealing book entitled *The Secret Powers Behind Revolution,* explaining that the aim of Freemasonry is to transform Christianity into a Masonic religion he called "atheist rationalism".

In his book, DePoncins writes about the need for the destruction of Christianity as being paramount to Freemasonry for the purpose of establishing "a new political and social city . . . in its place." DePoncins goes on to say:

> The great task of freemasonry is to spread ideas sometimes noble and beautiful in appearance but in reality destructive, of which the prototype is the famous motto: Liberty, equality, fraternity. Masonry, a vast organism of propaganda, acts by slow suggestion, spreading the revolutionary ferment in an insidious manner. The heads sow it among the inner lodges, these transmit it to the lower lodges whence it penetrates into the affiliated institutions and into the press, which takes in hand the public.

> Tirelessly and during the necessary number of years,
> the suggestion . . . works upon public opinion and fashions
> it to wish for the reforms from which nations die.[33]

Weishaupt's Conspiracy Exposed

In 1777, almost two years after Weishaupt founded the Illuminati he became a Freemason, and towards the end of 1778 he began working on the merging of the two secret societies. Four years later, at the Congress of Wilhelmsbad, on July 16, 1782, the merger between the Illuminati and Freemasonry was sealed in a secret alliance.[34] Nesta Webster writes: "What passed at this Congress will never be known to the outside world, for even these men who had been drawn unwittingly into the movement, and now heard for the first time the real designs of the leaders, were under oath to reveal nothing."[35]

It was not until April 1785 that four Freemasons, Utschneider, Cossandey, Grunberger, and Renner, all professors of the Marianen Academy, left the Order when they discovered its true aims. Shortly afterwards, all four men were summoned before a Bavarian court to give an account of the doctrines and methods of Freemasonry.[36]

When Weishaupt was confronted with their claims, it is said that he protested loudly that they had not been initiated into the inner mysteries of the Order.

On October 11, 1786, the Bavarian authorities searched the home of the Illuminati Zwack, a lawyer, and seized documents, which exposed the Order's doctrines and plans for inciting social revolution against the governments and monarchies of Europe.

Even after being discovered by the Bavarian authorities Illuminati members continued to proclaim their innocence, maintaining that the real purpose of the Order was to make the human race "one good happy family". In spite of their protests, however, the damming evidence was overwhelming, and revealed that the real aim of the Order was to bring an end to civilization through social revolution.

Fearing for the stability of Europe, the Bavarian authorities reprinted the Illuminati documents and circulated them as widely as possible to the people and governments of Europe. The publication was entitled *The Original Writings of the Order of the Illuminati.*

Shortly afterwards, the Bavarian authorities discovered an equally troubling problem. The Jesuit Abbe Barruel pointed out that the extravagance of the scheme made it impossible to believe, and the rulers of Europe dismissed it as being little more than "wishful thinking".[37]

Nevertheless, the Bavarian authorities took swift action against the sect, arresting several of its members. Zwack fled the country to England and Weishaupt, with a price on his head, took refuge at the estate of one of his converts, the Duke of Sax-Gotha.[38]

Bavaria's Final Warning

In 1814, some twenty-eight years after the Illuminati had been expelled from Bavaria, Francois Charles de Berckheim, who was the commissioner of police at Mayence, compiled an official report on the Secret Societies of Germany. The commissioner's dossier, from which the following extract has been taken, is registered under the following heading: Archives Nationales F' 6563 No. 2339, Serie 2, No. 49, states in part:

> The *Illumines* who remained in Bavaria, obliged to wrap themselves in darkness so as to escape the eye of authority, became only the more formidable: the rigorous measures which there the object, adorned by the persecution, gained them new proselytes, whilst the banished members went to carry the principles of the Association into other States.
>
> Thus in a few years Illuminism multiplied in hotbeds all through the south of Germany, and as a consequence in Saxony, in Prussia, in Sweden, and even in Russia . . . .
>
> The doctrine of Illuminism is subversive of every kind of monarchy, *unlimited liberty,* absolute leveling down, such is the fundamental dogma of the sect; to break the ties that bind the Sovereign to the citizen of a state, that is the object of all its efforts.

No doubt some of the principle chief amongst whom are numbered men distinguished for their fortune, their birth, and the dignities with which they are invested, are not the dupes of these demagogic dreams they hope to find in the popular emotions they stir up the means of seizing the reigns of power, or at any rate of increasing their wealth and their credit; but the crowd adapts believe in it religiously, and, in order to reach the goal shown to them, they maintain incessantly a hostile attitude toward sovereigns . . . .

The catechism of the sect is composed of a very small number of articles which might even be reduced to this single principle: "To arm the opinion of the peoples against sovereigns and to work by every method for the fall of monarchic governments in order to found in their place systems of absolute independence." Everything that can tend towards this object is in the spirit of the Association . . . .

As the principle force of the *Illumines* lies the power of opinions, they have set themselves out from the beginning to make proselytes amongst the men who through their profession exercise a direct influence on minds such as *litterateurs,* servants, and above all professors. The latter in their chairs, the former in their writings, propagate the principles of the sect by disguising the poison that they circulate under a thousand different forms. These germs, often imperceptible to the eyes of the vulgar, are afterwards, developed by the adapts of the societies they frequent, and the most obscure wording is thus brought to the understanding of the least discerning. It is above all the Universities that the Illuminism has always found and always will find numerous recruits.[39]

As you shall see, at the core of the Revolution movement emerged a deity that would champion its cause. And what better deity to champion that cause than the Great Goddess of antiquity—"queen of all gods," "goddess of war and battle," "queen of victory".

6

FRENCH REVOLUTION 1789

Two years before the suppression of the Illuminati, in Bavaria by the Bavarian authorities, Weishaupt sent his converts to France to begin the work of illuminating all Masonic lodges. Nesta Webster tells us that it was at the lodge of Amis Renis where members of the Masonic lodges from all over France gathered, and two German emissaries formally revealed the secret "Mysteries" of Weishaupt.[1]

By March 1789, the 266 lodges controlled by the Grand Orient were all illuminized. The following month the French Revolution broke out. The initial stages of the plot were called the "Orleaniste conspiracy," named after the Duc d'Orleans, the Grand Master of the Grand Orient lodges, who was one of the leading figures of the scheme to overthrow the French monarchy.

In the spring and summer of 1789, the first stage of the plan was put into action. It came in the form of an artificial grain shortage designed to create a famine and bring the French people to the point of revolt. By the time the aristocracy realized the severity of the problem it was too late. The plan was to hold up distribution of food supplies by blocking reforms in the National Assembly.

The plan worked! A food shortage created turmoil in Paris and swept across France. Unfortunately, it was not until the crisis arose that King Louis' court took action.

On July 11, the French treasurer, Jacques Necker, was dismissed by the King and sent into exile. The next day, when Necker's dismissal was learned by the people in Paris, there were cries of protest and violence in the streets. On the nights of July 12-13, Parisians set up their own militia and patrolled the streets at night with torches.

On July 14, the Bastille was stormed by a rioting mob. Revolutionaries claimed they wanted to set free the prisoners, but this was only a fabrication to hide their real aims. The American historian Douglas Johnson writes:

> On 14th July, still in search of arms, the Parisians invaded a great city arsenal, the Invadlides. Inside the gates, they overcame resistance, and seized four cannon and no less than 32,000 rifles.
>
> Using the cannon taken from the Invalides, and with the help of some sympathetic soldiers, they attacked the ancient fortress-prison of the Bastile. After a rather amateur attack of five hours, it finally surrendered. To the victors, it was a great symbol of defiance against the authority of the *ancien rigeme*. In fact, the real value of the event was small. The Bastile only held seven prisoners, two of whom were confined because they were mad. It was not much of a prize, but the triumph of the Parisians was linked with the idea of liberation, and the freed prisoners were escorted in a victory parade through the streets.[2]

Eight days later, on July 22, 1789, the bloodiest of the French revolutions began. It would later come to be known as "The Great Fear".

On that first day, the plan called for the revolutionaries to create a panic among the people throughout the country. Horsemen rode through towns and villages warning people of approaching vandals, saying, "all good citizens must take up arms". Several of the messengers carried placards stating: "Edict of the King: The King orders all chateaux to be burnt down; he only wishes to keep his own!"[3]

Desiring to be compliant with what was believed to be the king's Edict, peasants seized whatever weapons they could find and began destroying the homes and properties of landowners. "The object of the conspirators was thus achieved," says Webster.[4]

The Jacobins

During the first two years of the Revolution the Illuminati cloaked itself in yet another level of secrecy with the establishment of what was called the "Jacobin Clubs". Professor Robinson informs us that these societies were organized by the revolutionary committees of the Bavarian Illuminati, "who taught their method of doing business, of managing their correspondence, and of procuring and training their pupils."[5]

The plan was designed to give the "appearance" of a national uprising. Once their clubs were established throughout France, at a given signal, riots could be engineered to simultaneously take place in all parts of the country.

By 1790, the Jacobins had 1,100 members in France alone, and their political influence had become great. As the movement grew in numbers the Jacobins adopted Weishaupt's plan for enlisting women, promising them *emancipation* from a Man dominated world. The plan was to work on the passions of the women who attended their meetings, called "Societies Fraternalles," which were held three times per week. Nesta Webster says that the Jacobins "fanned their fury into flame and prepared those terrible bands of harpies who committed the atrocities of August 10th."[6]

True to the Illuminati aim to overthrow all monarchies and ordered governments, on August 10, 1792, a mob of revolutionaries broke into the royal palace, killing the King's Swiss Guards, imprisoning the King and his family, and eventually executing them.[7]

A Revolution of "Liberty, Equality, Fraternity"

On the 10th of August the French tricolor flag was replaced by the red flag of social revolution and the cry of "Vive norte rio d' Orleans" ('Long live the King Orleans') gave way to the Masonic watchwords "Liberty, Equality, Fraternity".[8] It is said that one of the female revolutionaries, George Sand, who was a member of Grand Orient Freemasonry, boasted long after the Revolution that the creed "Liberty, Equality, Fraternity" was hatched long before the French Revolution. Quoting Sand's very own words, Nesta Webster writes: "Half a century before those days marked out by destiny the French Revolution was fermenting in the dark and hatching below ground. It was maturing in the minds of believers to the point of fanaticism, in the form of universal revolution."[9] Webster goes on to say:

> We know . . . that George Sand was right in attributing to the Secret Societies the origin of the revolutionary war-cry "Liberty, Equality, Fraternity." Long before the Revolution broke out the formula "Liberty and Equality" had been current in the lodges of the Grand Orient—a formula that sounds wholly pacific, yet which holds within it a whole world of discord. For observe the contradiction: it is impossible to have complete liberty and equality, the two are mutually exclusive. It is possible to have a system of complete liberty in which every man is free to rob or to murder, to live, that is to say, according to the law of the jungle, rule by the strongest, but there is no equality there. Or one may have a system of absolute equality, of cutting every one down to the same level, of crushing all incentive in man to rise above his fellows, but there is no liberty there. So Grand Orient Freemasonry, by coupling together two words for ever incompatible, threw into the arena an apple of discord over which the world has never ceased to quarrel from that day to this, and which has throughout divided the revolutionary forces into two opposing camps.[10]

Robert Bork, the constitutional scholar, judge, and author says in his book entitled *Slouching Towards Gomorrah: Modern Liberalism and American Decline:* "From the French Revolution to the Sixties rebellions, radicals who worship liberty and equality also invariably yearn for fraternity, community, brotherhood. They will never achieve it, because the dynamic of radicalism in general and modern liberalism in particular is to shatter society. Talk of fraternity refers only to the rebels; everybody else is despised and to be coerced."[11]

Class Warfare

Contrary to the misconception of many, Karl Marx (1818-1883), and Friedrich Engels (1820-1895), who co-authored the *Communist Manifesto,* first published in 1848, were not the first to perfect the idea of "wage slavery" ('class warfare'). Rather, the French historian Fantin Desoards, a contemporary of the 1789 Revolution, informs us that it was the Jacobins with their watchwords "Liberty, Equality, Fraternity," who first used class warfare to bring about the revolt of the French populace, saying: "The plan of the Jacobins was to stir up the rich against the poor and the poor against the rich."[12]

The Liberal Left's Campaign of Class Warfare

Today, one does not have to go to France, Russia, Spain, or Greece to witness the Liberal Left's campaign of class warfare. It can be seen in our own halls of Congress, our courts, the executive branch, and various liberal media outlets on a daily basis.

One current example is that of liberal politicians, educators, and various media outlets pitting the middle class and poor against the "rich," demanding that corporations and independent business people pay their "fair share" when the top 5 percent already pay over 50 percent of all federal taxes.

Remarkably, at a time when some 21.6 million Americans are either unemployed or underemployed and the national debt is over $16.7 trillion, increasing each day by $4 billion, liberal elected officials and news media outlets are engaged in demonizing small business owners and corporate executives. Perhaps the most troubling part of this war against America's business community is that President Barack Obama has become the Liberal Left's most outspoken advocate of class warfare.

Unable to remain silent any longer, in July 2011, Senator Marco Rubio went to the floor of the Senate and said: "Its class warfare, and its the kind of language that you would expect from the leader of a third world country, not the President of the United States."

Abolition of Private Property

Another important figure of the French Revolution was Maximilien Robespierre (1758-1794), a Brother Mason, who was also a disciple of Jean Jacques Rousseau. True to Rousseau's idea that in order to truly be free and happy Man must return to his natural state, Robespierre advocated the abolition of private property, saying: "The property of man must return after his death to the public domain of society."[13]

In 1795, the Communist Noel Babeuf (1760-1797) said of Robespierre's aims to establish *equality* among the French people by abolishing the private ownership of land:

> He thought that equality would only be a vain word as long as the owners of property were allowed to tyrannize over the great mass, and that in order to destroy their power and to take the mass of citizens out of their dependence there was no way but to place all property in the hands of the government.[14]

The Liberal Left's Campaign to Nationalize America

Contrary to the misconception of many, it is a matter of record that when FDR, a Thirty-second Degree Mason, became President of the United States of America, in 1933, he placed all property, business, and labor of the American people under the control of the U.S. government. During FDR's first hundred days he achieved the long sought after goal of the radical Illuminati—the nationalization of America—with the following Acts:

* ★ March 9: The Emergency Banking Act—complete control of all banks, gold and silver, currency and transactions.

* March 31: The Civil Conservation Act—an act to control the use of all natural resources.

* April 19: The Abandonment of the gold standard—the seizure of all privately owned gold.

* May 12: The Agricultural Adjustment Act—the government control of all production and pricing of agricultural commodities.

* May 18: The Tennessee Valley Authority Act—the nationalizing of all utilities.

* May 27: The Truth Securities Act—government control of private financing.

* June 5: The House Joint Resolution 192—the abrogation of the gold clause in public and private contracts—the control of all contracts.

* June 13: The Home Owner's Loan Act—the government control of financing and prices of homes, and the bail out of all banks.

* June 16: The Railroad Coordination Act—the nationalization of transportation.

* June 18: The National Industrial Recovery Act—the nationalization of industry and labor.[15]

From this point on the nationalization of all banks, currency, industry, labor, natural resources, farm commodities, transportation, and land was complete.

Much like the classical feudalistic period of Common-Law England, when the king owned all the land and allowed his subjects to live on the land and operate it as long as they did not fall out of favor with the king, the property of the American people became subject to seizures, fines and encumbrances by the U.S. government.

Historical documents, however, clearly establish that this was not the case in early America. As evidence, we have enclosed the following copy of the original land grant deed found in Deed Book A, page 305 (Lauderdale County, Alabama, Court Records), which was made to this writer's third great grandfather, Jonathan W. Rhodes (1765-1830) and his heirs. It is dated April 4, 1825, granting seventy-nine and ninety four-hundredths acres to Jonathan W. Rhodes and his heirs, signed by President John Quincy Adams.

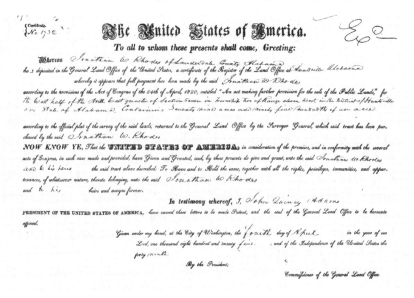

**Land Grant Deed from the United States Government
to Jonathan W. Rhodes, 1825.**

Notice that, at that particular time, the U.S. Congress issued the above land grant "to Jonathan W. Rhodes and his heirs and his assigns *to have and hold together with all the rights, privileges, immunities, and appur. tenances, of whatsoever nature . . . forever.*"

Under the leadership of FDR, the above U.S. Congressional land grant was made null and void. FDR's "New Deal" with the American people forever changed those early American property rights.

Now, instead of having property rights that are immune from government taxation, regulation, etc., extended to one's heirs forever, the Congressional Record of the 73rd Congress, 1st Session, Senate

Document No. 43, plainly states that the American people are merely the "users" of property. Reading the Congressional Record verbatim, we find the following statement:

> The ownership of all property is in the State, individual so-called "ownership" is only by virtue of Government, *i.e.,* law, amounting to mere user; and use must be in accordance with law and subordinate to the necessities of the State.[16]

Depopulation

At the time of the French Revolution, in 1789, it is estimated that the population of France was about 25 million. By 1793, after the destruction of the aristocracy and town magistrates there wasn't enough bread, money, or work for the millions of unemployed. Robespierre and his "Death Council" came up with the perfect solution—Depopulation! Babeuf wrote: ". . . this is the horrible conclusion . . . a portion of *sans-culottes* must be sacrificed, that this rubbish could be cleared up to a certain quantity, and that means must be found for doing it."[17]

Once the Death Council's decision was made, it is said that the revolutionary committees placed in charge of the extermination worked night and day studying maps spread out before them, pointing out towns and villages, calculating how many heads must be sacrificed in each town.

Thus began the final solution to the destruction and ruin brought about by the radical Jacobin motto: "Liberty, Equality, Fraternity," commonly called the "Great Fear," in which there were mass suspicions, trials, and executions. Professor Douglas Johnson writes: "No one could feel safe under the shadow of the guillotine, either in Paris or in the provinces. France was in the bloodiest phase of her history."[18]

The total number of victims drowned, guillotined, or shot all over France is uncertain. One account places the number at 300,000, and another at 5 million. In one case alone, at the town of Nantes, it is said that 500 children were slaughtered and 144 women, who sewed shirts for the army, were thrown into the river.

One of the primary aims of the depopulation plan was the elimination of priests and clergymen. In the September 1792 massacre of Catholic priests, six victims, including the Archbishop of Paris and four other priests, who had been imprisoned seven weeks earlier, were shot down in cold blood at the prison of La Roquette.

Robespierre and his comrades demanded death to anyone who disagreed with the Robespierre policy, saying the Republic "owes good citizens its protection. To the bad ones it owes only death." One of the revolutionary devotees, Jean-Paul Marat, echoed the sentiments of Robespierre in his newspaper *L'ami Du Peuple,* "Friend of the People," saying: "Let the blood of the traitors flow! That is the only way to save the country."

Joseph Fouche, who had been a headmaster at a Catholic school but renounced his Catholic faith to become a revolutionary, became a leader of the anti-Christian campaign. Traveling from town to town he closed down churches, ridiculed priests as "imposters," and outlawed celibacy.[19]

Because the people of Lyon, the second largest city in France, resisted Fouche's anti-Christian campaign, the convention deputy Bertrand Batere ordered Lyon to be destroyed, and a monument erected on its ruins that said: "Lyon waged war against liberty; Lyon is no more."[20]

One contemporary estimated that 8,000 Frenchmen were executed on September 2 alone. Another put the number at 28,000. During the purge none were spared—the poor, women, old men, and even young children. At one prison, the La Conciergerie, it is said that 378 of 488 prisoners were executed in one day. Prisoners were dragged into the courtyard and shot or cut to pieces with swords. Their bodies were dumped in the fields like garbage, or down a well.

By June of 1793, the Jacobins had seized complete control of the Republic. In October the revolutionary Paris Commune banned ministers from performing religious services. All religious holidays were banned and in their place were put "Feasts of Reason," accompanied by parades that exalted the "Goddess of

Reason". In November 1793, the Notre Dame Cathedral was renamed "The Temple of Reason".[21]

At least fifty people per day were executed at the guillotine that was set up next to a statue of the "Goddess of Reason,"[22] the forerunner to the "Goddess of Liberty" of the second French Revolution, in 1848, which became the prototype for Bartholdi's gigantic Goddess statue *Liberty Enlightening the World*. It is said that more than three thousand aristocrats were dragged to the guillotine, to the sounds of huge crowds of cheering men and women.

The Liberal Left's Campaign of "Social Engineering"

In the 1930s, Margaret Sanger published a magazine entitled "The Birth Control Review," which openly supported the "infanticide program" publically championed by Adolf Hitler and his Nazi regime as a goal of Aryan white supremacy. A strong advocate of population control, Sanger openly supported the Nazi plan for genetic engineering of the German population, and the propagation of a "super race," that was rooted in the occult and became a "religion of the blood".

Unknown to many, both Margaret Sanger and Adolph Hitler were disciples of Madame Blavatsky, the founder of a religion that worshiped Lucifer.[23]

During Hitler's genetic engineering campaign, at least 400,000 Germans were sterilized for the following: blindness, epilepsy, homosexuality, mental depression, alcoholism, deafness, sexual promiscuity, and physical deformity. Hitler's genetic engineering program was accompanied with the termination of the genetically "unfit" by euthanasia, which provided the ultimate solution for the "Jewish problem" in the Nazi death camps.

As an advocate of the same genetic engineering program for America, Sanger publically spoke of sterilizing those she designated as "unfit," a plan she said would be the "salvation of American civilization".

During the years prior to World War II, Sanger enlisted the help of the Nazi member Ernst Rudin, who later became the director of the German Medical Experimentation Programs, to serve as an advisor to her American Birth Control League organization, which eventually became known as "Planned Parenthood".

In the 1910s and '20s, the entire U.S. medical, political, religious, and legislative system was against the idea and practice of population control in any form. The Comstock Law of 1873, named after its proponent Anthony Comstock, made it a crime to promote obscene writing, along with drugs, and devices and articles that prevented conception or caused abortion.

In 1922, Sanger wrote a book entitled *The Pivot of Civilization,* in which she called for "the elimination of 'human weeds,' for the 'cessation of charity' because it prolonged the lives of the 'unfit,' for the segregation of 'morons, misfits, and the maladjusted,' and for the sterilization of genetically inferior races."[24]

For Sanger, the Comstock Law was a serious threat to the liberty and equality of American women. With the opening of an office of the American Birth Control League in Washington, D.C., in 1926, Sanger set out to persuade Congress to abolish or amend the Comstock Law by lobbying Senators, holding public rallies, and writing articles that promoted her women's liberation organization.

Thirteen years later, in 1939, Sanger organized the "Negro project," a program designed to eliminate members of what she believed to be an "inferior race". Sanger justified her "Negro project," saying: "The masses of Negroes . . . particularly in the South, still breed carelessly and disastrously, with the result that the increase among Negroes, even more than among whites, is from that portion of the population least intelligent and fit . . . ."[25]

During this same period, in the early 1900s, Alice Bailey founded the "Lucifer Publishing Company," and promoted the idea of population control. She was married to Foster Bailey, a Thirty-second Degree Freemason, who became the National Secretary of the Theosophical Society, in 1919. Like Adolph Hitler and Margaret Sanger, Alice Bailey was also a disciple of the Luciferin teachings of Madame Blavatsky.

At that particular time, because the name "Lucifer" had such a bad connotation, Bailey changed the name of her organization from "The Lucifer Company" to "The Lucis Trust," which exists today and continues to influence life in America with the same dark spiritual teachings espoused by its founder. Even today, publications for The Lucis Trust regularly refer to as "The Plan" for humanity that has been established by "The Hierarchy".

In 1973, the Supreme Court's ruling on *Roe v. Wade* opened wide a door for the birth control and sexual emancipation of America women that began in the early 1900s by Margaret Sanger and Alice Bailey. According to the Centers for Disease Control (CDC), from January 22, 1973, to January 22, 2013, (forty years) there were 54, 559,615 abortions performed in the United States.[26] This means that since January 1973, each year in the United States, an approximate average of 1,363, 990 unborn children have been sacrificed on the Abortion Altars of sexual emancipation in the name of the revolutionary motto "Liberty, Equality, Fraternity".

Today, the greatest benefactor of the early twentieth century Margaret Sanger and Alice Bailey's women's liberation movements is Planned Parenthood. According to Planned Parenthood's own annual report, in 2011 Planned Parenthood was funded by $542 million tax payer dollars even though it has over $1 billion in assets, such as buildings, property, etc. That same year Planned Parenthood performed 333,964 abortions (more than 900 abortions every day), as compared to only 2,300 adoption referrals (about 6 per day).

Despite Planned Parenthood's claim that it offers prenatal care to thousands of women each year, in 2011, fewer than 30,000 women received prenatal care, which clearly establishes Planned Parenthood as an "Abortion Mill," operating primarily for the purpose of terminating the lives of unborn children.

Nevertheless, today the officials of Planned Parenthood feel comfortable enough to boast about Planned Parenthood's sinister "social engineering" beginnings. In 1985, the annual Planned Parenthood report bragged: "[We are] proud of our past, and planning for our future."[27]

Thus what began as Margaret Sanger's campaign to sexually *emancipate* American women and *eliminate the unfit* has been successfully developed into a $500 million plus annual federal funded tax payer's Abortion Mill that now has 129 affiliates, and operates 875 clinics throughout the United States.

Abolition of God, Morality, and Marriage

In November 1793, the campaign against the churches, beginning with the massacre of the priests in September of the preceding year, was carried out all over France. In Paris, churches were desecrated and burnt to the ground.

In many churches, images of the saints were broken; pictures of Mary and Jesus were torn and burned; and men played cards on the high altar, while others mounted the pulpit and blasphemed the name of God. So great was their hatred for Christianity, one English contemporary of the French Revolution, in Paris, wrote: "Who cannot understand that to pray is a crime, and to kneel down before God an offense to humanity."[28]

True to the anti-Christian doctrines of Rousseau, Voltaire, and Weishaupt—that Reason should be the only code of man—the public worship of God was abolished and the Feasts of Reason were celebrated in the churches of Paris. Professor Robinson says that the actual ceremonies, which took place when women of easy morals were enthroned as goddesses, were modeled on Weishaupt's plan for an "Eroterion" or festival in honor of the "Goddess of love".[29]

During the destruction of the St. Eustache church, it is said that a crowd of "female patriots," who were participating in the "Love Feast," were chanting: "Marriage citizenesses, is the greatest error of ancient history. To be married is to be a slave!"[30]

One woman is said to have shouted: "The matrimonial state is a perpetual crime against morality . . . . We, the illegitimate companions, will no longer suffer the legitimate wives to usurp rites they no longer possess and which they ought never to have had at all. Let the degree be modified. All for free women, none for the slaves."[31]

Thus it was that what we know as the modern day "Feminist Movement" actually began in the late eighteenth century, which was precisely the time the Jacobins began to recruit women for their revolution of "Liberty, Equality, Fraternity".

Richard N. Rhoades

The Liberal Left's Campaign against God in Public Schools

The late D. James Kennedy, pastor of Coral Ridge Church, in Fort Lauderdale, Florida, once pointed out in his sermons that almost all the historic universities of America, including Harvard, Yale, Princeton, Dartmouth, Columbia, and many others, were founded as Christian institutions dedicated to the study of the Holy Scriptures, which was essential for the development of character and leadership.

Indeed, from the mid-1800s to the mid-1900s the preferred textbooks for America's public grade schools were *McGuffy's Eclectic Reader,* which were filled with passages of Scripture, as well as character building articles written by different writers. Some of the subjects in *McGuffy's Reader* are titled as follows: "The Creator" (4th Grade), "The Right Way" (4th Grade), "The Golden Rule" (4th Grade), "Dare to do Right" (4th Grade), "The Sermon on the Mount" (4th Grade), "The Righteous Never Forsaken" (5th Grade), "The Goodness of God" (5th Grade), "The Hour of Prayer" (5th Grade), "Religion the only Basis of Society" (5th Grade), "The Bible the Best of Classics" (5th Grade), "God is Everywhere" (6th Grade), "Observance of the Sabbath" (6th Grade), "God's Goodness to Such as Fear Him" (6th Grade), and "Immortality of the Soul" (6th Grade), just to name a few.[32]

In *McGuffy's Primer Reader,* one lesson is about the Creator. At the beginning of the lesson is an art drawing, showing a huge oak tree on the side of a hill with a little girl standing below it and looking up at it, as if wondering about the mystery of that great oak tree. The lesson reads as follows:

> Do you see that tall tree? Long ago it sprang up from a small nut.
>
> Do you know who made it do so?
>
> It was God, my child. God made the world and all things in it. He made the sun to light the day, and the moon to shine at night.
>
> God shows that he loves us by all that he has done for us. Should we not then love him?[33]

Unfortunately, all this spiritual and moral (especially Judaic-Christian) education of our children began to change when FDR became President of the United States of America. Roosevelt immediately took action to increase the number of justices on the Supreme Court. He believed that if he could increase the number of justices he could appoint like-minded justices and change the Constitution, which led to cries that Roosevelt was trying "to stack the court".

Congress refused to increase the number of justices. But it proved to be immaterial in the end. Due to resignation and death, Roosevelt was able to appoint enough like-minded Masonic justices to control the court to his liking.

The noted author, lecturer and radio host Dr. Stanley Monteith writes:

> The Masonic Order controlled the United States Supreme Court between 1941 and 1971, and drastically changed our society. Four of the six Supreme Court Justices who voted to remove God and prayer from public schools were Masons: Tom Clark, William O. Douglas, Earl Warren, and Hugo Black.[34]

Likewise, Paul Fisher says in his widely read book entitled *Behind the Lodge Door:*

> Indeed, between 1941-1971, the Supreme Court was dominated by Masons in ratios ranging from 5 to 4 (1941-1946, 1969-1971) to 8 to 1 (1949-1956). During that 30-year-period, the Court erected "a wall" separating things religious from things secular. It was an epoch when prayer and Bible reading were deracinated from public education . . . . Masons have succeeded in having their religion dominate American society.[35]

From the beginning of FDR's "New Deal" Court the objective was to reduce the influence of God, prayer and the Bible in the public arena. In one of the most important rulings of the Supreme

Court, *Everson v. Board of Education* (1947), Justice Hugo Black, a Brother Mason, wrote the majority opinion, saying:

> The "establishment of religion clause" of the First Amendment means at least this: Neither a state nor the Federal Government can set up a church. Neither can pass laws that aid one religion, aid all religions, or prefer one religion to another . . . . In the words of Jefferson, the clause against establishment of religion by law was intended to erect "a wall of separation between church and State."[36]

The problem with this interpretation is that nowhere in the Constitution is there any reference to the idea of "separation between church and state". That phrase was lifted from a private letter of Thomas Jefferson to the Danbury Baptist Association, in 1802, regarding the "free establishment of religion". Addressing the concerns of the Baptist Association, Jefferson wrote the following words:

> Believing with you that religion is a matter which lies solely between Man and his God, that he owes account to none other for his faith or his worship, that the legitimate powers of government reach actions only, and not opinions. I contemplate with sovereign reverence that act of the whole American people which declared that their legislature should make no law respecting an establishment of religion, or prohibiting the free exercise thereof, thus building a wall of separation between Church and State.[37]

Clearly, the "wall" Jefferson was addressing was meant to protect religion from government intervention, not separation of the Church from the State. In fact, when George Washington left office he delivered what has been called his Farewell Address. Among the many things he addressed was a warning to the American people should they ever turn away from religion and morality, saying:

Of all the dispositions and habits which lead to political prosperity, religion and morality are indispensable supports . . . .

Let it simply be asked where is the security for prosperity, for reputation, for life if the sense of religious obligation desert?

And let us with caution indulge the supposition that morality can be maintained without religion.[38]

Yet, FDR's Masonic controlled Supreme Court took precisely the opposite view, which was the very same humanistic philosophy propagated by Rousseau and Voltaire, Brother Masons, who advocated the separation of church and state.

The Liberal Left's Campaign against Marriage

Accompanying the Liberal Left's campaign to sanitize God from public schools we are now witnessing the very same campaign being waged against the institution of marriage. The same perversion that brought ancient civilizations to ruin for more than five thousand years is now paraded in the public eye and today defended as an inalienable right.

Is it any wonder that over 50 percent of adults in this country now believe that homosexuality is an "acceptable lifestyle"? And thanks to the relentless programing in our public schools, 85 percent of high school seniors say homosexuality is acceptable. And thanks to the Liberal Left's indoctrination of our teenagers, 86 percent now say that homosexuality is determined at birth.

Assessing the impact of the ongoing Revolution of modern day intellectual liberalism, Judge Robert Bork says that nothing has been as destructive to traditional values of Western Civilization as the restructuring of society, morality, and human nature by radical feminism that has come down to us from the Sixties.[39] Judge Bork goes on to say:

Indeed, since feminists view the family as a system of oppression, and since feminism contains a large lesbian component, the marriages of men and women are often

seen as morally inferior to unions involving the other
three genders.

The hostility towards the traditional family goes hand
in hand with the feminists' hostility towards traditional
religion. They see religion as a male invention designed to
control women.[40]

Given the Liberal Left's hostility toward traditional marriage
we should not be surprised that in recent Supreme Court rulings
liberal judges are now redefining the institution of marriage as an
inalienable right. Beginning in 2003, the Massachusetts Supreme
Court gave the state legislature six months to enact a law granting
homosexuals the right to marry. Today there are thirteen states that
have legalized Same-sex marriage, including the nation's Capital.

On July 30, 2012, emboldened by President Barack Obama's
personal endorsement of Same-sex marriage, in May 2012, the
Democrat Party included an unprecedented Same-sex marriage
plank in the party's platform. That same day the New York *Daily News*
quoted *Courage California,* a California-based gay rights activist group
that called the Democrat Party's same-sex marriage plank "a historic
move by the Democrat Party that places it squarely on the right
side of history, alongside President Obama." The statement added:
"Today's move shows how far our nation has moved on this issue and
for anyone who claims there's no difference between the two parties,
this should make crystal clear which party stands for *equality* for all
Americans and which party still looks to divide our nation."

A Revolution of Destruction and Ruin

Although the revolutionaries failed in their attempt to establish
France as a model for their revolution of "Liberty, Equality,
Fraternity," history concurs that they did succeed in the complete
destruction of the country.

In 1790, the noted British statesman Edmund Burke
(1729-1797) wrote in his book entitled *Reflections on the Revolution
in France:*

> Oh! What a revolution! . . . little did I dream that I
> would have lived to see disaster fallen upon (the throne
> of France) in a nation of gallant men, in a nation of men
> of honor . . . . But the age of chivalry is gone. That of
> sophisters, economists, and calculators, has succeeded; and
> the glory of Europe is extinguished for ever.[41]

Eight years after the Great Fear ended, in 1802, an Englishman named Redhead Yorke visited France and could not believe the devastation and carnage that still existed. He wrote: "France still bleeds at every pore—she is a vast morning family, clad in sackcloth."[42]

A Revolution Rooted in Freemasonry

Even today, liberal politicians, educators, and journalists continue to spin the truth of what really happened in the French Revolution of 1789. For instance, on July 1, 2000, an editorial of the *New York Times* stated that the French Revolution of 1789 had helped launch a worldwide movement, claiming that the Declaration of the Rights of the French citizens inspired democratic reforms and reinforced the ideas of America's own revolution of Independence.[43]

But for those who personally experienced the deadly purge of the Great Fear and lived to tell about it, nothing could be farther from the truth. In 1793, one journalist of the French *Journal de Vienne* wrote:

> It is not the French who conceived the great project
> of changing the face of the world; this honor belongs to
> the Germans. The French can claim the honor of having
> begun its execution, and of having followed it out to its
> ultimate consequences, which, as history is there to prove,
> were in accordance with the genius of this people—the
> guillotine, intrigue, assassination, incendiarism, and
> cannibalism . . . . Whence comes the eternal Jacobin refrain
> of universal *liberty* and *equality,* of the suppression of kings
> and princes who are merely tyrants, of oppression by the

clergy, of necessary measures for annihilating the Christian religion and establishing a philosophic religion—a refrain that reminds everyone of the declarations of Mauvillon, a notable Illuminatus, touching Christianity, of those Knigge and Campe touching State religion? Whence comes it that all this harmonizes with the "Original Writings," of the Illuminati if there is no alliance between the two sects (Freemasonry and Illuminati)?

Whence comes it that Jacobinism has partisans everywhere, even in the most distant countries, and how can we explain that these, as far as researches can extend, have been in touch with the Illuminati?[44]

Aloys Hoffman, the editor of the same *Journal de Vienne,* later wrote: "I shall never cease to repeat that the Revolution has come from masonry and that it was made by writers and the Illuminati."[45]

Although American Masons argue that American Masonry is entirely different from the violent European model, as we have just seen the goal of the Liberal Left to establish a New Secular Order based on the Law of Humanism remains the same. Indeed, the noted author William Still tells us that in Continental Masonry "the emphasis has been shifted towards world domination by a violent revolution, whereas the more gentile Anglo/American Revolution version inspired by Lord Francis Bacon, stresses a revolution of enlightenment."[46]

Revival of Great Goddess Cult

For centuries, under the reign of Christian emperors and kings, beginning with the Christian Roman Emperor Theodosius, in 381 C.E., who abolished the worship of the old pagan deities of Rome and made Christianity the official State religion, the public worship of the Great Goddess was suppressed. But gradually, with the emergence of Freemasonry, in the 1700s, the cult worship of the Great Goddess was revived.

Nowhere was her revival more prominent than during the French Revolution of 1789, when she was given the name "Goddess of Reason" by the Illuminati and Masonic Jacobins.

In 1794, the Revolutionary Convention decreed the existence of the "Supreme Being," which was unlike the God of Christianity.[47] Simply because the main tenet of Masonry's new religion was the worship of Nature.[48]

By mid-1795, the cult worship of the "Supreme Being" began to decline. As France struggled to establish a capable government during the reign of Napoleon Bonaparte (1804-1815), Louis Phillippe XVIII (1815-1824) and Charles Phillippe X (1824-1830), the Masonic Revolutionary Goddess of Reason and Goddess of Nature were replaced with the Goddess of Liberty.

Looking back to the Revolution of 1789, France's new Goddess of Liberty would be portrayed by the French artist Eugene Delacroix, in 1830, as the the great female liberator of the people.

Liberty Guiding the People.

Notice that Delacroix's painting portrays the Goddess Liberty as bear breasted, representing her new found freedom; carrying a pike in her left hand, symbolic of her war-like attributes that were meant to be used in leading the people to Liberty, Equality, Fraternity.

By 1848, during the Second Republic, the French artist A. L. Janet-Lange portrayed the Goddess Liberty as the *personification* of the Republic of France.

The Republic Enlightening the World.

Notice that in the above painting the Goddess Liberty, who is *personified* as the Second Republic of France, sits on her royal throne in the midst of the carnage, holding aloft in her left hand the torch of enlightenment and in her right hand the scales of justice. Under her left foot is a Book of the Law (Masonic Law—'the law of humanism') and standing at her right knee is a rooster, symbolizing the morning hour of awakening.

7

REVOLUTION
COMES TO AMERICA

A<small>FTER THE SUCCESSFUL OVERTHROW</small> of the French monarchy
and aristocracy the Masonic Jacobin revolutionaries turned their
attention across the Atlantic to the fertile land of the New Republic.
With Freemasonry firmly established in the thirteen states the
Jacobins streamed to U.S. lodges where they were readily accepted
as Brothers and hailed as liberators. By painting a picture that was
totally opposite from what really happened in France the Jacobin
revolutionaries were successful in duping American leaders and
winning a significant measure of popular support.[1]

So great was the enthusiasm over what the American
people believed to be a victory, entire cities, such as Boston and
Philadelphia, held huge celebrations to honor their Brother Masons.
It is said that more gunpowder was fired celebrating their so-called
"victory" than was fired during the entire War of Independence.[2]

Even Thomas Jefferson spoke about the French Revolution
in glowing terms. In 1791, Jefferson described it as "so beautiful
a revolution," saying that he hoped it would "sweep the world".[3]
Rebutting those who claimed that the French Revolution was
carried out by a group of Jacobin revolutionaries, Jefferson
maintained that he believed most Frenchmen were Jacobins, saying:
"Their excesses, if one called them such, reflected that national
will."[4]

For some, however, Jefferson's support of the French revolutionaries was unconscionable. Secretary of Treasury Alexander Hamilton openly criticized Jefferson, claiming that he had helped to foment the French Revolution. In May 26, 1792, Hamilton wrote to a friend, saying that Jefferson "drank freely of the French philosophy," and had a role in the Revolution "in the moment of fermentation, which he had a share in exciting."[5]

Hamilton's charges were well founded. While minister to France, Jefferson had drafted a Charter of Rights for the revolutionaries to be presented to the king.[6]

Despite Hamilton's criticism, Jefferson continued to affirm his support for the Jacobins and French Revolution. On May 8, 1793, Jefferson wrote a letter to the Frenchman Brissot de Warville from Philadelphia, saying that he was "eternally attached to the principles" of the French Revolution.[7]

Interestingly enough, even the former Communist leaders of Russia, who viewed the French Revolution as the model for its own Bolshevick Revolution, regarded Thomas Jefferson as the most prominent of the Founding Fathers. During the visit of the Soviet leader Mikhail Gorbachev, a Thirty-third Degree Mason, and his wife to the United States, in 1987, Mrs. Rasha Gorbachev made it a point to visit the Jefferson Memorial, and was quoted by the press as saying that Jefferson was "one of the world's greatest thinkers".[8]

Illuminati in Early America

On July 16, 1782, the year after the War of Independence ended, the secret societies of the world convened at the Congress of Wilhelmsbad and formed an alliance between the Illuminati and Freemasonry. Less than three years later, on March 2, 1785, the Bavarian government banned both the Illuminati and Freemasons, forcing Weishaupt to leave the country. That same year, in 1785, the first Illuminati lodge was established in Thomas Jefferson's state of Virginia. Shortly thereafter, fourteen more lodges were established in the thirteen Colonies.

One such lodge was the Columbian Lodge, which was established in New York City, in 1785. Some of its distinguished members were Governor DeWitt Clinton, who became the General Grand High Priest of the United States[9]; the New York Assemblyman Clinton Roosevelt, a family predecessor of Franklin D. Roosevelt; and Horace Greeley, the influential owner of *The New York Tribune* and *New Yorker* magazine.[10]

Clinton Roosevelt, a zealous advocate of the Illuminati teachings of Weishaupt, wrote a book on socialism entitled *The Science of Government Founded on Natural Law* in which he set forth his philosophy of God, saying: "There is no God of justice to order things aright on earth; if there is a God, he is a malicious and vengeful being, who created us for misery."[11]

In his book, Roosevelt described himself and other Illuminati members as "the *enlightened* ones". For Roosevelt, the U.S. Constitution was a flawed document that was "put together hastily," and therefore in need of revision.[12]

Not surprisingly, this is precisely how Clinton Roosevelt's descendent Franklin D. Roosevelt also viewed the Constitution. As you shall soon see, there was a major difference between the two men. Clinton Roosevelt merely wrote books about the need to revise the Constitution. As President of the United States of America, FDR suspended the Constitution with his declared State of Emergency Proclamation 2039, on March 9, 1933.[13] He then appointed like-minded Supreme Court Justices who changed the Constitution's "original understanding" to that of an "evolutionary document".[14]

America's First Democratic Clubs

In 1793, the new French revolutionary government sent a young man named Edmond Genet (1763-1834) to serve as its ambassador to the United States. Less than a year earlier, Genet had been expelled as ambassador to Russia for instigating political unrest among the Russian people.

Officially, as an ambassador to the new Republic, Genet's mission was to secure repayment of the debt owed to France, which was incurred during the War of Independence. The plan of the revolutionary French government was that the collected monies would be used to finance the continuation of the French

Revolution in England. "From this point on," says William Still, "the history of Europe can only completely be understood in light of this continuing World Revolution movement marching across its face."[15]

On April 8, Genet arrived in Charleston, South Carolina, on the French warship *Embuscade*. Instead of traveling to the then-capital of Philadelphia to meet with President Washington, Genet stayed in South Carolina and began organizing what he called "Democratic Clubs" in the frontier regions of the new states.[16] Unofficially, Genet's mission was to foment discontent among the colonists by championing causes that pitted the colonists against their own government.

Before long, Genet was being hailed by the frontier settlers as a champion of their civil liberties. It is said that Genet became so popular that at one festival held in his honor the people toasted Genet but refused to extend the same honor to President Washington.[17]

News of Genet's popularity soon spread to the cities, as well as Congress, where it became apparent to several representatives that Genet and his Democratic Clubs had become a serious threat to the new government. Noah Webster, the great educator, warned Congress that if the Democratic Clubs were not "crushed in their infancy . . . they would certainly crush the government."[18]

The Whiskey Rebellion

In the early 1790s, the new Secretary of Treasury Alexander Hamilton was instrumental in persuading Congress to levy a tax on all distilled liquor. At that particular time Congress was in dire need of funds to run the new government. The authority of Congress also needed to be solidified among the frontier people living on the edges of the new states. Hamilton, a religious man, believed liquor to be a sin condemned in the Bible and thought it especially appropriate that all distilled liquor should be taxed.

Among the populace, it was the corn farmers living on the western frontier who would be hit the hardest by such a tax. Due to rough roads, which frontier-farmers had to travel to reach towns to deliver their produce, it was extremely difficult to haul heavy wagons loaded with corn to the market-place. So to make their corn more transportable they distilled it into whiskey.

Genet and his Democratic Clubs seized upon the whiskey tax issue as a matter of civil liberties. Before long, the anger of the frontier corn farmers had been so inflamed that an anti-government riot broke out in Harrisburg called the "Whiskey Rebellion".

When word of the rebellion reached President Washington he dispatched 15,000 troops for Harrisburg. The rebels were unprepared for such a show of force. At the sight of Washington escorting 15,000 troops the insurrection was quickly brought to an end, and order was restored to the frontier.

Shortly afterwards, President Washington condemned the rebellion, its illuminati supporters in Congress and the French government, saying:

> I consider this insurrection as the first formidable fruit of Democratic Societies . . . instituted by artful and designing members (of Congress) . . . . I see, under a display of popular and fascinating guises, the most diabolical attempts to destroy . . . the government.
>
> That they have been the fomenters of the western disturbance admits of no doubt. (If) this daring and factious spirit (is not crushed), adieu to all government in this country, except mob and club government.[19]

When President Washington left public office he remained in retirement for only two years. In 1798, when war with France was threatening over the continued interference with the struggling nation, Washington came out of retirement and accepted the appointment of Commander-in-Chief of the Army under President John Adams.

So great was the fear of the Illuminati disguised as Jacobins that Congress passed a law called "The Alien and Sedition Acts," which was designed to protect the United States from French Jacobin agent's involvement in the affairs of the new government.[20]

By the time John Quincy Adams became the sixth president of the United States the Illuminati had successfully infiltrated the American lodges of Freemasonry. President Adams warned the American people that the Parisian Jacobins had "perfectly affiliated" themselves with the lodges of Freemasonry, saying:

I do conscientiously and sincerely believe that the Order of Freemasonry, if not the greatest, is one of the greatest moral and political evils under which the Union is now laboring . . . .

(It is) a conspiracy of the few against the equal rights of the many . . . . I am prepared to complete the demonstrations before God and man, that the Masonic oath, obligations and penalties cannot be reconciled to the laws of morality, of Christianity, or of the land.[21]

A Day of Trouble, Rebuke and Blasphemy

By 1798, as a result of the Democratic Club inspired Whiskey Rebellion and books written on the French Revolution by such men as the British statesman Edmund Burke and Professor John Robinson, the American people were beginning to understand the serious threat the Illuminati posed to the New Republic. As the Order grew in numbers and influence, clergymen began sounding the alarm from their pulpits.

On May 9, 1798, at Charlestown, the Reverend Jedediah Morse preached a message on Illuminism, taking for his text: "This is a day of trouble and of rebuke and blasphemy" (2 Kings 19:3), saying in part:

Practically all of the civil and ecclesiastical establishments of Europe have already been shaken to their foundations by this terrible organization; the French Revolution itself is doubtless to be traced to its machinations; the successes of the French armies are to be explained on the same ground. The Jacobins are nothing more nor less than the open manifestation of the hidden system of the Illuminati. The Order has its branches established and its emissaries at work in America. The affiliated Jacobin Societies in America have doubtless had as the object of their establishment the propagation of the principles of the Illuminated mother club in France.[22]

In July of that same year, Timothy Dwight (1725-1817), president of Yale University and grandson of the highly respected Jonathan Edwards, delivered a sermon to the people of New Haven, warning them of the anti-God teachings of the Illuminati, saying:

> No personal or national interest of man has been invaded; no impious sentiment of action against God has been spared; no malignant hostility against Christ and His religion has been unattempted. Justice, truth, kindness, piety, and moral obligation universally have been not merely trodden underfoot . . . but ridiculed, spurned, and insulted as the childish bugbears of driveling idocy . . . . For what and shall we be connected with men of whom this is the character and conduct?
>
> Is it that our churches may become temples of reason, our Sabbath a decade, and our psalms of praise Marseillaise hymns?
>
> . . . Is it that we may see the Bible cast into a bonfire, the vessels of the sacramental supper borne by an ass in public procession, and our children either wheedled or terrified, uniting in the mob, chanting mockeries against God, and hailing in the sounds of the "Ca ira" the ruin of their religion and the loss of their souls?
>
> . . . Shall our sons become the disciples of Voltaire and the dragoons of Marat, or our daughters the concubines of the Illuminati?[23]

On another occasion, in 1812, the Reverend Joseph Willard delivered a sermon in Lancaster, New Hampshire, warning of the attempt of the Illuminati to undermine the sacred values and institutions of the New Republic, saying:

> There is sufficient evidence that a number of Societies, of the Illuminati, have been established, in this land of Gospel light and Civil liberty, which were first organized from the grand Society in France. They are doubtless, secretly striving to undermine all our ancient institutions, civil and sacred. These societies are closely

leagued with those of the same order, in Europe; they have all the same object in view.[24]

Although greatly outnumbered, influential Illuminati members and their supporters fired back at their Christian accusers. The editor of *The Independent Chronicle* spoke of "the incorrigible impertinence of the clergy in turning aside from their legitimate functions to spread alarm about Illuminism."[25] And Thomas Jefferson, whom Reverend Morse claimed was an Illuminist, described Weishaupt as merely "an enthusiastic philanthropist".[26]

America's First Central Bank

In January 1779, the Continental Note was trading 8 to 1 against the Spanish Dollar, and by November of that same year it was trading 39 to 1. In January 1781, it was trading 100 to 1, and by May of that same year the Continental Note quietly died a natural death as legal Continental currency.[27]

Thus when it came time to establish a stable and honest monetary system for the New Republic, Congress mandated the use of gold and silver and established precious metals as the official currency of the United States though the Constitution, which states as follows:

* The Congress shall have Power . . . To coin Money, (and) regulate the Value thereof, and of foreign Coin, and fix the Standard of Weights and Measures.

Article 1, S 8, U.S. Constitution

* No state shall . . . coin Money; emit Bills of Credit; make any Thing but gold and silver Coin a Tender in Payment of debts . . . .

Article 1, S 10, U.S. Constitution

Acting upon the powers granted to them by the Constitution, Congress ratified the Coinage Act on April 2, 1792, which specified U.S. currency to be only gold and silver coin, and the standard unit of weight for a Dollar to be:

* Silver—412.9 grains, 90% pure, 10% alloy added for strength and durability.

* Gold—27.5 grains, 90% pure, 10% alloy added for strength and durability.

Thus by establishing the New Republic's monetary system on gold and silver through the U.S. Constitution the 1792 Congress was declaring that the mistakes of the past would not be repeated, as with the ever inflating Continental Note. But even as the ink dried on the new constitutional mandate the powerful Rothschild banking family was laying the groundwork among members of Congress for its abolishment and replacement with a central banking system.

At that particular time the Rothschild family was the most quietly hidden power in Europe. Over the years they had carefully established their financial empire by gaining control of scores of industrial, commercial, mining, and tourist corporations. Now they wanted to control the New Republic's monetary system.

The Rothschild family had learned hundreds of years earlier that once you control the credit of a nation you control its economy. It is said that in an unguarded moment Baron Nathan Mayer de Rothschild, a member of the Lodge of Emulation in London, boasted during a party in his mansion: "I care not what puppet is placed upon the throne of England to rule the Empire on which the sun never sits. The man that controls Britain's money supply controls the British Empire, and I control the British money supply."[28] Rothschild is also reputed to have said: "Let me issue and control a nation's money, and I care not who writes the laws."[29]

At the time, unlike Europe's central banking system, America's banking system was made up of independent locally-owned banks, which valued their independence. The Rothschilds knew that any attempt to take away their autonomy would be met with strong resistance and, therefore, would have to include the U.S. money powers.

Consequently, in order to gain control of America's banking system the Rothschilds had to find a man who was not only respected by the money powers but could command the respect of Congress. They found such a man at the highest level of the new government, Secretary of Treasury Alexander Hamilton, a Brother Mason.

The Rothschilds also knew that the new government would need a powerful incentive to make such a move, such as a monetary windfall for the U.S. Treasury. For the Rothschilds, that would be no problem. The new government was in dire need of money, having incurred an enormous debt during the War of Independence.

The voices for the support of a Central Bank, led by Hamilton, succeeded in convincing the members of Congress that the constitutional phrase ". . . to coin Money, (and) regulate the Value thereof . . ." was not to be taken literally but only as "implied or suggested powers". Interestingly, both Alexander Hamilton and George Washington supported a Central Bank while Jefferson opposed it. In a stern warning to the Congress about adopting such a system Thomas Jefferson warned the American people, saying:

> The Central Bank is an institution of the most deadly
> hostility existing against the principles and form of our
> Constitution. I am an enemy to all banks discounting
> bills or notes for anything but coin. If the American
> people allow private banks to control the issuance of
> their currency, first by inflation and then by deflation, the
> banks and corporations that will grow up around them
> will deprive the people of all their property until their
> children will wake up homeless on the continent their
> fathers conquered.[30]

Despite Jefferson's warning, the promise of $8 million dollars, which would immediately be realized from the sale of shares in a Central Bank, was much too enticing for the new Congress to pass up. On February 25, 1791, Washington signed the bill passed by Congress, and the first Central Bank of the United States was born, giving the new Bank a twenty-year charter.

Of the twenty-five thousand shares, which were sold at $400 each, the new government owned only twenty percent. Eighty percent of the new Republic's Bank of the United States was owned by private shareholders. Of that eighty percent, Baron James de Rothschild, a Thirty-third Degree Scottish Rite Mason of Paris, was the principle shareholder and, therefore, the principle power behind credit and economy of the New Republic.[31]

A Den of Thieves and Vipers

In 1811, because of stiff opposition from locally owned state banks, Congress refused to renew the Central Bank's charter. But congressional refusal proved to be only a temporary measure. In 1816, the powerful influence of the international money brokers prevailed and, once again, Congress chartered the privately owned Central Bank.

In 1832, shortly after Andrew Jackson ('Old Hickory') became President, he discovered that the U.S. government owned only twenty-four percent of the shares in the Bank of the United States, while the international bankers owned seventy-six percent. Jackson was outraged. When it came time to renew the bank's charter he promptly vetoed the bill's renewal.

The following year Jackson ordered all U.S. funds to be withdrawn from the Bank of the United States and transferred to various state banks. Mincing no words, "Old Hickory" told the money powers: "You are a den of thieves—vipers. I intend to rout you out and by the eternal God, I will rout you out."

Nicholas Biddle, head of the U.S. Central Bank and a hireling of the Rothschild interests, responded by ordering a sharp reduction in loans throughout the banking system. First, there was a drastic decline in business activity. Then an economic panic swept across the country. Biddle's message to Congress and President Jackson was loud and clear: "Re-charter the Bank!"

For Jackson, Biddle's new banking policy was economic blackmail. Nevertheless, "Old Hickory" stood his ground and told the American people that the bold effort of the Central Bank to control the government "is but a premonition of the fate that awaits the American people should they be deluded into perpetuation of this institution or the establishment of another like it."[32]

A brilliant military strategist, Jackson first brought an abrupt halt to the banking cartel's powerful hold on America's monetary system. He then re-established the constitutional currency of gold and silver coin.

Three years later, on January 8, 1835, President Jackson made the final payment on the national debt—a feat no other president has accomplished!

Although Jackson won the battle, the struggle for America's economic soul was far from over. When Abraham Lincoln became president he too recognized the money power's efforts to gain control of America's monetary system, and said:

> I see in the near future a crisis approaching that unnerves me and causes me to tremble for the safety of my country; corporations have been enthroned, an era of corruption in high places will follow, and the money power of the country will endeavor to prolong its reign by working upon the prejudices of the people until the wealth is aggregated in a few hands, and the Republic is destroyed.[33]

President Jackson and President Lincoln's fears were well founded. As you shall see, not only did the Money Powers gain control of America's monetary system, but in the entrance of their new "Federal Reserve" building was placed an image of the Great Goddess of antiquity.

8

THE FEDERAL RESERVE

In 1907, Jacob Schiff, a member of the B'nai B'rith (secret Jewish Masonic Order meaning "Brothers of the Covenant"), and the head of the New York investment firm of Kuhn, Leob & Co., warned the New York Chamber of Commerce that if a Central Bank was not established there would be a financial crisis that would devastate the country. Schiff reportedly said: "Unless we have a Central Bank with adequate control of credit resources, this country is going to undergo the most severe and far reaching money panic in its history."

That same year, Paul Warburg, the brother of Max Warburg, who headed the Rothschild-allied family banking interests in Frankfurt, Germany, was sent to America. Shortly after he arrived in America there was a major run on the banks across the country. Des Griffin says in his book entitled *Descent Into Slavery:*

> The United States plunged into a monetary crisis that had all the earmarks of a skillfully planned Rothschild "job." The ensuing panic financially ruined tens of thousands of innocent people across the country—and made billions for the banking elite. The purpose of the "crisis" was two-fold: (1) To make a financial "killing" for the Insiders, and (2) to impress on the American people the "great need" for a central bank.[1]

The 1907 banking crisis was so devastating to the economy of the country that Congress authorized a National Monetary Commission, headed by the powerful Senator Nelson Aldrich from Rhode Island, who was also the primary power broker for the Rothschild-allied banking family. Shortly afterwards, Senator Aldrich's daughter married John D. Rockefeller, Jr., bringing about a family union of the most powerful politician in the U.S. Senate and the wealthiest man in the world.[2]

It was at this particular time that the Rothschild banking cartel, led by Nelson Aldrich (a Mason who also served as treasurer of the Grand Lodge of Rhode Island [3]), made its move to establish a third U.S. Central Bank. According to the researcher James Perloff, in 1910, Aldrich met secretly with top representatives of the J. P. Morgan and Rockefeller interests at Morgan's hunting club on Jekyll Island, off the coast of Georgia. There the plan was devised in secret to establish a new Central Bank.

The meeting was later confirmed by one of its original designers, Frank Vanderlip, president of one of the nation's largest banks, Kuhn, Loeb's National City Bank of New York. In the *Saturday Evening Post,* February 8, 1935, Vanderlip recalled the fateful event, saying:

> . . . There was an occasion near the close of 1910 when I was as secretive, indeed as furtive, as any conspirator. I do not feel it is any exaggeration to speak of our secret expedition to Jekyll Island as the occasion of the actual conception of what eventually became the Federal Reserve System.
>
> We were told to leave our last names behind us. We were told further that we should avoid dining together on the night of our departure. We were instructed to come one at a time . . . where Senator Aldrich's private car would be in readiness, attached to the rear end of the train for the South.
>
> Once aboard the private car, we began to observe the taboo that had been fixed on last names. Discovery, we knew, simply must not happen, or else all our time and effort would be wasted . . . .[4]

Shortly after the Jekyll Island meeting Nelson Aldrich introduced to Congress what was called the "Aldrich Plan," which was a bill to establish a U.S. Central Bank. But there was a problem. Because the bill was named after Aldrich himself, and because Aldrich was closely connected with the Morgan and Rockefeller banks, congressmen became suspicious of the bill and it was killed in committee.

Undaunted, in 1913, its supporters re-submitted a second bill. Only this time they submitted it under the name "The Federal Reserve Act". Congress passed it!

Upon its passage, Congressman Charles A. Lindbergh, Sr. (1859-1924), the father of Charles Lindbergh (1902-1974), the "Lucky Lindy" of the Spirit of St. Louis, said:

> This Act establishes the most gigantic trust on earth. When the President signs this Act the invisible government by the Money Powers, proven to exist by the Money Trust Investigation, will be legalized. The new law will create inflation whenever the trusts want inflation. From now on depressions will be scientifically created.[5]

Since the monetary policies in the Federal Reserve Act were the creation of Paul Warburg, a partner of Kuhn, Loeb & Company, it was no surprise that the Kuhn, Loeb & Company National City Bank would control the largest number of shares, and therefore be the principle power behind America's new central banking system, the "Federal Reserve".[6]

At that particular time the banking house of Kuhn, Loeb & Company had been identified by Senator Robert L. Owen as representing the European Rothschild-allied banking family in the United States. Colonel Elisha Ely, in his book entitled *Roosevelt, Wilson and the Federal Reserve Law,* tells us that it was Paul Warburg who put the Federal Reserve Act together after the Aldrich Plan failed to pass Congress, claiming that Baron Alfred Rothschild of London was the mastermind behind both plans.[7]

Nevertheless, under the name "Federal Reserve" America's new Central Bank survived and became even stronger than before.

Although the Federal Reserve had become America's new Central Bank, President Woodrow Wilson, who was a major supporter, soon became concerned about its increasing control over America's economy. Three years later, Wilson admitted:

> ...The growth of the nation ... and all our activities are in the hands of a few men .... We have come to be one of the worst ruled; one of the most completely controlled and dominated governments in the civilized world ... no longer a government by conviction and the free vote of the majority, but a government by the opinion and duress of small groups of dominant men.[8]

Wilson's fears were well founded. But it was too late. From this point on President Wilson, as well as each future president, would bow at the altar of the Federal Reserve, where the high priests of the money powers preform their mystical rites of creating money out of thin air.

Nelson Aldrich, as the primary power broker for the Rothschild banking interest and one of the secret planners for a U.S. Central Bank at Jekyll Island, was rewarded handsomely. When Aldrich entered the Senate, in 1881, he was worth $50,000. When he left, in 1911, he was worth $30 million.[9]

The Great "Federal Reserve" Misconception

This year, on the one hundred year anniversary of the Federal Reserve Act passed by Congress, in 1913, most Americans still believe that the Federal Reserve is a government institution. According to the testimony of its own officers, however, the Federal Reserve Bank is *not* a government institution.

For example, in 1921, William P. G. Harding, Governor of the Federal Reserve Board, was invited to speak before the Washington Chamber of Commerce and explain to its members the role of the Federal Reserve Bank in America. Harding told his audience:

From a legal standpoint these banks are private corporations, organized under a special act of Congress, namely, the Federal Reserve Act. They are not in the strict sense of the word Government banks.[10]

Even more revealing is the sworn testimony Harding gave under oath, when he was called before members of Congress to give a statement about the private ownership of Federal Reserve Bank. Harding admitted:

The Federal Reserve Bank is an institution owned by the stockholding member banks. The government has not a dollar's worth of stock in it.[11]

More recently, on February 16, 1982, the *Olympic Herald* newspaper featured an article about Senator Jack Metcalf, a Washington state legislator, who introduced Senate Resolution No. 127, which challenged the constitutionality of the creation of U.S. currency by the Federal Reserve. In his bill, Senator Metcalf stated: "The Federal Reserve System is nothing more than a group of private banks which charge interest on money that never existed."

In the Senate report and text of *Information Prepared for Washington State Senate in Consideration of State Concurrent Resolution #127*, the following Senate discussion states in part:

Senator McCaslin: Reading your Resolution, are you really telling us that the Federal Reserve Banking System is a private banking system?

Senator Metcalf: Like most Americans, I believed the Federal Reserve was a party of the Federal Government. It is not! It is a federally chartered private banking corporation which has by law—not the Constitution, but by law—been given the power to control and issue money used in the U.S.

Today, only a few of our elected representatives understand that the Federal Reserve is not a government institution. But as you shall soon see, even when a majority of elected representatives were fully aware that the Federal Reserve was a private corporation owned and operated by a select group of Insiders and international bankers who were plundering the wealth of the American people they refused to do anything about it.

An American Patriot Remembered

On December 15, 1931, Congressman Louis T. McFadden, who was chairman of the House Banking and Currency Committee, from 1920-1931, voiced his concerns about the Federal Reserve to his elected colleagues, saying:

> The Federal Reserve Board and banks are the duly appointed agents of the foreign central banks of issue and they are more concerned with their foreign customers than they are with the people of the United States. The only thing that is American about the Federal Reserve and banks is the money they use.[12]

One month later, on January 13, 1932, due to Congress' failure to take action, Congressman McFadden introduced a resolution indicting the privately owned and operated banking cartel of the Federal Reserve Board of Governors for criminal conspiracy. The resolution stated in part:

WHEREAS I charge them jointly and severally, with the crime of having treasonably conspired and acted against the peace and security of the United States and having treasonably conspired to destroy Constitutional government in the United States. Resolved, that the Committee on the Judiciary is authorized and directed as a whole or by subcommittee to investigate the official conduct of the Federal Reserve Board and agents to determine whether, in the opinion of the said committee, they have been guilty of any high crime or misdemeanor which in the contemplation of the Constitution requires the interposition of the Constitutional powers of the House.[13]

During the next six months Congressman McFadden tried to enlist the support of his colleagues to launch a united front against the powerful Federal Reserve banking cartel. As earlier, however, there was little interest.

Finally, on June 10, 1932, McFadden took his fight to the House floor, saying:

Mr. Chairman, we have in this country one of the most corrupt institutions the world has ever known. I refer to the Federal Reserve Board and the Federal Reserve Banks . . . . Some people think the Federal Reserve Banks are United States Government institutions. They are not government institutions. They are private credit monopolies which prey upon the people of the United States for the benefit of themselves and their foreign customers; foreign and domestic speculators and swindlers; and rich predatory money lenders. In that dark crew of financial pirates there are those who would cut a man's throat to get a dollar out of his pocket; there are those who would send money into the states to buy votes to control our legislation; and there are those who maintain an international propaganda for the purpose of deceiving us and wheedling us into the granting of new concessions which will permit them to cover up their past misdeeds and set again in motion their gigantic train of crime.[14]

McFadden's plea for congressional action was both eloquent and direct. But, once again, his argument fell on deaf ears. Out of the entire House membership only five representatives were courageous enough to take a public stand against the Federal Reserve money powers.

For many, McFadden's failure to rally the House to take action was interpreted as a political victory for the opposition. The House Republican majority leader boasted: "Louis T. McFadden is now politically dead."[15]

For McFadden, the fight to restore America's constitutional monetary system was far from over. In another bold attempt, McFadden introduced a resolution to impeach President Herbert Hoover, a strong supporter of the Federal Reserve. McFadden's Impeachment Resolution states in part:

> WHEREAS the said Herbert Hoover, President of the United States has in violation of the Constitution and laws of the United States permitted irregularities in the issuance of the Federal Reserve which have occasioned great losses to the United States and have deprived the United States of legal revenue and has permitted the Federal Reserve Board and the Federal Reserve Banks unlawfully to take and use government credit for powerful gain and has permitted grave irregularities in the conduct of the United States Treasury, which violations make him guilty of high crimes and misdemeanors and subject to impeachment . . . . [16]

When McFadden's Impeachment Resolution was brought to the House floor for a vote it was overwhelmingly rejected by a vote of 361 nay, 8 yea, and 60 abstaining.[17]

Although Congressman McFadden failed in his attempt to persuade Congress to take action against the Federal Reserve banking cartel, he was still viewed as a threat by those who supported the Federal Reserve System. In the next congressional election, huge contributions found their way into the coffers of his opponent. As a result of his character assassination by his congressional colleagues and the liberal press, combined with the high-dollar campaign out-spending by his opponent, McFadden was overwhelmingly defeated in his bid for another term.[18]

For this great American patriot the worst was yet to come. In October 1936, the newspapers reported that Louis McFadden had "mysteriously died". During his fight with the Federal Reserve banking cartel there had been three attempts on his life; the last of which was fatal. It is believed that Congressman McFadden died of poisoning. Reporting on his "mysterious" death after a bout with the "intestinal-flue," on October 2, 1936, *Pelley's Weekly* of October 14 stated:

> Now that this startling American patriot has made the Passing, it can be revealed that not long after his public utterances against the encroaching powers (Federal Reserve), it became known among his intimates that he had suffered two attacks against his life. The first attack came in the form of two revolver shots fired at him from ambush as he was alighting from a cab in front of one of the Capital hotels. Fortunately both shots missed him, the bullets burying themselves in the structure of the cab. He became violently ill after partaking of food at a political banquet in Washington. His life was only saved from what was subsequently announced as a poisoning by the presence of a physician friend at the banquet, who at once procured a stomach pump and subjected the Congressman to emergency treatment.[19]

The Fed's New Economic Order

Between the years 1923 and 1929 the Federal Reserve flooded the nation's money supply with new money (the printing of Federal Reserve Notes) by sixty-two percent.[20] As a result, in 1928, the year before the Great Crash of 1929, five hundred banks failed nationwide.

Addressing the Great Crash of 1929, Congressman Louis McFadden said:

> It was not accidental. It was a carefully contrived occurrence . . . . The international bankers sought to bring about a condition or despair here so that they might emerge as rulers of us all.[21]

The Great Depression followed the Crash through the remainder of Herbert Hoover's presidency, when FDR was swept into office in the presidential election of 1932. The stage was now set for the complete take-over of America's monetary system by the privately owned and operated money powers of the Federal Reserve.

On March 2, 1933, Herbert Hoover wrote a letter to the Federal Reserve Board of New York, asking them for a recommendation for dealing with the situation at that time.[22] The Federal Reserve Board members responded with a Resolution they had adopted, which states in part as follows:

Resolution Adopted By The Federal Reserve Board Of New York

> Whereas, in the opinion of the Board of Directors of the Federal Reserve Bank of New York, the continued and increasing withdrawal of currency and gold from the banks of the country has now created a national emergency . . . . [23]

Until this time, from 1913 to 1933, when the Federal Reserve was authorized to be America's Central Bank, one of the primary purposes for the creation of a Central Bank was, among other things, for its function as a secure repository for the gold of the American people. During that time Federal Reserve Notes were redeemable in gold on demand. But all of that was about to change.

In 1933, due to the Great Depression, Americans were struggling to stay alive, keep their families fed, and save their businesses and farms from economic ruin. As a result, people were coming to the banks and wanting their gold on demand. However, since the

Federal Reserve Board had ordered the printing of more Federal Reserve Notes than the gold the banks had on hand its obligation to redeem Federal Reserve Notes for gold was now creating what the Board called a "national emergency".

The Federal Reserve Board placed the blame for the "national emergency" squarely on the backs of the American people, and called on the President to declare a bank holiday, stating:

> Now, Therefore, Be It Resolved, that, in this emergency, the Federal Reserve Board is hereby requested to urge the President of the United States to declare a bank holiday, Saturday, March 4, and Monday, March 6 . . . .

> Whereas, it is provided in Section 5 (b) of the Act of October 6, 1917, as amended that "the President may investigate, regulate, or prohibit, under such rules and regulations as he may prescribe, by means of licenses or otherwise, any transactions in foreign exchange and the export, hoarding, melting, or earmarkings of gold or silver coin or bullion or currency," ★ ★ ★ . . . . [24]

On March 5, 1933, the day following Franklin D. Roosevelt's inauguration as President, on March 4, he called for an extraordinary session of Congress to be held on the 9th of March.[25] The next day, on March 6, FDR declared a state of emergency under the War Powers Act of October 6, 1917, as amended by the Act of March 9, 1933, and issued Proclamation 2039, which states as follows:

> Whereas there have been heavy and unwarranted withdrawals of gold and currency from our banking institutions for the purpose of hoarding . . . .

> Whereas, it is provided in Section 5 (b) of the Act of October 6, 1917, (40 Stat. L. 411) as amended, that "the President may investigate, regulate, or prohibit, under such rules and regulations as he may prescribe, by means of licenses or otherwise, any transaction in foreign exchange

and the export, hoarding, melting, or earmarkings of gold
or silver coin or bullion or currency," ★   ★   ★ . . . . [26]

Here we see FDR using the exact same wording and punctuation used by the money powers in their Federal Reserve Board Resolution. Moreover, like the Federal Reserve Board, FDR placed the blame squarely on the American people for withdrawing their own gold from the banks, which by law was redeemable with the Federal Reserve Notes they had been given in exchange.

It is significant for us to understand that in the above paragraph of Section 5 (b), at the place of the three asterisks, "★   ★   ★," the remainder of the original Section 5 (b) of the War Powers Act of October 6, 1917 states: "(other than credits relating solely to transactions to be executed wholly within the United States)." [27] By including this phrase Congress made certain that the Constitutional rights, property and business transactions of the American people were protected from the government in time of war.

In Roosevelt's amended Act of March 9, 1933, however, the remainder of Section 5 (b), at the place of the three asterisks, "★   ★   ★," now read as follows:"by any person within the United States or any place subject to the jurisdiction thereof."[28]

In other words, under FDR's amended emergency powers Act of March 9, 1933, Congress removed that original phrase, which protected the American people's Constitutional rights and, instead, made the American people themselves, their property and business transactions, subject to government imprisonment, fines, and seizure, just as was any foreign person or persons who lived in the United States and conspired with the enemy at the time of war.

On March 9, 1933, at noon, Congress convened in a special session to bring President Roosevelt's emergency War Powers Act of October 6, 1917, as amended by the Act of March 9, 1933, to a speedy vote and confirmation.

To expedite a quick vote, only one copy of the bill was made available to the entire congressional membership to read, and only for about forty minutes.

One of the first voices to be heard on the House floor was that of Congressman Louis McFadden. The 73rd Congressional Record on FDR's national emergency Act of March 9, 1933, reads in part as follows:

> **Mr. McFadden:** Mr. Speaker, I regret that the membership of the House has had no opportunity to consider or even read this bill. The first opportunity I had to know what this legislation is, was when it was read from the clerk's desk. It is an important bill. It is a dictatorship over finances in the United States. It is complete control over the banking system in the United States .... It is difficult under the circumstances to discuss this bill. The first section of the bill, as I grasped it, is practically the war powers that were given back in 1917, with some slight amendments. The other gives supreme authority to the Secretary of the Treasury of the United States to impound all the gold in the United States in the hands of individuals, corporations, or companies for the purpose, I suppose, of bringing together that gold and making it available for the issuance of Federal Reserve notes. The third section deals with how banks are to be handled under this authority, how bank assets are to be frozen and deals with the question of limited receiverships and receiverships. The last section of the bill provides for the issuance of new money. I am a little at a loss, in the hurried way I have had to read this bill, to understand just how this new money is to be handled. Under the Federal Reserve Act obligations that are deposited as the security and gold for reserve notes are placed in the hands of the Federal Reserve agent. I would like to ask the chairman of the committee if this is a plan to change the holding of the security back of the Federal Reserve notes to the Treasury of the United States rather than the Federal Reserve agent?[29]

As earlier noted, prior to March 9, 1933, the Federal Reserve Banks held the deposited gold of the American people as security in return for gold certificates, which could be redeemed at any time. Now, Congressman McFadden is asking if this proposed bill is a plan to change the holder agency of that security from the Federal Reserve Bank to the Treasury of the United States (*i.e.,* the property, labor, assets, and business transactions of the American people).

Congressman Henry Steagall responded to McFadden's question, saying:

> **Mr. Steagall:** The provision is for the issuance of Federal Reserve bank notes, not for Federal Reserve notes (gold certificates); and the security back of it is the obligations, notes, drafts, bills of exchange, bank acceptances, outlined in the section to which the gentleman has referred.
>
> **Mr. McFadden:** Then the new circulation is to be Federal Reserve Bank notes and not Federal Reserve notes (gold certificates)? Is that true?
>
> **Mr. Steagall:** Insofar as the provisions of this section are concerned. Yes . . . . These notes are to be secured by assets that are approved, that are turned over by financial institutions to the Treasury of the United States. (Applause.) Mr. Speaker, I yield 3 minutes to the gentleman from Maryland (Mr. Goldsborough).
>
> **Mr. Goldsborough:** Mr. Speaker, in time of storm there can only be one pilot. In my judgment, the House of Representatives realize that the pilot, in this case must be the President of the United States, and they will steer their course by him. (Applause.) Mr. Speaker, in my deliberate judgment, under the leadership of the President of the United States, there will shortly be brought from the Committee on Banking and Currency carefully considered legislation which will relate and stabilize the currency of this country. (Applause.) Mr. Speaker, those two measures, if enacted into law will speedily give the people of this country such prosperity we have never had before in all of its history. (Applause on the Democratic side.) Mr. Speaker, I yield the remainder of my time to the gentleman from Mississippi (Congressman Busby).
>
> **Mr. Thomas Busby:** Mr. Speaker, in order for business to carry on, it is necessary to have a medium of

exchange. In this country our medium of exchange is based on currency and on bank credits. For several months some of us have seen the bank-credit situation breaking down and going out of use. The condition in which we find ourselves today is absolutely no surprise to me, and it is no surprise to some of the other gentlemen who have studied the question. The house had to fall upon us (referring to the Crash of 1929) to get some of the gentlemen who are responsible (Rep.) for our condition to understand our predicament. I have hoped, and others have hoped, for a restoration of the currency and of the mediums of exchange in this country—to no avail. We have come to the point where we are willing to endorse in a formal way an Executive fiat on this question; and I want to follow on, because I want the people of this country to have currency and mediums of exchange with which to do business. (Applause.)

Mr. Steagall: Mr. Speaker, I move the previous question on the passage of the bill.

The Speaker: Under the unanimous-consent agreement the previous question is considered as ordered.[30]

The bill was ordered to be read a third time, was read the third time, and passed. On the motion of Mr. Steagall a motion to reconsider the vote by which the bill that was passed was laid on the table.[31]

Afterwards, Congresswoman Janette Rankin, the first Congresswoman of the United States, took the floor, saying: "Mr. Speaker . . . it is the beginning of a new day—a turning point in the economic affairs of the American people, if not the entire world."[32]

Indeed, it was a new day for the American people, as well as the peoples of the entire world. But it came at a high price for the working people of America. From this point on the money backing the U.S. Treasury would be the property, business transactions, and labor of the American people.

Addressing Congress just before a vote on the Farm Bill, Congressman James Beck said:

I think of all the damnable heresies that have ever been suggested with the Constitution, the doctrine of emergency is the worst. It means that when Congress declares an emergency, there is no Constitution.

This means its death. It is the very doctrine that the German chancellor is invoking today in the dying hours of the parliamentary body of the German republic, namely, that because of an emergency, it should grant to the German chancellor absolute power to pass any law, even though the law contradicts the Constitution of the German republic, Chancellor Hitler is at least frank about it. We pay the Constitution lip-service, but the result is the same . . . . But the Constitution of the United States, as a restraining influence in keeping the federal government within the carefully prescribed channels of power, is moribund, if not dead. **We are witnessing its death-agonies, for when this bill becomes law, if unhappily it becomes law, there is no longer any workable Constitution to keep the Congress within the limits of its Constitutional powers.**[33] (Emphasis added.)

It is significant for us to understand that when FDR declared a national emergency, on March 9, 1933, he not only suspended the Constitution and gave "the President" (present and future presidents) broad executive powers, but declared that his Proclamation 2039 could continue until such time as another proclamation is made by "the President," a generic term which can equally apply to any President from FDR to the present and beyond.[34]

The concept of constitutional dictatorship goes back to the Roman Republic, which determined that, in times of dire emergencies, the Constitution and the rights of the people could be suspended temporarily, until the crisis, whatever the cause or reason, could be resolved. But once the crisis was resolved, the Constitution was to be returned to its peacetime position of constitutional authority.[35]

On March 9, 1933, however, when FDR declared state of national emergency he gave "the President" broad executive powers that have not been terminated to this present date. Affirming this fact, in 1973, Senate Report 93-549 was issued, which states in part:

> A majority of the people of the United States have lived all their lives under emergency rule .... For 40 years, freedoms and governmental procedures guaranteed by the Constitution have, in varying degrees, been abridged by laws brought into force by states of national emergency.[36]

Once FDR declared a national emergency and suspended the Constitution with the War Powers Act of October 6, 1917, as amended by the Act of March 9, 1933, Congress had an unlimited source of secured credit (*i.e.,* the property, business transactions, and labor of the American people). Needless to say, the domestic Insiders and international banking cartel of the Federal Reserve could have not been more pleased.

Recorded in the Congressional Record, March 9, 1933, on HR 1491, p. 83, Congressman Wright Patman said:

> Under the new law the money is issued to the banks in return for government obligations, bills of exchange, drafts, notes, trade acceptances, and bankers acceptances. The money will be worth 100 cents on the dollar because it is backed by the credit of the Nation. It will represent a mortgage on all the homes and other property of all the people of the nation.[37]

Two Governments of the United States

From this point on, the American people had a new unelected, unconstitutional, and unaccountable government at the helm of their economic destiny. Congressman Patman stated that the Federal Reserve constituted a "dictatorship on money matters by a banker's club."[38]

Later, in 1952, Congressman Patman told the American people: "This international banking cartel, as will be shown, manages the credit of the United States for the profit and advantage of its foreign and domestic members. In doing so, the Federal Reserve exploits the entire producing strata of the American society for the gain of a select few, non-producing few."[39]

Again, in 1964, on two different occasions, Congressman Patman told the House Banking and Currency committee:

> In its 50-year history, the Federal Reserve System has never been subjected to a complete, independent audit, and it is the only important agency that refuses to consent to an audit by the Congress' agency, the General Accounting Office . . . . As things now stand, the only information that we can get on programs of the Fed is what the Fed itself wants us to have.[40]

> . . . In the United States today, we have in effect two governments. We have the duly constituted government. Then we have an independent, uncontrolled government in the Federal Reserve System, operating the money powers which are reserved to Congress by the Constitution.[41]

Although Congressman Patman tried to awake his elected colleagues to the threat and unconstitutional power of the Federal Reserve, like Congressman McFadden, his appeals fell on deaf ears. During his tenure as a Texas Congressman, from 1928-1975, he was unable to persuade a majority in Congress to change the Federal Reserve in any way.

The Fed's Creation of Money

Unknown to most Americans, when Congress passed the Federal Reserve Act of 1913, under the Wilson administration, our elected representatives not only handed over to the domestic and international bankers the power to create money in the form of any denominational Note for pennies on the dollar, but bestowed on them the license to plunder the wealth of the American people, as well as the peoples of the world, in a way that could not have been imagined by the Founding Fathers.

In a special report on the cost of the actual printing of Federal Reserve Notes, William H. Ferkler, Manager of Public Affairs at the Department of Treasury, Bureau of Engraving and Printing in Washington, D.C., addresses the Fed's cost of printing Federal Reserve Notes, saying:

> As we have advised, the Federal Reserve is currently paying the Bureau approximately $23 for each 1,000 notes printed. This does include the cost of printing, paper, ink, labor, etc. Therefore, 10,000 notes of any denomination, including the $100 note would cost the Federal Reserve $230. In addition, the Federal Reserve must secure a pledge of collateral equal to the face value of the notes.[42]

Simply stated: the Federal Reserve, by printing 10,000 Notes into existence at a total cost of $230 dollars to the Federal Reserve, obtains a pledge of collateral equal to the face value of each $100 Note printed, namely $1 million dollars. This pledge is made to the banking cartel of the Federal Reserve by Congress in the form of U.S. Government Bonds, and the collateral which Congress pledges is the property, labor, assets, and business transactions of the American people.

Once again, citing the Senate report and text of *Information Prepared for Washington State Senate in Consideration of State Concurrent Resolution #127*, as revealed in the *Olympic Herald* newspaper, on February 16, 1982, we find the continued discussion among Senate members regarding the Fed's creation of money:

> **Senator Guess:** How does the Federal Reserve create money?
>
> **Senator Metcalf:** This will have to be an over-simplification; the actual operation is very complicated. However, this is an accurate summary of what happens. The Federal government is going into debt about a billion dollars a week. (Now $4 billion per day.) Where does that money come from? The government prints a billion dollars' worth of interest-bearing U.S.

Government bonds, takes them to the Federal Reserve, the Federal Reserve accepts them and places $1 billion in a checking account. The government then writes checks to a total $1 billion. The crucial question is: "Where was that $1 billion just before they touched the computer and put it in the checking account?" The answer: "It didn't exist." We, the people, allowed a private banking system to create money at will—out of absolutely nothing—to call it a loan to our government and then charge us interest on it forever.

Senator Quigg: Are you saying the Federal Reserve System implemented under the Federal Reserve Act of 1913 allows the banking system, as a system, to create money, in addition to what you have said about the Federal Reserve specifically?

Senator Metcalf: Yes, the Fractional Reserve System implemented under the Federal Reserve Act of 1913 allows the banking system, as a system, to create money to expand the money supply.

Dishonest Weights and Measures

It is important for us to understand that God requires us to operate according to His righteous standards of honesty and justice when trading in the market place. This is precisely the reason He addressed this issue before the people of Israel crossed the Jordan River to enter the land of Canaan, saying:

> 13 You shall not have in your bag differing weights, a large and a small. 14 You shall not have in your house differing measures, a large and a small. 15 You shall have a full and just weight; you shall have a full and just measure, that your days may be prolonged in the land which the Lord your God gives you. 16 For everyone who does these things, everyone who acts unjustly is an abomination to the Lord your God (Deut. 25:13-16; NASV).

In the ancient world it was the practice of dishonest merchants, when they bought produce from a farmer to sell to the general public, to have a bag containing differing weights and measures they would use to defraud their fellow man. For example, when a dishonest merchant purchased wheat from a farmer, he would use a set of heavy weights, which included a fifty shekel weight that actually weighed sixty shekels. During the course of the transaction, the dishonest merchant would pay the farmer for only fifty shekels of wheat. In other words, at the farmer's expense, the dishonest merchant created for himself 10 shekels of wealth (in the form of wheat) out of nothing through the use of dishonest weights.

Then, when this same dishonest merchant sold this wheat to a housewife in the marketplace, he would use a set of light weights, which included a fifty shekel weight that weighed only forty shekels. During the course of this transaction, he would use a fifty shekel weight to weigh out forty shekels of wheat, but he charged her for a fifty shekel weight of wheat.

Once again, this dishonest merchant created wealth (a second ten shekels from the same product) out of nothing through the use of dishonest weights.

In ancient Israel, the shekel was a gold or silver coin that weighed .533 of an ounce. This was considered to be an honest weight because of its gold or silver content. Because of this, shekel weights were used not only as an honest standard of weight when weighing anything on a set of scales but it also served as an honest form of currency for payment of goods, wages, and debts.

At the time of Isaiah's ministry, about 740-697 B.C.E., one of the great sins of Jerusalem's merchants was not only the using of dishonest weights and measures in the market place, but also the diluting the silver shekels (currency) and the hin (gallon) as another way to plunder the wealth of their fellow man. Denouncing this dishonest practice, the prophet Isaiah said:

> 21 How the faithful city has become a harlot, she *who w*as full of justice! Righteousness once lodged in her, but now murderers. 22 Your silver has become dross, your drink diluted with water (Isa. 1:21-22).

In Isaiah's day the dishonest money changers would melt down the silver shekel, add dross metal, re-mint the coins, and then spend them back into circulation. While this practice created more coins, the dross metal was lighter and cheaper than the silver, making the re-minted coins worth less than an honest silver shekel weight.

In time, the decrease in silver combined with the increase in the number of coins (money supply) caused the value (purchasing power) of each coin to decrease. As a result, it took more of the devalued shekels (money) to buy the same amount of goods and services. This is what is called the "debouching of the currency," which always produces higher prices, or inflation.

Likewise, in the days of Amos, (about 765-755 B.C.E.), the same dishonest practice existed. At that particular time the two kingdoms of Judah (in the south) and Israel (in the north) were at the height of their material and political success. But their prosperity had caused the people to forget the Lord and His command to practice righteousness in all their dealings. This was especially true of the rich and privileged classes, who were using their corrupted power to exploit the poor.

Addressing this dishonest practice, Yahweh told Amos to speak to the people, saying:

> 2 . . . "The end has come for My people Israel. I will spare them no longer. 3 The songs of the palace will turn to wailing in that day," declares the Lord God. "Many *will be* the corpses; in every place they will cast them forth in silence."
>
> 4 Hear this, you who trample the needy, to do away with the humble of the land, 5 saying:
> "When will the new moon be over,
> So that we may sell grain,
> And the sabbath, that we may open the wheat *market,*
> And to cheat with dishonest scales,
> 6 So as to buy the helpless for money
> And the needy for a pair of sandals,
> And *that* we may sell the refuse of the wheat?"
> (Amos 8:4-6).

At the time of Isaiah and Amos' ministries the dishonest merchants thought they could defraud their fellowman with impunity. But in 745 B.C.E., Amos' prophecy was fulfilled. Tiglath-Pileser III marched his Assyrian army against the northern ten tribes of Israel and the neighboring peoples, destroying their towns and villages, taking them captive and deporting them to Assyria.

Later, between 597 and 586 B.C.E., the Babylonian King Nebuchadnezzar brought all his military might against the people of Judah. Nebuchadnezzar's generals burned and plundered all the cities of Judah, including Jerusalem, and the great Temple of Solomon, killing thousands by fire, the sword, and starvation, and took thousands more into captivity, ending the kingdom of Judah.

Fractional Banking

During the middle ages, in Europe, people began to leave their gold on deposit with the goldsmith to keep it from being stolen by robbers. In receipt of their gold, the goldsmith would issue them paper notes, which were also much easier to carry.

People soon discovered that the local merchants would accept those notes for payment the same as when they paid in gold. This worked great until one day the goldsmith realized that people had become so accustomed to using their gold receipts that they seldom withdrew their gold. The goldsmith then began to apply the principle of dishonest weights and measures to go into the loan business.

He did this by simply writing (printing up) more gold receipts, which were used to make loans. The problem was he didn't have enough gold deposited in his bank to back up his newly printed receipts. But this is how the principle of fractional banking works. The goldsmith created money out of nothing in the form of paper loans and extended credit simply by writing out (printing up) more gold receipts and charging interest on the loans he had made.

As his loan business increased, the number of gold receipts (money supply) also increased in the market place. Eventually, the market place became saturated with paper receipts, which in turn reduced their purchasing power. *Webster's Twentieth Century*

Dictionary defines *inflation* as "an increase in the quantity of money or credit or both that causes a sharp and sudden drop in value, and a rise in prices."

As the devalued paper receipts became worth less and less, people began to redeem them for gold at the goldsmith shop. But since the goldsmith had only a *fraction* of gold on deposit for the amount of gold receipts in circulation, he quickly ran out of gold, and the people were stuck with worthless paper. This is the origin of what is called "fractional banking," and was but one more scheme that dishonest merchants used to create wealth out of nothing at the expense of an unsuspecting public.

U.S. Fractional Banking

Since 1979, Federal Reserve member banks have been required to set aside a certain amount of their money supply to satisfy reserve requirements. Over the years the reserve requirement has changed. In the late 1980s, the reserve requirements were set at sixteen percent of a bank's money supply. Today, the reserve requirements are set at ten percent, which means that when the Federal Reserve injects $1 billion in new reserve deposits, the banking system can immediately realize $900 million of it in new loans, simply by setting aside $100 million to satisfy the ten percent reserve requirement. It doesn't matter which banks get the deposit accounts; the new deposits immediately become the basis for new lending. The banks set aside ten percent of the $900 million and loan another $810 million, and so on. Those loans immediately become new deposits again and permit more new lending. Each time a loan is made the assets of a bank are increased by the same amount, except for the ten percent that has to be set aside to satisfy the reserve requirement. Using this principle, a bank can increase its assets by millions of dollars. This multiplication process continues until the banks exhaust the lending capacity created for them by the $1 billion injected into the banking system by the Federal Reserve. Eventually, the original $1 billion injected by the Federal Reserve will become more than $5 billion in new deposits that were created out of thin air with the stroke of a banker's pen; deposits that are loaned to the public in the form of paper loans and extended credit, which have to be paid back to the bank, generating money and interest on the entire amount.[43]

Larry Bates, a Christian businessman and former member of the Tennessee House of Representatives, who chaired the Committee on Banking and Commerce, writes about his experience as a banker in his book entitled *The New Economic Disorder*, saying:

> As a former banker, I have literally created millions of dollars out of thin air with the stroke of my pen. It works like this:
>
> One day I made a loan to a customer in the amount of $100,000, thereby increasing my assets in loans by $100,000. This customer was a good customer, and I deposited the $100,000 loan proceeds to my customer's checking account, thereby increasing my liabilities on the liabilities side of my bank ledger by $100,000.
>
> At the end of the day when I totaled my statement of condition, by the stroke of my pen I had increased the size of my bank by $100,000.
>
> All I have to do legally is to keep 10 percent of the $100,000 I deposited to my customer's checking account, or $10,000, in reserve. I subtract this $10,000 from the $100,000 deposit, and I now loan my next customer $90,000 of their money and repeat the process.[44]

The World's Central Bank

In the late 1970s, the powerful banking cartel of the Federal Reserve System set its sights on becoming the Central Bank of the world. According to the financial journalist Martin Mayer, it was the Eurodollar market that put the Federal Reserve into the international business in a big way.[45]

At that particular time foreign interests were borrowing heavily from U.S. banks even though they paid a higher interest rate than Americans. President John Kennedy imposed an interest equalization tax that was meant to put a lid on foreign borrowing. Heavy borrowing by foreign interests was having a negative impact on the U.S. economy. This caused the Fed to print more Federal Reserve Notes, increasing the money supply which, in turn, caused inflation.

Much to everyone's surprise, instead of diminishing foreign borrowing, Kennedy's interest equalization tax created a whole new market for U.S. dollars. Now, instead of American banks making foreign loans, the bankers of London cashed in on the foreign market's demand for U.S. dollars. Suddenly, the Federal Reserve was confronted with a whole new opportunity to establish a U.S. dollar market separate from the American dollar market, which was not subject to the same requirements that existed in the United States. It was this new set of circumstances that enabled the Federal Reserve to become a major player in the international markets and eventually become the world's Central Bank.

In 1979, the Federal Reserve Board led an effort to establish an Interagency Country Exposure Committee (ICEC) made up of three members each from the Federal Deposit Insurance Corporation (FDIC), and the Office of the Comptroller of the Currency (OCC).[46]

The purpose was to rate "country borrowers" with loans from American banks. Through the years 1979-1982, the Fed made loans to less developed countries at record high interest rates.[47]

From this point on, given the dominance of the U.S. dollar, the giant banks of Europe and Latin America were virtually forced to have separately capitalized subsidiaries or active branches in the United States.[48] In 1990, Alan Greenspan, the chairman of the Federal Reserve Board, boasted to the House Committee of the Federal Reserve's emerging role as the world's Central Bank, saying that four American banks do half of all the international business done by American banks.[49] "The international role of banks," he added, "has changed from one of simply extending credit to one of facilitating transactions."[50]

By the beginning of the twenty-first century the Federal Reserve's Bank had become the Central Bank of the world. On the back cover of Martin Mayer's book, *The Fed,* Adam Smith, chairman of Adam Smith Global Television, affirms what is now acknowledged by economists and financial institutions worldwide, saying: "America in the new millennium is not only the military superpower but the financial superpower as well, and at the heart of the system is the Fed, now the central bank to the entire world."

The Fed's Exaltation of the Great Goddess

In the main lobby of the Federal Reserve marble building, which sits just east of the Lincoln memorial, in Washington, D.C., are portraits of Woodrow Wilson, the Fed's founding President, and Senator Carter Glass of Virginia, who successfully guided the Federal Reserve Act through Congress, in 1913. On the lobby's ceiling is a plaster relief of Greek coins surrounding the Goddess Cybele.[51]

Why is this relief of the Goddess Cybele on the ceiling of the lobby of the Federal Reserve significant? As you shall see, it is the binding-tie that links the Great Goddess of antiquity to the Federal Reserve.

Affirming the link of the ancient cult worship of Cybele to that of the great pagan female deity of Babylon, Semiramis, the Scottish theologian Alexander Hislop writes:

> In the records of antiquity the existence of any *god* of fortifications has been commonly overlooked . . . . But the existence of a *goddess* of fortifications, everyone knows that there is the amplest evidence. That goddess is Cybele, who is universally represented with a mural or turreted crown, or with a fortification, on her head. Why was Rhea or Cybele thus represented? Ovid asks the question and answers it himself; and the answer is this: The reason he says, why the statue of Cybele wore a crown of towers was, "because she first erected them in cities." The first city in the world after the flood . . . that had towers and encompassing walls, was Babylon; and Ovid himself tells us that it was Semiramis, then, the first queen of that city and tower whose top was intended to reach heaven, must have been the prototype of the goddess who *'first* made towers in cities.'[52]

155

Here we see the Fed's exaltation of the Goddess Cybele linked to the Great Goddess of Babylon, Semiramis. But even more important is the Fed's practice of dishonest weights and measures in the market place, which links the fraudulent character of the Federal Reserve to the unrighteous character of the Great Goddess.

At the time of Zechariah, shortly after the Babylonian captivity, this great pagan female deity was known as "Wickedness" (Zech. 5:8), which in Hebrew is pronounced *resha,* meaning "iniquity, wickedness, godlessness, unrighteousness (Ps. 5:4; 45:7), lawlessness, injustice (Ecc. 3:16), dishonestly, *fraudulent scales* (Mic. 6:11), falsehood (Prov. 8:7), *unlawful gain, wealth which was obtained in a wicked way* (Mic. 6:10)."[53]

Moreover, since the establishment of the Federal Reserve, in 1913, most of the banks and financial institutions in the cities of America, especially those in New York City, have been built as towers. Indeed, since 9/11/01 the most famous of these towers were the Twin Towers of the World Trade Center.

PART III

American Foundations
Of The
Great Goddess

9

'LET'S OFFER THE AMERICANS A STATUE OF LIBERTY'

T HIS STORY, WHICH HAS often been told, but never fully, by Lady Liberty's many chroniclers, has usually resulted in the spinning of patriotic myths. Thus for most Americans, we should not be surprised that *The Statue of Liberty* is viewed as our great national icon of justice and freedom.

This view, however, was not always the case. During the early stages of the statue's development the entire project nearly collapsed for lack of funding. Neither the French or American peoples were interested in giving their hard earned money toward the building of a gigantic statue.

For Americans, there were several reason, the most important being the economy. At that particular time the American people were still emerging from the Civil War while, at the same time, engaged in the transformation of an agricultural country into a rapidly growing industrialized nation.

Had it not been for the spinning of patriotic myths by Liberty's many chroniclers the statue *Liberty Enlightening the World* (now called *The Statue of Liberty*) may well have become little more than just another great work of art that remained on par with other great works of statuary. In fact, most chroniclers agree that Bartholdi never believed his statue would one day become America's most treasured national icon.

Thus the real significance of this story is not to be found in the spinning of more patriotic myths. Rather, it is in the understanding of the pagan origin of the French Masonic statue *Liberty Enlightening the World,* which is rooted in the ancient cult worship of the Great Goddess of the Orient, and her more recent exaltation by the secret society of Freemasonry, in the late eighteenth and nineteenth centuries.

The Visionary Professor

After the French Revolution of 1789, a succession of regimes maintained their fragile hold on the government by stifling all political opposition with the threat of execution and imprisonment. Even with this show of force, the energy of the Masonic motto "Liberty, Equality, Fraternity," which had been set in motion during the Revolution, could not be stifled. The dissatisfaction of splinter groups continued to foment under the surface even after the restoration of the monarchy in 1815, and erupted again in 1830, 1840, 1848, and 1871. As a result, the revolutionary idea of a model society built on liberty and equality had become little more than an on-going cycle of political and social chaos, which had divided the nation against itself.

During the mid-1860s and early 1870s, for most French liberals and moderate republicans, who both opposed the oppressive rule of Napoleon III, the success of the American people to unify the nation, free the slaves, and maintain a constitutional form of government became their ideal model.

Among those who looked to America as the ideal nation, where the rank and file governed themselves, was a man named Edouard-Rene de Laboulaye (1811-1883).

A highly respected man both in America and France, in 1865, then in his fifties, Laboulaye was a holder of the Chair of Comparative Law at the College de France in Paris, a successful businessman, author, chairman of the French

Edouard-Rene Lefebvre de Laboulaye

Anti-Slavery Society, and his country's most outspoken advocate of the United States and its people.

A devout Catholic and a Mason, Laboulaye credited his initial interest in America to his reading of a book written by the Protestant theologian and abolitionist, Dr. William Ellery Channing of Boston. On the walls of his apartment in Paris, as well as his country home in Glatigny (near Versailles), hung pictures of Washington, Jefferson, Franklin, and Horace Mann, along with framed membership certificates in the New York and Philadelphia Union League clubs. On his desk were letters from Senator Charles Sumner (the great abolitionist), Edward Everett, and James Russell Lowell, along with a note on Executive Mansion stationary signed "A. Lincoln".

Among Laboulaye's many works included a *History of the United States,* written for the purpose of informing the French people on the "durable conditions of liberty," which presented Washington as the great revolutionary hero "who had reconciled the world with liberty." Some of Laboulaye's other works included a study of the American Constitution, a translation of works by Benjamin Franklin and William Ellery Channing, and *Paris in America,* a critical satire of French attitudes toward things American, especially liberty.

In Laboulaye's *Paris in America* he characterizes himself as the Frenchman who, upon his return to France from a visit to America speaks only of liberty and when criticized he defends himself, saying: "the madness of liberty is never cured."

Laboulaye was not alone in his passion for American liberty. It was shared by many other freedom loving Frenchmen, especially in 1865. Upon hearing of the assassination of President Lincoln there was a great outpouring of French sentiment. Numerous letters were sent from all parts of the country to the American representative in Paris, John Bigelow (who would later play an important role as an intermediary between the French and American statue organizers). One letter, signed by the people of Caen, stated that America's "sorrow is the sorrow of all good men" because Lincoln had met his tasks and overcome them "without veiling the statue of Liberty."

Seizing the opportunity to take advantage of the political capital that could be gained from Lincoln's death, a group of Laboulaye's friends placed an ad in the rural newspaper *Le Phare de la Lorie,* appealing for funds for a gold medal to be presented to Mary Todd Lincoln, President Lincoln's wife. When the ad was discovered by Napoleon's secret police it was ordered to be removed. The donated monies were confiscated, and the list of its supporters was destroyed.

Despite attempts to suppress the French people's admiration and tribute to President Lincoln, by the end of 1866, a gold medal was presented to Mrs. Lincoln. Laboulaye's group gathered enough cash to have the medal made in Switzerland. It was then smuggled to John Bigelow, at his office in Paris, and later delivered to Mrs. Lincoln in America.

On the medal's face, surrounding a profile of President Lincoln, were inscribed the words: "Dedicated by the French Democracy to Lincoln, twice elected President of the United States." On the reverse side, along with a replica of the Great Seal of the United States, were inscribed the following words: "Lincoln, an honest man; abolished slavery, saved the republic, and was assassinated on the 15th of April, 1865," and in bold letters the Masonic revolutionary motto: "Liberty, Equality, Fraternity".[1]

An accompanying letter to Mrs. Lincoln was signed by Laboulaye and twenty-six of his friends, including France's greatest living novelist and poet, Victor Hugo, who was still a legendary figure of French libertarianism, and Luis Blanco, the radical Socialist who helped lead the 1848 French Revolution.

The Famous Dinner Party

On a warm summer night in 1865, Laboulaye hosted a dinner party at his estate in Glatigny for some of his most important republican friends. Politicians, intellectuals, writers, and artists had been invited for the purpose of discussing the re-kindling of France's former relationship with America. Many of these men were well known, such as the Count de Gasparin (the Christian moralist), Charles de Remusat (the scholarly count), Frederic Auguste Bartholdi (the celebrated thirty-one-year-old sculptor, who was at the time working on a sculpture of his host), as well as M. Henri Martin[2] (the historian and Master of a Masonic lodge).[3]

Other prominent Masons who were a part of the statue's early beginnings included C. F. Deitz-Monnin, Jean Mace, and Victor Borie.[4]

At the time, the French government was in a state of turmoil, which gave Laboulaye and his friends an additional reason to desire a stronger bond with America. Up until this point in time none of the French revolutions, beginning with the Revolution of 1789, had succeeded in bringing about the type of government Laboulaye and his friends desired.

For Laboulaye, the great American experience had proven that a just government "of the people, for the people, and by the people" was not merely wishful thinking. Laboulaye was convinced that the same experience could be achieved in France.

It is reportedly said that after dinner Laboulaye turned the conversation to the subject of France's relationship with nations it had helped in the past. "What about Italy?" one man said. "France came to Italy's aid to protect Rome from Garibaldi's revolutionaries. Yet, today the Italians hate France!"

"Yes, but what about the United States?" asked another. At that point it is said that Laboulaye stood to his feet and said: "We know that America has not forgotten Lafayette and his volunteers, who helped the colonists win their War for Independence. There," he declared, "we have the basis for a feeling that honors the Americans as well as us . . . and if a monument should rise in the United States, I should think it fitting if it were built by both our nations."[5]

Before the evening ended, Laboulaye's words ignited a flame in the hearts of his republican friends, especially the young sculptor. Bartholdi later wrote in his notes that Laboulaye's idea "interested me so deeply that it remained fixed in my memory."

Although Laboulaye's idea was received with enthusiasm, everyone agreed that the time was not right. Napoleon III was still the emperor, and Laboulaye knew that such an effort would be resisted. With this in mind, Laboulaye's idea of building a great monument to commemorate American liberty was put on hold until the end of the Second Napoleon Empire.

The Gifted Sculptor

Frederic Auguste Bartholdi

Frederic Auguste Bartholdi (1834-1904) was born in Colmar, in the French province of Alasce, to a prosperous middle-class family. His father died when he was young, leaving him to be reared by his devout Protestant mother, who was both strong-willed and pushy, but whom Bartholdi adored. As a young man he showed a talent for drawing, and was enrolled as a student of the acclaimed painter Ary Scheffer, who was known for his devotion to the republican cause.

From the very beginning of Bartholdi's work as a sculptor he showed a particular interest in large-scale statues designed for public places in the outdoor. When Bartholdi was only nineteen the city of Colmar commissioned him to do an outdoor twelve-foot-high statue of General Jean Rapp, a Colmar native who had served under Napoleon. Among Bartholdi's other statues included one of Admiral Jean Bruat in Colmar, Lafayette in New York, and a statue of the defenders of the French city of Belfort during the Franco-Prussian War, which was constructed from several cut stones as a huge lion, roaring defiance.

In 1855, at the age of twenty-two, Bartholdi had a life-shaping experience when he accompanied Leon Gerome, Bally, and Berchere—a group of orientalist painters—on a trip to the Nile Valley in Egypt. During Bartholdi's lengthy visit, he studied the craftsmanship of Egypt's great monuments: the Sphinx, the Pyramids, and the huge animal gods that filled ancient temples. As a lover of ancient art, Bartholdi had already studied other great classical works, such as *Athena* and *Zeus* of Phidias, and the *Colossus of Rhodes.*[6]

It was during Bartholdi's visit to Egypt, however, that he became intrigued with the idea of becoming a sculptor of colossal art-works that would endure the test of time.

Bartholdi's First Design of the Goddess

Like many well-meaning ideas born during an impassioned appeal over dinner, for the first few years Laboulaye's dream of a colossal monument went nowhere. It would be five years later before Bartholdi made a serious attempt to begin the Liberty project. During that interval period Laboulaye concentrated on his teaching at the College de France and, at the same time, worked on things which would help France become the Republic he admired across the Atlantic.

In 1867, Bartholdi's dream of crafting a gigantic Goddess statue in the style of the great works of Eastern antiquity seemed to be on the verge of becoming a reality. Bartholdi had been reading in the press about the Khedive of Egypt, Ismail Pasha, who had commissioned a Frenchman, Ferdinand de Lesseps, to supervise the excavation of the Suez Canal. Ismail, who wanted to modernize Egypt, and was the rage of Paris society, struck Bartholdi as being a modern day version of the ancient pharaohs, and the work on the Suez as being on the same scale of the ancient Egyptian builders.

When the Khedive visited Paris that same year to attend the Universal Exposition, Bartholdi submitted a sketch to Ismail for an immense lighthouse that would be erected at the entrance of the canal. Its form was that of a robed woman, many times life-size, and holding aloft a torch. Bartholdi named his Goddess lighthouse design *Egypt bringing the Light to Asia,*[7] which was a recreation of the Egyptian Goddess Isis meant to represent both ancient and modern Egypt, recalling the reign of the pharaohs of Alexandria and Ismail's desire to Europeanize Egypt.

Bartholdi's sketch for Egypt Bringing the Light to Asia.

When Ismail first saw the design and liked it Bartholdi believed he had finally found both the project and man who would help him realize his dream: to build a colossal work of art on a scale similar to the great works of ancient Egyptian statuary.

During the next two years Bartholdi worked intermittently on the Suez project, experimenting with the figure of a robed female goddess, designing her in a number of sketches and small clay models.

**Bartholdi's miniature clay designs for Egypt
Bringing the Light to Asia, 1867-70.**

Shortly before the canal's re-opening, in 1869, Bartholdi learned from De Lesseps, who knew Ismail well, that whatever the Khedive had previously said about his idea for a lighthouse he didn't have the financial resources to pay for such an undertaking. Bartholdi, nevertheless, attended the dedication ceremony and, once again, submitted his design for a lighthouse to the Khedive. This time, however, it became apparent to Bartholdi that there would be no commission to build a gigantic lighthouse statue that would be placed at the entrance to the canal.

Years later, while being interviewed by an American reporter, Bartholdi insisted that his design of *Egypt Bringing the Light to Asia* or *Progress* project ended with the Suez Canal's re-opening, and that the similarity to his design of *Liberty Enlightening the World,* erected in New York Harbor, was only a coincidence. It is said that Bartholdi told the reporter that at the time of the Suez project his statue of

Liberty did not exist, even in his imagination, and that the only thing similar between the drawing he submitted to the Khedive and his statue of Liberty was that both held aloft a light.

Bartholdi reportedly replied: "Now . . . how is a sculptor to make a statue which is to serve the purpose of a lighthouse without making it hold the light in the air? Would they have me make the figure . . . hiding the light under its petticoat not to say under a bushel?"

Disputing Bartholdi's claim, the noted art historian Marvin Trachtenberg writes: "Bartholdi forgot that in the case of both the Suez *Progress* and the original idea for the New York Liberty the lighthouse beacon was not planned for the torch, but was to radiate from the forehead of the figure; the torch was to be purely symbolic."[8]

Trachtenberg tells us that Bartholdi tried to evade the obvious design of both projects, which featured two gigantic, robed, torch-bearing female deities designed as lighthouses, located at two major gateways of the ancient world and the new world "symbolizing twin deities in the nineteenth century pantheon—Liberty and Progress—in both cases actively passing their message from one continent to another."[9]

Bartholdi's Lack of Originality

Although Bartholdi was a gifted sculptor, Liberty's chroniclers agree that most of his work was based upon the works of other great artists. The Liberty authors Christian Blanchet and Bertrand Dard tell us that although Bartholdi was a remarkable individual he, nevertheless, was "lacking in originality".[10] Trachtenberg simply says that Bartholdi's work "bears little discernible stamp of formal originality, and resembles the output of a hundred other sculptors and monument-makers of his time."[11]

La Republique, Ary Scheffer, 1848.

Earlier art works indicate that Bartholdi may have very well got the idea for his statue from other great artists, such as his master, Ary Scheffer, who in an official competition, in 1848, sketched an image of the new French Republic.[12]

The Great Commission

Once again, in the spring of 1871, Laboulaye invited the young sculptor and his republican friends for dinner at his Glatigny estate. The guests included Oscar de Lafayette, Louis Wolowski, Count Charles de Remusat, and Count de Gasparin. This time Bartholdi was more experienced and, having recently been involved with his design of the Suez lighthouse project, had some ideas of his own.

It is said that during dinner Laboulaye raised his glass of wine and told his guests that there could be little doubt that the hundredth year anniversary of the United States of America would revive strong feelings for France in America. Reportedly, Laboulaye said: "Would this not be the time for the American monument we had proposed six years ago?" Bartholdi stood to his feet and replied: "I think it would be well to offer the Americans a statue—a statue of Liberty."[13]

Much to the delight of Laboulaye and his guests, Bartholdi had made an admirable choice. What better gift to give to the people of America than a statue of the French Goddess Liberty, who had been *personified* as the French Republic, in 1848; whose image had been struck on French coins, and represented by great French works of art as the Goddess of enlightenment.

That night Bartholdi was given the commission to build a statue of the French Goddess Liberty, which he enthusiastically accepted. Before the meeting concluded, one of the guests asked Bartholdi: "What kind of statue will it be?" Bartholdi reportedly said: "It ought to be a statue that can be seen from the shores of America to the coast of France."[14]

The Perfect Site

Once the idea for a gigantic statue of the Goddess Liberty was agreed upon, Laboulaye told Bartholdi to visit America, promising him letters of introduction to his circle of friends at the Union League Club and elsewhere.[15]

On May 18, 1871, Bartholdi wrote Laboulaye, informing him of his upcoming visit to America to do preliminary groundwork for the Liberty project, requesting Laboulaye's promised letters of introduction to U.S. government officials, members of the press, and art associations. In his letter, Bartholdi told Laboulaye that he not only hoped to make an acquaintance with lovers of art, but most important, he hoped that his contacts would be helpful in the realization of his plan for his statue of Liberty in honor of American independence. Concluding his letter, Bartholdi said: "I will try especially to glorify the Republic and Liberty over there, hoping that I will one day find them back here, if possible."

As soon as Bartholdi received Laboulaye's letters of introduction he left for America, on June 8, aboard the steamer *Pereire,* promising Laboulaye that he would send him word of his impressions of both the country and its people. But even more important was the need to find the perfect site for his statue, hopefully at the gateway to America, in New York Harbor.

The concept of a gateway setting for a patron deity of a city or country was hardly an original idea. It goes all the way back to the first races of men who settled in the fertile land of Mesopotamia after the Great Flood. One of the first things they did was to erect an image of their patron deity at the entrance of their cities.

The most famous patron deity of these first races of men was the Babylonian Goddess Ishtar, whose image was placed at the most important gateway to the great city of Babylon—the Ishtar Gate.[16]

As a lover of ancient art, Bartholdi was well-acquainted with this ancient concept. Among the great art works of antiquity Bartholdi believed that the *Colossus of Rhodes* was the most celebrated. The *Colossus of Rhodes* was a bronze statue of the Sun-god Helios designed by Chares of Lindus, a pupil of the famed Greek sculptor Lysippus. Chares worked on the *Colossus* statue for twelve years before its official dedication.

It is reputed to have been over 100 feet high, and was commissioned to commemorate the successful defense of the island against the Macedonian king Demetrius I, in 305 B.C.E.

According to legend the statue was made from the bronze weapons and armor left behind by Demetrius' retreating army. Tradition holds that the statue of Helios originally straddled the harbor and that ships passed between its outspread legs. It was toppled by an earthquake in 280 B.C.E., and its metal fragments laid where they fell for nine hundred years before they were hauled off and sold for scrap.

In 1725, the artist J. B. Fisher von Erlach made a painting of the Sun-god Helios, straddling the entryway to the harbor, wearing a spiked crown with a flaming torch in his uplifted hand, which served as a beacon of light for ships in the night.

Colossus of Rhodes

Apparently, Bartholdi's interest in the *Colossus* Sun-god Helios statue went much deeper than the gigantic work of art it represented. In the *Bartholdi Museum*, in Colmar, France (Bartholdi's hometown), is a photo of Bartholdi's studio. On the rear wall is an image of a radiant sun—Bartholdi's family crest—with a small model of the statue of the Goddess Liberty in the forefront.

Bartholdi's studio.

On the morning of June 21, when the *Pereire* arrived at the bay of New York Harbor, Bartholdi already had a good idea of where he wanted his statue to be erected. He only needed to find the perfect site.

That morning, as the *Pereire* slowly made its way up the bay in the harbor, as soon as Bartholdi set his eyes on the bay he knew he had found the perfect site. Bartholdi wrote to Laboulaye about the magnificent scene he witnessed when his ship arrived in New York Harbor: the great cities of New York and Brooklyn, with rivers stretching as far as the eye can see, filled with steamboats and vessels of every kind. Bartholdi wrote: "If I myself felt that spirit here, then it is certainly here that my statue must rise, here where people get their first view of the New World, and where Liberty casts her rays on both worlds."

As the *Pereire* moved into the harbor, two island fortresses caught Bartholdi's attention: Governor's Island and Bedloe's Island fortress—Fort Wood (1808-1811)—by far the most impressive. In a letter to Laboulaye, Bartholdi wrote: "I've found an admirable spot. It is Bedloe's Island in the middle of the bay . . . . The island belongs to the government; it's on national territory, belonging to all the States, just opposite the Narrows, which are, so to speak, the gateway to America."

Preparing the "Fertile Soil"

Once ashore, armed with Laboulaye's letters of introduction, Bartholdi began calling on some of the most influential men in America. In Long Branch, New Jersey, he was received by President Ulysses S. Grant at his summer cottage. Bartholdi also talked with Peter Cooper, a civic minded industrialist and philanthropist who had financially backed the cross-Atlantic cable to France laid by Cyrus W. Field. In Philadelphia, he met with Colonel John W. Forney, publisher of the *Press* and a civic and political leader of considerable influence. In Nahant, Massachusetts, on several occasions he visited Henry Wadsworth Longfellow, who expressed both his admiration and encouragement for the project. In Washington, D.C., on the 4th of July, Senator Charles Sumner, a friend of Laboulaye, took Bartholdi for a tour of the city. And during his stay in Washington, he was received by the White House, shook hands with senators, and met several generals, including Sherman and Sheridan.

One of Bartholdi's most important meetings was with Richard Morris Hunt, a well-known architect. As a youth, Hunt had studied at the Ecole des Beaux-Arts in Paris and was its first American graduate (1846-1855). He had also worked on the Louvre Library Pravilion in Paris, which Bartholdi knew well. After the Civil War, Hunt returned to New York and became a successful society architect, building mansions in New York and magnificent summer cottages in Newport for his wealthy American clients.

During Bartholdi's visit with Hunt it is said that the two men discussed pedestals and their importance in complementing the work they supported. Oddly enough, there is no mention in Bartholdi's notes that he discussed with Hunt the idea of building a colossal statue of Liberty without discussing the pedestal on which it would stand.

Bartholdi spent three-and-a-half months traveling across the U.S. by train, trying to gain a better understanding of the American people and the country, hoping to fill out his own idea for his statue of Liberty. From Boston, Bartholdi traveled to Westfield, Hartford, and New Haven in Connecticut, and through New York, visiting Niagara Falls. His train route took him west to Omaha and then across the great prairie to the Rocky Mountains.

While in Sacramento, Bartholdi visited several historic landmarks. He then traveled on to San Francisco and saw the famous bay, where thousands of men had journeyed to San Francisco by ships from all over the world, in 1849-1855, with hopes of "striking it rich" in the gold fields of northern California.

On Bartholdi's return trip his train crossed the Rocky Mountains and onto the Great Plains, where buffalo herds could still be seen roaming the prairie. On his cross-country journey, he saw ranches, factories, oil wells, growing cities, and industrious people of every race, color, and creed. Everywhere he went there was bustling enterprise. But most important, Bartholdi believed that the time was right for the building and erection of a gigantic statue of the French Goddess Liberty at the gateway to America, in New York Harbor.

Near the end of his trip, Bartholdi reportedly wrote to Laboulaye, saying: "In every town I visit I look for people who might be interested in taking part in our enterprise. So far, I have found them everywhere. The ground is well prepared . . . only the spark will have to be provided by France."

When it came time to return to France, despite Bartholdi's good report and the many influential men he had met, there were no secured commitments, no signed documents, and no subscription funds to take home to Laboulaye. Nevertheless, as Bartholdi's steamer weighed anchor, he knew that he was not returning to Paris empty handed. Now more than ever, he was convinced that his dream of building a gigantic statue of the French Goddess Liberty would finally become a reality.

Bartholdi's Ideal Image

For most Liberty chroniclers, Bartholdi's ideal image for his statue can be traced all the way back to the Roman Goddess Libertas, in the third century B.C.E. In ancient Rome, the Goddess was portrayed as a robed woman, holding a scepter denoting self-rule, with a crushed vase-of-confinement at her feet, and wearing the Phrygian cap that was given to slaves when awarded their freedom.

The problem with this analysis is that the origin of the Goddess Libertas did not begin with the Romans. Ancient historians inform us that her cult worship began at a much earlier date. Servius records that there was an ancient Goddess worshiped by the Sabines called "Feronia," who was believed to be the "goddess of *liberty*" because at Terracina (or Anxur) slaves were emancipated in her temple (Servius, in *Aeneid,* viii. v 564, vol. I, p. 490), and because the freedmen of Rome are recorded on one occasion to have collected a sum of money for the purpose of offering it in her temple.[17]

The Sabines were an Italic tribe that lived in the central Appennines of north-eastern Italy before the reign of the third king of Rome, Tullus Hostilius 673-642 B.C.E. Scholars tell us that Faronia was a Sabine Goddess, whose annual festivals occurred as early as the reign of Tullus Hostilius, and were attended by great numbers of people who brought offerings of gold and silver to a sacred grove at the foot of Mount Soracte,[18] where Feronia, the "goddess of *liberty*," was worshiped along with a youthful divinity, regarded as a "youthful Jupiter".[19]

The recorded worship of this Sabine Goddess of Liberty, along with a youthful male deity called "Jupiter," is highly significant. Because ancient historians tell us that it was the practice of the cult worship of the Great Mother Goddess to include the worship of a youthful male deity, known by the ancients to be the reincarnation of Nimrod, the Sun-god.

In Babylon, Nimrod, as a "youthful Tammuz," was worshiped along with his deified mother, Semiramis. In Egypt, Nimrod was worshiped along with his deity mother, Isis, as a "young Horus". In Asia, he was worshiped as a "youthful Desius," the son of Cybele. In India, he was adored as a "youthful Crishna," the son of Devaki. Among the ancient Sabines, he was regarded as a "youthful Jupiter," who was worshiped along with Feronia, the "goddess of *liberty,*" in a grove.

Alexander Hislop tells us that "both of them, under the names Rhea and Nin, or 'goddess Mother and Son,' were worshiped with an enthusiasm that was incredible, and that their images were everywhere set up and adored."[20]

Over the course of time, the cult worship of the Great Mother Goddess overshadowed that of her deified son. "So great was the devotion to this goddess queen," says Hislop, "not of the Babylonians only, but of the ancient world in general, that the exploits of Semiramis has, in history, cast the exploits of her husband Ninus or Nimrod, entirely into the shade."[21]

Thus there can be little doubt that the ancient origins of the Roman Goddess Libertas, from which Bartholdi derived his inspiration for his gigantic statue of the French Goddess Liberty, goes all the way back to the first deified queen of Babylon, who was later worshiped by the Italic Sabines as the "goddess of *liberty*" in a sacred grove at the foot of Mount Soracte. Nor can there be little doubt that the Romans, who were known for adopting the deities and cult worship of the peoples they conquered, adopted the worship of this pagan female Goddess from the Italic Sabines.

History concurs that when the Sabines moved to the city of Rome they brought with them the ancient cult worship and rites of their great female deity Feronia—the "goddess of *liberty*". It is also a matter of record that by the third century B.C.E. her worship among the Roman people had become so popular that a temple was built for her on Aventine Hill, where she was exalted by the Romans as Libertas.

Liberty's Political Transformation

Although most chroniclers of the *Statue of Liberty* are faithful to record its French origins, little, if nothing, is ever written about the revival of the cult worship of this ancient Goddess by the secret societies of the eighteenth century. History concurs, however, that the revival of the cult worship of this pagan female deity did indeed take place among the revolutionary Freemasons of the late eighteenth century. Berry Moreno, the historian and librarian at the Statue of Liberty National Monument and Ellis Island, says:

> Libertas enjoyed a revival as a philosophical and political symbol of liberty and democracy in the eighteenth century. The form of the antique deity, once conspicuous on Roman coinage, now found herself on modern French and American coins and medals . . . . The

revival of the goddess on coinage, medals, paintings, and other forms of art established the precedent necessary for her ultimate return in the form of the statue *Liberty Enlightening the World.*[22]

In the mid-1700s, the traditional Roman concept of the Goddess was portrayed by Cesare Ripa as "Faith," who wore a helmet and classical robe. Cradling in her left arm, together with an open book on the New Testament, Liberty displayed the Law of Moses on a tablet. With her right hand she raises aloft a heart with a flaming candle, a symbol of her illuminating powers which she used to dispel ignorance and superstition.

Fede Cattonica, 1776.

"Thus she is," says Trachtenberg, "along with everything, a seer and a prophetess. Considered in this way, her tablet bears not so much a remembrance as an implicit commandment—Seek Liberty!—and a prophecy: Liberty, as achieved in America in 1776, shall spread throughout the world, and most importantly, to France."[23]

Verita, 1776.

In 1776, Cesare Ripa portrayed the

Liberte, 1810.

Goddess as a nude woman partially clad in a flowing robe, holding aloft in her right hand a radiant image of the Sun-god. Her right foot sits on a globe, symbolizing the world over which she reigns.[24]

In 1810, J. B. Huet portrayed the Goddess as a robed woman, holding a scepter (indicating her sovereignty), accompanied by a freedom loving cat alongside a broken jug at her feet (a symbol of confinement now ended), and wearing a Phrygian cap.[25]

From the late 1700s to about the mid-1800s, the above traditional image of the Goddess continued to be struck on U.S. coins, as either sitting on a rock (an Americanized version of a European throne) and holding a staff (her scepter) topped with a Phrygian cap, or as a classical bust wearing the Phrygian cap, or an inscribed crown. Even the bronze statue of *Armed Liberty*, designed by Thomas Crawford and completed in 1863, on the dome of the Capital in Washington, D.C., is a representation of the traditional concept of the great female deity.

With the advent of political and social change in France, in the late 1700s, the traditional concept of the Goddess became a matter of political expediency. By the 1800s, she had become the embodiment of French politics. Trachtenberg writes: "To be properly understood, the origins of the *Statue of Liberty* must be seen in the context of French politics in the 1860s, French notions of liberty and republicanism . . . and especially Laboulaye's political philosophy. For although the statue was destined to become a personification of the United States, it began as an expression of French ideas."[26]

France's political transformation of the Goddess was also reflected on coins, as during the Second Republic (1848-1852), where the official expression of the Goddess of Liberty heralded back to the Revolution of 1789. The Masonic motto "Liberty, Egalite, Fraternity" usually appeared on the Reverse side of French coins, but on the silver 5 francs it appeared on the front along with a representation of the twin deities Liberty and Equality, standing on each side of Hercules.

5 Francs, 1849.

In the years 1860 to 1870, the Goddess was portrayed by the Grand Lodge of France in the *La Chain d'Union* publication as "Truth".

Truth, LaChain d'Union.

As "Truth," the Goddess is in the body of a nude woman, except for a flowing robe. In her right hand she holds aloft a mirror, a symbol of truth. In her left hand is a triangle, a symbol of justice. Her sovereignty over these two concepts is symbolized by a nude woman standing atop the world. Other visible symbols are the five-pointed star on her head, and the radiant sun behind her. On her pedestal are the words: "I Emancipate. I Pacify. I Enlighten".

Marvin Trachtenberg informs us that the term "enlighten" is derived from the French word "eclairant," which means "to *illuminate*".[27] Trachtenberg goes on to say: "The fate of Bartholdi's program included as well the explicit theme of the project—the still unexplained fact that his *Liberty* was conceived, in a mode that we might call gerundive allegory, as 'enlightening the world'. ('Enlightening', translated from 'eclairant', carries here the archaic sense of 'illumination' as well as the more specific 'instruction' it has become. An up-dated translation of the original French title might well be *Liberty Illuminating the World*.)"[28]

Liberty's Masonic Influence

In the middle 1800s, as a result of France's many revolutions, the country's Masonic lodges became closely involved with political

178

causes. Beginning with the Revolution of 1789, France had experienced nine major governmental changes. Each change was marked by a cycle of political, social, and religious upheaval.

By 1870, the French people had been under the dictatorship of Napoleon III for eighteen years. During that time they were constantly harassed and censored by Napoleon's secret police. The greater the oppression, however, the greater became the people's resolve to one day have a republic governed by law. Thus it was in this political context that Masonic lodges of France became centers for rallying like-minded Frenchmen to join the republican cause.

Less than a month after Napoleon entered into war with Prussia, both he and 83,000 of his troops were captured in the battle at Sedan. Then, on January 28, 1871, France was forced to sign an armistice in which Alsace and part of Lorraine, both provinces of France, were ceded to Germany, which was a devastating blow for Bartholdi. Bartholdi's hometown of Colmar, where his beloved mother lived, was in the province of Lorraine.

After the war, Bartholdi resettled in Paris, refusing to go back to Colmar except for brief visits with his mother. For Bartholdi, Colmar was occupied territory and he was an exile. Up to this time Bartholdi's one driving ambition in life was to be a sculptor of great works of art. But by the spring of 1871, Bartholdi had become politicized by the war. When he returned to Paris from America, in the fall of 1871, he was firmly committed to the republican cause.

In 1872, Bartholdi joined the Masonic Lodge of Alsace-Lorraine (named after his home province), in Paris. The accompanying photo shows Bartholdi hiding his hand inside his coat, revealing what is called in Masonry "the hidden hand," which is related to the "Mysteries" of Freemasonry.

The historian Henri Martin, a Master of a Masonic lodge, as well as an important backer of Liberty's statue, was one of the regular visitors to Laboulaye's estate in Glatigny, where Bartholdi met Martin and was encouraged to join Freemasonry.[29] From

Bartholdi the Mason, in 1880.

that point on Masonic officials were often involved with the design of Bartholdi's statue, and in various ceremonies dedicated to it.[30]

Thus it was no accident that when Bartholdi returned to Paris from his visit to America he joined the Masonic Lodge of Alsace-Lorraine, located in Paris. Nor was it a coincidence that the statue of the Goddess Liberty he fashioned was made in the image of the great French Goddess of Enlightenment.

Liberty's Robe

Although the Goddess of Masonry was often portrayed as nude, Laboulaye, as a devout Catholic, shunned those nude expressions. It is said that at Laboulaye's insistence, Bartholdi covered his statue of the Goddess with a robe from neck to toe.

Liberty's Tablets

In finding a substitute for the broken jug at Liberty's feet, Bartholdi designed a broken chain to place at her feet. Until mid-1875, Bartholdi had planned to put the links of the classical broken chain in Liberty's left hand. But at the urging of Laboulaye and his Masonic brethren, Bartholdi agreed to change the position of the arm and put into its crook an "intimation" of the Mosaic tablets, portraying the Goddess as a divine seer and prophetess.[31]

"The ancient Goddess of Liberty," says Trachtenberg, "had thus become not only a reincarnation of such old themes as Faith and Truth, but assumed in her own right a multiplicity of roles: martyr, secular saint, prophetess and romantic heroine."[32]

Liberty's Torch

In finding a substitute for Delacroix's flintlock held in the hand of the revolutionary Goddess Liberty, Bartholdi placed a torch. Both Bartholdi and Laboulaye believed that it was important to stress that the purpose of Liberty's flame, which was to spread "enlightenment," not to set fires ('war and revolution').

In April 1876, a gala benefit performance took place at the Paris Opera, where the renowned French musician Charles Francois

Gounod presented a Liberty cantada. After it concluded, Laboulaye is said to have made a passionate appeal for funds, saying: "Ours, in one hand holds the torch,—no, not the torch that sets afire, but the flambeau, the candle-flame that *enlightens*. In her other, she holds the tablets of the Law . . . . This statue, symbol of Liberty lives only through Faith and Truth and Justice, Light and Law. This is the Liberty that we desire, and that will remain forever the emblem of the alliance between America and France."

By the mid-1800s, the French Goddess was portrayed as the Goddess of Enlightenment.

On the cover of the *Free Mason* magazine, founded in 1847, the Masonic Goddess holds the candle-flame that enlightens in her right hand. In her left hand is the unrolled scroll of the Law, as she stands atop the world she rules. On her forehead is the five-pointed star, which represents "Omniscience, or the All-seeing Eye . . . the emblem of Osiris, the Creator."[33]

Le flambeau, non la torche.

In July 1876, a drawing of Auguste Bartholdi appeared in the *Irish World Centennial Supplement*,[34] portraying a statue of the Goddess of Liberty, with her right hand holding aloft the flame of "enlightenment".

In the other hand she holds the tablets of the Law, while standing on her own pedestal atop of the world over which she rules.

Liberty on top of the world, July 1876.

Liberty's Crown

In finding a substitute for the five-pointed star of Liberty's crown, Bartholdi selected a seven-pointed crown. Marvin Trachtenberg writes: "It is likely that Bartholdi was aware that the seven canonical rays that his statue's head emanates symbolized, in their original context, the sun's radiance to the seven planets, just as Liberty 'enlightens' the seven continents and seven seas of the world."[35]

Christian Blanchet and Bertrand Dard tell us that perhaps Bartholdi's choice of a crown of rays was because the Sun was also an important Masonic symbol: ". . . that may explain Bartholdi's choice, particularly in the light of one sentence of Masonic ritual that ran: 'The Great Architect of the Universe has given the Sun to the world to enlighten it, and Liberty to sustain it.'"[36]

10

'To Build a Shrine for Her'

W HEN BARTHOLDI'S SHIP REACHED Le Harve, on a wintery day in 1872, Paris was in political turmoil and eastern France was still under the occupation of Prussia. What had once been beautiful cobblestone boulevards in Paris were now littered with the charred ruins of civil war.

In 1871, when one faction of Parisians, the *Communards,* angered at the monarchists for accepting a humiliating peace treaty with Prussia, set up their own provisional government and drove the monarchists out of Paris. As a result, the monarchists fled to Versailles, Paris was put to the torch, and France was bitterly divided between two factions that were fighting for the control of the country.

Disheartened by the chaos, Bartholdi and Laboulaye agreed that this was not the time to pursue their dream of building a colossal statue of the Goddess of Liberty as a memorial to American independence. Before such an effort could succeed the political climate would have to dramatically improve.

In the meantime, Bartholdi kept himself busy with other projects, such as the monumental fountain for the 1876 Philadelphia Centennial Exhibition; a statue of Lafayette, which France would present to New York; and the celebrated Lion of Belfort, carved from a stone mountainside.

Laboulaye stayed busy by heading an effort to establish a French republic that would be governed by a constitution, which proved to be an impossible task. Laboulaye found himself caught in the middle of two volatile groups, the radical *Communards,* led by Illuminati atheists, and the monarchists, who cared little about the needs of the French people.

Not wanting to abandon the Liberty project, in 1874, Laboulaye spearheaded an effort with his inner circle of devoted friends to quietly form the Franco-American Union, which would become the Liberty project's administrative and financial operation.

In the meantime, in spite of the country's many problems, the effort to establish a constitutional government was making headway. On January 30, 1875, the National Assembly narrowly passed an amendment for the establishment of the French Republic. The vote was 353 to 352.

By spring of that same year there was a dramatic change in the political climate of the country. It soon became apparent that a new day had arrived in France. Laboulaye's dream of having a constitutional government had finally become a reality. Now, although quite elderly, he would devote his full attention to his beloved Liberty memorial project.

Financing the Dream

As is customary with most charitable causes begun with only a small group of devoted individuals, several prestigious honorary members were added to the Union for the purpose of generating public interest in the project. Chief among the notables selected were Elihu Washburne, the American ambassador to France, Philippe Bartholdi, a distant cousin of the sculptor and France's ambassador to America, who had also just been named one of France's Commissioners to the upcoming Philadelphia Centennial Exposition, and John Forney, a Philadelphia politician and journalist, who was the Commissioner-General of the United States in Europe for the Exposition. Other prestigious members included descendants of Lafayette, Rochambeau, Alexis de Tocqueville, and several members of the new French parliament. Laboulaye was elected the Union's president.

The next step was the establishment of a prestigious downtown office in Paris. On September 28, 1875, the Union published its first public appeal for funds in two Paris newspapers, which states in part:

The great event which is to be celebrated on the 4th of July, 1876, allows us to celebrate with our American brothers the old and strong friendship which for a long time has united the two peoples.

The New World is preparing to give extraordinary splendor to the festival. Friends of the United States have thought that the genius of France ought to display itself in a dazzling form.

A French artist has embodied that thought in a plan worthy of its object, and which is approved by all; he has come to an understanding with our friends in America and has prepared all the means for enacting the plan.

It is proposed to erect, as a memorial of the glorious anniversary, an exceptional monument. In the midst of the harbor of New York, upon an islet which belongs to the Union of the States, in front of Long Island, where was poured out the first blood for independence, a colossal statue would rear its head . . . . On the threshold of that vast continent, full of new life, where ships arrive from everywhere, it will rise from the waves, representing "Liberty Enlightening the World."

Although the Union's first public appeal was informative it was grossly overstated, claiming that during Bartholdi's visit to America he had "prepared all the means for executing the plan . . . which is approved by all." As earlier noted, at the time Bartholdi returned home to France, there were no American commitments, no signed documents, and no subscription funds for the project. In fact, at that point in time the Union had no assurance that the American government would accept the French statue, let alone allocate a site for its placement. All President Grant had told Bartholdi was that congressional approval would be necessary to secure Bedloe's Island. Moreover, America's hundred year anniversary, July 4, 1876, was only nine months away, which made it virtually impossible to complete the Liberty project in such a short period of time.

Nevertheless, within a few days the same appeal appeared in other newspapers across France. Much to the delight of Laboulaye and Bartholdi the first responses were encouraging. Newspaper editorials wrote favorable about the project. Entire cities collected subscription funds and mailed them to the Union's office in Paris. One metal manufacturer even offered to provide all the copper for the statue's body.

Union members were encouraged by the response and made plans to hold a fund-raising banquet at the Hotel du Louvre on November 6, and another was planned two weeks later at the Palace of Industry.

One of the primary objectives of the Union's kick-off banquet was to bring out the different political factions of Paris, which included an impressive list of dignitaries. Among those who attended were the Minister of Finance and the Minister of Education, representing the French President, Marshal MacMahon. The U.S. Ambassador Washbourn attended, representing America, including several high ranking city officials and members of the new parliament. Commissioner Forney, along with a number of American merchants whose offices were in Paris, was in attendance. There were also several pro-American French liberals and aristocrats who came out to witness the grand event, all friends of Laboulaye and members of the Union.

In the banquet room the tables were arranged in a horseshoe, with shields in the center that displayed portraits of Washington, Franklin, Lafayette, Rochambeau, Lincoln, and Grant. The walls were decorated with French and American flags. A model of the statue *Liberty Enlightening the World,* which Bartholdi had finished in August, stood at the end of the hall, displayed against a large velvet curtain.

When the banquet concluded there was little doubt among those who attended that it had been a success. Numerous pledges had been made, and the after-dinner speeches ended with a final toast by Laboulaye to the eternal friendship of France and the United States.

Union members scheduled more banquets in Paris, Le Havre, and other cities. Only this time the primary objective was to involve the French municipalities, which were the usual sources of support for civic monuments.

Under the leadership of Laboulaye and Henri Martin the Franco-American Union, sponsored by many members of the Masonic Fraternity, made another important fund-raising objective: the Masonic Brotherhood. At one banquet 200 guests dined on a 14-course meal, which included *filet de boeuf Lafayette* and *croustades a la Washington,* and a 45 minute address by Laboulaye. Money flowed in during those first few days. The Liberty author Oscar Handlin tells us that "the Freemasons and some other business firms responded to the tune of some 200,000 francs."[1]

Despite the excellent start, it wasn't long before elation turned to despair. By the time the Union held its banquet at the Palace of Industry, in October, donations had fallen off dramatically. The reason was obvious: though France was now a republic the country was still suffering from the wounds inflicted by civil war. The vast majority of Frenchmen were still poor. Some could give no more than a sou (half-a-cent). And many of the bourgeois were reluctant to give their hard earned money to fund a gigantic goddess statue that would grace the harbor of a far-off country, even if that country was the United States.

Desperate for funds, Laboulaye made an appeal to French businessmen in New York but found little interest in the project. Leaving no stone unturned, Laboulaye called on prominent American businessmen to donate to the cause. One such man was Adolf Salmon, who was an honorary member of the Franco-American Union. Laboulaye asked him to conduct a fund-raising drive aimed at New York businessmen.

Reluctantly, but as a favor to Laboulaye, Salmon placed a few ads for donations in a popular France-American newspaper. But this too produced little response. Like many new projects run amuck, it was now beginning to appear as though Laboulaye's Liberty project would die a premature death due to a lack of cash flow.

Just when it looked as though the Liberty project had ended, Bartholdi, who was resolved to complete the project, came up with a bold idea. In November 1875, Bartholdi placed an ad in the newspapers promising companies that made a financial contribution to the Liberty project the right to use his copy-righted image of *Liberty Enlightening the World* to promote their products. The ad states:

The Committee of the Franco-American Union has decided that the right to reproduce the Centennial monument, which is a copyrighted artistic property, will be granted to all those manufacturers, sales agents and mercantile houses which have businesses in the United States or any other country, and wish to associate their product with the image of this work, which is certain to become a national emblem of American independence. The price paid for this right will be turned over to the subscription fund.

U.S. patent design of Bartholdi's statue.

The idea worked! Within one month after making the proposal scores of French and American businessmen were signing up to use the image of Bartholdi's yet un-built statue. By 1876, the image of Bartholdi's statue could be found on billboards all across France, promoting some of the country's best known products.[2]

To the delight of Laboulaye and his friends, Bartholdi's idea to involve the business community raised 200,000 francs. But as late as mid-summer 1879, the Union was still 200,000 francs short. Having exhausted most of their sources for funding, the Union appealed to the Ministry of the Interior for permission to hold a national lottery.[3] As a result of Laboulaye's influential friends, permission was granted.

Once again, Union members appealed to the business community. Only this time the appeal was made to donate gifts that could be given as prizes for the lottery. As before, the business community saved the day, contributing over 500 valuable prizes.

Within a few months some 300,000 lottery tickets went on sale. This time the Union's objective was to involve the middle working class.

In June 1880, the final drawing was held. On July 7, a Union spokesperson proudly announced that it had raised the necessary 600,000 francs ($400,000 U.S. dollars) to fund the building of the colossal French Goddess Liberty statue. Contributors included over

100,000 individuals, 181 cities, 10 chambers of commerce, and many school children.

"The Arm"

By January 1876, the Union realized that it would be impossible to complete the Liberty statue and have it in America for the opening of the Philadelphia Centennial Exposition in May. There was only one other option: the Committee announced that Liberty's right hand, holding aloft the torch, would be shipped across the Atlantic for the opening of the Exposition.

But when the time arrived for the opening of the Exposition, in May, even this pledge of the Union failed to be kept. "The Arm," as referred to by Bartholdi in his letters, missed both the May and July 4th celebration dates. It wasn't until August 14 that the Arm arrived at an American port aboard the steamer *Labrador.*

In spite of the Arm's late arrival, it was set up on the Exposition grounds and quickly became a powerful attraction to visitors. For a small donation, which would go to the Franco-American Union, people could purchase a ticket to enter the Arm and walk up a stairway to the torch. When the Exposition ended the Arm was then sent to New York, where it would remain in Madison's Square for the next four years.

"The Arm," Centennial Exposition, Philadelphia, Pennsylvania, 1876.

Fashioning Liberty's Image

Like most projects that begin before they are fully funded, the Liberty project was no exception. Bartholdi began work on his statue long before the needed funds had been raised. With his four-foot model of the statue as his guide, Bartholdi made a plaster model over nine feet tall. From it, he made another plaster model which towered thirty-six feet. With each model he carefully adjusted the dimensions to make certain that its proper form would be retained.

Once the thirty-sixth model had been shaped to his liking, Bartholdi divided and outlined its surface into some 300 sections. Each section was then enlarged four times to meet the dimensions of the final design. Altogether, some 9,000 measurements were made back and forth from the plaster model's surface to each enlarged section, which was built with thin strips of wood that were later covered with a coat of plaster. Using this method, the statue had 300 large plaster shaped sections. Strong laminated wooden molds were then made from each section, which became the mold used to shape the individual copper sheets that would become the statue's body.

Liberty's left hand and arm frame being constructed in the Gaget–Gauthier workshop in Paris. Bartholdi in the lower right corner (without hat).

Liberty's Body

When shaping Liberty's body cooper sheets would be hoisted into the laminated molds and forced into the proper shape by pressing it with levers and beating it into place with wooden mallets. For complicated sections, such as the torch, the cooper sheet was molded to the craftsman's liking and was then lifted out of its wooden mold and hammered on the outer surface to enhance its appearance, as with the eyes, nose, ears, and mouth. When finished, it gave the appearance of a giant life-like goddess.

After visiting the Gaget-Gauthier workshop, one writer for the *New York World* newspaper wrote about his experience, saying:

> The workshop was built wholly and solely for the accommodation of this one inmate and her attendants, some 50 workmen hammering for their lives on sheer copper to complete the toilet of her tresses for the show. The Lillputians reached her back hair by means of ladders running from stage to stage on a high scaffolding. I mounted the scaffolding with them and stood on a level with her awful eye—some 30 inches from corner to corner—to be engulfed in her gaze.

In the summer of 1878, Bartholdi completed a bust of his statue, and made it ready for display at the Paris Universal Exposition. On June 28, Liberty's bust was placed in a large wagon drawn by several teams of horses and hauled across the city to the Exposition grounds located near the Seine River. As the wagon made its way through the streets of Paris, crowds of onlookers began running toward it shouting, "Vive la Republique!"

The next day, one reporter wrote about the Liberty wagon, saying: "The bust is resting on a thick pile of branches, and at every turn in the route it sways a little, which gives it the air of nodding in salute to the curious crowd swarming around it. The effect is imposing; in spite of oneself one raises his hat to return the courtesy."

When the wagon reached the Exposition grounds it was unloaded and Liberty's bust was set up in front of the Pavilion of the Nations building, where visitors lined up to climb its interior stairway to the platform inside her crown. Once there, as many as forty people at one time could gaze at the horizon through the windows in her crown.

Liberty's bust displayed in Paris.

Liberty's Face

Bartholdi's mother.

Although there is no documentation regarding the model Bartholdi used for Liberty's face, most Liberty chroniclers believe that it was the face of Bartholdi's mother. One recorded incident seems to support this idea.

In 1884, at a banquet held in honor of Bartholdi, the French Senator Jules Francois Jennotte-Bezerian, in his after dinner speech, recalled an experience he had shared with the sculptor, saying: "Several days after having met Monsieur Bartholdi for the first time, he invited me to the opera. In entering the stage box,

I noticed an aged woman sitting in a corner, and when the light fell on her face, I turned to Bartholdi and said to him: 'Why, that's your model for Liberty Enlightening the World!' 'Yes,' he answered calmly. 'It's my mother!'" Then, it is said that Bartholdi's eyes filled with tears, though he never said a word.[4]

Another tradition holds that Bartholdi's model for Liberty's face might well have been that of a young middle-class Alsatian woman named Jeanne-Emilie Baheux de Puyieux, whom the sculptor met on his first trip to the United States, in 1871, and later married on December 21, 1876.[5] It is said that Jeanne-Emilie spent long hours posing as a model for Liberty.

Liberty's Skeletal Frame

In 1789, Bartholdi turned his attention to the construction of Liberty's skeletal frame. Just before its construction began, Eugene Emmanuel Viollet-le-Duc, the engineer Bartholdi put in charge of the project, unexpectedly died.

At the time it was thought that Viollet-le-Duc's sudden death was a tragic loss to the Liberty project. To many, most certainly to Bartholdi, Viollet-le-Duc was considered to be one of the world's leading structural engineers. But there was a problem. It soon became evident that Viollet-le-Duc still held onto some of the old medieval ideas of structural engineering, which he planned to use to secure Liberty's statue.

Before Viollet-le-Duc's death he recommended that the statue's interior be filled with sand up to the hips. This was a

method used on medieval statues, which not only anchored them to the ground but gave them tremendous support in times of high winds and storms. But because of the fierce storms along the Atlantic coastline, had Viollet-le-Duc lived and his plan been implemented, it is almost certain that Liberty's statue would not be standing today.

To replace Viollet-le-Duc, Bartholdi enlisted the help of a man named Gustave Eiffel, a Brother Mason. Eiffel was a man

Gustave Eiffel

who had introduced new concepts in the structural design of railroad bridges, such as the Garabit railroad bridge and later, his most famous achievement, the Eiffel Tower, which has Masonic significance, was built in 1889.

Eiffel's design for the statue's interior support called for a strong center pylon of four iron beams rising from its base to its neck. Like the backbone on a skeleton this center pylon would project smaller beams toward the outer skin that would be connected by spring-like rods to a webbing of iron straps lining the inside of the statue's skin. Thus the hundreds of spring-like rods attached to each section of the statue's copper skin would be flexible and allow them to float when buffeted with strong winds. Consequently, when each section was secured to the center pylon and joined together, Liberty's body not only had flexibility but strength to withstand sudden changes in temperature and wind velocity.

Assembling Liberty's frame.

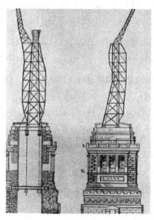

Liberty's completed frame.

To secure Liberty's torch and arm, which soared some sixty feet and nearly straight up, Eiffel designed a separate extended girder which branched off the center pylon's shoulder. Strong and flexible, it allowed the arm to sway in heavy gales but remain safe enough for someone to climb up into the torch to service its lights.

It took Eiffel the entire year of 1880 just to design and build Liberty's frame. When completed, it weighed 120-tons and stood almost ninety-eight feet tall. When asked how long he expected his design to withstand the elements of time, Eiffel simply said, "It will hold."

In early 1884, after Liberty's arm and torch were returned to Paris from New York, the statue was assembled at the Gaget-Gauthier workshop in downtown Paris. With scaffolding still reaching to its shoulders, the statue towered above the neighboring buildings, appearing like a great goddess of antiquity that, in some miraculous way, had just been transported through time to modern day civilization.

Liberty's statue assembled in Paris.

Liberty's Home Site

In December 1876, several prominent New Yorkers joined together and formed an American organization to work in concert with the Franco-American Union in France. It was called The American Committee for the Statue of Liberty. At its head was William Evarts, a Brother Skull & Bonesman, who had served as Secretary of State in the Rutherford B. Hayes administration. Other influential members included Richard Butler, a New York businessman, Edwin D. Morgan, a former New York governor and senator, Parke Godwin, editor of the *New York Post*, and the celebrated poet William Cullen Bryant[6]: now the core of the Committee, their combined influence gave the Liberty project a much needed boost of credibility.

The first official act of the Committee was to submit a formal request to President Grant for securing Bedloe's Island as the official site for Liberty's statue, and petition the President to submit its request to Congress for approval.

On February 9, 1877, President Grant sent a resolution to Congress to accept the offer of the French people and designate a suitable spot on the Federal Government properties of Bedloe's Island or Governor's Island in New York Harbor for the placement of the statue.[7]

At this particular time the Constitution was still understood as a document of "original understanding". Under the original understanding of the Constitution only Congress had the authority to set aside land for a national park. Consequently, at that particular time it was understood by all three branches of government that the Constitution gave Congress the sole authority to grant such a request, and only on the condition that the statue would serve as a beacon.

Under the Constitution, beacons came under the authority of Congress to regulate commerce. Therefore, included in Grant's resolution was a paragraph which stated that the island would serve for both "the inauguration of the statue and its maintenance as a lighthouse."

Upon receiving President Grant's resolution, the House manager of Commerce, Abraham Hewitt, another important recruit of the Committee, expedited it through committee and brought it before the House for a vote. President Grant's resolution not only passed, both Houses of Congress passed it on February 22, 1877, George Washington's birthday. President Grant then signed it into law on March 3, his last official day in office.[8]

Liberty's Official Debut

By October of 1881, the craftsmen had completed most of the copper pieces for Liberty's body. On October 24, the one hundredth anniversary of the Battle of Yorktown, won by both Washington and Layfette's troops, Levi Morton, the new American ambassador to France, drove the first ceremonial copper rivet into one of Liberty's feet.[9]

Two hundred people attended the ceremony, including Bartholdi, the management and craftsmen of Gaget-Gauthier and Company, DeLesseps, Eiffel, as well as other American and French dignitaries. The special guests of honor were Laboulaye and his close associate in the Union, the Masonic lodge Master Henri Martin.[10] This, however, would be the last time either man would attend a ceremony honoring their beloved Liberty statue. Both men died in 1882.

Until this time most of the primary movers of the Liberty project were Freemasons. It wasn't until the 11th hour, when the success of the project was assured, that French officials stepped in and informed Ambassador Morton that the French government would take a more active role in the remaining work of the Franco-American Union; that France would provide a warship to transport Liberty's statue to New York; and proposed a date of July 4th, 1884, to formally transfer the ownership of the statue to the United States government.[11]

Liberty's Transfer of Ownership

Although Congress had earlier signed a resolution that would appropriate an island in New York Harbor as the official site for the statue, there was still no official commitment on the part of the U.S. government to take possession of it. Thus when the French government proposed a date for the transfer of ownership of Liberty's statue to take place on July 4th, Ambassador Morton was caught off-guard.

Not knowing how to respond to the proposed transfer of ownership, Morton quickly dispatched a message to the U.S. State Department, requesting instructions on how to proceed. Four days before the scheduled ceremony, Morton received a message from the State Department, authorizing him to accept the statue on behalf of the U.S. government.[12]

On July 4, the day finally arrived for the formal transfer of Liberty's statue to the U.S. government. The outdoor foundry yard around the huge workshop area of Gadget-Gauthier and Company was decorated with red, white, and blue flags, and a speaker's platform had been set up directly in front of Liberty's enormous feet.

Some two hundred people who had gathered in the courtyard were waiting for the ceremony to begin, when DeLessepes, who had taken Laboulaye's place as president of the Union, and Ambassador Morton, arrived promptly at 11:30 A.M. Both men went directly to the speaker's platform where they took their place among the seated guests and dignitaries.

As the crowd of people stood at the base of Liberty's towering copper body, glistening in the noon-day sun, DeLesseps stepped forward to the podium and presented Bartholdi's statue *Liberty Enlightening the World* to the United States government "in the name of the French people." When DeLesseps finished speaking, Ambassador Levi Morton stepped to the podium and accepted the statue "in the name of the American people." Morton then read a telegram of congratulations from U.S. President Chester Arthur (1881-1885), who praised Bartholdi along with others, and warmly thanked the people of France for the Goddess statue *Liberty Enlightening the World.*

After the final speech, a formal document of transfer was passed around to be signed by the official representatives of the French and American governments, including the Franco-American Union. The U.S. flag was then raised to Liberty's torch, and as the Liberty deed, in its gold case, was handed over to Ambassador Morton, the band played the *Marseillaise,* the *Star Spangled Banner,* and *Hail Columbia.*[13]

11

'A Stand Shall Be Erected For Her'

Aftter the transfer of the ownership ceremony, on July 4, Liberty's statue was left standing in the Gaget-Gauther foundry yard for the remainder of the year. Both French and American Committee officials felt that shipping the massive statue across the Atlantic during the winter could be much too dangerous. For the next few months the statue remained on display in Paris and became the city's main attraction, as crowds of Parisians jammed the streets just to gaze at Liberty's towering figure.

In December, the workmen began dismantling the 151-foot-high statue for its trans-Atlantic voyage to New York Harbor. Each section was carefully removed, labeled, numbered and packed in a wooden crate. More than two hundred wooden crates were loaded onto wagons drawn by huge teams of horses and taken to the Paris railway terminal where a seventy-car train would transport them to the French port of Rouen, near the mouth of the Seine River. At Rouen, the wooden crates, weighing a total of 220 tons, of which the copper itself weighed 88 tons, was loaded aboard the French warship *Isere*.

On May 21, 1885, after several more speeches were delivered during a downpour of rain, two French warships, the *Isere* and its escort, the *Flore,* weighed anchor and began the long journey across the Atlantic to New York.

On June 18, both warships arrived off Sandy Hook in the lower bay of New York Harbor. Upon learning of the *Isere's* arrival, General Charles Stone, the chief engineer of the pedestal project, and several New York aldermen boarded a tug-boat and went down to the lower bay to meet the *Isere* and take possession of its prized cargo. Upon boarding the *Isere,* General Stone was taken to the captain's cabin where he was handed the official documents that conveyed ownership of the statue to the United States of America.

Two days later, on a sunny cloudless morning, the French warships slowly made their way up the bay toward Bedloe's Island for the cargo unloading. When the *Isere* arrived at the harbor entrance four U.S. naval ships, which carried the Mayor of New York and several other dignitaries, led the way to Bedloe's Island. Because of the advanced publicity, as the small armada of ships slowly moved into the harbor, crowds of people were already waiting on the Battery. The sound of their cheers, accompanied with band music, saluting cannons, and a fleet of small boats, made a spectacular welcome for the two French warships that had just crossed the Atlantic.

Once the ships had docked and their passengers disembarked there were more speeches, more celebrations, and more ceremonies. But unlike previous occasions, this time there was a serious problem that threatened the entire project: there was still no pedestal upon which to stand Bartholdi's statue *Liberty Enlightening the World*. Eight years had passed since the founding of the American Committee, and there were still no funds in the Committee treasury to build a pedestal.

During the Committee's first few years it had been successful in getting Congress to pass a resolution that would make available either Governor's Island or Bedloe's Island as Liberty's official home site. Both islands had been made into fortresses in the early 1800s to protect New York City from enemy ships passing through the Narrows. Of these two islands, Bartholdi preferred Bedloe's Island, which not only had a commanding presence in the bay, but as a former Army fortress with its massive outside walls that formed an eleven-pointed star, made it the ideal site for America's new Goddess statue, *Liberty Enlightening the World.*

Shortly after the resolution for Liberty's home site was signed by President Grant, General William Tecumseh Sherman, the Civil War hero and Commanding General of the Army, personally inspected both islands and selected Bedloe's Island, the former Fort Wood Army fortress, as the most appropriate site, much to Bartholdi's delight.[1]

There were several reasons the American people were not interested in supporting the pedestal project. At the time the country was still recovering from the depression of 1873. Many people had lost their farms and were forced to move to cities in search of work. In addition, the country itself was going through a major change. It was the beginning of the American industrial revolution. New breakthroughs in technology, medicine, and manufacturing were being made.

America was a nation on the move. The American people had little time to think about financing a giant Goddess statue that had no practical value to the nation, the economy, or their own personal lives. Equally significant, large numbers of immigrants were now pouring into the country's cities, placing additional strain on an already over-burdened job market.

At that particular time large groups of people were moving west. People were selling everything they owned and buying wagons, oxen, horses, and mules that would take them from the Eastern part of the country to Oregon and California.

Equally important, there was a strong anti-NewYorker sentiment among most of the people living in other parts of the country. For most Americans, New York was the state of wealthy bankers, greedy lawyers, and rich stock brokers. So if money was needed to fund a particular project, especially if that project benefitted New York, the prevailing attitude was: "Let the New Yorkers pay for it."

But when it came to funding Liberty's pedestal, New York's wealthy had no more interest in supporting it than the poor, or those living outside the state. Even New York's wealthy patrons of the arts questioned the "artistic value" the statue would add to the state.[2]

Then there were the out-spoken Protestants and Catholics, who opposed Bartholdi's Goddess statue on biblical grounds, calling it "pagan and idolatrous".[3] John Gilmory Shea, who later became the first president of the Catholic Historical Society of the United States, wrote in one Catholic article entitled *Our Great Goddess and Her Coming Idol:*

. . . ere long the idol of the goddess "Liberty Enlightening the World" will be set up on Bedloe's Island, doubtless as was Nabuchodonoser's great statue of old, with sound of harp and sackbut and psaltery, and woe will betide the man who does not at the sound fall down and worship.

. . . Some antiquated persons with medieval ideas may choose to believe in One Who proclaimed His doctrine eighteen centuries ago in Palestine and look up to Him as "the true Light that enlighteneth the world," and believe that man can be really free only "with the freedom wherewith He hath made us free" but as their voices are not likely to be heard amidst the shouting, and the music, we may in advance enter our protest.

Designing Liberty's Pedestal

After eight years of existence, in 1881, the American Committee had accomplished little more than securing a site for Liberty's statue. As a result, much of the Committee's efforts to fund the pedestal had come to a grinding halt. Not only was the project floundering, it was receiving bad reviews in the press, and had become a thing of public ridicule.

William M. Evarts

Just when things looked the worst, the Committee received news of the Franco-American Union's successful fund-raising campaign. William Evarts, the Committee Chairman, packed his bags and boarded a steamship to Paris. Evarts wanted to personally meet with members of the French Union and hear for himself the progress they had made.

Upon arriving in Paris, Evarts met with French Committee members, and immediately dispatched a telegram to the American Committee with instructions to "move with promptness and energy" to complete the pedestal and prepare for receiving the great "contribution of French genius, with friendship and enthusiasm."[4]

Until this time, much of the pedestal project was still in the planning stages. Several designs were submitted to the Committee but none had yet been approved. Among the many designs submitted to the Committee from both American and French artists were two that stood out in particular. They were drawings for the pedestal by the celebrated sculptor himself, Auguste Bartholdi, which were in the shape of a flat-platformed pyramid.

Bartholdi's 1880 sketch of pedestal.

Bartholdi's accompanying 1880 sketch of pedestal with Goddess atop.

Within Masonry the pyramid is one of its most important symbols. Among the ancient Egyptians, the pyramid of Gizah was believed to be the tomb of the god Hermes, who was the personification of "universal wisdom". It is a pyramid without a capstone.

Manly Hall says in his book entitled *The Lost Keys of Freemasonry*:

> The Master Mason becomes the capstone of the Universal Temple. He stands alone on the pinnacle of the temple. One stone must yet be placed, but this he cannot find. Somewhere it lies concealed. In prayer he kneels,

asking the powers to aid him in his search. The light of the sun shines upon him and bathes him in a splendor celestial. Suddenly a voice speaks from the Heavens, saying "The temple is finished in my faithful Master is found the missing stone."

. . . The Master Mason embodies the power of the human mind, that connecting link which binds heaven and earth together in an endless chain. He . . . has become the spokesman of the Most High. He stands between the glowing fire light of the world [the sun]. Through him passes Hydra, the great snake, and from its mouth there pours to man the light of God.[5]

Here we see the Masonic significance of Bartholdi's drawing of the unfinished pyramid pedestal on which the Goddess statue *Liberty Enlightening the World* was to stand, holding aloft her torch of enlightenment. Standing atop Bartholdi's unfinished pyramid pedestal sketch, the essence of his Great Goddess statue is revealed once and for all.

But there is more. Manly Hall says that the "light of God" that passes through the Master Mason is "Hydra, the great snake" ('Lucifer'). Hall writes: "When the Mason learns that the key . . . is the proper application of the dynamo of living power, he has learned the Mystery of his Craft. The seething energies of Lucifer are in his hands."[6]

For Luciferians, Lucifer has a dual nature: the female principle, Isis, as well as the male principle, Osiris.[7] The word "Lucifer" means "Light Bearer". Thus, among the elite of Masonry, the female principle of Lucifer is viewed as the *Enlightener (or 'Illuminator') of the World,* and Masons are the "children of light". The Masonic writer Foster Bailey says:

Stage by stage They [the Masters of Wisdom] assist at the unfolding of the consciousness of the candidate until the time comes when he can "enter into light," and, in his turn become a Light-Bearer, one of the Illuminati who can assist the Lodge on High in bringing humanity to light.[8]

The Gifted Architect

On December 6, 1881, after rejecting all the submitted pedestal designs, including Bartholdi's design, the American Committee selected a well-known American architect. The Committee then established a projected cost and completion date for the pedestal—$250,000 dollars and nine months.

Richard Morris Hunt

The architect the Committee selected was Richard Morris Hunt, a Brother Mason, whom Bartholdi had met on his first visit to the United States, in 1871.

Born in 1828 to a prosperous New England family, Richard Hunt was sixteen when his mother took him to Paris where he studied under the renowned architect, Hector Lefuel. When Hunt was nineteen he enrolled in the famed *Ecole des Beaux-Arts* school and was its first American graduate.[9]

Hunt's architectural talents were quickly recognized, and shortly after completing his education he was placed in charge of constructing an addition to the famed Louvre, the *Pavillion de la Bibliothique* in Paris. For those who knew Hunt's skill as an architect there was little doubt that had he wanted to remain in France he would have had an exceptional career. But at the age of twenty-seven Hunt returned to the United States, where he soon became a leader of American Renaissance architecture.

Among some of his more notable projects were the Astor Library and the Metropolitan Museum in New York, the dome of the Capitol building in Washington, D.C., the famed Vanderbilt "Biltmore" estate near Ashville, North Carolina, the "Breakers" in Newport, Rhode Island, and the Administration Building of the World's Columbian Exposition at Chicago.

Upon accepting the pedestal commission, Hunt's initial design was a scaled down version of Bartholdi's 1880 flat-platformed pyramid drawing. Instead of shaping it in the form of a massive flat-platformed pyramid with two smaller tapered platforms, Hunt reduced the size and made it into four-broad tapered platforms rising from its base to a height of 114 feet, with a stairway entrance on each side.

But even this design was rejected by the Committee, claiming that it was too large and would overpower the statue. Hunt then scaled down the pedestal to ninety-eight feet, which not only accentuated the statue but made it more affordable, and much more to the liking of the Committee.

Construction of Liberty's Pedestal

By 1883, the Committee was still far short of reaching its financial goal of $250,000 dollars. Nevertheless, the prevailing feeling among Committee members was that the work on the pedestal had to begin. The man selected to be in charge of the pedestal's construction was General Charles Stone, who had received his training as an engineer at West Point Academy.

After the Civil War, in 1865, General Stone resigned from the Army and was employed as an engineer for a mining company. Then, in 1870, he was invited by Ismail Pasha, the Khedive of Egypt, to assist DeLesseps with the excavation of the Suez Canal—the same project which inspired Bartholdi's design of *Egypt Bringing the Light to Asia.*

Charles P. Stone

In April 1883, more than one hundred men began excavation behind the fortress walls of old Fort Wood. Their first task was to dig a huge hole that would later be filled with cement, which would become the pedestal's foundation. In October, the actual pouring of cement began and continued through winter until March, when the cement reached ground level.

In June of 1884, after eight months of pouring some 24,000 barrels of cement, the foundation was completed. It stood fifty-two feet above the ground and was heralded as the largest single block of cement ever to be formed. Protruding from its base were huge steel beams which would anchor Eiffel's skeleton frame as though it were attached to solid rock.

Construction work on Liberty's pedestal;
Harper's Weekly, **July 12, 1884.**

Though the foundation of the pedestal was finally completed, its completion came at a high cost. The Committee's funds had been depleted in the process. A new campaign had to be launched to raise more cash.

Volunteers were sent to factories, workshops, and offices in search of donations.

Six-inch models of Liberty's statue were sold for $1 dollar. Public appeals were made at art shows, fairs, and all types of community functions. Even school children were encouraged to donate a penny toward the pedestal's completion.

By July 4, 1884, the day the ownership of Liberty's statue was transferred to the United States government, in spite of a massive effort to raise the necessary funds to complete the pedestal: the Committee had raised only $20,000 dollars.

From a public relations standpoint things couldn't have been worse. Public ridicule became the headline of the day. The *New York Times* suggested that the giant statue be placed at the Battery to make it easier for people to scrawl their names on it. One newspaper editorial titled "Looking a Gift Horse in the Mouth" lamented:

> The painful parsimony of the Frenchmen who have undertaken to present this city with the statue of "Liberty Enlightening the World" is simply disgusting. They have, in effect, told us that we cannot have the statue unless we provide it with a pedestal. This effort to compel us to pay out of our own money for the embellishment of our harbor has not yet been condemned by the press with the severity it deserves.

The writer concluded his comments by saying that the French people ought not only to pay for the pedestal but also pay the United States $10,000 for the rent of Bedloe's Island.

The Gifted Poetess

In October 1883, Committee officials decided to sponsor an art and literary auction as a pedestal fund-raiser. William Evarts asked some of the country's most celebrated writers, such as Walt Whitman, Mark Twain, and Bret Harte, to contribute one or more of their writings to the pedestal project. Among some of the better known New York writers, Evarts contacted a young poetess named Emma Lazarus.

Emma Lazarus

Born in 1849, Emma was neither poor nor an immigrant. Her parents were of Portuguese-Jewish descent and belonged to the Sephardic Jewish community of New York.

Even as a young girl Emma demonstrated a special talent for learning poetry and languages. Unlike other children, most of Emma's education came from private tutors. Emma's father, whom she adored, was a wealthy sugar refiner and was not hesitant when it came to providing the best for his daughter.

When Emma was only seventeen her father had her first book of poetry printed. By the time Emma was thirty-one, she had published a novel and a play, as well as more poems.

As the daughter of a prominent Jewish family, Emma was well known in most circles of New York society. Among Emma's many friends, one of her most cherished friendships was the Concord poet Ralph Waldo Emerson, whom she had met at a party and cultivated a friendship through correspondence.

For most of Emma's life, she kept herself busy as a New York socialite, and had little interest in her Jewish heritage. It is said that when her rabbi, Dr. Gottheil, asked Emma if she would write a poem for his Hebrew hymn book she replied: "I will gladly assist you as far as I am able; but that will not be much . . . I feel no religious fervor in my soul."

At the time Emma wrote those words she had no idea that her life was about to abruptly change, which began with the death of her mother. When Emma's mother, Esther, died Emma felt that her life too had ended. No longer could she go to her mother for council or comfort.

One day a close family friend, Edmund Stedman, a banker, who was also a poet, suggested to Emma that she could find comfort in turning to her Jewish heritage as an artistic expression. Emma replied: "I am proud of my blood and linage but the Hebrew ideals do not appeal to me."

It was about this time, in 1879, that the infamous Russian Pogroms (the structured extermination of the Jewish people and their faith), which were ordered by the Russian Tsar Alexander III, swept through Bulgaria, Rumania, and other neighboring countries.[10]

By 1881, hundreds of thousands of Jews had already fled eastern Europe. Another 300,000 were systematically eliminated. One editorial in the London *Times* stated: "These persecutions have taken every form of atrocity in the experience of mankind . . . . Men have been cruelly murdered, women brutally outraged, children dashed to pieces or burned alive in their homes."

Thousands of homeless Jews made their way across the Atlantic to New York as a massive wave of anti-Semitism spread across Europe. At that particular time there was no Ellis Island for receiving and processing immigrants. The thousands of Jewish immigrants coming into the country were taken to Wards Island in New York's East River, where they were held-over in large government sheds. Caught unprepared, the government was understaffed and unable to handle the massive numbers of destitute Jewish immigrants. To help in the recovery phase, volunteer rescue societies were hastily organized to feed and clothe the thousands of homeless Jewish refugees that had fled their homeland in Europe and made their way to America.

Inspired by George Eliot's novel *Daniel Derronda,* Emma decided to visit Wards Island with a small group of women. Like most volunteers, Emma was unprepared for what she encountered. Until that time Emma had only read about the pogroms and atrocities committed against the Jewish people. Now she was personally witnessing the plight of her own people in a way she could never have imagined. Everywhere Emma looked she saw people herded together in huge sheds like cattle; fearful, confused, sick, and possessing little more than the clothes they were wearing.

From that point on Emma's life changed. Never again would she live the glamorous lifestyle of a New York socialite. Nor would she ever again be indifferent toward her Jewish heritage.

In 1882, Emma began attending protest rallies and writing articles for prominent magazines on the plight of the Jewish people. She began to learn Hebrew, and took an active interest in the newly founded Zionist movement, which was established to help exiled Jews return to their homeland in Israel. Most important, with a renewed love for her Jewish heritage, Emma began writing again. This time she authored a book of poems entitled *Songs of a Semite.* In one poem entitled *The New Ezekiel,* Emma wrote:

> The Spirit is not dead; proclaim the word. Where lay dead bones, a host of armed men stand; I open your graves, my people, saith the Lord, I shall place you living in the land.

In 1883, at the age of thirty-four, Emma, for the first time, visited Europe and her family's native homeland in Spain. Unlike earlier years, Emma was now set on learning everything she could about her Jewish heritage. While in Europe she worked with other Jews to help broaden the cause for Jewish nationalism.

When Emma left Spain to return to her home in New York that same year, her passion for the plight of her people burned brighter than ever.

On the day Emma arrived at her home there was a large stack of mail waiting for her. One of the letters was from William Evarts, requesting her to write a poem in her own hand that the Committee could auction off during its next fund raising drive. Exhausted from her trip, Emma sat down and pinned a brief note to Evarts, saying: "I am not able to write to order."

Two days later, with the plight of the Jewish people still on her mind, on November 2, 1883, Emma sat down and pinned a poem she entitled *The New Colossus* and sent it off to Evarts. Interestingly, Emma had never personally seen Bartholdi's statue. She only knew about it from pictures and articles she had seen in newspapers and magazines, which often compared the similarity of Bartholdi's statue of the Goddess Liberty to that of the Greek *Colossus of Rhodes* Sun-god statue.

On December 3, the opening night of The Bartholdi Statue Pedestal Art Loan Exhibition, held in the National Academy of Design, F. Hopkinson Smith gave the first public reading of Emma's poem, saying:

> Not like the brazen giant of Greek fame,
> With conquering limbs astride from land to land,
> Here at our sea-washed, sunset gates shall stand
> A mighty woman with a torch, whose flame
> Is the imprisoned lightning, and her name
> Mother of Exiles. From her beacon-hand
> Glows worldwide welcome; her mild eyes command
> The air-bridged harbor that twin cities frame.
>
> "Keep, ancient lands, your storied pomp!" cries she
> With silent lips. "Give me your tired, your poor,

Your huddled masses yearning to breathe free,
The wretched refuse of your teeming shore.
Send these, the homeless, tempest-tost to me.
I lift my lamp beside the golden door!"

That night Emma's sonnet brought only $1,500.[11] Three years later, on October 28, 1886, when Bartholdi's statue, *Liberty Enlightening the World,* was dedicated on Bedloe's Island, Emma, now very ill, was unable to attend the ceremony. Nor was there any mention of her poem.

The following year, on November 19, 1887, the day of Emma's thirty-eight birthday, Emma died of Hodgkins disease, never knowing that her poem would one day become synonymous with Bartholdi's colossal statue, *Liberty Enlightening the World.*

For another six years Emma's poem remained in obscurity. Then, in 1903, Georgiana Schuyler, a sculptor and friend of Emma, found a copy of the sonnet in a New York bookstore. When Georgiana read it she was so moved by the words that she contacted the Liberty Park officials and spearheaded an effort to have Emma's poem memorialized along with Bartholdi's statue, *Liberty Enlightening the World.*

Arrangements were soon made to have Emma's sonnet engraved on a bronze plaque and placed inside the pedestal. On the plaque are inscribed the full text of Emma's *New Colossus* poem, concluding with the following words: "This tablet, with her sonnet to the Bartholdi Statue of Liberty engraved upon it, is placed upon these walls in loving memory of Emma Lazarus."

By this time the constant flow of immigrants to America from the Old World had become the very embodiment of Emma's poem. For multitudes of new immigrants now pouring into New York Harbor, Bartholdi's gigantic Goddess statue, *Liberty Enlightening the World,* had indeed become "The Mother of Exiles".

On the day Emma's poem was memorialized there were no speeches, no ceremony, and no press coverage. Yet, Emma's sonnet was reprinted again and again in newspapers and magazines across the country. By 1949, Emma's poem had become synonymous with Bartholdi's Goddess statue, *The Statue of Liberty,* and its last five lines were set to music in the Broadway musical *"Miss Liberty,"* composed by Irving Berlin.

Cornerstone Ceremony

By July 1884, there was only $20,000 dollars left in the Committee's bank account, which was barely enough to lay the first two levels of the pedestal. William Evarts knew that something had to be done soon to demonstrate that the project was going forward. Otherwise, whatever momentum had been gained would soon be lost.

Chairman Evarts contacted the Grand Lodge of the Free and Accepted Masons of the State of New York. Evarts, a Skull & Bonesman, wanted to continue the Brotherhood tradition of having the cornerstone of major public and private monuments "consecrated" with full Masonic rites ever since George Washington, in 1793, personally laid the cornerstone of the Capital Building, with the assistance of the Grand Lodge of Maryland.

Once arrangements were made, Evarts made a public announcement that the pedestal cornerstone would be laid on August 5, and that the Reverend "Worshipful" Franck R. Lawrence, the Deputy Grand Master of the Grand Lodge of the State of New York, and its officers, were invited to preside over the ceremony.[12]

The Committee made all the necessary preparations for the upcoming event, contacting the press, preparing the site, and sending out invitations to all the appropriate people, especially dignitaries. When the day finally arrived the Committee became acutely aware that everything had been taken into account except one important factor—the weather!

That morning an early August storm unleashed a record downpour of wind and rain upon the 1,500 guests and dignitaries who gathered on Broadway to make up a procession to the Battery. Congressmen, senators, mayors, ambassadors, the presidents of the different French societies, and Freemasons who had come from every state in the Union scrambled to board the steamer *Bay Ridge,* which was decorated with the tricolors of France and the Stars and Stripes of the U.S., as it prepared to cross a choppy bay.

When the *Bay Ridge* arrived at Bedloe's Island its rain-soaked passengers made their way through the mud and standing water to the sixty-seven-foot concrete foundation, where they huddled under their umbrellas, shivering in the cold while waiting for the ceremony to begin

The Cornerstone Ceremony; *Harper's Weekly,*
August 16, 1884.

The cornerstone itself was an immense block of Leetes Island granite, 6 feet 10 inches long, 3 feet 8 inches wide, and 2 feet 6 inches high, weighing six tons. At the northeast corner of the foundation there was a square hole to place the copper box containing special articles. A derrick held the cornerstone, suspended by cables, which was ready to be lowered over the copper box and cemented in place by a silver trowel.

At 2 o'clock, the band played the *Marseillaise* and *Hail Columbia,* which was the signal for the ceremony to begin. After the opening prayer, General Stone opened the copper box to receive the name-cards of those present. Then Edward Ehlers, Grand Secretary and member of the Continental Lodge No. 287, read aloud the items that had already been placed in the copper box: copies of the Constitution and Declaration of Independence; George Washington's Farewell Address; 20 bronze medals of Presidents (including Washington, Monroe, Jackson, Polk, Buchanan, Johnson, and Garfield, who were proven Masons); copies of New York City newspapers; a portrait of Bartholdi; a copy of *Poem on Liberty* by E. R. Johnes; and a list of the Grand Lodge of Masons of the State of New York.[13]

When the lid was secured the copper box was laid in its place and the cornerstone was lowered over it. The Deputy Grand Master, "Worshipful" Lawrence, solemnly declared the cornerstone "plumb, level and square."[14] He then cemented it, tapped it three times with a mallet, and announced that the cornerstone was duly laid.[15] The Masonic "consecration" elements of wheat, wine, and oil were then sprinkled over it.[16]

One reporter for the *New York Times* wrote that after a twenty-one gun salute from the battery of old Fort Wood, the "Worshipful" Deputy Grand Master Lawrence delivered a Masonic address, saying in part:

> Never since the building of the Temple of Solomon have Masons participated in a work more exalted than that now in progress upon this spot. The colossal statue to be placed upon this massive base is grand in its origin, its execution and its proportions—grand as representing a pure and ennobling friendship between two great nations of free men, at peace with one another and at peace with all the world, who, thus happily circumstanced, erect an enduring monument to typify and illustrate to all the earth their love and liberty.[17]

Despite the continuing downpour more speeches were delivered, followed by a chorus of *Old Hundred*. Episcopal Bishop Henry C. Potter, a Brother Mason, concluded with the benediction and everyone made a mad dash through the water and mud to the dock for the return trip on the *Bay Ridge* steamer.

The next day, one newspaper reporter wrote: "those who attended the grand event would have been less wet if they had swam back to the Battery."

The Gifted Journalist

With all the press coverage and fanfare given to the cornerstone ceremony there was still little public interest in the pedestal project. For the next six months small gifts from veterans and various patriotic groups, civic clubs, and philanthropic societies trickled into the pedestal fund. By March 1885, the Committee's bank account totaled only $2,885 out of the $182,491 raised. It would take another $100,000 to finish the pedestal, and time was not on the Committee's side.

On March 10, the Committee ordered General Stone to halt work on the pedestal. The following day front page headlines heralded the shutting down of the pedestal operations, and a new wave of ridicule began. In a cartoon drawing one newspaper portrayed Liberty as an old woman, sitting on a rock in the harbor with a look of disgust on her face because she still had no pedestal on which to stand. In terms of negative publicity, things could not have gotten much worse.

Joseph Pulitzer

It was at this time that Joseph Pulitzer, a Hungarian born immigrant of Magyar-Jewish descent, came on the scene.

Born in Hungary in 1847 and immigrating to America in 1864, Pulitzer landed in St. Louis, Missouri, and took a job as a reporter with a German newspaper.

At the age of twenty-two Joseph Pulitzer entered politics and was elected to the Missouri state legislature.

In 1878, Pulitzer bought the bankrupt *St. Louis Dispatch* for $2,500 and merged it with the struggling *Post,* making the *Dispatch-Post* one of the most successful newspapers in St. Louis. Instead of just reporting the news, Pulitzer made the *Dispatch-Post* a staunch advocate for the plight of the common man.

In 1883, Pulitzer became restless with his life in St. Louis and began looking for a greater challenge. This time the mid-West reporter set his sights on New York City. On May 10 of that same year, Pulitzer bought the struggling *World* newspaper from Jay Gould for $346,000.

Once Pulitzer took the helm of the *World* it didn't take him long to make his mark on New York. Pulitzer knew that the secret to success in journalism was found not only in informed reporting, but also in entertainment and, more importantly, in championing the causes of the underdog. Pulitzer's *World* gave New Yorkers massive doses of each.

Interestingly enough, Joseph Pulitzer is credited as being the first to run the comic-strips, and have special investigative reporting. But where Pulitzer really made his mark was when he championed the causes of the common man in opposition to the pet projects of New York's elected politicians. In this arena, Pulitzer was fearless.

It wasn't long after arriving in New York City that Pulitzer found out about the on-again-off-again plight of the American Committee's pedestal project. With so many millionaires in town Pulitzer argued that it was a disgrace that New York City's wealthy had not responded to the Committee's many appeals for funds. In one editorial, Pulitzer wrote:

> Here in the commercial metropolis of the Western
> world, where hundreds of our citizens reckon their wealth
> by millions, where our merchants and bankers and brokers
> are spoken of as 'princes,' we stand haggling and begging
> and scheming in order to raise enough money to procure
> a pedestal on which to place the statue . . . . The dash of
> one millionaire merchant's pen ought to settle the matter
> and spare the city further information . . . .

Although Pulitzer's appeal was direct and forceful his challenge went unanswered, and the Committee's funding plight for the pedestal project continued. But this was about to change.

By 1885, the *World* had become one of New York's most read newspapers, outdoing almost every other newspaper in the city. Pulitzer, knowing exactly how to harness the power of his readership, took it upon himself to champion the cause of the pedestal project.

On March 15, just five days after the pedestal work was halted, Pulitzer launched his own fund-raising campaign. He began by personally contributing $1,000. He then offered to print in the *World* the names of every person who mailed in a subscription, regardless of how little the amount. Pulitzer's appeal stated in part:

> It would be an irrevocable disgrace to New York city and the American Republic to have France send us this special gift without our having provided even so much as a landing place for it . . . there is but one thing that can be done. We must raise the money.
>
> The *World* is the people's paper, and it now appeals to the people to come forward and raise this money. The $250, 000 that the statue had cost was paid by the masses of the French people—by the workingmen, the tradesmen, the shop girls, the artisians—by all, irrespective of class or condition. Let us respond in like manner. Let us not wait for the millionaires to give the money. It is not a gift from the millionaires of France to the millionaires of America but a gift of the whole people of France to the whole people of America.
>
> Take this appeal to yourself personally . . . give . . . something however little . . . let us hear from the people.

Day after day Pulitzer's appeal was printed on the front page of the *World,* displaying a cartoon of Uncle Sam holding his hat in his hand. The response was overwhelming. In the first week, readers mailed in over $2,000. Funds were pouring in not only from *World* subscribers but from people who mailed in a donation and bought the paper just to see their name in print.

To add an element of human interest Pulitzer often published excerpts from some of the letters people would send to the *World.* One said: "I am a little girl nine years old and I will send you a pair of my pet game batams if you will sell them and give the money to the statue." A man wrote: "Since leaving off smoking cigarettes I have gained twenty-five pounds, so I cheerfully enclose a penny for each pound."

Before long, other newspapers, which had taken note of the *World's* success, began making their own pedestal funding appeals. Contributions were even coming in from other parts of the country.

One Northern Baptist Church in Philadelphia announced that it would take up a special collection on Sunday, May 31, 1885. Its pastor, Reverend H. H. Barbour, said that the church's special day was "a particularly appropriate occasion to appreciate liberty which enables people to worship in perfect freedom." Other churches, as well as synagogues, followed suit.

In just two months, the *World* received $52,203.41 towards the pedestal project. By August, Pulitzer announced that the people had given $109,191.41. Of the 121,000 Americans who sent money to the *World,* most of them were New Yorkers, and 80 percent of the money given was in sums of less than $1.

In just five months, Pulitzer not only raised the funds needed to complete the pedestal, but had boosted the subscriber circulation of the *World* to 150,000 copies, which was seven times greater than it had been before the fund raising drive began.

Pulitzer sent a check for $100,000 to the American Committee and spent the balance on a silver marbled gift for Bartholdi. It was a replica of Liberty's hand, holding aloft her torch placed atop a round globe, which featured the images of Bartholdi's bust and a robed woman with her right hand outstretched, pointing to Bartholdi. Her left hand grasped a shield.

Bartholdi's trophy.

Once the fund-raising campaign was finished Pulitzer turned his attention to the people who had sent in their money. In a *World* editorial, he wrote: "The statue itself gains an inestimable value from this fact. It is not only an ideal of Liberty—but an attestation of Liberty in every stone—the people have done their work well—their liberality has saved the great Republic from disgrace."

Liberty's Completed Pedestal

In the spring of 1886, the last stone of the pedestal was set in place. On April 22, another ceremony was held, accompanied with more speeches and celebrations.

BY AUTHORITY OF THE AMERICAN COMMITTEE OF THE STATUE OF LIBERTY.

Hunt's "Fortress of Liberty"
design of Liberty's pedestal.

Notice that in the above photo, Richard Hunt's design of Liberty's pedestal included forty shields, representing the forty states of the Union. According to Marvin Trachtenberg, the pedestal's forty shields represent the "Fortress of Liberty" notion.[18]

Interestingly enough, Alexander Hislop tells us that the "Goddess of Fortifications" idea goes all the back to the first deified queen of Babylon, Semiramis, saying:

> . . . the existence of a goddess of fortifications, every one knows that there is the amplest evidence . . . . The first city in the world after the flood . . . that had towers and encompassing walls, was Babylon; and Ovid himself tells us that it was Semiramis, the first queen of that city, who was believed to have "surrounded Babylon with a wall of brick."[19]

In May 1886, work began on anchoring and erecting Eiffel's enormous iron pylon and framework on the pedestal. On a hot July day another ceremony was held to commemorate the assembly of the first two copper sections on the statue's skeletal frame, ceremoniously named "Bartholdi and Pulitzer".

Assembling Liberty's Statue

In July, the American Committee notified the Department of State that work on the statue was almost completed and proposed September 3 as the date for its official inauguration. But it soon became apparent that the inauguration date would have to be moved to a later date: attaching the copper sections proved to be far more difficult than first believed.

When the statue was dismantled in France and placed in wooden crates many of its pieces had been wrongly numbered and labeled. Some of the larger sheets had been packed too tight, causing them to lose their shape. Before many of the pieces could be reattached to Liberty's frame, workers had to identify them and re-form those that had lost their shape.

Assembling Liberty's statue on its pedestal.

Finally, in October 1886, Bartholdi's gigantic Goddess statue, *Liberty Enlightening the World,* was set atop its own pedestal on Bedloe's Island in New York Harbor.

12

'LIBERTY HAS HERE MADE HER HOME'

O N OCTOBER 25, 1886, Bartholdi arrived in New York Harbor aboard the *La Bretagne* steamship. For the first time he would now see his life-long dream as a reality. "I am much pleased," he told the reporters surrounding him at Bedloe's Island, as he stood gazing at his towering statue. Then, after a brief pause, Bartholdi said: "I was worried about some of the lines . . . it is a grand sight. It is a success."

On Thursday, October 28, the day for the dedication ceremony had finally arrived. The mayor of New York City proclaimed Thursday an official holiday and invited everyone to share in the grand event. City newspapers heralded it as "a day like no other." President Grover Cleveland would grace the day's events with his presence, having accepted an invitation from the American Committee to preside over the ceremonies.

By mid-morning New York City was transformed into a French-American metropolis. City Hall, civic and office buildings, homes, hotels, and restaurants were decorated with French and American colors. In front of the *World* building was hanging a huge banner that stretched across Park Row, saying in French: *"La Belle France—The United States: Vive l' entente fraternal des deux republiques"* ('Long live the fraternal union of the two republics').

On every street, French and American colors heralded the rekindling of an old relationship that had not existed since the days ofWashington and Lafayette. One newspaper editorial described the scene as "something analogous to the bright spirit of rejoicing that stirred in every human breast." Another boasted that a record one million people had come out to share in the festivities and witness the dedication of the statue *Liberty Enlightening the World.*

That day everything came together to make Liberty's dedication ceremony one of the most celebrated events in American history, except for the weather! The night before the city had experienced a torrential downpour. The next morning the entire city, as well as the harbor, was covered with fog, which was so thick that Bartholdi's gigantic statue was hidden from view. It was as though God Himself was hiding from heaven the "great event" that was about to take place.

The next day one foreign reporter commented: "Not a square centimeter of the streets were clear." A Cuban correspondent for an Argentinian newspaper wrote: "The day was bleak, the sky was leaden, the ground muddy, the drizzle stubborn. But human joy has rarely been so bright."

That morning President Cleveland arrived from Washington and was received at the elegant home of his Secretary of the Navy, William C. Whitney, at Fiftieth Avenue and Fifty-Seventh Street. Shortly afterwards, because the parade was scheduled to start from Madison Square, at 10:20 A.M., the dignitaries emerged from the Whitney mansion and climbed into their awaiting carriages.

As the presidential procession moved down Fifth Avenue the President was greeted by cheering crowds of people lining both sides of the street. At 10:45 A.M., President Cleveland's carriage reached the reviewing stand, where he was escorted to his place among other French and American dignitaries. Members of the French delegation were then presented to the President, which included Bartholdi and DeLesseps, with his white upturned mustache. Upon greeting Bartholdi, President Cleveland remarked: "You are the greatest man in America today!" To which Bartholdi replied: "Through your courtesy Mr. President."

As soon as Bartholdi appeared on the reviewing stand he was easily recognized by the nearby crowd from his picture in the Liberty memorial program, and the many newspaper articles which had been written about him. Before Bartholdi could take his seat, people began shouting his name. Within minutes, the crowds of people on both sides of the reviewing stand were chanting "Bartholdi! Bartholdi! Bartholdi!"[1]

The next day one reporter wrote: "The crowds on the avenue curbing's up and down, heard the name and passed it to the others in the Park and side streets until the air was shaken with a roar of cheers that must have gladdened the heart of the artist, who bowed at his acknowledgments."[2]

At 11:30 A.M., more than twenty thousand parade marchers began their three hour celebration past the reviewing stand led by the Marine band, and followed by a battalion of 250 police.[3] Next came the Engineers Corps which consisted of 250 men.[4]

The Second Regiment then fell in line, together with two hundred men, composing a detachment of the Massachusetts Volunteer Militia.[5] These were followed by the Seventh, Eighth, Twelfth, Eleventh and First regiments, and the French societies, numbering 2,500 men.[6]

The governors of Massachusetts, Main, Vermont, Connecticut, Rhode Island, New Jersey, New York, and Maryland, together with the United States judges, entered carriages and fell into line behind the French associations.[7]

The third Division, consisting of mayors and municipal officers, a battalion of police of Philadelphia, 400 men, a battalion of police from Brooklyn and Jersey City, veterans of the War of 1812, veterans of the Mexican War and the Military Order of the Royal Legion completed the division.[8]

The Fourth Division was made up of war veteran military organizations of New York City, New Jersey, and other states.[9]

The Fifth Division was also composed of Grand Army posts. Colonel Locke Winchester acted as the Marshal of the Sixth Division, which numbered 500 men belonging to the Washington City Continental Guard, with General Washington's carriage, the old Washington Continental Guard, Sons of Revolution and Sons of Veterans.[10]

The Seventh Division comprised some 300 men who represented the different education institutes.[11]

The Eighth Division was made up of independent military organizations.

The Ninth Division was comprised of representatives of the Brooklyn Fire Department, the Association of Old Brooklynites, the mayor of Brooklyn and city officials.[12]

The Tenth Division was comprised of the Volunteer Firemen's Association, the Board of Trade and Transportation, uniformed Knights of Pythias of Indiana, Knights of Pythias of New York, Freemasons, and other secret societies, 1,500 men.[13]

During the parade, DeLesseps was asked by one of the reporters if the splendor of the military pageant impressed him as being sufficiently worthy of the event it commemorated. DeLesseps replied: "It is grand sir; truly grand."

At 1:15 P.M., the leading vessels of the naval fleet anchored to the southeast of Bedloe's Island. The ships formed a line that extended from North to South and comprised the Alliance, the Tennessee, the Jamestown, the Saratoga, and the Portsmouth.[14]

The next day, one reporter wrote: "Here was gathered a fleet of vessels that can be better imagined than described. All manner of craft were at anchor in the waters about the great statue. There was no feeling except that of patriotism."[15]

Three hours later President Cleveland, having reviewed the marchers, accompanied by members of his Cabinet, the governors of several states, French dignitaries, and many other notables, was taken by carriage to the Hudson River at West Thirty-Third to board the USS *Dispatch,* which would take him to Bedloe's Island for the Unveiling ceremony. Once aboard the *Dispatch* the accompanying Navy ships anchored in the harbor gave the President a 21-gun salute.

Although a thick fog remained in the harbor, obscuring from view the upper part of Liberty's towering figure, nearly 300 vessels of all types, French warships, excursion steamers, and tugboats slowly made their way toward Bedloe's Island. One reporter described the scene as an "extraordinary spectacle," saying: "Ahead of us, behind us, all around is a flotilla, or rather an entire fleet, which is heading for Bedloe's Island. Everything that floats in New York, Brooklyn or Jersey City—steamers, ferry boats, yachts—has lit its boilers for this ceremony. All these boats are bedecked with colors . . . and all are crowded, to the point of being in danger of floundering with enthusiastic and joyous throng."

With an estimated one million people, both ashore and afloat, President Cleveland and all the 2,500 dignitaries disembarked on the island and took their seats on a temporary platform at the base of Liberty's pedestal. Everyone that is, except for Bartholdi, who with his three helpers had climbed up the 167 steps from the ground to the top of the pedestal. Then, walking inside Liberty's statue, Bartholdi climbed another 168 steps from her enormous feet to her massive head, and the final 54 steps of a ladder to her towering torch.

At the proper moment, which was to be signaled from the ground, Bartholdi and his three helpers would pull loose the huge French flag that was draped over Liberty's face.

At 3:00 P.M., as President Cleveland appeared the band struck up "Hail to the Chief," and everyone broke out in a shout of cheers, which lasted several minutes. Even the ships in the harbor joined the cheering, blowing their horns, as warships fired their guns.

The Congregational minister Dr. Richard Storrs, stepped to the podium to give the invocation prayer and raised his hands, trying to quiet the crowd. But to no avail. Finally, Dr. Storrs began his prayer. The next day one reporter wrote:

> With his hands outstretched and his eyes cast heavenward, he besought the blessings of the Almighty upon an event which betokened the friendship of nations and the promise of peace which would be lasting and glorious between the great Republics. Dr. Storrs prayer was brief but exquisitely pathetic.[16]

When Dr. Storrs finished his prayer, Ferdinand de Lesseps stepped to the podium to make a brief speech. As had been the case with Dr. Storrs, the cheering of the crowd and noise from the boats and ships surrounding the island continued. DeLesseps wryly noted that "steam which had done so much good . . . is at present doing us harm."

By the time DeLesseps finished his speech the crowd was shouting for Bartholdi but, unknown to those who wanted to hear from the artist himself, Bartholdi was not on the platform. Instead, he was perched high inside Liberty's torch, waiting for the signal from below to unveil his gigantic statue to the world.

William Evarts, who was now a Senator of New York and still the chairman of the American Committee, stepped to the podium and said:

> The scene upon which this vast assemblage is collected displays a transaction in human affairs which finds no precedent on record in the past nor will the future, we may feel assured, ever confront us with its counterpart or parallel. I declare in your presence and in the presence of these distinguished guests from France, and of this assemblage of honorable and honored men of our land, and of this countless multitude, that this pedestal and united work of two Republics is completed and surrendered to the care and keeping of the Government and the people of the United States.

Just as Evarts paused to rest his voice, the boy on the ground, who was to give the signal to Bartholdi perched high in Liberty's torch, thought the senator had finished speaking. The boy began waving his arms at Bartholdi, who was some 300 feet above the crowd. At that moment, Bartholdi and his three helpers pulled on the ropes, releasing the huge French flag that slid off Liberty's face.

Before Evarts could say another word a great roar of shouts and cheering bellowed across the bay from the massive crowd of onlookers, ships blew their whistles, a broadside was fired from the flagship of the U.S. naval squadron, and the Marine band struck-up a rendition of "My Country Tis of Thee."

Evarts tried to continue his speech but the noise was so loud that it was pointless. After several minutes, when the noise began to subside, President Cleveland stepped to the podium and addressed the assembly. He was then followed by M. Albert Lefaivre, the French Consul General to New York. Then the featured speaker of the day, New York Senator Chauncey M. Depew, a Brother Skull & Bonesman, who was a strong advocate of a new world order that would now be enlightened by *Liberty Enlightening the World*, stepped to the podium and delivered the final speech.

The Unveiling of Liberty Enlightening the World.

As the ceremonies concluded, the entire crowd sang the Doxology as the band played *"Praise God from Whom all Blessings Flow"*.[17] Henry C. Potter, the highly respected Mason and Bishop of the Episcopal diocese of New York, pronounced the benediction.

The next day, on October 29, 1886, the *Augusta Chronicle* gave a full account of the entire dedication ceremony, including President Cleveland's speech. One *Augusta Chronicle* reporter wrote the following account, stating:

The ropes leading from the platform to the flag, which still covered the face of the Goddess, was seen to sway, a sharp pull was given and the banner fell to the pedestal. The countenance of the statue was uncovered above the great assembly, and M. Bartholdi's life work was formally declared live—as a work of art. From that moment began the existence of the Statue of Liberty Enlightening the World.

President Cleveland then stepped forward and said: "We are not here today to bow before the representation of a fierce and warlike God, filled with wrath and vengeance, but we joyously contemplate instead our own deity, keeping watch and ward before the open gates of America, and greater than all that have been celebrated in ancient song. Instead of grasping in her hand thunderbolts of terror and death she holds aloft the light which illumines the way to man's enfranchisement.

"We will not forget that Liberty has here made her home; nor shall her brazen altar be neglected. Willing votaries will constantly keep alive its fire, and shall gleam upon the shores of our sister Republic in the East. Reflected thence and joined with answering rays, a stream of light shall pierce the darkness of ignorance and man's oppression until liberty enlightens the world."[18]

13

'SHE HAS BECOME US'

THROUGHOUT HISTORY THERE HAVE only been a few great works of art that have had the power to invoke an attitude of awe and reverence, and become universal shrines. Among some of these ancient works of art include the Egyptian Pyramids and great Sphinx, the Greek statues of Athena and Zeus, the Colossus of Rhodes, and the Roman pantheon.

In much the same manner, from the time the Franco Union began raising funds for the Liberty project, Bartholdi's statue of the French Goddess of Liberty was destined to join the ranks of earlier great works of art. As a gigantic Goddess statue, Bartoldi's imposing life-like image captured not only the minds and hearts of the American people, but also the peoples of the world.

The American historian Edward Robb Ellis says in his classic work entitled *The Epic of New York City:*

> It was done. The world's best-known statue had been dedicated, and from this day forward it stood at New York's doorway, a permanent reminder of an elusive idea. Spiritually it belonged to all mankind—not just to New Yorkers, not just to Americans. It developed into a shrine, where all might worship.[1]

Unlike many of the great art works of antiquity, which over time became shrines, people from all over the world began making pilgrimages to visit *Liberty Enlightening the World* from the very beginning. A Visitors Book shows that by September 1890, some 88,000 people visited Bedloe's Island to look upon the gigantic Goddess statue as Bartholdi had first conceived her.[2]

On a single day in August, 1894, the same register noted that sixty-nine people had visited the island. They had come from eleven states and eight foreign countries.[3]

In September 1937, Bedloe's Island came under the control of the National Park Service, and with each passing year, the number of people visiting what became known as "Liberty Island" steadily increased. According to the Liberty Park Service Department, in 1945, the island was visited by 501,040 people. By 1955, the number had increased to 739,364. By 1964, for the first time the total number of visitors exceeded one million people—1,026, 466, and kept climbing, stopping short of two million in the early 1980s. In 1987, more than three million people visited the island.[4]

Today, more than 5 million people make the pilgrimage to visit Liberty Island each year. Liberty Park Service Rangers tell us that on any given day, rain, snow, or shine, about half the people visiting the island are not from America. Each week the concession building sells multiple thousands of postcards, souvenir ball-point pens, ice-cream bars, hamburgers, and miniature statues of the Goddess.[5]

Although Bartholdi constantly referred to Bedloe's Island as "Liberty Island," and often expressed a desire that the island's name be officially changed, nothing was done until more than fifty years after his death. On August 3, 1956, the island's name was changed to Liberty Island by a joint resolution of Congress, and signed into law by President Dwight D. Eisenhower.

Goddess of the Nations

Remarkably, just like the exaltation of the Great Goddess among the nations of the ancient world, since the building and erection of Bartholdi's statue, *Liberty Enlightening the World,* on Bedloe's Island, in 1886, her cult following among the peoples of the world has indeed been revived. Hundreds of images of the Goddess have been built and erected worldwide. For example, in Paris, France, alone there are four different locations where replicas of Liberty's statue have been erected. Other French cities include Bordeax, Barentin, Saint-Cyr-sur-Mer, Colmar, etc.

Statues of the Goddess can also be found in the following countries: Austria, Germany, Kosovo, Denmark, Norway, Spain, Ukraine, United Kingdom, Ireland, Argentina, Brazil, Ecuador, Peru, China, Israel, Japan, Philippines, Taiwan, Vietnam, and Australia.

Luxembourg, Paris.   **Leicester, England.**   **Lviv, Ukraine.**

Bangy, Brazil.   **Baquio City,**   **Arraba, Israel.**
Philippines.

In the United States, which has by far the greatest number of Liberty statues, replicas of Bartholdi's statue can also be found in the following cities and states: Duluth, Minnesota; Bozeman, Montana; Madison Avenue in Manhattan; Sioux Falls, South Dakota;

Vestaia Hills, a suburb of Birmingham, Alabama; Buffalo, New York; the Marysville Bridge, north of Harrisburg, Pennsylvania; San Marcos, California; Memphis, Tennessee; Tahlequah, Oklahoma; Lebanon, Tennessee; Fargo, North Dakota; Topeka, Kansas; Webster, Massachusetts; New York City (42 different locations); Seattle, Washington; Fayetteville, Arkansas; Sioux City, Iowa; Fairfield, Iowa; Orlando, Florida; Dalton, Georgia; Milwaukie, Oregon; Forney, Texas; Houston, Texas; Neenah, Wisconsin; Waukegan, Illinois; South Bend, Indiana; Burns, Oregon; Las Vegas, Nevada; Legoland California amusement park; Yankee Stadium, New York City; Garden City, Idaho, art gallery; Brooklyn Museum of Art; the Metropolitan Museum of Art in New York City, etc.

A Living Goddess

From the very beginning of Bartholdi's conception of his statue, Liberty was viewed as an image that would invoke strong emotions in the minds of people. None were greater than the sense that her statue would become a "living Goddess" to those who would visit her.

On June 30, 1984, the *New York Times* featured an article on *The Statue of Liberty* entitled "Special Feelings about Work on a Special Statue." The reporter interviewed several men working on the restoration of the statue, which they all affectionately referred to as "The Lady".

Among those who were interviewed, one worker on the crew that built the scaffolding recalled how he was one of the first to reach the level of Liberty's face and look into her enormous eye. As he stood gazing into her eye he leaned forward and gave her a kiss.

One supervisor of the restoration project recalled that when he arrived at Liberty Island early in the morning before any of the other workers, he couldn't help but notice her many life-like features. While looking at her in the early morning light he was compelled to reach out and touch her face.

Addressing the life-like qualities of Bartholdi's Goddess statue, Christian Blanchet and Bertrand Dard write:

The statue of 1886 was promoted, built, and publicized by strong, and distinctive individuals—a liberal scholar, a sculptor, a crusading newspaper editor. When she was finished her head was in the clouds, and her feet in the dirt and casual anarchy of an unsupervised Bedloe's Island. She was like the humanity she was meant to enlighten.

. . . Bartholdi built a goddess of liberty, with a classic, imposing stride and posture. But she became a goddess with whom her devotees feel very much at home.[6]

Liberty's Altar

On October 28, 1886, at the dedication ceremony, President Grover Cleveland pledged in his speech "not to forget that Liberty has here made her home, nor shall her brazen altar be neglected." True to his pledge, in September 1937, an altar was set up at Bedloe's Island to commemorate the 150th anniversary of the U.S. Constitution and honor America's great national icon, *The Statue of Liberty*.

Liberty's altar, which bore a resemblance to the ancient alter of the Roman Goddess of Liberty, was set up in front of the stairway that entered the portals of the pedestal.

The front of the altar was decorated with thirteen stars at the top. In the center of the altar, below, was a large image of the Liberty Bell: on the left side was the date "1787," and on its right side was "1937". Standing on the altar itself was a four foot replica of Liberty's statue. On either side of the statue were two large candlesticks each fitted with three tall white candles, and two small American flags. Draped behind the altar was a huge American flag. Wreaths and flowers were placed at the base of the altar as though they were offerings or tributes to the Goddess.[7]

During the ceremony, which was sponsored by the Mayor's Committee and National Park Service, speeches were given and an actor did an impersonation of George Washington. The ceremony concluded with a cloud of black smoke rising in the sky from Liberty's torch, as though a burnt offering was being made on behalf of America.[8]

Liberty's Personification *as* America

For the devotees of Lady Liberty, the placement of her statue on Bedloe's Island in New York Harbor was not enough. By the early 1900s the U.S. government launched a massive propaganda campaign to personify in the minds of people the idea that America and the *Statue of Liberty* were one and the same. Blanchet and Dard write:

> Then, with the government's propaganda campaign in World War I, the statue became the figure immediately identifiable as America, first joining and then more or less displacing Uncle Sam and 'Colombia.' Originally it had suggested France-American friendships and international peace. Now it became "Americanized," a process that had deep repercussions on how often and in what light it was portrayed. In the United States, the statue was treated with a strange, democratic mixture of veneration and easygoing familiarity—a goddess on one hand, and an image as popular as a comic-strip heroine or movie star on the other. It became something of a media figure in a society that the media were learning to dominate. In the world at large, it came to stand for "the American way" in all its implications, at a time when America emerged as a superpower and self-proclaimed worldwide defender of the non-Communist world.[9]

Between the years 1916 to 1947, in order to personify Liberty *as* America, government officials placed her image in a number of patriotic partnerships with popular American figures, such as the Founding Fathers, the American eagle, and the U.S. flag.

One of the most common methods employed was to place a profile of Liberty's head on a common U.S. postage stamp.

Another technique used to personify Liberty *as* America was to strike her image on U.S. coins.

From 1916 to 1947 the Treasury Department portrayed Liberty on U.S. coins, as with the President's $1 dollar coin.

During this same period, another popular method used to personify Liberty *as* America was to place her image on U.S. war bonds.

Here Liberty is personified *as* America "the Great Defender," wearing the flag and holding in her left hand a shield bearing the Great Seal of the United States while a Boy Scout kneels before her, handing her a sword bearing the Scout Motto: "Be Prepared".

In 1949, the musical Broadway production *Miss Liberty* opened at the *Imperial Theater* on July 15, 1949 and closed on April 8, 1950, following 308 performances. It was based on *The Statue of Liberty*, with the music and lyrics written by Irving Berlin. In the last Act, the musical concluded with the words of Emma Lazarus' poem, *The New Colossus*, personifying the Goddess *as* America, saying:

> "Keep ancient lands, your storied pomp!" cries she
> With silent lips, "Give me your tired, your poor,
> Your huddled refuse of your teeming shore.
> Send these, the homeless, temptest-tost to me.
> I lift my lamp beside the golden door!"

During the years that followed hundreds of books were written about *The Statue of Liberty*, endearing Lady Liberty as the very embodiment of Liberty, Equality, and Justice.

Perhaps no chronicler has better expressed the meaning of what Lady Liberty has become to the people of America as the noted author Richard Schneider, whose "Foreword" to his book entitled *Freedom's Holy Light* was written by President Ronald Reagan. Schneider writes:

> At her 1886 dedication, she was seen as a symbol of America's fight for independence. Today most American's think of Concord Bridge and the Liberty Bell in this respect.
>
> Instead, the tall torchbearer in classic gown has become something uniquely her own, a *personification* of America.
>
> She has become the cashier at the check-out counter, the worker on the auto assembly line, the farmer, the girl at the word processor, the carpenter, the miner, the husband, the mother.
>
> She has become *us.*
>
> When we look at her we see home, we see our cities and villages, our schools and town halls, our churches and synagogues.[10]

PART IV

Biblical Foundations
Of The
Great Goddess

14

FIGURATIVE LANGUAGE IN THE BIBLE

O<small>NE OF THE PRIMARY</small> problems that arises in the interpretation of Scripture is that commentators and interpreters often fail to take into account the fact that much of the Bible is written in the ancient form of figurative language, or *figures,* which was a common form of communication among the people of that day.

Today, the term "figurative" is often used in a sense that lessens the power or force of a word or idea, implying that its meaning is weakened, or that what one is talking about has quite a different meaning, or that it really has no meaning at all. But such was not the case with the use of *figures* during the times of the Bible.

One of the foremost modern day scholars of this ancient use of figurative language is the late E. W. Bullinger (1837-1913), who was an Anglican clergyman, theologian, and language scholar. Dr. Bullinger's three great works are as follows: *A Critical Lexicon and Concordance to the English and Greek New Testament* (1877), *Figures Of Speech Used In The Bible* (1898), and the *Companion Bible,* as general editor (published in 6 parts 1909-1922), which was completed after his death by his associates. It is also worthy to note that Theodore Herzl (1860-1904), the Father of modern Zionism, was among Dr. Bullinger's personal friends.

In 1867, at the age of 29, Dr. Bullinger accepted a position at Trinity Bible Society as the Clerical Secretary, where he served until his death. During his distinguished tenure, Trinity Bible Society achieved several important objectives, including the following: 1) the completion and publication of the Hebrew version of the New Testament; 2) the publication of Ginsburg's first edition of the Tanakh (*Introduction to the Massoretico-Critical Edition of the Hebrew Bible*); 3) the formation of the Brittany Evangelical Mission Society and translation of the Bible into the Breton language; 4) the translation and publication of the first-ever Protestant Portuguese Reference Bible; and 5) the distribution of a Spanish language Bible in Spain after the Spanish Revolution of 1868.

Although the use of figurative language was a common form of communication among most peoples of the ancient world, it wasn't until the time of the Greeks that the use of *figures* was reduced to a science, giving names to more than two hundred *figures.* When the Romans came into power, they built upon the science of *figures* established by the Greeks.

Among the Greeks the many different forms of *figures* were called "Schema," meaning *shape*. The Romans called it "Figura".[1] Thus in the ancient world the employment of *figures* was an important part of communication. With the decline of the Middle-Ages, however, the knowledge of the ancient use of *figures* almost died out.

Since that time only a handful of scholars have revisited the study of this ancient form of communication and written about it. For example, in 1625, Solomon Glassius (1593-1656), a distinguished German Jewish theologian, published the *Philologia Sacra,* in which he includes an important treatise on "Sacred Rhetoric". In 1682, Benjamin Keach (1640-1704) published his *Troposchemalogia: or, a Key to Open the Scripture Metaphors and Types.* This was followed by John Holmes, in his work entitled *Rhetoric Made Easy* (1755). G. W. Hervey's book was entitled *System of Christian Rhetoric* (1873). E. W. Bullinger researched this ancient use of *figures* and wrote the classic work entitled *Figures Of Speech Used In The Bible* (1898).

Unfortunately, today little is known about this ancient form of figurative language. This is especially true among modern day Bible scholars, as well as higher schools of learning. Thus it is no exaggeration to say that except for the above few works the knowledge of this ancient use of *figures* has all but died out.

An "Accidental" Discovery

One day while browsing in a Christian book store in Amarillo, Texas, this writer "accidently" came across a copy of Dr. Bullinger's classic work entitled *Figures Of Speech Used In The Bible*. Due to a lack of interest, Dr. Bullinger's book had been relegated to the "bargain book" section where its price had been drastically reduced for a quick sale.

After scanning the book's pages I was impressed with its well-documented scholarship but had absolutely no idea as to its significance. I set Dr. Bullinger's book back on the bargain book pile and said to myself: "I'll come back next week. If it's still here I'll buy it." The following week Dr. Bullinger's book was still in the bargain book pile. That very day I purchased Dr. Bullinger's book but still had no idea as to the significance of its contents. What I soon discovered changed my understanding of the Scriptures.

How important was Dr. Bullinger's treatment of *figures* in the preparation for writing this book? Of this fact I am firmly convinced: had I not had Dr. Bullinger's work on *Figures Used In The Bible* this book would have never been written. To this end I am forever indebted to the late Dr. E. W. Bullinger.

The Great Misconception of Biblical Figures

For most of us the term "figurative" means the use of words as "symbols" or as a "metaphor". *Webster's Twentieth Century Dictionary* defines the term "figurative" as follows: "**1 a:** representing by a figure or resemblance: EMBLEMATIC. **2** expressing one thing in terms normally denoting another with which it may be regarded as analogous: METAPHORICAL." Simply stated, in modern day thought the employment of figurative language is understood as having "less meaning," depriving words of their force and power.

In the ancient world, however, the use of *figures* meant exactly the opposite. For example, in Bible times the employment of a *figure* always denoted a particular form, such as a *simile, metaphor, parable, personification, word-picture,* etc., which a word or sentence took that was different from its ordinary use.[2] Equally significant, the use of a *figure* was meant to add more force, more life, intensified feeling, and greater emphasis to what was being said.[3]

What most modern day students of the Bible fail to understand is that the profuse use of *figures* in the Bible establishes, beyond any possible contradiction, that figurative language was an important form of communication among the people of that day. Even more important, however, the profuse use of *figures* in Scripture establishes that the figurative language of that day was a form of communication chosen by Yahweh Himself. Dr. Bullinger says, "Jehovah has been pleased to give us the revelation of His mind and will in words. It is therefore absolutely necessary that we should understand not merely the meanings of the words themselves, but also the laws which govern their usage and combinations."[4]

With this understanding we should not be surprised that one of the primary problems of the interpretation of Scripture is the failure to understand when the words of Scripture are to be understood in their original or simplest form, as being *literal,* and when they are to be understood as a *figure.* Dr. Bullinger tells us that whenever and wherever possible, the words of Scripture are to be understood *literally,* but when a statement appears contrary to a plain statement of fact, or revealed biblical truth, then it is reasonable to expect that a *figure* has been employed.[5]

For example the following statement, "Blessed are the undefiled in the way, who walk in the law of the Lord" (Ps. 119:1), is a matter-of-fact statement. But the words, "Quicken me after thy loving kindness; so shall I keep the testimony of thy mouth" (v. 88), are written as a *figurative* statement that has been given additional force and meaning to what has already been said.

Likewise, the following passage in Romans 11:18: "Boast not against the branches. But if thou boast, thou bearest not the root, but the root thee," is written in the form of a *figure;* whereas the passage, "Behold therefore the goodness and severity of God: on them which fell, severity; but toward thee, goodness, if thou continue in his goodness: otherwise thou also shalt be cut off" (v. 22), is a matter-of-fact statement.

Unfortunately, today in the interpretation of Scripture these two forms of communication are often viewed as one and the same. The English use of a *figure* is often understood as the exact opposite of what is really being said, or something not meant to be taken *literally*. And herein lies much of the problem of understanding what the Hebrew writers were communicating to the people of that day. Dr. Bullinger says:

> From non-attention to these Figures, translators have made blunders as serious as they are foolish. Sometimes they have translated the figure literally, totally ignoring its existence; sometimes they have taken it fully into account, and have translated, not according to the letter, but according to the spirit; sometimes they have taken literal words and translated them figuratively. Commentators and interpreters, from inattention to figures, have been led astray from the real meaning of many important passages of God's Word; while ignorance of them has been the fruitful parent of error and false doctrine. It may be truly said that most of the gigantic errors of Rome, as well as the Lord's People, have their root and source, either in figuratively explaining away passages which should be taken literally, or in taking literally what has been thrown into a peculiar form or Figure of language: thus not only falling into error, but losing the express teaching, and missing the special emphasis which the particular Figure was designed to impart to them.
>
> This is an additional reason for using greater exactitude and care when we are dealing with the words of God. Man's words are scarcely worthy of such study. Man uses figures, but often at random and often in ignorance or in error. But "the words of the Lord are pure words." All His works are perfect, and when the Holy Spirit takes up and uses human words, He does so, we may be sure, with unerring accuracy, infinite wisdom, and perfect beauty.[6]

For this reason we have chosen to use Dr. Bullinger's book entitled *Figures of Speech Used In The Bible* to understand the meaning of Zechariah's use of *figures* to communicate his Divine revelation about a *Woman* called "Wickedness" (Zech. 5:8), whose image was predicted to be built, erected, and set upon its own pedestal in the latter day "land of Shinar" (v. 11).

In the same manner, we also will use Dr. Bullinger's work on *figures* to understand the Apostle John's use of *figures* to communicate his Divine revelation about a *Woman* called "the great whore" and "Mother of Harlots" (Rev. 17:1, 5), who is later identified as "that great city . . . Babylon" (v. 18; 18:2).

As you shall soon see, the significance of Yahweh's use of *figures* in Scripture cannot be overstated. The nineteenth century Bible scholar Thomas Boys put it well when he addressed this ancient form of communication in his *Commentary* on 1 Peter iii., saying:

> There is much in the Holy Scriptures, which we find it hard to understand: nay, much that we seem to understand so fully as to imagine that we have discovered in it some difficulty or inconsistency.
>
> Yet the truth is, that passages of this kind are often the very parts of the Bible in which the greatest instruction is to be found: and, more than this, the instruction is to be obtained in the contemplation of the very difficulties by which at first we are startled. This is the *intention* of these apparent inconsistencies.
>
> The expressions are used, in order that we may mark them, dwell upon them, and draw instruction out of them. Things are put to us in a strange way, because, if they were put in a more ordinary way, we should not notice them.[7]

15

'The Woman Is Wickedness'

5 Then the angel who was speaking with me went out and said to me, "Lift up now your eyes and see what this is going forth." 6 I said, "What is it?" And he said, "This is their appearance in all the land.7 (and behold a lead cover was lifted up); and this is a woman sitting inside the ephah." 8 Then he said, "This is Wickedness!" And he threw her down into the middle of the ephah and cast the lead weight on its opening. 9 Then I lifted up my eyes and looked, and there two women were coming out with the wind in their wings; and they had wings like the wings of a stork, and they lifted up the ephah between the earth and the heavens. 10 I said to the angel who was speaking with me, "Where are they taking the ephah?" 11 Then he said to me, "To build a temple for her in the land of Shinar; and when it is prepared, she will be set there on her own pedestal" (Zech. 5:5-11; NASV).

About two thousand five hundred years ago the Hebrew prophet Zechariah was given a Divine revelation about a *Woman*, and was informed by an Angel that she would be transported to a latter day country called "the land of Shinar," where a temple would be built and erected for her, and when it was prepared she would be set there on her own pedestal.

Zechariah, meaning "the Lord remembers," was of priestly descent, a son of Berechiah and grandson of Iddo, the head of one of the twelve priestly families, or courses, who returned from Babylon with Zerubbabel. Zechariah himself succeeded his grandfather Iddo as head of his priestly course (Neh. 12:4, 16), and began his ministry about 520 B.C.E., shortly after the fall of the great Babylon Empire, in 586, by the Medes and Persians.

It had been nearly twenty years since the Jewish people had returned from Babylonian exile, and only the foundation of the Temple was completed. Apparently, there was an attitude of complacency when it came to the rebuilding of the Lord's House. The prophet Haggai, a contemporary of Zechariah, walked the streets of Jerusalem, declaring: "Is it time for you yourselves to dwell in your paneled houses while this house *lies* desolate?" (Hag. 1:4).

While Haggai challenged the people to rebuild the Temple and focused on the immediate blessing of Yahweh, Zechariah looked to a future time of Judah's restoration as a People and rise among the nations of the earth (Zech. 8:3); the rebuilding of the Temple and return of the Lord to Jerusalem (1:16); the re-gathering of the Jewish people from their worldwide dispersion (8:7, 8); Yahweh's dwelling among the Jewish people in Jerusalem (8:3); a time in which there will be a great peace, prosperity, and joy (3:10; 8:12); the establishment of Jerusalem as the Holy City of Truth (8:3); the coming of the Gentile nations to Mount Zion to worship the Lord (2:15; 8:20-23); and the honoring of the Jewish people by the nations of the world (8:23).

Thus for most Bible scholars the first eight chapters of the Book of Zechariah were written on end-time events. For example, the noted Christian scholar George Robinson regards the Book of Zechariah as "the most Messianic, the most truly apocalyptic and eschatological of all the writings of the O.T."[1] The scholars of the *Jewish Encyclopedia* tell us that Zechariah was "one of the Minor Prophets, to who is attributed the collection of prophecies and apocalyptic visions constituting the book bearing his name."[2] And the Catholic scholar John McKenzie writes: "The dominate note of Zc. 1-8 is messianism. The prophet proposes a revelation of a new national-religious messianic community to be established in Palestine with its center in Jerusalem."[3]

Nothing New Under the Sun

It is significant for us to understand that the Scriptures clearly teach that history has so been designed by Yahweh that it is bound to repeat itself. The writer of Ecclesiastes plainly states: "The thing that hath been, it *is that* which shall be, and that which is done *is* that which shall be done: and *there is* no new *thing* under the sun" (Eccl. 1:9; AKJV).

Bible scholars agree that history has indeed repeated itself again and again. Few, however, have understood that the modern day exaltation of the statue *Liberty Enlightening the World / Statue of Liberty* is directly linked to the pagan cult worship of the Great Mother Goddess of antiquity. Even fewer have entertained the idea that ancient history would repeat itself in a latter day country code-named "the land of Shinar".

Zechariah's Latter Day Revelation

Scholars agree that the Book of Zechariah is filled with the same figurative language found in the Apocalypse. The Hebrew scholar Joseph Good says: "The style of writing found in Zechariah is the same style found in the Book of Daniel and the Book of Revelation, and was understood by the people of that day as dealing with the subject of the Day of the Lord."[4]

With this understanding, based upon the laws which govern the use of *figures* in the Bible, the following can be established: 1) the *Woman* in the ephah described by Zechariah as "Wickedness" is destined to be judged by Yahweh Himself; 2) that the ephah in which the *Woman* sits in the midst is symbolic of trade and commerce; 3) that the *Woman* described as "Wickedness" is, in fact, an ancient pagan female deity, whose origins are rooted in a historic *Woman*; 4) that a primary character trait of this female deity is moral unrighteousness, especially as it relates to the practice of dishonest weights and measures; 5) that the *two women* described as having "wings like those of a stork" are two great Peoples, who had a major role in transporting the *Woman* in the midst of the ephah to the peoples of the white race living in the northern peninsula (now

249

Europe); and 6) that the final destination of the *Woman* sitting in the midst of the ephah is a *literal* latter day country code-named "the land of Shinar" ('Babylonia'), where a shrine/temple will be built for her, and when it is prepared she will be set there on her own pedestal.

Ephah going Forth

> 6 "This is the ephah going forth."

Zechariah's latter day vision begins with the Angel showing him an image of an *ephah going forth,* which is called a *Hypotyposis,* or *Word-Picture.*[5] Dr. Bullinger tells us that "the name is given to this figure because it describes an action, event, person, condition, passion, etc., in a lively and forcible manner, giving a vivid representation of it."[6]

In Jewish thought the *ephah* is often used as a prescribed standard of measurement for doing business in the marketplace. Dr. G. Campbell Morgan says: "The ephah is the symbol of commerce . . . . Thus the principle of wickedness is to find its last vantage ground in commerce."[7]

Indeed, we find the term *ephah* employed again and again in the Hebrew Scriptures when addressing the dishonest practice of using a different set of weights and measurements in the act of conducting business with the intent to defraud people for personal gain (Lev. 19:35-36; Ezek. 45:10; Deut. 25:13-16; Mic. 6:10-11; Prov. 11:1; 20:23; Isa. 1:21-22).

The Angel then says: "This is their appearance ('*resemblance*') in all the land" (v. 6). The Hebrew scholars of *Gesenius' Hebrew-Chaldee Lexicon* tell us that the word "land" in Hebrew, *erets,* means "*a land, country,* as found in Gen. 21:32; Ex. 3:8; 13:5; Neh. 9:22."[8] In fact, this is the very same word the Angel employs in Zechariah 5:11, when speaking about the "land ('*erets*') of Shinar". Thus from the very beginning of Zechariah's vision we know the Angel is speaking about a *literal* latter day country code-named "the land of Shinar" ('Babylonia'), which will be characterized by *trade* and *commerce.*

Lead Cover

7 And behold, a lead cover was lifted up . . . .

Continuing on with the employment of the figure *Hypotyposis,* or *Word-Picture* the Angel employs the *figure* "lead cover" as a vivid and forcible *representation* of Divine judgment.

In Hebraic thought the *figure* "lead cover" is *owphereth* or *ophereth,* meaning "lead weight," with the feminine part of *aphar* meaning "to be gray, or rather to pulverize, to be dust."[9]

Expanding on this Hebraic concept the scholars of *Unger's Bible Dictionary* inform us that "in Zech. 5:8 the 'lead weight' is *'eben ha 'operet,* 'stone of lead.' . . . the use of *'eben,* 'stone,' in the sense of a weight, is early and familiar in Heb.; thus Isa. 34:11, *'plummet of desolation,'* and so in various references."[10]

Moreover, the Hebrew word used for the word "lifted" is *nasa,* a Niphal participle, which is a verbal adjective in the passive voice, indicating continued simple action.[11] The Hebrew scholars of the *Gesenius' Hebrew-Chaldee Lexicon* inform us that the Hebrew word *nasa,* written in the Niphal stem means *"to lift up oneself, to be elevated, to be lifted up, high."*[12]

Here Zechariah is told by the Angel that the *figure* "lead cover" (*'plummet of desolation, to pulverize, to be dust'*) is a vivid and forcible *representation* of Divine judgment.

Woman sitting inside Ephah

7 ". . . this is a woman sitting *inside* the ephah."

Continuing on with the figure *Hypotyposis,* or *Word-Picture,* the Angel *describes* an action of the *Woman* "sitting inside the ephah".

For most theologians, however, the *Woman* represents the sins of the people of Israel. For example, the fourth century Roman Catholic Cardinal Jerome says:

> The angel bids him behold the sins of the people of Israel heaped together in a perfect measure, and the transgressions of all fulfilled, that the sins which escaped notice one by one,

might, when collected together, be laid open to the eyes of all, and Israel might go forth from its place, and it might be shown to all what she was in her own land.[13]

The noted Bible commentator Matthew Henry (1662–1714), says that the *Woman* is "the sinful church and nation of the Jews, in their latter and corrupt age."[14] Henry goes on to say:

> Guilt is upon the sinner as a weight of lead, to sink him to the lowest hell. This seems to mean the condemnation of the Jews, after they filled the measure of their iniquities by crucifying Christ and rejecting his gospel. Zechariah sees the ephah, with the woman thus pressed in it, carried away to some far country. This intimates that the Jews should be hurried out of their own land, and forced to dwell in far countries, as they had been in Babylon. There the ephah shall be finally placed, and their sufferings shall continue far longer than in their late captivity.[15]

David Baron (1855–1926), whose commentary on Zechariah was noted by the Bible scholar and teacher W. H. Griffith Thomas as "a book of genuine help and spiritual profit . . . . The best available book on the subject," writes:

> We regard, therefore, the woman in this vision, not as a personification of the Jewish people, nor as a collective representation of individual sinners who are finally gathered into one heap in the ephah, *but as delineating the (then as yet hidden) moral system of which the ephah is the emblem.*
> . . . in its essence is the worship of Mammon, should be represented by a woman, "because of the power it displays as a temptress, whereby it exercises such an enticing and dangerous influence over the souls of men." Or as Grotius observed: This form of wickedness is here described as a woman "because she is the mother of thefts and perjuries, and of all crimes."[16]

The problem with these interpretations is that they fail to take into account the biblical uses of *figures,* which is a major factor in Zechariah's vision about the *Woman* "sitting inside the ephah".

As earlier noted, in the Scriptures the *ephah* is often used as a prescribed standard of measurement for doing business in the marketplace, which is a symbol of *commerce.* So here is the critical question: What country in the ancient world was known for its great *commerce* and *trade?* Most certainly it was not Israel, which was primarily an agricultural society. Nor was it Egypt or Assyria, whose economies were dependent on farming. Rather, it was the land of Shinar, the home of the great deified queen of Babylon, Semiramis.

Ancient clay tablets record that the Gulf was a valuable maritime trade route for both imports and exports. During the early Dynastic period one account records that timber was supplied to Ur-Nanshe of Lagash, and later texts from Lagash mention the import of copper ore and exports of wool, cloth, silver, fat and resin.[17] Inscriptions from Ur, the home of Abraham, showed that trade in the Gulf was conducted by merchants who were financed by the Temple of the Goddess Nanna ('Inanna') or Ishtar, the reincarnation of Semiramis, in Ur, "with whom most goddesses in later times were identified."[18]

As the self-proclaimed Virgin of Prophecy, one of her most esteemed titles among the peoples of that day was *"Woman".*[19] Indeed, scholars agree that there was only one *Woman* who was exalted among the nations of the ancient world as the Great Mother Goddess—Semiramis.[20]

For many, she was the "Mother of grace and mercy," the celestial "Dove," and "the hope of the world".[21] Among the ancient Sumerians she was called "Nanna". To the Babylonians she was known as Ishtar. In Egypt, she was worshiped as Isis. In Asia, she was known as Cybele the Great Goddess. In Asia Minor, she was called Artemis by the Greeks and Diana by the Romans. Among the apostate Israelites she was called the "Queen of Heaven". Jeremiah writes: "The children gather wood, and the fathers kindle the fire, and the women knead their dough to make cakes to the queen of heaven" (Jer. 7: 18).

Among the faithful worshipers of Yahweh, however, her exaltation and cult following was utter detestable (1 Kings 15:13). Thus we should not be surprised that Zechariah was given a latter day vision of the exaltation of this ancient deified *Woman,* who had exerted such a powerful influence over the peoples of the earth, as well as the people of Israel.

Woman is Wickedness

8 Then he said, "This is Wickedness!"

In this passage the Angel employs the figure *Prosopopceia,* or *Personification.* Dr. Bullinger informs us that this is "a figure by which things are represented or spoken of as persons; or, by which we attribute intelligence, by words or actions, to inanimate objects or abstract ideas."[22] Dr. G. Campbell says, ". . . according to the distinct prophecy, the woman sitting in the midst of the ephah is the personification of wickedness."[23]

The scholars of *The Complete Word Study Old Testament* tell us that the term "wickedness" comes from the Hebrew word *rishah,* which is the feminine counterpart of *risha,* meaning "wickedness, moral unrighteousness, specially fraud, dishonest, deceitful, fraudulent scales (Mic. 6:11), falsehood, (Prov. 8:7), unlawful gain, wealth which was obtained in a wicked way (Mic. 6:19)."[24]

With this understanding it becomes evident that Zechariah's vision of the *Woman* personified as "Wickedness" is not only the embodiment of moral unrighteousness, but also identified with the dishonest weights and measures that will be used in the commerce and trade of this latter day country code-named "the land of Shinar". The Angel says: *"This is the ephah that goeth forth,"* and adds the *descriptive* words: *"This is their appearance ('resemblance') in all the land."*

Two Women

9 I looked up again and saw two women come . . . .

Continuing on with the *figure* called *Prosopceia,* or *Personification,* Zechariah addresses *two women,* who had "wings like a stork". Dr.

Bullinger tells us that this *figure* "is employed when the absent are spoken of as alive, or when anything (*e.g.,* a country) is addressed as a person."[25] In this particular case the Angel's reference to *two women* was meant to *represent* two whole Peoples.

The fact that Zechariah is addressing two whole Peoples, or nations as *women* can easily be established in Scripture. For example, Isaiah 32:9-12 addresses a whole People as a class of *women,* saying: "Rise up, ye women that are at ease: hear my voice, ye careless daughters: give ear unto my speech." Again, we find this same *figure* employed in Isaiah 3:18-26; Micah 7:8-10, etc.

Indeed, throughout Scripture this same *figure* is used to *personify* a whole People as both a *woman* and *women,* as in Ezekiel 16 & 23; Hosea 2, etc., which establishes that the employment of this *figure* was a common practice among the people of that day.

Wind in their Wings

9 . . . coming out with the wind in their wings . . . .

Continuing on with the employment of the figure *Hypotyposis,* or *Word-Picture,* Zechariah *describes* in a vivid and forcible manner the actions of the *two women* ('two whole Peoples').

In Hebrew the word for "wind," *ruach* primarily means the "breath, as in the breath of one's mouth, or the air put in motion by divine breath."[26] It can also mean the human spirit as breathed by God into man (Gen. 2:7; Job 27:3), as well as the rational mind as the seat of the senses, affections, and emotions (Gen. 41:8; Josh. 2:11; 5:1; Prov. 25:28; Eccl. 7:8; Dan. 2:1).

The scholars of *Strong's Exhaustive Concordance* inform us that the Hebrew word for "wings," *kanaph* conveys the meaning of not only of the wings of a bird, but also the *overspreading* ('like feathers on a bird's wings') of established boundaries or borders.[27]

As earlier noted, in 334 B.C.E., Alexander the Great invaded Western Asia and conquered the mighty Persian and Phoenician Empires of Western Asia. Some two hundred years later, about 197, Rome defeated the Macedonians at Thessaly and afterwards, went on to conquer Western Asia.

Wings like the wings of a Stork

9 . . . they had wings like the wings of a stork . . . .

In this phrase Zechariah employs the figure *Simile,* or *Resemblance.* Dr. Bullinger says that this *figure* is "a declaration that one Thing *resembles* another; or, Comparison by *Resemblance.*"[28]

The scholars of *Unger's Bible Dictionary* tell us that the white stork is a bird which was common to the land of Israel at the time of Zechariah; that among the Israelites the white stork was considered to be an "unclean bird"; that "it is a migratory bird, going to Northern Europe in the summer, flying high in the heaven (Jer. 8:7), and making a rushing noise ('the wind in their wings,' Zech. 5:9)."[29]

The scholars of *World Book* tell us that the white stork's migratory flight path includes Western Asia and into the north part of the African continent, Egypt.[30] The scholars of *The Illustrated Bible Dictionary* state that the stork is one of the most striking migratory birds of Palestine, slowly traveling north especially along the Jordan valley in March and April; Jer. 8:7 says that "the stork in the heavens knows her times . . . ."[31] And the scholars of the *Jewish Encyclopedia* describe the stork as an "unclean bird," saying: "The name alludes to the filial piety and devotion attributed by the ancients to the stork. Both white and black storks occur in Palestine: the former is a migrant, passing through in April; the latter is especially abundant in the neighborhood of the Dead Sea."[32]

Remarkably, one only has to look at a map of ancient Western Asia to see that the routes taken during the military campaigns of Alexander the Great and the Roman soldiers were basically the same. Both military campaigns began in the northern peninsula (now Europe) and went deep into Western Asia, across the land of Israel and into the North African Continent, Egypt, which is precisely the same flight path of the migrating white storks in Zechariah's vision.

Lifted up Ephah

> 9 . . . they lifted up the ephah between the earth and
> the heavens.

Continuing to employ the figure *Hypotyposis,* or *Word-Picture,*
Zechariah *describes* the actions of the *two women* ('two whole
Peoples'), who "lift up" the *Woman* sitting inside the ephah. Once
again, Zechariah employs the Hebrew word *nasa,* meaning *"to lift
oneself up, to be elevated, to lift up, high."*[33]

When understood from a historical perspective it becomes
evident that Zechariah was speaking about two pagan Peoples of
the white race, who would adopt the idolatrous religion of this great
Asian female deity, and take it back to their homeland where she
would be "lifted up" ('exalted') in the north peninsula (now Europe).

The Great Question

> 10 "Where are they taking the ephah?"

Here we see Zechariah asking the Angel the great question.
Until this time Zechariah knew that the idolatrous religion of this
pagan female deity had been confined to Western Asia. Now he asks
the Angel where the *two women* ('two whole Peoples') are taking the
ephah with the *Woman* personified as "Wickedness" sitting inside.

The Revealing Answer

> 11 "To build a temple for her in the land of Shinar . . . ."

Continuing on with the employment of the *figure* called
Hypotyposis, or *Word-Picture,* the Angel *describes* the future actions
of the *two women* ('two whole Peoples'), who "lift up" ('exalt')
the *Woman* sitting inside the ephah, saying: "to build (Heb. *banah,*
meaning "to build, to erect, as a house, a temple"[34]) it a shrine (Heb.
bayith, "temple; used of the temples of idols"[35]) in the land (Heb.
erets, "land, continent, a country"[36]) of Shinar (Heb. *shinvar,* "the
plain of Babylon"[37]).

257

The scholars of *Unger's Bible Dictionary* inform us that the land of Shinar "was celebrated in the ancient world not only by the Babylonians but also by the Greeks and Romans as a region of prodigious fertility."[38] In other words, among the people of Zechariah's day the ancient land of Shinar was known as "the land of plenty".

As earlier noted, the Hebrew term employed for the word "temple," *bayith* comes from the word *banah,* "to build a house, temple—dwelling place."[39] The word "erected," Heb. *kun,* means "to set up, to erect, to set upright, as a throne."[40]

As we have already mentioned, the Hebrew word for "land" (v. 11) is *erets,* meaning "country".[41] So we know, beyond any possible contradiction, that the Angel is talking about a future whole People, a *literal* country code-named "the land of Shinar" ('land of plenty'), a land of great *commerce* and *trade,* where a shrine/temple will be built for the *Woman.*

Thus what we have is a *repetition* of history, just as the writer of Proverbs says: "The thing that hath been, it *is that* which shall be, and that which is done is that which shall be done, and *there is* no new *thing* under the sun" (Ecc. 1:9; AKJV).

Set on Her own Pedestal

> 11 ". . . and when it is prepared, she will be set there on her own pedestal."

Employing the figure *Hypotyposis,* or *Word-Picture,* the Angel concludes Zechariah's latter day vision by *describing* in a vivid and forcible manner precisely what will take place in regards to the exaltation of the *Woman* in the latter day country code-named "the land of Shinar," saying: "when it is prepared, she will be "set" (Heb. *nuwacvh,* meaning "to sit down, to reside, to remain"[42]) on her own "pedestal" (Heb. *mkunah* or *mkonah,* "place, base").[43]

In the Tanakh (JPS) this passage is translated as follows:

> 11 And he answered, "To build a shrine for it in the land of Shinar, [a stand] shall be erected for it, and it shall be set down there upon the stand."

In the J. P. Green Interlinear Hebrew-English Old Testament the same passage is translated as follows:

> 11 And he said to me, To build a house for it in the land of Shinar; and it shall be fixed and established there on its own place.

The translators of the New American Standard Version (NASV) translate the same passage as follows:

> 11 Then he said to me, "To build a temple for her in the land of Shinar; and when it is prepared, she will be set there on her own pedestal."

The great shrine of the ancient Goddess,
Liberty Enlightening the World, **set on its own pedestal in New York Harbor—the Gateway to America.**

16

'THE WOMAN IS THAT GREAT CITY'

4 And the woman was arrayed in purple and scarlet color, and decked with gold and precious stones and pearls, having a golden cup in her hand full of abominations and filthiness of her fornication:

5 And upon her forehead was a name written, MYSTERY, BABYLON THE GREAT, THE MOTHER OF HARLOTS AND ABOMINATIONS OF THE EARTH.

18 . . . And the woman which thou sawest is that great city, which reigneth over the kings of the earth (Revelation 17:4-5, 18; AKJV).

FOR MOST THEOLOGIANS THE *Woman* described in the above passage is the false religion of Babylon that has existed since the fall of Adam and Eve in the Garden of Eden. For example, Dr. G. Campbell Morgan says: "The name on the forehead of Babylon commences with the word 'Mystery.' Babylon stands for the whole system of organized godlessness in the history of the human race. In its course it has been surrounded by every kind of material splendor, 'arrayed in purple and scarlet, and decked with gold and precious stones and pearls.'"[1] The Christian theologian A. Plummer of the *Pulpit Commentary* states that the *Woman* of Revelation 17 is "the worldly portion of the Church, though nominally Christian, is in reality identical with the world, which is openly antagonistic to God."[2] And James Moffatt of the *Expositor's Greek New Testament* writes that the *Woman* of Revelation 17 is "Rome personified (so Sib. Or. iii 46-92, before 80 A.D.) as a feminine figure, rides on a beast of the same colour (sic) . . . ."[3]

The problem with the above analysis is the failure to take into account the ancient use of *figures* in Scripture. Once again, the words of Dr. E. W. Bullinger are worth repeating:

> Commentators and interpreters, from inattention to the figures have been led astray from the real meaning of many important passages of God's Word; while ignorance of them has been the fruitful parent of error and false doctrine. It may be truly said that most of the gigantic errors of Rome, as well as the erroneous and conflicting views of the Lord's People, have their root and source, either in figuratively explaining away passages which should be taken literally, or in taking literally what has been thrown into a peculiar form or Figure of language: thus, not only falling into error, but losing the express teaching, and missing the special emphasis which the particular Figure was designed to impart to them.[4]

Among the 200 *figures* catalogued by Dr. Bullinger, none are more important to our understanding of the *Woman* in the Apocalypse than the figure *Prosopoceia*, or *Personification*. Once again, Dr. Bullinger informs us that this *figure* "is employed when the absent are spoken of (or to) as present: when the dead are spoken of as alive: or when anything (*e.g.*, a country) is addressed as a person."[5]

Equally significant, among the six classes belonging to the figure *Personification*, one can be divided into the group where "a whole People or State" is spoken of as a *woman*.[6] For instance, in Isaiah 32:9-11, we read: "Tremble, ye women that are at ease." Here Isaiah is addressing the whole People of Israel as *women*. We also see this same *personification* of Israel as a *woman* in Isaiah 3:18-26; Micah 7:8-10, etc.

It can also be established that the term *woman* is used in Scripture to address a whole People as a *harlot*. Such was the case with the idolatrous nation of Israel, which was often spoken as an *adulterous woman* ('harlot'): Jer. 3:1, 3, 4; 4:30; Ezek. 16 & 17; Hos. 2, etc., which is based on passages as Ex. 34:15, 16; Deut. 31:16; Judges 2:17; Isa. 1:21; 23:15-17; 57:3; Nah. 3:4, etc.

Dr. Bullinger informs us that the figure *Personification* is also used in Scripture to address a "city spoken of as a Mother," especially a metropolitan city.[7] For example, in 2 Samuel 20:19, the figure *Personification* is used to address the city of Jerusalem as a *Mother*, saying: "*I am one of them that are* peaceable and faithful in Israel: thou seekest to destroy a city and a *mother* in Israel." And in Hosea 2:2, the prophet *personifies* the city of Jerusalem as a *mother*, saying: "Plead with your *mother*, plead: for she is not my wife, neither *am* I her husband . . . ."

The significance of this ancient use of the figure *Personification* cannot be overstated. Because we find it used again and again throughout the Scriptures to identify a whole People or nation as a *woman*, a *harlot* or *whore*, and a *mother*.

With this understanding we should not be surprised that the Hebrew writer of the Apocalypse employed this same ancient form of figurative language to *personify* the Great Mother Goddess of ancient Babylon as a great People/nation of the last days code-named "Babylon". Nor should we be surprised to learn that in many ways this great latter day nation is similar to historic Babylon, of which the Jewish people of that day were well-acquainted.

The genius of John's employment of *figures* in regards to the *Woman*, in Revelation 17 & 18, is that in doing so he was able to not only establish the character of the *Woman*, but also the character of the people connected to this great latter day nation code-named "Babylon".

As you shall soon see, even more remarkable is how well John's two thousand year old characterization of this *Woman* of the Apocalypse coincides precisely with the people and land of the United States of America.

The Great Whore

17 Come hither; I will show unto thee the judgment
of the great whore . . . . (Rev. 17:1).

Like Zechariah, John begins his latter day discourse on a note
of judgment, employing the figure *Prosopopceia,* or *Personification*[8]
to give his audience a visible *representation* of the *Woman,* who he
addresses as the "great whore".

As earlier noted, throughout the Hebrew Scriptures the prophets
employed the *figures* "whore," "harlot," etc., to *personify* the whole
People of Israel, as well as the city of Jerusalem as an adulterous
woman.

Why is this understanding of the use of the figure *Personification*
important? Because at that particular time the terms "whore" and
"harlot" were used by the faithful followers of Yahweh when
addressing the Great Goddess of Babylon. For example, the scholars
of *Unger's Bible Dictionary* tell us that "Herodotus refers to the
custom of the Babylonians, who compelled every native female to
attend the temple of Venus (identified with Ishtar, the reincarnation
of Semiramis) once in her life and to prostitute herself in honor of
the goddess . . . . It is interesting to note that men were not excluded
from the practice of temple prostitution (23:18, marg.)."[9]

Here we have the historical origins of the "great whore" of
Revelation 17, which was well-known by the people of that day. To
the faithful followers of Yahweh the idea of the "great whore" was
not a blind leap of faith in some kind of unknown spiritual entity.
Rather, it was rooted in the historic exaltation of the Great Goddess
of Western Asia, whose origins goes all the way back to the first
deified queen of Babylon, Semiramis. Alexander Hislop says: "Thus
was this Chaldean queen a fit and remarkable prototype of the
'Woman' in the Apocalypse, with the golden cup in her hand, and
the name on her forehead, 'Mystery, Babylon the Great, the Mother
of harlots and abominations of the earth.'"[10]

Sits upon Many Waters

> **17** . . . the great whore that sitteth upon many
> waters . . . . (Rev. 17:1).

In this passage John employs the *figure* called *Hypotyposis,* or *Word-Picture*[11] to give his audience a visible *representation* of the *Woman* as the "great whore". Once again, Dr. Bullinger's definition of this *figure* is worth repeating: "[*Word-Picture* is] the name given to this figure because it describes an action, event, person, condition, passion, etc., in a lively and forcible manner, giving a vivid representation to it."[12]

Explaining the *figure* "many waters," the Angel plainly says: "The waters which thou sawest, where the whore sitteth, are peoples, and multitudes, and nations, and tongues" (v. 15). The Greek scholars Ardnt and Gingrich inform us that the Greek word for "peoples" is *laoi,* meaning "a mass, *crowds.*"[13] The Greek word for "multitudes, *oxloi* means "crowds, throngs, (multitudes) of people."[14] The word "nations," *ethvn* is derived from *etho,* meaning "race, specifically non-Jewish—Gentile, heathen, nation, people."[15] And the word "tongues," *glossai* means "languages".[16]

Here we have a vivid description of the people connected to this latter day nation code-named "Babylon," which can be summarized as follows: 1) it is inhabited by a "mass, crowds of people," indicating large groups of people living close together in cities, as tribes; 2) that these "crowds of people are in the "multitudes"; 3) that they are of different ethnic races; and 4) that they speak different "languages".

Arrayed in Purple and Scarlet Color

> 4 And the woman was arrayed in purple and scarlet
> color, and decked with gold and precious stones and
> pearls . . . . (Rev. 17:4).

In this passage John is employing the figure *Prosopographia,* or *Description of Persons*[17] to give his audience a vivid *description* of the *Woman.*

Alexander Hislop tells us that the ancient queen Semiramis was arrayed in such splendor that it is said on one occasion her appearance quelled a rebellion among her people, and the people were so moved by her beauty they erected a statue of her.[18] Hislop goes on to say:

> This Babylon queen was not merely in *character* coincident with the Aphrodite of Greece and the Venus of Rome, but was, in point of fact, the historical original of that goddess that by the ancient world was regarded as the very embodiment of everything attractive in female form, and the perfection of female beauty.[19]

Among the people of that day, had there been any doubts as to the identity of the *Woman* John was addressing they would have been dispelled with his use of the words "having a golden cup in her hand."

In the work entitled *Kitto's Biblical Cyclopedia* the Great Goddess Queen is portrayed as having a cup in her hand.

The ancient historian Pliny refers to the cup in the *Woman's* hand as "the cup of Semiramis, which fell into the hands of the victorious Cyrus the Great, after the fall of Babylon."[20] Pliny says, "Its gigantic proportions must have made it famous among the Babylonians and the nations with whom they had intercourse. It weighed fifteen talents, or 1200 pounds (Pliny, Hist. Nat., lib. xxxiii, cap. 15).[21]

The Woman's "Golden Cup" of Abominations

4 And the woman was arrayed in purple and scarlet . . . having a golden cup in her hand full of abominations and filthiness of her fornication (Rev. 17:4).

In this passage John employs the figure *Characterismos*, or *Description of Character*[22] to give his audience a vivid *description* of the immoral character of the *Woman*.

As earlier noted, among the people of Zechariah's day she was known as "Wickedness" (Heb. *rishah*, "moral wrong, wickedness, unrighteousness (Is. 9:18; Mal. 3:15), fraud, falsehood (Prov. 13:6)." Thus to the faithful worshipers of Yahweh her cult worship, in whatever manner it was displayed, was utterly detestable (1 Kings 15:13).

As the Goddess of Byblos, she was worshiped as Anath. As the Goddess of the Canaanites, she was worshiped as Asherah. Regardless of where she was exalted, it is said that "the people became drunk with the wine of her fornication." The scholars of *Unger's Bible Dictionary* write:

At Byblos (biblical Gebal) on the Mediterranean, N of Sidon, a center dedicated to this goddess has been excavated. She and her colleagues specialized in sex and war, and her shrines were temples of legalized vice . . . . On a fragment of the Baal Epic, Anath ('Anat') appears in an incredibly bloody orgy of destruction. For some unknown reason she fiendishly butchers mankind, young as well as old, in a most horrible and wholesale fashion, wading ecstatically in human gore up to her knees—even up to her throat—all the while exulting sadistically.[23]

As you shall see, it can be established that John's vivid *description* of the immoral character of the *Woman* coincides precisely with what is now happening in the United States of America in the name of the Ancient Goddess of personal freedom—"Lady Liberty".

America's "Golden Cup" of Abominations

History concurs that over the centuries little has changed in regards to Man's exaltation of the Great Goddess, especially in America. For example, since the momentous *Roe v. Wade* decision, in 1973, some 55 million unborn children have been sacrificed on the abortion altars of America's Goddess of personal freedom—"Lady Liberty". Judge Robert Bork writes:

> The systematic killing of unborn children in huge numbers is part of a general disregard for human life that has been growing for some time. Abortion by itself did not cause that disregard, but it certainly deepens and legitimates the nihilism that is spreading in our culture and finds killing for convenience acceptable. We are crossing lines, at first slowly and now with rapidity: killing unborn children for convenience; removing tissue from live fetuses; contemplating creating embryos for destruction in research; considering taking organs from living anencephalic babies; experimenting with assisted suicide; and contemplating euthanasia.[24]

Indeed, much like the unrestrained sexual licentious practiced in ancient temples dedicated to the Goddess, today in America, liberal activist Justices of the Supreme Court have ruled that pornography and nude dancing in beer halls are protected by the constitutional right of free expression.

Even some of America's most respected hotels are cashing in on the "adult entertainment" craze. For example, in a recent PBS *Frontline* documentary entitled "American Porn," revealing a new trend among popular hotel chains, such as the Marriott, Westin, and Hilton that now make porn movies available to customers in their hotel rooms. Many other U.S. corporations, such as AT&T, News

Corporation, and Yahoo! are reaping huge profits by offering porn entertainment on cable and the Internet.

Scholars agree that in ancient cities where the Great Goddess was exalted images of the male erected phallus and female vagina could be seen engraved in stone and in other works of art everywhere. Today, in an American culture that exalts the Goddess of personal liberty, little has changed.

In the 1950s, a high school student named Hugh Hefner read Alfred Kinsey's *Sexual Behavior in the Human Male* and became so intrigued with the idea of liberating the sexual feelings of men and women that he created *Playboy* magazine. For the next thirty years pornography and nudity became a powerful driving force in American culture.

Today, Hefner's *Playboy* influence has invaded every aspect of American culture. One can hardly look at a magazine, newspaper, TV, the Internet, or simply stand in line at the local grocery check-out counter without being barraged with sexual images.

Just a few years ago, during the third quarter of one particular Super Bowl, the drug manufacturer Eli Lilly and Company paid over four million dollars to promote a sixty-second Cialis commercial that was seen by tens of millions of adults, teenagers and children, who were watching the game. The entire sixty second commercial was dedicated to explaining how Cialis can help men have an erection "when the moment is right." This was only a few minutes after Janet Jackson flashed her breast to an unsuspecting Super Bowl crowd while on national and international TV during the halftime show. Today, Cialis' male erection ads, as well as others, have become a prominent part of American culture.

In the ancient world, temple worship of the Goddess often included sexual orgies with multiple partners, as well as adult-child sex. Today in America, little has changed.

As a result of the 2003 *Lawrence v. Texas* decision, which struck down the state's anti-sodomy statute, polygamists are now pushing to have marriage with multiple partners legalized. Even the criminal acts of child sexual abuse, rape, and incest (now called "adult-child sex" and "inter-generational sex") are now gaining respectability.

For example, in the 2004 movie *Birth,* Nicole Kidman plays a young widow who fantasizes that her deceased husband has been reincarnated as a ten-year-old boy. In one scene, Kidman is shown seducing the boy by kissing him tenderly on the lips. In another scene, Kidman asks the boy if he has ever had sex. In yet another scene, the boy slowly undresses in front of Kidman before joining her in the bathtub.

Columnist John Leo of *U.S. News & World Report* called the course of American culture "decadent," saying that it is "associated one way or another with most of the high-profit acts, black and white, that are pumping nihilism into the culture . . . . We are living through a cultural collapse, and major corporations are presiding over the collapse and grabbing everything on the way down."[25]

Perhaps nothing better illustrates the moral decline in America today than the recent undercover videos that exposed Planned Parenthood officials discussing the process of harvesting baby parts for profit. In one video, an official was seen haggling over the price of baby parts "per specimen" and trying to get the most amount of money out of each part. One official was seen saying she "wants a Lamborghini" while negotiating pieces of baby parts. Another official was seen talking about the best way to harvest baby parts "intact," while eating a salad and sipping on a glass of wine. Incredibly, liberal politicians, including President Obama (who claimed he had not seen the videos) and presidential candidate Hillary Clinton, as well as the liberal press, defended Planned Parenthood, claiming that the videos were edited.

> Among the many who voiced their outrage, perhaps Dr. Ben Carson, the former distinguished neurosurgeon and presidential candidate, put it best when he said: "These recent videos show the atrocity and level of depravity we have sunk to as a nation."

Remarkably, some two thousand years ago the Hebrew prophet of the Apocalypse wrote about the immoral character of a historic *Woman*, the deified queen of Babylon, Semiramis, who he *personified* as a great latter day nation code-named "Babylon," saying:

4 And the woman was arrayed in purple and scarlet . . . having a golden cup in her hand full of abominations and filthiness of her fornication (Rev. 17:4).

Mystery, Babylon the Great

5 And upon her forehead was a name written, MYSTERY, BABYLON THE GREAT . . . (Rev. 17:5).

Continuing on with the figure *Characterismos,* or *Description of Character,* John gives his audience a vivid *description* of the occult character of the *Woman.* Alexander Hislop writes:

> Now, as the Babylon of the Apocalypse is characterized by the name of "MYSTERY," so the grand distinguishing feature of the ancient Babylonian system was the Chaldean "MYSTERIES" that formed so essential a part of that system . . . . The Chaldean Mysteries can be traced up to the days of Semiramis, who lived only a few centuries after the flood, and who is known to have impressed upon them the image of her own depraved and polluted mind.[26]

Interestingly enough, the Greek term for "Mystery," *musterion* is derived from *mustes,* meaning a "person initiated in sacred mysteries".[27] In the ancient world this was especially true of those initiated into the secret societies of the sacred "Mysteries" where certain information communicated to the initiated was to be kept secret.[28]

As you shall see, it can be established that John's vivid *description* of the *Woman's* commitment to the "Ancient Mysteries" coincides precisely with the commitment of the Founding Fathers, presidents, and secret societies of the United States of America to the "Ancient Mysteries".

The "Mystery" Cults of America

As earlier noted, from our nation's very beginning as a sovereign Republic the Founding Fathers, as well as much of the early American populace, were devotees of the Craft of Freemasonry. Since that time the "Mystery" cults of America's have become the chosen fraternities of presidents, legislators, justices, educators, government officials, generals and military personnel, business and religious men and women from every walk of life. Thus we should not be surprised that today America has more members in the "Mystery" cults than any other nation on earth.

As earlier noted, there have been sixteen confirmed American presidents as having been Masons: Washington, Monroe, Jackson, Polk, Buchanan, Andrew Johnson, Garfield, McKinley, Teddy Roosevelt, Taft, Harding, Franklin D. Roosevelt, Truman, Lyndon Johnson, Ford and Reagan. And according to a 1951 edition of the *Holy Bible, Masonic Edition,* there is abundant evidence that Thomas Jefferson, and Pierce and Taylor were also members.[29]

In addition, both Presidents George H. W. Bush and his son, George W. Bush, are Skull and Bonesmen; and President Bill Clinton, a member of DeMolay, all of which are allied Masonic fraternities. The *Masonic Bible* states that "for well over one hundred and fifty years, the destiny of this country has been determined largely by men who were members of the Masonic Fraternity."[30]

Given this understanding, the significance of the Hebrew writer of the Apocalypse's reference to the name "Mystery" on the *Woman's* forehead cannot be overstated. Because in Jewish thought the forehead is regarded as the seat where all the important decisions of life (or a nation's destiny) are made. For instance, the Hebrew Scriptures inform us that the high priest's crown was a gold plate inscribed with the words "Holiness to the Lord" that was placed directly on his forehead, representing the seat of his consecration (Ex. 29:6; 39:30; Lev. 8:9; 21:12).

Thus there can be little doubt that the people of that day would have understood that John's reference to the term "Mystery" written on the forehead of the *Woman* was a direct reference to her consecration to the "Ancient Mysteries".

Addressing the significance of the "Ancient Mysteries," Albert Mackey writes:

> Each of the pagan gods had (besides the *public* and *open*) a *secret worship* paid unto him; to which none were admitted but those who had been selected by preparatory ceremonies, called INITIATION. This *secret worship* was termed the MYSTERIES.[31]

Explaining the origin of the "Ancient Mysteries," Manly Hall says in his book entitled *What the Ancient Wisdom Expects Of Its Disciples:*

> In the remote past the gods walked with men and . . . they chose from among the sons of men the wisest and the truest.
> With these specially ordained and illuminated sons they left the keys of their great wisdom, which was the knowledge of good and evil.
> . . . these illuminated ones, founded what we know today as the Ancient Mysteries.[32]

Addressing the need to propagate the "Ancient Mysteries," the occult prophetess Alice Bailey says in her work entitled *The Externalisation Of The Hierarchy:*

> There is no question therefore that the work to be done in familiarizing the general public with the nature of the Mysteries is of paramount importance at this time. These Mysteries will be restored to outer expression through the medium of the Church and the Masonic Fraternity.[33]

Remarkably, some two thousand years ago the Hebrew prophet of the Apocalypse wrote about a historic *Woman,* the deified queen of Babylon, Semiramis, who he *personified* as great latter day nation code-named "Babylon," saying:

5 And upon her forehead was a name written,
MYSTERY, BABYLON THE GREAT . . . (Rev. 17:5).

Mother of Harlots

5 And upon her forehead was a name written . . . The
MOTHER OF HARLOTS . . . . (Rev. 17:5).

Continuing with the employment of the figure *Prosopopceia,* or *Personification,* John gives his audience a visible *representation* of the *Woman* as the "Mother of Harlots". Dr. Bullinger tells us that this *figure* is employed "when a city is spoken of as a Mother."[34]

The scholars of *Unger's Bible Dictionary* inform us that the *figure* "Mother" was understood by the peoples of the ancient world to be a reference to a whole People, or nation. One writer states: "As in English so in Heb., a nation was considered as a mother, and individuals as her children (Isa. 50:1; Jer. 50:12; Ezek. 19:12; Hos. 4:5)."[35]

Arndt and Gingrich tell us that the Greek word *porne* ('harlot'), used in a figurative sense, as in Revelation 17:5, is the equivalent of the Hebrew word *zanah* ('harlot') and is employed "as the designation for a government that is hostile to God and his people; Isa. 1:21; 23:15f; Jer. 3:3; Ezek. 16:30f, 35."[36]

The Original Webster's Unabridged Dictionary defines the term "harlot" as follows: "In *Scripture,* one who forsakes the true God and worships idols."[37]

Moreover, Alexander Hislop tells us that Semiramis "was worshiped as Rhea, the great 'Mother' of the gods, with such atrocious rites as identified her with Venus, the Mother of all impurity, and raised the very city where she had reigned to a bad eminence among the nations, as the grand seat at once of idolatry and consecrated prostitution."[38]

One Christian scholar says of her idolatrous worship by the Canaanites:

> Asherah was only one manifestation of a chief goddess of western Asia, regarded now as the wife, then

as the sister, of the principle Canaanite god El. Other names of this deity were Ashtoreth (Astarte) and Anath. Frequently represented as a nude woman bestride a lion, with a lily in one hand and a serpent in the other, and called Qudshu "the Holiness," that is, "the Holy One" in a perverted moral sense, she was a divine courtesan. In the same sense the male prostitutes consecrated to the cult of Qudshu and prostituted themselves to her honor were called qedeshim, "sodomites" (Deut. 23:18, marg.; 1 Kings 14:24; 15:12; 22:46).[39]

As you shall see, it can be established that John's vivid *description* of the immoral character of the *Woman* as the great "Mother of Harlots" coincides precisely with what is now happening in the United States of America in the name of the Ancient Goddess of personal freedom—"Lady Liberty".

America's Sexual Revolution

History concurs that the liberal revisionism of the courts, which began with the appointed FDR Supreme Court Justices of the late 1940s, has all but sanitized Judaic-Christian values from American culture.

For example, in 1948, in *McCollum v. Board of Education*, the Supreme Court ruled that public property may not be used for religious instruction or other activities that aid in the teaching of religion. In *Engel v. Vitale* (1962), the Court ruled against school prayer, saying that schools may not conduct devotional exercises, compose prayers, read the Bible, or participate in any other religious activity.

In *Abington Township, Pa. v. Schempp*, and *Murray v. Curlett* (1963), the Court prohibited Bible reading in school. In *Stone v. Graham* (1980), the Court struck down a Kentucky law permitting the posting of the Ten Commandments in the schoolroom. And in *Edwards v. Aguillard* (1987), the Court struck down a Louisiana law requiring that both creation science and evolution be given balanced treatment in the classroom. At the same time the Court ruled that nudity and sexual content in films, books, magazines, etc., were protected under the Free Speech Amendment.

As a result of these rulings pornography, nudity, occultism, violence and sex have become a multi-billion dollar business in America. In 1973, Americans spent about $10 million on pornography. By 1987, the amount had grown to more than $8 billion. Today, by some estimates, the amount exceeds $15 billion annually.

One of the many down-sides of the American sexual revolution is the high toll of sexual diseases that is now at epidemic proportions. Today, more than 65 million Americans are infected with sexually transmitted diseases (STDs), including Herpes, Hepatitis B, AIDS, and more than a dozen others—most of which have no known cures. Each year more than 15 million men and women are infected with STDs.

According to a report from the Reuters wire service, teen pregnancy has skyrocketed in recent years. The rate in the U.S. is more than four times higher than that of France, Germany, and Japan. For the first time, over 50 percent of American adults believe that homosexuality is an acceptable lifestyle. And in public schools, 85 to 90 percent of high school seniors say homosexuality is an acceptable alternative lifestyle.

In 1996, Congress passed the Defense of Marriage Act (DOMA). DOMA passed Congress with large bipartisan support: 85 votes in the Senate and 342 votes in the House, and Democratic President Bill Clinton signed it into law.

In the House Judiciary Committee report on DOMA, lawmakers affirmed that "civil laws that permit only heterosexual marriage reflect and honor a collective moral judgment about human sexuality. This judgment entails both moral disapproval of homosexuality and moral conviction that heterosexuality better comports with traditional (especially Judaic-Christian) morality."

Within just a few short years, however, DOMA was being reversed by liberal activist justices. For example, in November 2003, Chief Justice Margaret Marshall of the State Supreme Judicial Court gave the Massachusetts legislature six months to enact a law granting homosexuals the right to marry. Just four months earlier, in July, the U.S. Supreme Court laid the groundwork for Marshall's decision when it struck down the laws of seventeen states and declared homosexuality to be a constitutionally protected right. Following the decision, conservative Supreme Court Justice Antonin Scalia wrote the following comment:

> . . . state laws against bigamy, same-sex marriage, adult-incest, prostitution, masturbation, adultery, fornication, bestiality, and obscenity [are now] called into question . . . . The court has largely signed on to the homosexual agenda.
>
> . . . The court has taken sides in the culture war.

More recently, as a result of the Supreme Court's rulings, in June 2011, Governor Andrew Cuomo signed a bill that was narrowly passed by legislators that made Same-sex marriage legal in New York, becoming the sixth state where gay couples can now be legally married.

On May 11, 2012, President Obama told an ABC network interviewer that he supports Same-sex marriage. Celinda Lake, a Democratic pollster called Obama's endorsement "a sign of leadership and authenticity" to the liberal base and younger voters, in particular.

On November 6, 2012, voters approved Same-sex marriage in four states: Maine, Maryland, Minnesota and Washington. Gay rights activists singled out President Obama's new position in favor of Same-sex marriage as a key factor in Tuesday's victories. "His shift," said Jon Davidson, legal director for Lambda Legal, a gay rights organization, "caused a lot of other politicians to feel free to change their positions as well and made it easier for African-American churches to change their positions."

Shortly after President Obama came out in support of Same-sex marriage scores of elected lawmakers publically announced their support for Same-sex marriage. By March 2013, it was reported that only 10 of the Senate's 55 Democratic senators did not support Same-sex marriage.

On March 27, 2013, the noted conservative radio host Rush Limbaugh made a startling prediction about the survivability of Same-sex marriage in the U.S., saying: "The opponents say, 'Well, the country's changing and you better get with it because this genie's not getting back in the bottle.' And I think that's right . . . . I think the inertia is clearly moving in the direction that there is going to be gay marriage at some point in time *nationwide.*"

Three months later, on June 25, 2013, five Supreme Court Justices made two landmark rulings that will forever change the definition of marriage in the United States, as well as impact many other nations of the world. Those five Justices, including Justice Anthony Kennedy, the 1988 Ronald Reagan appointed "conservative"—leaning swing vote, ruled as unconstitutional Section 3 of the DOMA law, which recognizes "only marriage between a man and a woman." The five Justices also dismissed an appeal to uphold the California ballot proposition and state constitutional amendment passed by California voters in the November 2008 state elections, 7,001,084 (Yes – 52.24%) to 6,401,482 (No – 47.76%), which provided a new provision: Section 7.5 of the Declaration of Rights to the California Constitution—"only marriage between a man and a woman is valid or recognized in California."

In a blistering rebuke of Justice Anthony Kennedy's ruling in the 5-4 case, Justice Antonin Scalia said that it opened the door for a federal law allowing Same-sex marriages. Justice Scalia further wrote in his dissenting opinion:

> It takes real cheek for today's majority to assure us, as it is going out the door, that a constitutional requirement to give formal recognition to same-sex marriage is not at issue here—when what has preceded that assurance is a lecture on how superior the majority's moral judgment in favor of same-sex marriage is to the Congress's hateful moral judgment (DOMA) against it.
>
> By formally declaring anyone opposed to same-sex marriage an enemy of human decency, the majority arms well every challenger to a state law restricting marriage to its traditional definition. Henceforth those challengers will lead with this court's declaration that there is "no legitimate purpose" served by such a law, and will claim that the traditional definition has the purpose and effect

to disparage and injure the "personhood and dignity" of same-sex couples.

Remarkably, some two thousand years ago the Hebrew prophet of the Apocalypse wrote about a historic *Woman,* the deified queen of Babylon, Semiramis, who he *personified* as a great latter day nation code-named "Babylon," saying:

> 5 And upon her forehead was the name written . . . the MOTHER OF HARLOTS . . . (Rev. 17:5).

The Woman is that Great City

> 18 And the woman which thou sawest is that great city (Rev. 17:18).

Here John is plainly told by the Angel that the *Woman* being addressed is, in fact, the *Personification* of a great latter day "city" code-named "Babylon".

Explaining the early city-state make-up of the ancient land of Shinar ('Babylonia'), the British archaeologist Joan Oats says:

> . . . by the period early in the 3rd millennium which archaeologists call 'Early Dynastic', the city-state—a political institution unknown elsewhere at this early date—had come into being. Each such state consisted of a city, occasionally several cities, with its surrounding territory, including dependent towns and villages.[40]

History concurs that down through the centuries little has changed. Today, chief cities are often referred to as countries, or a State. For instance, Washington, D.C. is often spoken of when addressing the United States. The same is true when using Moscow for Russia, Paris for France, London for England, Berlin for Germany, Jerusalem for Israel, etc.

Yet, for most theologians, John's use of the *figure* "great city" is interpreted to mean the city of Rome. For example, Dr. Plummer of the *Pulpit Commentary* says: "Many writers have been led by this verse to believe that Rome, either pagan or papal, is thus pointed out as the antitype of the harlot. That this is one fulfillment of the vision need hardly be doubted."[41]

As you shall see, however, nothing could be further from the truth, because it can be established that the Angel's *personification* of the *Woman* as a "great city" coincides precisely with the United States of America.

The Great Communicator

On the night of August 23, 1984, President Ronald Reagan, often referred to as the "Great Communicator," addressed the delegates of the Republican National Convention, and said in part:

> The poet called Miss Liberty's torch "the lamp beside the golden door."
>
> Well, that was the entrance to America, and it still is. And now you really know why we're here tonight.
>
> The glistening hope of that lamp is still sure. For every promise, every opportunity is still golden in this land. And through that golden door our children can walk into tomorrow with the knowledge that no one can be denied the promise that is America.
>
> Her heart is full, her torch is still golden, her future bright. She has arms big enough to comfort and strong enough to support, for the strength in her arms is the strength of her people. She will carry on in the '80s unafraid, unashamed and unsurpassed.
>
> In this springtime of hope, some lights seem eternal, America is.

Then, on January 11, 1989, President Reagan gave his famous Farewell Address from the Oval Office to the American people, concluding with the following statement:

And that's about all I have to say tonight, except for one thing. The past few days when I've been at that window upstairs, I've thought a bit of the 'shining city on a hill.' The phrase comes from John Winthrop, who wrote it to describe the America he imagined.

What he imagined was important because he was an early Pilgrim, an early freedom man. He journeyed here on what today we'd call a little wooden boat; and like other Pilgrims, he was looking for a home that would be free. I've spoken of the shining city all of my political life, but I don't know if I ever quite communicated what I saw when I said it. But in my mind it was a tall, proud city built on rocks stronger than oceans, windswept, God-blessed, and teeming with people of all kinds living in harmony and peace; a city with free ports that hummed with commerce and creativity. And if there had to be city walls, the walls had doors and the doors were open to anyone with the will and heart to get here. That's how I saw it, and see it still.

Remarkably, some two thousand years ago the Hebrew prophet of the Apocalypse wrote about a historic *Woman,* the deified queen of Babylon, Semiramis, who he *personified* as a great latter day nation code-named "Babylon," saying:

18 And the woman which thou sawest is that great city (Rev. 17:18).

Babylon the Great

5 And upon her forehead was a name written . . . BABYLON THE GREAT . . . (Rev. 17:5).

Continuing to employ the figure *Hypotyposis,* or *Word-Picture,* John gives his audience a vivid *description* of the *Woman,* who he *personified* as a great latter day nation code-named "Babylon".

For most modern day theologians Babylon is a representation of all the idolatry, false religion, and immorality that has existed since the time of Adam and Eve. Little is ever said or written about the greatness of ancient Babylon. History concurs, however, that the early Babylonians made great contributions to civilization in the areas of science, medicine, agriculture, education, astronomy, writing, etc.

A highly inventive people, the early Babylonians developed the wheel, the sundial, the wedge-script cuneiform script, the plow, and many other inventions that are still in use today. The Babylonians were masters at building with little more than mud-bricks and mortar. They built dams and developed a highly sophisticated system of canals that were used for travel, commerce, and the irrigation of their crops.

Because of Babylon's fertile soil and abundance of water the Babylonian people were able to produce an abundance of fruits, grains, and vegetables, which allowed its mixed populace to pursue a variety of different trades and professions. And because of its abundant food production Babylon became the "Bread Basket" of the world. As earlier noted, Babylonia was known as "the land of plenty." Indeed, ancient tablets tell us that the Babylonian people were the best dressed, best fed, and best educated people in the ancient world.

Not only was Babylon the most beautiful city in the ancient world it was the financial capital of the world; the world's trading center, educational center and ethnic population center. Babylon was also the "melting pot" of the ancient world. Over the centuries, peoples from all parts of the world traveled to Babylon in hopes of making a new life for themselves and their families.

Moreover, because of Babylon's diverse ethnic population it was a land of many religions. Shrines, temples and synagogues could be found everywhere.

Although Babylon was known for its war-like character it was also known as a "liberator" and "peacemaker" among the nations of the world. On more than one occasion the kings of Babylon intervened in disputes among nations as "peacemaker". On one occasion, when King Nabopolassar, the father of Nebuchadnezzar, formed an alliance with Cyaxares the Mede and overthrew Nineveh, the capital of Assyria, he was hailed as a "liberator" by the peoples of the Middle East.

As a great military force Babylon was unequaled among the nations of the world. A fearless and warlike people the city of Babylon rose from obscurity to become a great empire in just a few short years.

In a day when most nations were ruled by sovereign kings, Babylon was ruled by a monarch but also had a representative form of government for its people. As a monarchial-representative type government the cities of Babylonia were governed by law with courts and police, and protection for the basic human rights. Transactions were governed by a law of contract. Because of its many laws Babylon was known as the "Mother of Laws".

At the height of Babylon's glory its vast empire was bordered by three great bodies of water: the Persian Gulf to the south, the Great Sea (Mediterranean) to the north, and the Red Sea to the west. And the city of Babylon was located between two great rivers, the Tigris and Euphrates Rivers.

Babylonia was also a land rich in gold. In Daniel's account of Nebuchadnezzar's dream of the image of a man whose head was of "fine gold" (Dan. 2:32), its head represented Babylon (v. 38).

In the Genesis account we are told that the river which flowed out of the Garden of Eden and separated into four different rivers. One of which was the river Havilah, which was on the northern boundary of Babylonia "as one goes toward Assyria."

How rich were those gold deposits? We don't know for certain. But the Bible says, ". . . the gold of that land is good" (Gen. 2:11-12). Some believe that it was the discovery and mining of the rich deposits of gold in northern Babylonia that made it financially possible for Nebuchadnezzar to make Babylon the greatest nation on earth.

Among Babylon's many characteristics none were more unique than its large Jewish population. Unlike the Jewish people's treatment in most nations, as captives of Babylon they were allowed to observe the Sabbath, the appointed festivals, and new moons. In fact, some were appointed to high positions in government, and many went on to become wealthy in business.

Professor George Stephen Goodspeed, the early twentieth century professor of Ancient History in the University of Chicago, writes about the greatness of ancient Babylon, saying:

Adornment and practical utility as well as defense were in the mind of Nebuchadnezzar when he put his hand to the rebuilding of Babylon.

He dug again the sacred canal and lined it with brick; he raised the sacred street; carrying it by a bridge over the canal and lifting higher the gates of the two city walls at the point where it passed through them. He built up the bank of the Euphrates with bricks, making splendid quays, which still exist, walled them in and opened gates at the point where the city streets came down to the water's edge. Later historians dwell on his magnificent hanging gardens, which rose somewhere near his palaces; they were built in lofty terraces to solace his Median queen for the absence of her beloved mountains. Across the river, in the twin city of Borsippa, he rebuilt the city wall and restored the temple tower of the god Nabu, son of Marduk. In time the two cities became more and more united. It is this double city which seems to be in the mind of Herodotus when he describes Babylon as a great square about fourteen miles on each side, the walls making a circuit of fifty-six miles and enclosing an area of two hundred square miles. While the Babylon of the Kaldi was much smaller than this, their devotion to it manifested itself in these initial works that in course of time produced the larger and more famous city. Already it contained at least two of the seven wonders of the world, and its beauty and wealth made it for a long time thereafter the chief centre (sic) of the east. "From Nebuchadnezzar to the Mongol invasion" it was well-nigh "the greatest commercial city of the world."[42]

Babylon: the greatest commercial city of the world.

As you shall see, it can be established that John's vivid *description* of the *Woman,* who he *personified* as "Babylon the Great" coincides precisely with the United States of America.

The Greatest Nation on Earth

Like ancient Babylon, America, in a short span of time, has also risen from insignificance as a nation to become the greatest nation on earth. Like the ancient Babylonians, the people of America have been the most inventive, industrious people on earth. Indeed, like the inventions and discoveries of the ancient Babylonians, the peoples of the world are still enjoying the inventions and scientific discoveries of Americans, such as Charles Goodyear (1800-1860), Samuel Colt (1814-1862), Thomas Edison (1847-1931), Alexander Graham Bell (1847-1922), Wilbur Wright (1867-1912) and Orville Wright (1871-1941), Jonas Salk (1914-1955), and a host of other American inventors and scientists.

The similarities of ancient Babylon and the United States of America can be summarized as follows:

• Like ancient Babylon, America is the commercial center of the modern day world. Since the 1920s the United States has been the world's largest national economy. In 2012, with only 4.46 percent of the world's population, its nominal GDP was estimated to be $15.7 trillion, approximately a quarter of the world's GDP. U.S. purchasing power is also the largest in the world, approximately a fifth of the world's GDP purchasing power. As of 2010, the U.S. remains the world's largest manufacturer, representing a fifth of the world's manufacturing output. Also, about 60 percent of the world's currency reserves have been invested in the U.S. dollar, and the New York Stock Exchange is the world's largest stock exchange.[43]

New York City: the financial center of the United States.

• Like ancient Babylon, America, with its abundant supply of water, canals, dams, and fertile land, has become the "Bread Basket" of the world. California alone, as a result of its mild climate, fertile soil, irrigation canals, dams, and agriculture technology, is ranked sixth among the nations of the world in annual gross revenue production.

• Like ancient Babylon, America is a land of diverse ethnic peoples, with different languages, who live together in their own ethnic communities in cities, as "tribes". Filled with the hope of finding a new life for themselves and their families, people from every nation in the world continue to come to America. Like ancient Babylon, it can truly be said that America is the "melting pot" of the world.

- Like ancient Babylon, because of America's diverse ethnic population it is also a land of many religions. Shrines, temples, churches and synagogues can be found everywhere.

- Like ancient Babylon, America is also known as a "liberator" and "peacemaker". From the time of the European wars of World War I and World War II, to this present date, America has been known as a liberator of the oppressed. Moreover, with the establishment of the United Nations, in New York City, the United States is unique among the nations of the world as a "peacemaker".

- Like ancient Babylon, America, originally formed as a Republic to be governed by the people, is governed by a "monarchial" type Executive Branch, granted emergency executive powers to "the President" that are still in effect from FDR's Proclamation 2039, March 9, 1933, with a representative form of government. According to the Federal Register the total number of Executive Orders issued by each President since FDR are as follows: Barack Obama (2009-2012)—**144**; George W. Bush (2001-2009)—**291**; Bill Clinton (1993-2001)—**364**; George H. W. Bush (1989-1993)—**166**; Ronald Reagan (1981-1989)—**381**; Jimmy Carter (1977-1981)—**320**; Gerald R. Ford (1974-1977)—**169**; Richard M. Nixon (1969-1974)—**346**; Lyndon B. Johnson (1963-1969)—**324**; John F. Kennedy (1961-1963)—**214**; Dwight D. Eisenhower (1953-1961)—**480**; Harry S. Truman (1945-1953)—**896**; and Franklin D. Roosevelt (1933-1945)—**3,726**.[44]

- Like ancient Babylon, the cities of America are governed by law with courts and police, and protection for the basic human rights. Transactions are also governed by a law of contract.

* Like ancient Babylon, America has become the "Mother of Laws". For example, beginning January 2013, 40,000 new federal, state and local laws went into effect across the United States, ranging from getting abortions in New Hampshire, learning about gays and lesbians in California, getting jobs in Alabama, light bulbs, and even driving golf carts in Georgia. Nearly 900 of those 40,000 laws were from California alone.

* Like ancient Babylon, since the discovery of gold in 1948 by John Marshall, at Sutter's Mill on the American River, in northern California, America has been known as a land "rich in gold". So rich were the gold deposits that people from every nation on earth left family and friends to come to California in hopes of "striking it rich". In the United States alone, gold production multiplied **seventy-three times** during the six years that began in 1848. Among the gold producing nations of the world, the United States made such rapid progress from 1851 to 1855 that it contributed nearly 45 percent of the world's total gold output. The historian A. F. Harlow said of 1849: "It is one of the three or four great milestones in history. Epochs ended and began with it. The golden fruitage of California's hills changed us in ten or fifteen year's time, from a weak, infantile, economically dependent nation, to what might almost be called a world power."

* Like ancient Babylon, America has a large Jewish population. Like ancient Babylon, American Jews have been treated unlike Jews of no other nation. American Jews worship in their synagogues, observe the seventh day Sabbath, the appointed festivals, and new moons. And like the Jews of ancient Babylon, American Jews have been appointed to high positions in government, and many have gone on to become wealthy in business and professional life.

Remarkably, some two thousand years ago the Hebrew prophet of the Apocalypse wrote about a historic *Woman,* the deified queen of Babylon, Semiramis, who he *personified* as a great latter day nation code-named "Babylon," saying:

> 5 And upon her forehead was a name written . . . BABYLON THE GREAT . . . (Rev. 17:5).

All Nations have Drunk of Her Wine

> 2 . . . and the inhabitants of the earth have been made drunk with the wine of her fornication (Rev. 17:2).

Continuing to employ the figure *Hypotyposis,* or *Word-Picture,* John gives his audience a visible *representation* of the *Woman's* immoral influence on the peoples of the earth.

The Greek scholars Arndt and Gingrich inform us that the term "fornication" (Gk. *porveias* means "prostitution, unchastity, fornication, of every kind of unlawful sexual intercourse").[45]

Equally significant, we are told that when used in a figurative sense the term "fornication" was employed "in accordance with an OT symbol of apostasy from God, or idolatry; from the time of Hosea the relationship between God and his people was regarded as a marriage bond. This usage was more easily understandable because many pagan cults (Astarte, Isis, Cybele et al.) were connected with sexual debauchery (cf. Hos 6: 10; Jer. 3: 2, 9) Rv 19:2."[46]

As you shall see, it can be established that John's vivid *description* of the *Woman's* immoral influence on the peoples of the earth coincides precisely with what is now happening in United States of America in the name of the Ancient Goddess of personal freedom—"Lady Liberty".

The Marketing of America's "Wine"

Today, beyond any possible contradiction, television and movies have become the primary mediums through which corporate

America is marketing sex, violence and profanity to the masses of people in America and around the world.

Indeed, since 1993, no media outlet has been able to capitalize on the worldwide youth market like MTV, the rock music television channel. For instance, by 1993, MTV's popular rock-and-roll programming was available on a daily basis to 210 million households in seventy-one countries.[47] Today, MTV can be seen in 330 million households in one hundred forty countries.[48]

The "Wine" of Profane Music

Perhaps the most potent impact on America's culture is the lyrics and obscene material in today's popular music, which is filled with lyrics that focus on the vulgar and profane.

One of the most popular groups of the 1980s and 1990s was the rock group Guns n' Roses. In 1987, their album *Appetite for Destruction* sold more than 12 million copies in America alone, exposing teenagers and preteens to profane and sexually explicit lyrics, such as follows:

> Panties round your knees, with your ass in debris . . . .
> Tied up, tied down, up against the wall
> Turn around bitch I got a use for you
> Besides you ain't got nothin' better to do
> —and I'm bored.

In 1991, the Guns n' Roses made a new CD that described a "bitch" who craved sexual abuse:

> She ain't satisfied without some pain
> Friday night is goin' up inside her—again.

The rappers known as the "Geto Boys" used violence and sadistic fantasies to popularize their album *Grip It! On That Other Level,* reaching the Top 30 most listened to albums, and was certified gold when it passed 500,000 copies.

After their first album, the Geto Boys made an equally violent and pornographic follow-up, which Warner-Elektra-Atlantic

Corporation (affiliated with the Time-Warner conglomerate) enthusiastically agreed to distribute to the worldwide market.[49]

During this same period another hard metal group, Motley Crue, capitalized on the popularity of hard rock violence and erotic stimulation in their sadistic song "You're All I Need":

> Laid out cold, now we're both alone
> But killing you helped me keep you home.

Expressing the sentiments of many, on September 18, 1991, the late Senator Robert Byrd made an impassioned speech on the Senate floor about the corrupting influence American music was having on young people, saying: "If we in this nation continue to sow the images of murder, violence, drug abuse, sadism, arrogance, irreverence, blasphemy, perversion, pornography and aberration before the eyes of millions of children year after year and day after day, we should not be surprised if the foundations of our society rot away as if from leprosy."

The "Wine" of Violence and Sex

While American attendance at the movie theater has dropped off in the past few years, the appetite for U.S. violent and sexually explicit movies in foreign countries has dramatically increased over the past two decades. Between 1985 and 1990 Hollywood revenues for U.S. feature movies increased 124 percent.[50] As a result, in the early 1990s half of all U.S. movie income was coming from the peoples of foreign countries. Today, real growth in the U.S. movie industry is coming from the peoples of foreign countries, and the foreign revenues for U.S. movies have skyrocketed.

During the weekend of July 22, 2011, *Harry Potter and the Deathly Hallows II* played in theaters across the U.S. Box office revenues for that weekend totaled $47, 422, 212 dollars. That same weekend the same movie, *Harry Potter and the Deathly Hallows II,* was shown in some twenty-two different countries: Argentina, Australia, Austria, Brazil, Chile, Columbia, France, Germany, Hong Kong, Italy, Japan, Mexico, the Netherlands, New Zealand, Portugal, Russia, South Korea, Spain, Switzerland, Taiwan, the U.K., and

Ireland. The combined weekend revenue for these countries totaled $98, 803, 547.[51]

Today, the greatest challenge for most Hollywood producers is trying to out-do the latest movie. For example, in the movie *A Kiss Before Dying* a cold-blooded conman (Matt Dillon) victimizes twin sisters with the promise of matrimony by murdering the first one on the day of their engagement, and makes plans to kill the surviving sister shortly after a lavish wedding.

In the movie *Naked Tango,* shortly after a wedding ceremony the new husband pressures his wife to have sex with another man. When she refuses he tries to stab her to death.

In the movie titled *Marrying Man,* the husband (Alec Baldwin) and wife (Kim Basinger) marry and divorce three times in succession, with each marriage accompanied with alternating scenes of passionate lust and violent rage.

In *Voyager,* the father (Sam Shepard) becomes involved in an erotic, romantic affair with a teenager, which has photographed sex scenes. The shocker is when Shepard discovers that the teenager he is having sex with is his daughter.

In *Sleepwalker,* the Hollywood stars Alice Krige and Brian Krause play the part of intimate lovers. Throughout the film there is heavy breathing, nudity, passionate kissing, and sexual intercourse. The shocker in this film is that the sexual relationship is between mother and son.

In 1903, when the silent movie *The Great Train Robbery* became popular it is said that audiences left their seats during the scene which a bad-man pointed his pistol directly at the camera. Today, killing and violence is a major part of the American entertainment industry: the more killing and violence, the greater the impact and popularity. Action movies like *Die Hard 2* (with its 264 killings) and *Rambo III* (with its 106 killings) have now become classic films that are shown repeatedly on TV during the holiday season. This is especially troubling given the fact that America leads the nations of the world in crime, violence, and murder.

Not surprisingly, recent scientific studies have established a direct link between the increase in real crime and violence and Hollywood make-believe productions.

On July 3, 2006, the *Albuquerque Tribune* featured an article entitled "Violent TV can make children more aggressive." Dr. Victor Strasburger, professor of Pediatrics and chief of the Adolescent Medicine Division at the University of New Mexico, said:

> Research has clearly demonstrated that, first of all, media teaches children and teenagers. They are great teachers—they're funny and quite entertaining—and numerous messages about sex and violence kind of slip in the side door. Or barge in through the front door without even knocking.
>
> For example, a fairly consistent message in American media is that its OK to be violent, especially if you're the good guy beating up the bad guy. And there's more to that message: violence is an acceptable solution to some very complex problems.
>
> Other common messages are that everyone is having sex and no one's using birth control; and that everyone's drinking and smoking with no health consequences.
>
> That's just general TV programming; I'm not even talking about advertising. TV has a tremendous effect on our lives.

For many, the greatest shocker is that movies and TV programs that glorify sex and violence can be made at all for the general public's consumption. Today many ask: How did things get to such a state? The answer is quite simple: the Supreme Court has deemed the glorification of immorality, murder, and violence to be a constitutional right of "free speech" guaranteed by the First Amendment.

In a more recent landmark decision, on June 27, 2011, the Supreme Court struck down California's 2005 ban on the sale of violent video games to minors, extending the law of "free speech" rights guaranteed by the First Amendment. The California Lawmakers defined "violent" as activity involving "killing, maiming, dismembering, or sexually assaulting an image of a human being."

The conservative Justice Antonin Scalia wrote the ruling for the 7-2 majority, saying: "Even where the protection of children is the object, the constitutional limits on government action apply. Whatever challenges of applying the Constitution to ever-advancing technology, the basic principles of freedom of speech and the press, like the First Amendment's command, do not vary."

For those who ascribe to the absolute creed of *liberty* and *equality* there are no Constitutional or biblical limits. But for those who understand the powerful influence the Great Goddess had on the peoples of the ancient world there is a much deeper explanation to America's moral and spiritual decline. Alexander Hislop says: "wherever her worship was introduced, it is amazing what fascinating power it exerted. Truly, the nations might be said to be 'made drunk' with the wine of her fornication."[52]

The "Wine" of the Occult

Today, most of the masses of people in the United States and around the world regard Hollywood's exotic movies to be harmless entertainment. But a close examination of many of today's films reveals that they have become high-dollar propaganda productions for the occultists, radicals and secret societies of the Hollywood elite.

A decade ago, movies that displayed Masonic symbols were rare and far apart. In the last decade, however, masses of Americans, as well as masses of peoples around the world, have been deluged by movies displaying Masonic symbols.

For example, in *Conspiracy Theory* (1997), Mel Gibson, as a programed assassin turned cabbie, Jerry Fletcher, says, "I mean George Bush knew what he was saying when he said New World Order, you remember those fatal words, New World Order? Well he was a Thirty-third Degree Mason you know and an ex-director of the CIA." Julia Roberts, as a justice lawyer, Alice Sutton, says, "I suppose they have a secret handshake."

In *The End of Days* (1999), Arnold Schwartzenegger plays a former police officer who carries an amulet. At one point he says, "Now this amulet is from a Masonic Order in the former sub-heredom of the Vatican Knights, the Knights of the Holy See. They await the return of the dark angel to earth."

In *Erin Brockovich* (2000), featuring Julia Roberts, the cornerstone of the Barstow Courthouse displays a square and compass.

In *The Majestic* (2001), unrelated to the story, the square and compass symbol can be seen once on a mausoleum in the cemetery scene and once on a building on Main Street.

In *Bang Bang You're Dead* (2002), above a police station can be seen a square and compass.

In *Hollywood Homicide* (2003), featuring Harrison Ford, Keith David as Leon, Detective Joe Gavilan's supervising officer, wears a Masonic ring, clearly seen on the hand he's holding the phone with.

In *Bad Boys II* (2003), narcotics officers Mike Lowrey, played by Will Smith, and Marcus Bennet, played by Martin Lawrence, uses a tile installer's truck, with a square and compass sticker on the back door.

While some movies do not explicitly show Masonic symbols, hidden occult symbolism is still represented, such as in *The Lord of the Rings* (2001-2003), where the principles are traveling eastward and at one point pass between two pillars. Set in the mythological world Middle-earth, the three films follow Frodo Baggins, played by Elijah Wood, as he and a "Fellowship" embark on a quest to destroy the One Ring, and thus ensure the destruction of its maker, the Dark Lord Sauron.

In *The DaVinci Code* (2006), early in the film Tom Hanks, as Robert Langdon, stands in front of a display of "religious" symbols, including a Masonic square and compass. Langdon investigates a murder in Paris' Louvre Museum and discovers a battle between Priory of Sion (a secret society founded in 1099) and Opus Dei (an institution of the Roman Catholic Church) over the possibility of Jesus having been married to Mary Magdalene. At the end of the film, Langdon makes a passing reference to Freemasonry when he describes the symbols found in the Rosslyn Chapel.

In *National Treasure Two: Book of Secrets* (2007), artifact hunter Benjamin Franklin Gates, played by Nicholas Cage, Masonic references are limited to citations of a secret correspondence between Queen Victoria and Confederate General Albert Pike and a suggestion that the French Freemason Frederic Bartholdi incorporated a clue to the treasure in his design of his statue *Liberty Enlightening the World* because "Masons built clues into everything."

In *Into the Wild* (2007), directed by Sean Penn, both the Elks Hall and Masonic Temple in Fairbanks, Alaska, can be seen in the opening scenes.

In *Dance of the Dead* (2008), as zombies rise from the graveyard, a Masonic headstone is seen.

In *True Grit* (2010), Mattie, played by Hailee Steinfield, looks down at her dead father's belongings and among the items is a large gold square and compass emblem. An ashtray with a Masonic square and compass bordered by two pillars is also seen in half-shadow while Mattie is counting money.

For the elite of Masonry, the significance of the public display of occult symbols cannot be overstated. Foster Bailey, a Thirty-second Degree Mason, explains the esoteric power of Masonic symbols in his book entitled *The Spirit of Freemasonry*, saying: "A symbol veils or hides a secret, and is that which veils certain mysterious forces. These energies when released can have a potent effect."[53]

The "Wine" of Corporate Greed

In 2001, PBS (Public Broadcasting Station) ran a documentary on modern day American culture entitled *The Merchants of Cool*. The documentary focused on how young people have become the target of corporate America's $150 billion dollar dream. "Today," said the narrator, "five giant U.S. companies are responsible for selling nearly all of youth culture: Rupert Murdoch's Newscorp, Disney, Viacom, Universal Vivendi, and AOL/Time Warner."

These entertainment conglomerates, which own four of the five music companies that sell 90 percent of the music in the U.S. that is marketed domestically and internationally, also own all the film studios, all the major TV networks, all the TV stations in the 10 largest markets, and all or part of every single commercial cable channel.

In order to capture a large share of the "Mr. Cool" market corporate media executives have made the MTV channel the domestic and international champion of today's teens and preteens love for profane music, rebellion, and lust for pleasure and excitement.

Corporate executives openly admit that the motivation of these huge conglomerate companies is profit. "Everything on MTV is commercial," says one corporate executive. "There is no non-commercial part of MTV," whether it be marketing a soft drink, rap music, clothing, or a movie that's coming out of Hollywood. And unlike a few years earlier, there are no limits on the marketing of today's American "Gone Wild" culture.

With the advent of the Internet online pornography, every type of sexual experience, including child pornography, is literally only a *click* away from home computers. In many cases teenagers, as well as adults, don't have to go looking for it. They find their e-mail box filled with hardcore sexual images, which is a "protected right".

After extensive research, corporate executives found that by championing the *shocking* and *graphic,* the greater the response among teens and preteens. So whether the product being sold is a soft drink, clothing, music, or sex, the marketing idea is to make it as *shocking* and *graphic* as possible. Regardless of the "hook" being used, it is always followed by an ad to spend money on a movie, CD, DVD, Internet access, TV subscription, etc.

Remarkably, some two thousand years ago the Hebrew prophet of the Apocalypse wrote about a historic *Woman,* the deified queen of Babylon, Semiramis, who he *personified* as a great latter day nation code-named "Babylon," saying:

> 2 . . . and the inhabitants of the earth have been made drunk with the wine of her fornication (Rev. 17:2).

Reigns over the Kings of the Earth

> 18 And the woman which thou sawest is that great city, which reigneth over the kings of the earth (Rev. 17:18).

Continuing to employ the figure *Hypotyposis,* or *Word-Picture,* John gives his audience a visible *representation* of the dominance of the *Woman,* who he *personified* as a great latter day nation code-named "Babylon," over the rulers of the earth.

Arndt and Gingrich tell us that the Greek word for the term "reigneth," *basileiav,* means "royal," as in "the royal palace."[54] Moreover, the Greek term *basileia* comes from the same root or concept as *basileus,* which is derived from *basis* and means "to support," as in "the support of the people."[55]

Thus the point being made with the employment of the Greek term *basileia* conveys the idea of a great latter day nation code-named "Babylon" having a "royal palace," which reigns over the kings ('rulers') of the earth. In addition, *basileia* conveys the idea for the basis of that rule, which is "to support the people".

As you shall see, it can be established that John's vivid *description* of the *Woman's* reign over the rulers of the earth coincides precisely with America's dominance over the rulers of the earth.

The World Dominance of the White House

Immediately after World War II, it was from the White House that President Harry Truman, began America's huge postwar aid programs—the $13 billion dollar Marshall Plan for the re-building of Europe, and a similar foreign aid package for the re-building of Japan, which laid the groundwork for their economic and political resurgence as viable nations.

At that particular time the Organization for European Economic Cooperation was created to carry out the Marshall Plan, and successfully removed many economic controls and restrictions imposed by the war. By 1960, low-wage European merchants had flooded U.S. markets and the European people had achieved a new level of prosperity. In the process, the Europeans became financially dependent upon America's prosperity.

On the Pacific front, before World War II, the only cars on Japan's roads were U.S. imports. By 1970, with America's foreign aid and the lowering of tariffs on Japanese imports, Japan was selling a million cars in the U.S. Like Europe, Japan also became prosperous. And like the European people, the Japanese people became dependent upon American prosperity.

By the 1980s, as a result of President John Kennedy's Trade Expansion Act, U.S. trade concessions were also given to Third World countries, such as Hong Kong, Taiwan, Singapore, South

Korea, Indonesia, Malaysia, the Philippines, Thailand, and Latin America. In the process, like the peoples of Europe and Japan, the peoples of these countries also became dependent upon America's prosperity.

In the 1990s, Communist China, no longer able to resist the temptation of free enterprise, joined the other nations of the world and became one of America's biggest financial benefactors.

Then, in 1991, with the fall of the Soviet Union and the emergence of Russia's democratic reforms, the people of the new Russian state also became dependent upon billions of American dollars in the form of U.S. aid and business investments.

America's Dominance of the Rulers of the Earth

As a result of the removal of tariffs (taxes) on foreign imports and foreign aid the advocates of "Free Trade" have progressively built a global economy where the U.S. dollar dominates all other national currencies. Simply stated, in a world of almost 200 nations, the U.S. dollar has ruled since the end of World War II.

This means that since the presidency of FDR, each succeeding president has used the power of the U.S. dollar to influence the rulers ('kings') of the world to adopt U.S. policies. For example, in the Desert Storm War of 1991, from the White House, President George H. W. Bush brought together a coalition of 39 nations to join the U.S. in its war against Saddam Hussein. For most of these Muslim nations, their reason for joining the Bush coalition was not to unite in a common cause against Saddam Hussein. Rather, it was the U.S. dollar.

In the case of Egypt's participation, President Mubarak sent little more than an Egyptian flag to stick in the desert sand and received an $8 billion cancellation of U.S. debt. King Hussein of Jordan promised to stay out of the war and was rewarded $32 million to build a super four-lane highway across Jordan's desert sands. And King Assayd of Syria sent a handful of Syrian troops to join the battle for Bush's promise of $2 billion U.S. dollars.

In August 1991, an attempt to play down the White House's role in garnering international support for the Gulf War, a National Security Strategy of the United States report was personally signed by President George Bush, stating in part: "In the Gulf, we saw the United Nations playing the role dreamed of by its founders . . . . I hope history will record that the Gulf crisis was the crucible of the new world order."

Two months later, on October 1, 1991, an exuberant George Bush stood before the United Nations assembly and called on the rulers of nations to now support a "new world order of open borders and open trade."

Again, on March 25, 1999, after a heated comment from Russia's President Boris Yeltson, condemning President Bill Clinton's bombing of Serbia, the news media reported on Russia's "beggar-like" dependence on the United States. One reporter wrote that Russia's Prime Minister Stephashin had come to America with a "tin cup and an extended hand, hoping to repair relations with the United States and secure financial aid for his increasingly impoverished country."

In July 1999, in order to keep Israel on track to relinquish 13.1 percent of the West Bank (Judah/Sameria) to the Palestinian Liberation Organization (PLO), Clinton met with Israel's Prime Minister Ehud Barak and offered to increase military aid to Israel from $1.9 billion per year to $2.4 billion; promised U.S. financing for Israel's development of a third battery of Arrow anti-missiles; gave Israel permission to purchase 50 F-16 fighter jets; and promised the release of $1.2 billion dollars which the Clinton administration had suspended in response to former Prime Minister Benjamin Netanyahu's refusal to implement the Wye River Accords of 1998.

On July 20, 1999, President Bill Clinton traveled to Sarajevo, Bosnia-Herzegovina, to attend an international summit of some 40 nations, to consider a "stability pact" for bringing peace to the Balkins. To the surprise of most heads of state, Clinton submitted his own "stability pact," which included $700 million to help rebuild the area, which included a $150 million investment fund; a $200 million line of credit for business in the region; a regional equity fund; and a small business fund, most of which would be funded by the United States.

That same year, in November 1999, Clinton visited Bulgaria and offered $40 million dollars and U.S. incentives for businesses that invested in Bulgaria.

One month later, on December 10, 1999, when Russian President Boris Yeltson lashed out at President Clinton for his criticism of Russia's war in Chechnya, Clinton simply said: "I don't agree with what's going on there, and I think I have an obligation to say so." The next day, CNN's Wolf Blitzer reported on the dispute, saying: "U.S. officials know that Russia is dependent upon U.S. financing, and that's why the U.S. is not overly concerned."

On January 23, 2000, the *Associated Press* (AP) reported that a military coup to seize control of the government of Ecuador ended under pressure from the United States. The article stated in part:

> Ecuador's vice president assumed the presidency of this small Andean nation Saturday—ending, at least for now, a political crisis that exploded when Indian protestors aided by a cadre of junior military officers seized power and ousted a highly unpopular president.
>
> Vice President Gustavo Nobao's sudden ascension came after Ecuador's military chief, buckling to U.S. pressure, dissolved a three-man junta that had claimed power just a few hours earlier.
>
> . . . After military chief General Carlos Mendoza announced the end of the short-lived junta, he resigned from his army leadership post, saying . . . the decision to dissolve the junta was made after discussions with U.S. officials, who threatened to cut foreign aid and discourage investment if power was not restored to the elected government.

On May 9, 2001, the press reported that President George W. Bush warned the new Yugoslav president, Vojislav Kostunica, during his first visit to the White House, that U.S. aid to his country depended on Belgrade's cooperation to hand over former president Slobodan Milosevic to the U.N. war crimes tribunal at the Hague. Before leaving the White House, Kostunica assured President Bush that Belgrade would cooperate with the tribunal.

On June 27, 2001, the AP reported that U.S. pressure was key to Milosevic's extradition, saying:

Yugoslavia's president singled out U.S. pressure Tuesday as the main reason for his country's change of heart on extraditing Slobodan Milosevic to the UN war crimes tribunal.

. . . Washington has linked U.S. financial aid for Yugoslavia to Milosevic's extradition for trial for alleged Kosovo atrocities.

Keeping up the pressure for his handover, the United States has not said whether it will attend an international conference Friday in Brussels, Belgium, meant to raise the money Yugoslavia needs to rebuild after 13 years of misrule under Milosevic, Kostunica's predecessor.

On May 16, 2001, even Congress took action to pressure leaders of the Middle East to comply with an agreement previously made with Israel. The House passed a controversial amendment sponsored by Democratic Representative Tom Lantes of California that would withhold $625,000 dollars in aid to Lebanon until the country secured its borders near Israel. The measure, which passed 216 to 210, also directed the president to develop a plan for terminating millions of dollars in other aid if the Lebanese did not comply within six months.

On November 10, 2001, shortly after 9-11, the Pakistan president, General Pervez Musharraf, met with President Bush in New York City after attending a United Nations meeting and was offered a package of $1 billion in U.S. aid, debt reduction, a lifting of all U.S. sanctions, and a loan from the IMF for Pakistan's cooperation and assistance in America's fight against the Taliban and Al Qaeda terrorist network in Afghanistan.

At the same time, Sudan received the lifting of U.S. sanctions for joining the U.S. led coalition in the fight against terrorism, in spite of its horrible human rights record and well-known persecution of Christians.

During this same period, Jordan was given new free trade agreements with the U.S. for joining America's fight against terrorism. Before September 11, this would have been politically impossible due to disagreements over trade details.

In October 2003, Congress and the Senate jointly approved a spending bill of nearly $87 billion to rebuild Iraq and Afghanistan as democratic societies.

On November 6, this action to make the Middle East a democracy was followed by President George W. Bush's speech to the National Endowment for Democracy, where he called on the rulers ('kings') of Egypt, Iran, Saudi Arabia, and Syria to adopt democratic reforms, telling them: "it is the only path to national success and dignity."

Remarkably, some two thousand years ago the Hebrew prophet of the Apocalypse wrote about a historic *Woman*, the deified queen of Babylon, Semiramis, who he *personified* as a great latter day nation code-named "Babylon," saying:

> 18 And the woman which thou sawest is that great city, which reigneth over the kings of the earth (Rev. 17:18).

Makes Rich the Merchants of the Earth

> 3 . . . and the merchants of the earth are waxed rich through the abundance of her delicacies (Rev. 18:3).

Continuing to employ the figure *Hypotyposis,* or *Word-Picture,* John gives his audience a visible *representation* of the merchants of the earth who become rich through *commerce* and *trade* with the *Woman,* who he *personified* as a great latter day nation code-named "Babylon".

It is significant for us to understand that the Greek term for "merchants" (v. 3), *emporos* means "wholesale dealers" in contrast to *kapnlos* "retailer".[56] Here John is telling his audience that these merchants are not merely business people who sell their goods to the people of this great latter day nation code-named "Babylon". Rather, they are foreign "wholesale dealers," whose goods and products are manufactured in their own countries, and then brought to this great latter day nation to be sold by retail dealers.

Throughout history there have only been a few great nations which have had the economic prosperity capable of becoming the international trade centers of the world. In Daniel's day it was Babylon. In John's day it was Rome. In our day it is America.

As you shall see, it can be established that John's vivid *description* of the merchants of the earth becoming rich through their *commerce* and *trade* with the *Woman* coincides precisely with the "free trade" policies of the United States of America.

FDR's Apostle of "Free Trade"

Having been empowered by the Emergency War Powers Act of October 6, 1917, as amended by the Act of March 9, 1933, FDR gave his Secretary of State, Cordell Hull, a Brother Mason, free reign over America's trade policies.

As a member of the House Committee on Ways and Means, in 1913, Hull had drafted America's first income tax bill. His plan was to replace tariffs (taxes) on foreign imports with taxes on the labor and business transactions of the working people of American. For Hull, the American people's labor and business transactions were the one great untaxed source of revenue. And his job was to change that constitutional reality.

Under Hull, beginning 1934, tariffs were gradually phased out in favor of bilateral agreements. Within two years the State Department had negotiated bilateral tariff cuts with seven countries: Cuba, Belgium, Haiti, Sweden, Brazil, Canada, and the Netherlands. By the end of World War II, Hull's State Department had negotiated thirty-bilateral trade agreements.[57]

Thus began a sixty-year era of tariff cuts which would offer almost unrestricted access to U.S. markets by the wholesale merchants of the world. By 1990, customs duties that once produced 50-90 percent of U.S. revenue would produce only 1-2 percent. The benefits going to the wealthy American bankers, industrialists, and foreign wholesale merchants, while the lost tariff revenue to the government was made up by a progressive income tax placed on the working people of America.

After World War II, FDR's "Free Trade" doctrine was continued by the following Presidents: Harry Truman, Eisenhower, Kennedy,

Johnson and Nixon. President Ronald Reagan championed free trade with Canada. At the end of the Persian Gulf War, President George H. W. Bush announced the dawn of a new world order that would usher in a new era of free trade. And in 1993, under President Bill Clinton the long awaited NAFTA dream of the global elite became a reality, as Congress began selling their votes to the White House before the actual vote took place.

By this time America's trade deficit was already in serious trouble. In 1975, U.S. exports exceeded imports by $12.4 million, but that was the last trade surplus the U.S. would see. In 1987, the U.S. trade deficit was $153.3 million. In 2002, the U.S. ran a trade deficit of $484 billion. That same year the U.S. trade deficit with China alone was $103 billion. In 2003, it hit $124 billion. By mid-2004, the China deficit was approaching $150 billion a year. In 2011, China's trade deficit with the U.S. was $350 billion.

In 2003, the U.S. trade deficit hit $550 billion. By 2004, it was $600 billion.

In 1990, the U.S. cumulative trade deficit was $1.01+ trillion. In 2009, the U.S. cumulative trade deficit was $7.52 trillion.

Today, under the free trade policies of both Democrat and Republican administrations America has become the international trade center for the nations of the world, and the wholesale merchants of the earth have become rich beyond their wildest dreams.

Remarkably, some two thousand years ago the Hebrew prophet of the Apocalypse wrote about a historic *Woman,* the deified queen of Babylon, Semiramis, who he *personified* as a great latter day nation code-named "Babylon," saying:

> 3 . . . and the *emporos* ('wholesale merchants') of the earth are waxed rich through the abundance of her delicacies (Rev. 18:3).

The Slaves and Souls of Men

> 11 And the merchants of the earth shall weep and mourn over her; for no man buyeth their merchandise any more:

12 The merchandise of gold, and silver, and precious stones, and fine linen, and purple, and silk, and scarlet, and all thyine, wood, and all manner vessels of ivory, and all manner vessels of most precious wood, and of brass, and iron, and marble,

13 And . . . oil, and fine flour, and wine, and beasts, and sheep, and horses, and chariots, and *slaves* and *souls* of Men (Rev. 18:11-13).

Continuing to employ the figure *Hypotyposis,* or *Word-Picture,* John gives his audience a vivid *representation* of the "slaves" and "souls of men" who are connected to the *trade* and *commerce* of the *Woman,* who he *personified* as a great latter day nation code-named "Babylon".

Arndt and Gingrich inform us that the Greek term "slaves" (v. 13), *soma,* not only means "body" but is "often used by Greek writers for the bodies of men taken in war and made to be slaves, as in Revelation 18:13."[58] The Greek word for "souls," *pauche,* refers to the "life, spirit, and strength *of man.*"[59]

Equally significant, John writes the Greek word *swmatwv* ('salves') in the *genitive* case, which is the case of "belonging".[60] Simply stated, the use of the *genitive* shows an essential "relationship" between the term "slaves" and "wholesale merchandise". In other words, without the *swmatwv* ('slaves') there would be no great stream of wholesale merchants coming by ship to sell their goods and products to the peoples of this great latter day county code-named "Babylon".

As you shall see, it can be established that John's vivid *description* of the "slaves" and "souls of men," who are connected to the *commerce* and *trade* of the *Woman,* coincides precisely with the *commerce* and *trade* of the United States of America, which is made possible by the blood, sweat and tears of the working people of America.

The American People's Descent into Slavery

In 1909, William Howard Taft, a Mason, was elected to succeed Teddy Roosevelt, also a Brother Mason, having pledged himself to tariff reform. At that particular time progressive Republicans were beginning to join the camp of Democrat free traders, who demanded a cut in tariff rates.

After reaching a compromise agreement among the free traders and protectionists, a new issue dominated the debate: How was the lost tariff revenue to be replaced? The free traders set their sights on replacing the lost tariff revenue with a federal income tax. The historian William Gill writes: "The focus of the battle in Congress became not so much the tariff per se as the income tax which was to replace it."[61]

Until this time there had never been a personal income tax; only an indirect tax in times of national necessity to fund the government, such as during the Civil War. Congress introduced the income tax through the Revenue Act of 1861 and 1862, which levied a flat tax of 3-5 percent of people's income over $800. However, the Act also specified a termination of income tax in 1866, because the Constitution did not give Congress authority to place a permanent direct tax on the American people's property, labor, and business transactions. But that was about to change.

On June 16, 1909, with the Republican and Democrat free traders joining hands, President Taft, in an address to Congress, proposed a 2 percent federal income tax on corporations by way of an excise tax and a Constitutional amendment to allow a federal income tax. Congress adopted Taft's proposal by a 77-0 margin in the Senate and by 318-14 in the House.[62] The noted author and political analyst Pat Buchanan writes:

> This was a crucial moment in economic history. From Taft's initiative would come the Sixteenth Amendment and a permanent tax on the income of all Americans. This revenue engine would quickly replace tariffs as the prime source of federal income, and the immense stream of cash it would generate would be used to finance world wars, and expand federal power into every walk of American life. In one of the ironies of history, the federal income tax was the legacy of a Republican named Taft.[63]

A federal income tax amendment to the Constitution was first proposed by Senator Norris Brown of Nebraska, Senate Resolutions

No's 25 and 39. But neither resolution passed. The amendment proposal Senate Joint Resolution No. 40, introduced by Senator Nelson Aldrich, who was also the Senate Majority Leader and Finance Committee Chairman, was finally accepted.[64]

On July 12, 1909, the resolution proposing the Sixteenth Amendment was passed by the Sixty-first Congress and was submitted to the state legislatures.[65]

Oddly enough, support for a federal income tax was strongest in the western states and opposition was strongest in the northeastern states.

In 1910, New York Governor Charles Evans Hughes spoke out against the income tax amendment. While he supported the idea of a federal income tax, Hughes believed the words "from whatever source derived" in the proposed amendment implied that the federal government would have the power to tax state and municipal bonds. He believed this would excessively centralize governmental power and "would make it impossible for the state to keep any property."[66]

Nevertheless, from this point on the financing of the so-called "free trade" of America was placed squarely on the backs of the working people of America.

Remarkably, some two thousand years ago, the Hebrew prophet of the Apocalypse wrote about a historic *Woman,* the deified queen of Babylon, Semiramis, who he *personified* as a great latter day nation code-named "Babylon," linking its diverse international commerce to . . .

> 13 . . . the *soma* ('slaves') and *pauche* ('souls') of men
> (Rev. 18:13).

The Great Merchants of the Earth

> 23 . . . for thy merchants were the great merchants of
> the earth (Rev. 18:23).

Continuing to employ the figure *Hypotyposis,* or *Word-Picture,* John gives his audience a vivid *representation* of the great merchants of the *Woman,* who he *personified* as a great latter day nation code-named "Babylon".

Arndt and Gingrich inform us that the words "great merchants," in Greek, *megistaves,* which comes from the same root word *megas,* means "great men, rulers, *more prominent* or *outstanding* because of certain advantages."[67]

As you shall see, it can be established that John's vivid *description* of the "great merchants" of the *Woman* coincides precisely with the great merchants of the United States of America.

The Great Merchants of America

Today, when comparing American corporations with the corporations of the world there can be little doubt that the merchants of the U.S. are indeed the greatest merchants in the modern day world. According to the *Forbes Global 2000* magazine among the top 200 business leaders, from 2004 to 2012, the United States has by far the world's largest public corporations.[68]

For example, in only 200 of the world's largest public corporations listed in *Forbes Global 2000,* represented by 26 nations, the United States has three times more companies than its nearest competitor.[69] Among those 200 nations the top five nations, with a combined number of 64 companies, have a combined sales of $5,068.6 trillion, as compared to the United States, which has 60 companies that have a combined sales of $4,893.1 trillion. Those five nations are listed as follows:

China (14)	$940.8 B	United States (60) $4,893.1 T
Japan (14)	$1,092.6 T	
United Kingdom (13)	$935.6 B	
France (12)	$978.6 B	
Germany (11)	$1,121.0 T	
Total combined sales (64)	$5,068.6 T	Total U.S. sales (60) $4,893.1 T[70]

Among America's greatest merchants listed in *Forbes Global 2000* are the following top twenty:

Wall-Mart	285.22 B	Hewlett-Packard	81.85 B
ExxonMobil	263.99 B	Berkshire Hathaway	74.21 B
General Motors	193.45 B	Verizon Commun.	71.28 B
Ford Motor	170.84 B	Bank of America	65.45 B
General Electric	152.36 B	Procter & Gamble	54.19 B
Chevron Texaco	142.90 B	Boeing	52.46 B
ConocoPhillips	118.72 B	Pfizer	52.52 B
Citigroup	108.28 B	Fannie Mae	52.12 B
American Intl Group	95.04 B	JP Morgan	50.12 B
IBM	96.29 B	Johnson & Johnson	47.35 B[71]

For good reason, many of America's corporations have their headquarters in New York. Edward Ellis writes:

New York is one of man's greatest achievements. There has never been another city like it. Only superlatives can express its magnitude, power, and renown.

New York is the capital of the world because it contains the headquarters of the United Nations. It is the best known city on earth. It is the wealthiest city of modern times. Its influence is felt in every corner of this planet. It has the world's largest educational system. It is the biggest and busiest manufacturing city in the world. Robert F. Wagner once saying of New Yorkers "make more, sell more, buy more, eat more and enjoy more than the citizens of any other state in the world."

It is the financial capital of the world. It is the headquarters for most of the biggest corporations in existence.[72]

Remarkably, some two thousand years ago the Hebrew prophet of the Apocalypse wrote about a historic *Woman,* the deified queen of Babylon, Semiramis, who he *personified* as a great latter day nation code-named "Babylon," saying:

> 23 . . . for thy merchants were the *megistaves* ('great merchants') of the earth (Rev. 18:23).

By Her *Pharmakeia* all Nations were Deceived

> 23 . . . for by her sorceries were all the nations deceived (Rev. 18:23).

Continuing on with the employment of the figure *Hypotyposis,* or *Word-Picture,* John gives his audience a vivid *representation* of the deceptive and harmful effects of the "sorceries" of the *Woman,* who he *personified* as a great latter day nation code-named "Babylon".

It is significant for us to understand that John's employment of the Greek word *pharmakeia,* meaning "sorceries, magic," which is derived from the word *pharmakeus,* "mixer of poisons, magician," comes from the word *pharmakon,* meaning "a druggist ('pharmacist') or poisoner—a magician; a sorcerer."[73]

Equally significant, the Greek word *eplavntnsav,* meaning "to deceive," which is derived from *planao,* means "to lead astray, deceitful, deceitful spirit, imposter, *to roam from safety.*"[74]

In the ancient world it was believed that illness and disease were caused by evil spirits and could be cured by magic potions and sorcery. Ancient tablets inform us that the practice of *pharmakeia* goes all the way back to the ancient Babylonians.

The scholars of *The Illustrated Bible Dictionary* inform us that "prognostic magic, *i.e.,* divination," played an important role in the "defensive and curative" magic employed by magicians or sorcerers of Babylon to deliver people from affliction, illness, demonic possession, etc.[75] Moreover, the scholars of *Unger's Bible Dictionary* write:

> Magic may be divided into two classes—natural or scientific, and supernatural or spiritual—the one attributed its wonders to a deep, practical acquaintance

with the powers of nature; the other to celestial or infernal agency. But both systems seem to have taken their origin in traditional accounts of early miracles—in attempts to investigate how such miracles were performed, and whether it were possible or not to imitate them. The theory of atoms held by the Epicureans appear to have been the basis of most magical speculations.

It may be expressed somewhat after this manner: All changes in nature take place by the operation of atoms and must *ultimately,* therefore, be effected by mechanical action. Wherever man can substitute artificial action of the same kind, he can produce the same effects as those of nature. It required, in the first place, a knowledge of the mode in which nature acted; and, second, the power of applying the same agencies.[76]

With this understanding Man began to cure sickness and disease by trying to duplicate nature through the use of medical prescriptions, utilizing raw materials such as milk, snake skin, turtle shell; plants such as cassia, myrtle, asafoetida and thyme; and products of the willow, pear, fir, fig and date.[77]

The remedies prescribed were both salves and filtrates that were taken internally, often dissolved in beer.[78] The British archeologist Joan Oats tells us that ancient tablets indicate that the early Babylonians were acquainted with chemical operations and procedures, such as with "potassium nitrate (saltpetre)".[79]

Although the Babylonians attributed many diseases to demons in a patient's body, the practice of early medicine was often independent of incantations or spells. According to the Catholic historian John McKenzie, much of the magical formulae of Mesopotamia passed into Europe and has survived even in modern times, and that the ancient Babylonians seem to be the single most important source of "magical practice" in the western world.[80]

As you shall see, it can be established that John's vivid *description* of the deceptive and harmful effects of the "sorceries" (*'pharmakeia'*) of the *Woman* coincides precisely with the deceptive and harmful effects of the mega-prescription drug industry of the United States of America.

America's Prescription Drug Epidemic

While it cannot be disputed that modern medical science has developed many drugs that have benefitted mankind, several medical doctors are now beginning to publically come out against the medical profession's reliance on drugs as the cure-all for disease and illness. One such person is Dr. Arabella Melille, a doctor of psyco-pharmacology. Dr. Melille and Colin Johnson, a journalist and medical writer, state in their book entitled *Cured to Death:*

> Western medicine has made a fundamental error in allowing itself to become reliant on the universal use of drug therapy. It is an error of philosophy and of tactics. Our examination of the effects of prescription drugs on patients, doctors and institutions of health care has led us inevitably to this conclusion. Our statement runs counter to accepted wisdom, contradicts many popularly held beliefs and is contrary to the ideology and motivation of some of the largest and most powerful interests in the world. We are convinced that the evidence is irrefutable and cannot be interpreted in any other way. We ask you to consider the possibility that drugs, rather than helping or curing, are actually doing harm.
>
> It is true that through vaccination, some infectious diseases can be eradicated; that drugs provide effective therapy for previously fatal conditions and that analgesia and anesthesia make life more bearable. The problem is one of perspective. Drugs have become the predominant force in health care, to the detriment of other approaches.
>
> The spectacular beginning of the modern drug age may blind us to the fact that *all* drugs, whatever their virtues; are inherently dangerous.
>
> The nature of the substances that the pharmaceutical industry produces is such that, inevitably, unforseen disasters will happen.[81]

Given today's strong drug therapy culture, most people forget that drug companies are a profit making business, just like any other incorporated profit making business. And like any other business, the primary reason drug companies are in business is to make money. Lots of it!

In July 2004, the widely read *U.S.A. Today* ran a special article on major drug companies that were profiting from strong gains of cholesterol-lowering drugs and anti-depressants. No. 1 Pfizer reported that its revenue was $12.3 billion, up 24 percent from the same period last year. Pfizer's cholesterol drug, Lipitor, posted a 17 percent increase in sales to $2.4 billion. Revenue from the anti-depressant Zoloft grew 25 percent to $789 million. Merick saw its sales of Zocor, another cholesterol drug, rise 12 percent. Revenue reached $6 billion, up 9 percent from a year ago. The drug company Wyeth increased its sales of the anti-depression drug Effexor by 31 percent, increasing its revenues to $832 million. Wyeth's revenue rose 13 percent to $4.2 billion.

Unlike most foreign drug companies, American drug companies, which spend millions on lobbying Congress, are allowed to advertise their own products. Dr. John Abramson, a family M.D., who is on the clinical faculty of Harvard Medical School, tells us that in 1991 drug companies spent $55 million on advertising drugs directly to the public. During the next eleven years, drug companies increased their advertising budget to over $3 billion.[82]

Their advertising campaign worked. Consumers began forming their own opinions as to which drugs they believed they needed and began requesting, and then demanding, the latest drugs and tests advertised by the drug companies.[83]

The Gatekeepers

As a matter of public safety, in most countries, governments have established a degree of control over the activities of drug manufacturers, and to some degree monitor the uses to which their products are sold. For instance, in the United States drug manufacturers are regulated under the Food and Drug Administration (FDA).

Within the FDA there is a team of doctors, scientists and statisticians dedicated to evaluating the data provided by the drug companies, which seek to justify their claims as to safety and effectiveness of new drugs. But with the discovery of new drugs a new problem arose. As drug companies began to submit more and more drug products for approval, the FDA became understaffed, underfunded, and under greater pressure. One British journal, *The Lancet,* claimed that the FDA was being influenced by the drug companies so much that it had become "a servant of industry."[84]

While there are many examples of the drug industry's powerful influence on the FDA, one stands out in particular. In the late 1980s, due to the growing AIDS epidemic and the call from AIDS activists to find a quick cure, political pressure was put upon the FDA to speed up the process of approving new drugs. As a result, in 1992, Congress passed the Prescription Drug User Fee Act, which allowed drug companies to pay a $300,000 fee for each new drug application. In return, the FDA agreed to adhere to a speeder timetable for approving new drugs. Where the FDA normally took twenty months to approve a new drug, it now only takes six months.

Needless to say, these changes have resulted in a serious safety loss factor. For example, in 1993, the *Los Angeles Times* reported that new drugs were suspected of causing more than 1,000 deaths. According to the *Los Angeles Times,* "the FDA approved each of those drugs while disregarding danger signs or blunt warnings from its own specialists." Four years later, between 1997 and 2000, it was found that some 22 million Americans had taken a drug that later was withdrawn from the market.[85]

Prescription Drugs "Gone Wild"

Today, due to carefully crafted advertising, expensive drug lobbying (the drug industry presently has 625 lobbyists, more than one for each member of the House and Senate[86]), and manipulation of the media coverage, America is now experiencing a prescription drug abuse of epidemic proportions.

For example, on April 9, 2001, *Newsweek* featured a special report on America's abuse of prescription pain medication, stating that while the pharmaceutical market doubled to $145 billion between 1996 and 2000, the painkiller market tripled to $1.8 billion over the same period, and that in 1999 an estimated 4 million Americans used prescription pain relievers, sedatives, and stimulants.

Among the pain relievers used the most abused prescription drug included oxycodone, which contains potentially addictive opioids. Emergency Room (ER) Data revealed that there were dramatic rises of prescription drug abuse during this same time period. Emergency Room visits involving medications like Vicodin and Lortab jumped from an estimated 5,100 incidents in 1992 to more than 14,000 in 1999. Abuse of oxycodone pain relievers like Percodan and OxyCotin rose from 3,750 to 6,430, and the anti-anxiety drug Xanas increased from 16,000 to more than 20,500.

On April 10, 2001, the government reported that 4 million Americans were abusing prescription drugs, including sleep-deprived people who became addicted to sedatives, and family members who sell spare pills on the street.

On November 18, 2003, *U.S.A. Today* reported that in the past decade, the number of prescriptions written by doctors for narcotic pain relievers had increased an average of nearly 500 percent per drug.

On August 20, 2004, the FDA admitted that many of the anti-depressant drugs being prescribed to children may be causing thoughts of suicide and announced that it would take new steps to warn the public.

On August 30, the *Los Angeles Times* reported that in a study of prescription drug abuse, Duke University researchers found that about 21 percent of elderly patients had taken prescription drugs, such as anti-depressants, pain relievers such as Demerol, and sedatives such as Valium, that were known to cause harmful side effects in men and women over the age of 65.

On September 30, Merck, the maker of the pain reliever Vioxx announced that it was voluntarily withdrawing the drug because of new data showing it increases the risk of heart attacks and strokes. The officials of Merck reported that 84 million people worldwide had taken the heavily promoted drug, available in the U.S. since May 1999.

On August 17, 2006, Merck & Company was stung with two major legal setbacks over the withdrawn painkiller Vioxx when a federal jury ordered the drug-maker to pay $51 million to a heart attack victim, and a state judge in New Jersey overturned a November verdict favoring Merck & Company. The New Orleans jury found that Merck "knowingly misrepresented or failed to disclose" information about Vioxx to retired FBI agent Gerald Barnett's doctors.

In New Jersey, state Superior Court Judge Carol Higbee ruled evidence uncovered since the November verdict showed that Merck withheld information showing heart attacks could come with the use of Vioxx for less than 18 months. Merck had consistently maintained in the trial that a person had to be on Vioxx for 18 months to be at increased risk of a heart attack. Christopher Seeger's attorney said: "That was false. They had data that people were having heart attacks within weeks."

On November 1, 2011, Elizabeth Cohen, a senior medical correspondent, reported on CNN that the Center for Disease Control has just labeled deaths caused by prescription pain relievers to be an "epidemic," with 15,000 deaths in 2008 compared to only 4,000 deaths in 1999. The deaths from prescription pain relievers in 2008 were more than all the deaths from cocaine and heroin combined.

America's Drugstore Explosion

Since the turn of the new millennium, in order to keep up with the increased number of "Baby-boomers" now reaching their 60s, U.S. drugstore companies have been making plans for expansion. For example, on October 11, 2003, Walgreen Company, the parent company of the Walgreen drugstores, the largest drugstore chain in America, with 4,227 stores, announced plans to open 450 more stores in 2004. Eckerd, which has 2,720 stores in 21 states, announced its plans to open 250 new stores in the remaining six months of 2003. And CVS Corp., the nation's second largest drugstore chain, with 4,124 locations in 32 states, recently announced that it is looking at markets with "growing populations".

The primary motivation for this accelerated increase in drugstore expansion is, of course, profit. With "Baby-boomers" getting older, especially with today's strong emphasis on health care, the drug industry knows that the demand for prescription drugs will dramatically increase over the next few years. Today, it is estimated that America spends $183 billion a year on prescription drugs. This does not include the billions spent on over-the-counter drugs. Concerned medical doctors believe this spending on prescription and over-the-counter drugs will increase significantly in the next few years. And so will the American people's dependency on drugs.

America's Dominance of the International Drug Market

As earlier noted, the primary reason for the existence of drug manufacturers is profit. And like the need for prescription drugs, profit has no geographical boundaries. U.S. drug manufacturers have been engaged in marketing their drugs to an ever expanding worldwide market for several decades.

For example, in 1974, R.W. Lang, in his book entitled *The Politics of Drugs*, cited a report of America's Pharmaceutical Manufacturers' Association, saying: "The U.S. pharmaceutical manufacturers have 227 plants, 367 sales offices and 554 distributors in various parts of the world. Of the plants, 39 percent are located in Latin America and 29 percent in Europe."[87]

By the 1980s, three major U. S. pharmaceutical companies were firmly established in the following foreign countries:

Pfizer with subsidiaries in Argentina, Australia, Belgium, Brazil, Canada, Chile, Colombia, England, France, Germany, Greece, India, Italy, Japan, Mexico, Nigeria, Pakistan, Philippines, Spain, Sri Lanka, Taiwan, Turkey, Venezuela and Zimbabwe.

Merck with subsidiaries in Argentina, Australia, Bermuda, Brazil, Canada, Colombia, England, France, Germany, Holland, Hong Kong, Italy, Japan, Mexico, Pakistan, Panama, Peru, Philippines, South Africa and Thailand.

Sterling with subsidiaries in Argentina, Australia, Brazil, Canada, Chile, Colombia, Costa Rica, Dominican Republic, Ecuador, El Salvador, England, France, Ghana,

Guatemala, Honduras, Italy, Jamaica, Malayisa, Mexico,
New Zealand, Nicaragua, Peru, Philippines, Puerto Rico,
South Africa, Trinidad and Venezuela.[88]

By the end of the 1980s there was hardly a country in the
non-Communist world that did not have at least one United States
drug manufacturer's subsidiary. Even at that time, among the top 30
multinational drug manufacturers, the United States had three times
the drug subsidiaries of any other nation.[89]

The Overdosing of Pharmaceutical Companies

In another highly revealing work, Jay S. Cohen, M.D., author
of the book entitled *Overdose: The Case Against the Drug Companies,*
makes the case that U.S. pharmaceutical drugs are often harmful
because of inadequate research and poorly designed drug doses.

For example, Dr. Cohen points out that when birth control
pills were introduced in America, in 1960, they contained 300 to
600 percent more estrogen than necessary. Within two years there
were reported cases of blood clots in the legs, clots moving to the
lungs, strokes, and deaths. Dr. Cohen writes: "These and other side
effects were dose-related and could have been avoided if the drug
companies had taken the time to develop lower, safer doses—just as
birth control pills contain today."[90]

It took nearly a decade for medical research to establish that it
was birth control pills that were causing blood clots, heart attacks,
and strokes. During this time, millions of women continued to
receive high-dose birth control pills, with thousands developing
severe side effects, and hundreds dying.

At the same time the FDA did little to address the problem.
Instead, it was British researchers who established that it was
high-dose pills that were causing severe health problems, as well as
causing hundreds of deaths. Dr. Cohen writes:

> In Britain, the authorities didn't hesitate to act. By
> 1969, doctors were directed to use lower-dose pills, and
> by 1970 the high-dose pills virtually vanished from the
> British market.

Similar actions in other European countries led to a rapid drop in the number of serious reactions involving birth control pills. But in the U.S., rather than act directly to change the methods of the drug companies and doctors, the FDA simply added warnings to the package inserts and notified doctors by letters.[91]

Some will argue that the above case is merely an outdated example of how U.S. drug companies use to operate. But this is not true. Dr. Cohen documents a host of other drugs, such as Celebrex, Vioxx, Motrin, Prozac, Lipitor, Zocor, Viagra, Claritin, Allegra, etc., which have caused harmful side effects from improper research and poorly designed drug doses.

On the back cover of Dr. Cohen's book is the following statement: "This 'side-effect epidemic' is due mainly to unnecessarily high medication doses that are developed by drug companies and approved by the FDA."

For the peoples of third world countries the harmful side-effects of FDA approved prescription drugs is highly problematic since they can buy them over the counter like sweets or candy, with little or no monitoring.

Remarkably, some two thousand years ago the Hebrew prophet of the Apocalypse wrote about a historic *Woman,* the deified queen of Babylon, Semiramis, who he *personified* as a great latter day nation code-named "Babylon," saying:

> 23 . . . for by her *pharmakeia* ('sorceries') were all nations *eplavntnsav* ('led astray') (Rev. 18:23).

How Much She hath Glorified Herself

> 7 How much she hath glorified herself, and lived deliciously (Rev. 18:7).

Continuing on with the employment of the figure *Hypotyposis,* or *Word-Picture,* John gives his audience a vivid *representation* of the self-glorification and sensual lifestyle of the *Woman*, who he *personified* as a great latter day nation code-named "Babylon".

Arndt and Gingrich inform us that the Greek word for "deliciously," *streniao* comes from the same concept as *strenos,* meaning "to live in luxury, to live sensually."[92] The scholars of the *Complete Word Study New Testament* inform us that the words "how much," Gk. *osos,* is written as an *anarthrous,* whose primary function is to point out the *quality* of something, as in *quality* of life.[93]

In ancient Babylon, one of the major characteristics of the Babylonian people was that they were great builders. Scholars agree that during the golden age of Babylon's existence, Babylon was the most magnificent city in the ancient world. The hanging gardens Nebuchadnezzar built for his wife had rising terraces that supported full grown trees, which to the Greeks were one of the Seven Wonders of the ancient world.

The height of Babylon's glory as a great empire was relatively brief, about eighty-eight years. During that time Nebuchadnezzar spared no expense to make Babylon the most magnificent city in the ancient world.

Ancient tablets describe Babylon as great in size, beauty, and strength. The people's large two story homes, fashionable clothes, abundance of food, and prosperity were unequaled among the peoples of the ancient world. How appropriate are the words Daniel recorded of the great King Nebuchadnezzar as he stood in his palace overlooking Babylon, declaring: "Is this not Babylon the great, which I myself have built as a royal residence by the might of my power and for the glory of my majesty?" (Dan. 4:30).

As you shall see, it can be established that John's vivid *description* of the self-glorification and sensual lifestyle of the *Woman* coincides precisely with the self-glorification and sensual lifestyle of the United States of America.

American's Luxurious Lifestyle

Today, beyond any possible contradiction, the cities of America are the most magnificent in the world. Indeed, America's large homes, fashionable dress, abundance of food, prosperity, and luxurious lifestyle have made the American people the envy of the world. The following is a brief summary of what is now commonly referred to as "the American way of life".

The Accumulation of "Things"

In January 2000, the *Sacramento Bee* newspaper featured an article on the new American phenomenon: "Suburbia's new Toy Room: a four-car garage." One real estate agent said of the new growing demand for homes with a four-car garage: "People have a lot of toys these days—boats, jet skis, lawn mowers—so there is a big demand for it." The article went on to say that some four-car garages top 1,000 square feet—longer than a typical apartment, wide enough for a Ford Expedition, and deep enough for a squash court.

The Obesity Crisis

Another clear indication of the American people's sensual lifestyle is obesity. Today, two-thirds of the American people, more than 190 million Americans are overweight or obese. In fact, one out of every three children is either overweight or obese. During the last thirty years childhood obesity has tripled.

One of the primary reasons given for America's obesity crisis is that the American people have become a food driven society. Turn on the TV and one is bombarded with food and drink advertisements. Drive down the highway and there are endless miles of billboards advertising food, food, and more food.

In order to attract customers, restaurants, especially fast-food restaurants, have menus that include larger portions, bigger drinks, and all you can eat buffets. Regular hamburgers are now advertised as "the Whopper!" Ordinary burritos, tacos and soft drinks are now marketed as "the Super Burrito," "the Super Taco," and "the Super Drink!"

How serious is America's obesity problem? Obesity in America has become so serious that major corporations are now cashing in on it in a big way. America's grocery store shelves are filled with new products advertised as "Diet," "Fat Free," and "Healthy Choice". Restaurants, especially fast-food restaurants are now offering salads, fruits, and calorie labeled meals. TV commercials are filled with advertisements on weight-reducing programs that feature exercise DVDs, home gyms, and oil-free cookware.

Perhaps one of the best examples of cashing in on today's obesity crisis is the popular TV show called "The Biggest Looser". In the early 2000s the executives of NBC got together and came up with an idea for a show that has become one of TV's most successful programs. Obese men and women across America are recruited as contestants: women who weigh 250-400 pounds, and men who weigh 300-500 pounds. The idea is to see who can lose the most weight over a three month period where contestants participate in a supervised training program at what is called "The Ranch". At the end of the three month period the person who loses the most weight wins the title "Biggest Looser" and $250,000.

The Love of Pleasure

Perhaps the most poignant indicator of America's sensual lifestyle is the American people's insatiable appetite for pleasure.

Today, recreation, sports, and entertainment in America have become big business, with private business joining in partnerships with cities and states to gain commitments from major league sport teams and theme parks. For example, when Walt Disney opened his first theme park, in 1955, the city of Anaheim was little more than a back-water town of motels, fast-food restaurants, souvenir shops, and orange groves, with a population of 30,000 people. But after an investment of over $4.2 billion by Disney, the city of Anaheim, and the State of California, the back-water town of Anaheim has been converted into an international home-base for tourists and vacationers from around the world.

This was only the beginning. Recognizing the American people's appetite for greater thrills, on February 8, 2001, Disney opened a second theme park, *Disney's California Adventure,* on a 55-acre park, just a few hundred feet away from the original *Disneyland.* With this new theme park, Disney and the city of Anaheim have attracted some 7 million new visitors each year, on top of the 14 million per year that already visit *Disneyland.*

Government Spending

Today, one of the great issues in America is our national debt, which presently is an astounding $18.8 trillion, increasing at the rate of $4 billion dollars each day! Government spending is at an all-time high, and it appears that there is no end in sight. Economists agree that no nation in the history of mankind has spent the amount the United States annually spends on itself.

How did our country get in such dire financial straits? It was simple. With the passage of the Federal Reserve Act, in 1913, Congress handed over to the international banking cartel of the Federal Reserve the authority to create money out of nothing.

With FDR's "New Deal" for the American people, making the labor, business transactions, and property of the American people as security for the U.S. Treasury and the federal government's unlimited line of credit with the Federal Reserve, in 1933, America's plunge into the abyss of economic ruin was only a matter of time.

Beginning with 1969, each year Congress spent more money than its income revenues. What began as billions of dollars of indebtedness has now become double-digit trillions.

Thus for the past forty plus years the spending of Washington's elected officials has been out of control, and is now threatening the financial stability of both America and world economy. Not surprisingly, America's rapidly increasingly indebtedness now has many world leaders concerned.

For instance, on August 1, 2011, the Prime Minister of Russia (now President), Vladimir Putin, speaking to a pro-Kremlin youth group, said: "The U.S. is a living parasite of the global economy." Putin continued, saying that the U.S. is living beyond its means and "shifting a part of the weight of its problems to the world economy."

One of the best examples of America's self-glorification can be found in President Barack Obama's 2010 budget request, totaling $3.55 trillion, which can be broken down as follows:

Mandatory Spending: $2.173 trillion (+14% increase).
★ $695 billion (+4.9%)—Social Security.
★ $571 billion (+58.6%)—Other mandatory programs.

* $453 billion (+6.6%)—Medicare.
* $290 billion (+12%)—Medicaid.
* $164 billion (+18%)—Interest on National Debt.

Discretionary Spending: $1,378 trillion (a +13.8% increase)
* $663.7 billion (+12.7%)—Department of Defense.
* $78.7 billion (–1.7%)—Department of Health & Human Services.
* $72.5 billion (+2.8%)—Department of Transportation.
* $52.5 billion (+10.3%)—Department of Veterans Affairs.
* $51.7 billion (+40.9%)—Department of State.
* $47.5 billion (+18.5%)—Department of Housing & Urban Development.
* $46.7 billion (+12.8%)—Department of Education.
* $42.7 billion (+1.2%)—Department of Homeland Security.
* $26.3 billion (–0.4%)—Department of Energy.
* $26.0 billion (+8.8%)—Department of Agriculture.
* $23.9 billion (–6.3%)—Department of Justice.
* $18.7 billion (+5.1%)—National Aeronautics & Space Administration.
* $13.8 billion (+48.4%)—Department of Commerce.
* $13.3 billion (+4.7%)—Department of Labor.
* $13.3 billion (+4.7%)—Department of Treasury.
* $12.0 billion (+6.2%)—Department of the Interior.
* $10.5 billion (+34.6%)—Environmental Protection Agency.
* $9.7 billion (+10.2%)—Social Security Administration.
* $7.0 billion (+1.4%)—National Science Foundation.
* $5.1 billion (–3.8%)—Corps of Engineers.
* $5.0 billion (+100%)—National Infrastructure Bank.
* $1.1 billion (+22.2%)—Corporations for National & Community Service.
* $0.7 billion (0.0%)—Small Business Administration.
* $0.6 billion (–14.3%) General Services Administration.
* $11.0 billion (+275%) Potential Disaster Costs.
* $19.8 billion (+3.7%) Other Agencies.
* $105 billion—Other.[94]

Government Entitlements

Perhaps nothing better illustrates America's sensual driven lifestyle as the growing availability of government entitlements. Based on recent Means-Tested reports in the past twenty years there has been a dramatic increase in entitlement spending, such as follows:

1991: entitlements, such as welfare, food stamps, and housing, was 9 percent of federal spending.
2011: entitlements consumed 16 percent of federal spending—almost a 100 percent increase.
Sources: OMB and Census.

1991: 41 million people who lived in a household received federal aid outside of Medicare and Social Security.
2011: 107 million people who lived in a household received federal aid—an increase of 161 percent.
Sources: OMB and Census

1991: 23 million people received food stamps.
2011: 45 million people received food stamps—about a 100 Percent increase.
Source: USDA

Nov. 1992: 3.45 million people were on disability.
Nov. 2012: 8.8 million people were on disability—an increase of 154 percent.
Source: SSA

Interestingly enough, the possibility of this very scenario was predicted two hundred years ago by Thomas Jefferson and Alexander Hamilton, who agreed that when the public Treasury becomes a "trough," and when the voters realize this they will only send to the government people who promise to give them a bigger piece of the government Treasury. Today, Jefferson and Hamilton's "trough" case scenario has become a reality. For the first time in history, America has become an "Entitlement Nation": the government's entitlement spending has now reached over 50 percent of the American population.

Richard N. Rhoades

Government Debt

In January, 2009, at President elect Barack Obama's inauguration the National Debt was $10.6 trillion. As of December 16, 2015, the National Debt was $18.8 trillion, making President Obama's seven year $8.2 trillion increase nearly double the combined Debt of all previous presidents.

On the current financial course the debt deficit for 2021 is projected to be $22 trillion, but at the rate it is now increasing under Obama the economists are predicting that this number will easily be reached in the next two to three years.

Although other nations are in serious debt to the tune of billions, America is the only nation on earth whose debt deficit is measured in the trillions.

Remarkably, some two thousand years ago the Hebrew prophet of the Apocalypse wrote about a historic *Woman,* the deified queen of Babylon, Semiramis, who he *personified* as a great latter day nation code-named "Babylon," saying:

> 7 How much she hath glorified herself, and lived deliciously (Rev. 18:7).

Come Out of Her My People

> 4 And I heard another voice from heaven, saying, Come out of her my people, that ye be not partakers of her sins, and that ye receive not of her plagues (Rev. 18:4).

In this passage John employs the figure *Prosopographia,* or *Description of Persons,* giving his audience a vivid *representation* of the people Yahweh has called to leave the *Woman,* who is *personified* as a great latter day nation code-named "Babylon".

For most theologians, the term "My people" in the above passage is a direct reference to Christians to come out of some so-called evil worldwide system called *Ecclesiastical Babylon, Commercial Babylon,* and *Political Babylon.* For example, Dr. A. Plummer of the

326

Pulpit Commentary writes: "Since the harlot, who is identified with Babylon, is representative of the faithless part of the Church of God, these words form a direct warning to Christians."[95] And the Jewish author Steve Wohlberg says in his book entitled *Exploding the Israel Deception,* whose Foreword is written by Doug Batchelor, the Director of *Amazing Facts* radio and television ministries:

> Inside spiritual Babylon today are large numbers of true Christians who are serving the Lord to the best of their ability. This applies to many who are even now teaching false prophecy. Yet God still calls them "my people." The Lord mercifully sees them as part of His spiritual Israel. But they are confused! The word "Babylon" means "confusion." Because of today's global religious confusion . . . millions of the Lord's people now believe false theories about the end time. Yet according to Revelation 18:4, Jesus Christ is now calling us all to "come out" of spiritual confusion and *into the truth of His Word.*[96]

The problem with these analysis is that they interpret the words "My people" *spiritually* when they were meant to be taken *literally.* But even more important, they completely ignore the biblical use of the term "My people," which is an exclusive expression throughout the Scriptures for the physical people of Israel.

For example, the scholars of *Strong's Exhaustive Concordance* establish that the term "My people" is employed a total of 266 times in the Hebrew Scriptures, and is always used as a direct reference to the physical children of Israel. In the New Testament, with the one exception of 2 Corinthians 6:16, the term "My people" is found a total of 9 times as a direct reference to the physical children of Israel.

Yet, in spite of this overwhelming evidence, Christian scholars, prophecy teachers, and Bible students maintain that the words "My people," in Revelation 18:4, are a direct reference to Christian Believers to come out of some so-called evil worldwide system called "*spiritual* Babylon".

The noted Bible scholar and author Dr. S. Franklin Logsdon (1907–1987), former pastor of the Moody Memorial Church in Chicago, says of this misconception:

> Is this a call for the Church? No. A challenge for present-day believers? No. Of course, the Lord calls upon His people every day to separate from all deception and confusion, from all that is contrary to His holiness, but the Church, the members of the body of Christ (Colossians 1:18), are not in view here. They will have been caught up by this time to be with the Lord (1 Thess. 4:16). They will be gone from the scene. The alarm is divinely sounded, therefore, for His saved people of the Tribulation period.
>
> . . . And should the endtime nation that God has in view be the U.S.A., then it would mean that He will evacuate the Jews (at least those saved after the Church is raptured, together with all others who have believed the Gospel), even as He took righteous Lot out of Sodom before He let fall His hand of judgment upon that city.
>
> . . . Those who will pack up and leave and go to Palestine will have a striking testimony. We read, "The voice of them that flee and escape out of the land of Babylon, to declare in Zion the vengeance of the Lord our God . . ." (Jeremiah 50:28).[97]

The End-time Gathering of God's "Elect"

Some will argue that this end-time scenario could never happen because Matthew 24:29-31 plainly teaches that Christ will not return until "after the tribulation" to gather together His "**elect**". Quoting Yeshua's (Jesus) own words, Matthew writes:

> 29 Immediately after the tribulation of those days . . . .
>
> 30 And then shall appear the sign of the Son of man in heaven . . . .
>
> 31 And he shall send his angels with a great sound of a trumpet, and they shall gather together his **elect** from

the four winds, from one end of heaven to the other (Matt. 24:29-31).

The problem with interpreting the "**elect**" as being general, as meaning "all Believers," is that the Greek term Matthew uses for the word "**elect**" is *ekegomai;* Hebrew *bakhar,* meaning "to choose, select".

In Jewish thought, the "**elect**" or "**chosen**" are those selected for a particular purpose by someone. For example, the Hebrew Scriptures clearly teach that the people of Israel were chosen by God for a specific purpose on earth: 1) "God hath **chosen** thee to be a special people unto himself" (Deut. 7:6); 2) "The Lord hath **chosen** thee to be a peculiar people unto himself" (Deut. 14:2); 3) "O ye seed of Israel his servant, ye children of Jacob, his **chosen** ones!" (1 Chr. 16:13); 4) "The people whom he hath **chosen** for his own inheritance" (Ps. 33:12); 5) "O ye seed of Abraham his servant, ye children of Jacob his **chosen**" (Ps. 105:6); 6) "He brought forth his people with joy, and his **chosen** with gladness" (Ps. 105:43); 7) "For the Lord hath **chosen** Jacob unto himself, and Israel for his peculiar treasure" (Ps. 115:4); 8) "For Jacob my servant's sake, and Israel mine **elect** . . . ." (Isa. 45:4); 9) "I will bring forth a seed out of Jacob . . . mine **elect** shall inherit it" (Isa. 65:9); and 10)" . . . the days of my people, and mine **elect** shall long enjoy the work of their hands" (Isa. 65:22).

Thus when Christ spoke to the Jewish people of His day, saying, ". . . but for the **elect's** sake those days shall be shortened" (Matt. 24:22), who was He speaking about? In the historical context of that day there can be little doubt that the Jewish people would have understood Christ's use of the Greek term *eklegomai;* Hebrew *bakhar* to mean the redeemed people of Israel.

Did John understand this latter day Hebraic teaching on the gathering of God's "**elect**"? Indeed he did! Some two thousand years ago John wrote about a historic *Woman,* the deified queen of Babylon, Semiramis, who he *personified* as a great latter day nation code-named "Babylon," saying to its Jewish inhabitants:

4 . . . Come out of her My people, that ye be not partakers of her sins, and that ye receive not of her plagues (Rev. 18:4).

Her Sins have reached unto Heaven

5 For her sins have reached unto heaven, and God hath remembered her iniquities (Rev. 18:5).

Continuing on with the employment of the figure *Hypotyposis,* or *Word-Picture,* John gives his audience a vivid *description* of the "sins" of the *Woman,* who he *personified* as a great latter day nation code-named "Babylon".

Arndt and Gingrich inform us that the Greek word for "sin" is *amartia,* meaning "every departure from the way of righteousness, both human and Divine."[98] And the word "iniquities," *adiknma,* which is derived from *adikeo,* means "to *do wrong* of any violation of human or divine law . . . to be in the wrong, to do wrong to someone, to treat someone unjustly."[99]

Moreover, it is significant for us to understand that the operative word in verse 5 is the primitive Greek particle *gar,* meaning "for," which is the "assigning a *reason*" for what has already been stated, such as in verse 4: ". . . Come out of her my people, that ye be not partakers of her sins, and that ye receive not of her plagues." Employing the Greek particle *gar,* John goes on to say: "For her sins have reached unto heaven, and God hath remembered her iniquities" (v. 5).

With this understanding there can be little doubt that John's use of the Greek particle *gar,* meaning "for," establishes that the *amartia* ('sins,' meaning "the departure fr. the way of righteousness, both human and divine"[100]) and *adiknma* ('wrongdoing,' meaning "to do wrong to someone, the treating of someone unjustly"[101]) is related to the future *unjust treatment* of the Jewish people living in a great latter day nation code-named "Babylon".

Anti-*Semitism* in America

Many will argue that a violent outbreak of anti-*Semitism* against the Jewish peoples of America could never happen. But if the outbreak of anti-*Semitism* in Germany during the late 1930s to the mid-1940s teaches us anything it is a foreboding example of how quickly an entire nation's attitude towards its Jewish inhabitants can suddenly turn into a raging fire of anti-Jewish sentiment.

Contrary to the misconception of many, history concurs that when anti-*Semitism* began to raise its ugly head most of the educated and intellectual Jews of Germany refused to believe that their own lives, as well as the lives of their loved ones, family and friends, were in danger. But when their synagogues were burned; when their businesses were raided; when their homes were set on fire; when Chancellor Adolf Hitler declared that Jews were no longer German citizens; that Jews and Germans could no longer marry, or have intimate relations, they knew it was time to gather what belongings they could and leave Germany.

Today in America, beyond any possible contradiction, there is a concerted effort by the Liberal Left to appeal to people's feelings rather than sound reasoning; refuse to investigate the facts objectively and present them to the American people without bias and according to the rule of law. Instead, the Liberal Left's aim is to present only that aspect of truth which is favorable to their own side; censure and disregard all other facts and truth in opposition to their position; and use the liberal media to acquire and maintain political power, implement their own policies, and influence public opinion to accept those policies.

While we the People are being told by our elected officials that America is moving in the right direction, there is an ideological war now being waged for the soul of America and the forces of darkness, which we have already addressed, are in control and winning.

Equally troubling, accompanying the spiritual darkness that is now manifesting itself in America is a strong undercurrent of Jewish hatred. For example, from 1979 to 1989 there were more than 9,617 recorded Jewish hate crimes in America, which included 6,400 cases of vandalism, bombings and attempted bombings, arsons and attempted arsons, and cemetery desecrations.[102]

In June 2002, a nationwide survey released by the Anti-Defamation League (ADL) showed an increase in the number of Americans with anti-Jewish attitudes, reversing a ten year decline and raising concerns within the Jewish community that an under-current of Jewish hatred persists in America.

Between April 26 through May 26, 2002, a national poll of 1,000 American adults was conducted and found that 17 percent of Americans—about 35 million adults—hold strong anti-Jewish views. Nearly three-quarters, 72 percent, believe that Jews have too much power. The most anti-Jewish Americans were four times, 42 percent, as likely to believe that Jewish leaders have too much influence over U.S. foreign policy. The break-down of different ethnic groups is as follows:

* ★ 17 percent of Anglo Americans
* ★ 35 percent of Hispanics
* ★ 44 percent of foreign-born Hispanics
* ★ 20 percent of Hispanic Americans born in the U.S.
* ★ 35 percent of African-Americans.[103]

Among the anti-Jewish organizations are Christian Churches, including fundamentalist churches, the Nation of Islam, the Ayran-White Resistance, the Kuklux Klan, the American Nazis, and the gangs of skinheads.

On April 3, 2006, the U.S. Commission on Civil Rights reported that anti-*Semitism* is a "serious problem" on college campuses throughout the United States.

In 2010, the FBI reported that there were 1,147 hate crimes committed against American Jews and only 197 committed against American Muslims, making crimes of violence against Jews in America approximately 10 times greater than Muslims.[104]

For the first time, Jewish leaders are now saying that anti-Israel attitudes are triggering anti-*Semitism* in America. More than ever, the negative attitudes towards Israel and what is happening in the ongoing "land for peace" debate is fueling concern that American Jews have too much influence over U.S. Middle East policy.

Today, more than half of Americans, 51 percent, maintain that the U.S. has been tilting too much toward Israel, while three-quarters of the most extreme anti-Jewish Americans said they feel this way.[105] Abraham H. Foxman, the ADL National Director, recently said:

We have said that anti-Israel feelings are linked to anti-Semitism, and the responses from Americans in this poll make this connection clear. Anti-Israel sentiments are used in this country to fuel, legitimize and rationalize anti-Semitism.

. . . While there are many factors at play, all of the evidence suggests that a strong undercurrent of Jewish hatred persists in America.[106]

Remarkably, some two thousand years ago the Hebrew prophet of the Apocalypse wrote about a historic *Woman,* the deified queen of Babylon, Semiramis, who he *personified* as a great latter day nation code-named "Babylon," saying to its Jewish inhabitants:

4 . . . Come out of her My people, that ye be not partakers of her sins, and that ye receive not of her plagues.

5 For her *amartia* ('departure from the way of righteousness, both human and Divine') have reached unto heaven, and God hath remembered her *adiknma* ('unjust treatment of His people') (Rev. 18:4, 5).

"I Sit As A Queen"

7 . . . for she saith in her heart, I sit as a queen, and am no widow, and shall see no sorrow (Rev. 18:7).

Continuing on with the employment of the figure *Hypotyposis,* or *Word-Picture,* John gives his audience a vivid *description* of the *Woman,* who views herself as "queen of the nations".

As you shall see, it can be established that John's vivid *description* of the *Woman,* who says in her heart: "I sit as a queen," coincides precisely with how the Founding Fathers viewed the New Republic of the United States of America.

Today, there can be little doubt that America is viewed by most Americans, as well as most peoples of the world, as the greatest nation on earth. Indeed, with its majestic mountains, flowing rivers, beautiful lakes, fertile fields, great metropolitan cities, prosperity, learning and medical institutions, standard of living, and massive armed fortifications have made America the "queen of the nations" among the peoples of the earth.

History concurs that this is precisely how the elite of Freemasonry perceived the New Republic from its earliest beginnings as a sovereign State. As earlier noted, on March 25, 1780, Congress commissioned the second Great Seal committee that was comprised of the following Masons: John Scott of Virginia, James Lovell of Massachusetts, and William Houston of New Jersey,[107] to resolve the problem of the first committee.

On the reverse side they designed a seated figure of the Goddess Columbia, *personifying* the New Republic as a "sitting queen," holding a staff topped with the Phrygian slave's cap, with the word SEMPER ('eternal') above, and the date of the United States of America's Independence, in Roman numerals, below. (The accompanying illustration with the word "SEMPER," meaning "eternal," has been crossed out and above is written "Virtute prennis," meaning "Everlasting because of virtue".)

Second design of Reverse side of the Great Seal, 1780.

Remarkably, some two thousand years ago the Hebrew prophet of the Apocalypse wrote about a historic *Woman,* the deified queen of Babylon, Semiramis, who he *personified* as a great latter day nation code-named "Babylon," saying:

> 7 . . . for she saith in her heart, I sit as a queen, and am no widow, and shall see no sorrow (Rev. 18:7).

17

'BABYLON IS FALLEN, IS FALLEN'

18 And after these things I saw another angel come down from heaven, having great power: and the earth was lightened with his glory.

2 And he cried mightily with a strong voice, saying, Babylon the great is fallen, is fallen, and is become the habitation of devils, and the hold of every foul spirit, and a cage of every unclean and hateful bird (Rev. 18:1-2; AKJV).

HISTORIANS TELL US THAT ancient Babylon was the most fortified city in the ancient world. Alexander Hislop says that "it was Semiramis, the first deified queen of that city, who was believed to have 'surrounded Babylon with a wall of brick.'"[1] From that point on Semiramis was identified with Babylon as "the *goddess* of fortifications".[2]

Babylon's massive fortifications included an inner 300 foot double wall that was 85 feet thick, wide enough to race four chariots side-by-side at its top. The outer wall was 25 feet thick. Beyond the outer wall was a wide mote filled with water from the Euphrates. Between the inner and outer walls there was piled rubble. Watchtowers stood every 65 feet apart on the 300 foot walls.[3]

Throughout Babylon's brief history it was called "Babylon the Invincible". Yet, Babylon's demise came suddenly and unexpected by a militarily inferior people, the Medes and Persians, who devised a plan that brought an end to the great Babylonian Empire in a matter of hours of one day.

Upriver on the Euphrates River, at its lowest point, the Medes and Persians dug a channel to divert the flow of the river.[4] At a pre-selected time in the darkness of night, the channel was opened and water from the river was diverted so that the water flowing under the great walls of the city would subside enough to allow a small group of men to enter the city undetected and open the city gates from within.

Another important part of the plan was to launch the attack when the Babylonians were celebrating one of their festivals.[5] The Babylonians loved to celebrate holidays, which gave them a reason to enjoy their favorite pastime: feasting, drinking, and sexual orgies.

Apparently, the Jewish festivals were no exception. According to Daniel's account, the attack of the Medes and Persians took place after sundown on the appointed day of Yom Kippur.

Ancient tablets record that beer was the most favorite of their alcoholic beverages. The British archeologist Joan Oats tells us that the wheat and barley grown by the Babylonians not only provided flour for unleavened bread, but also the raw material for the brewing of beer. One ancient tablet stated that beer was "the liquid which 'makes the liver happy and fills the heart with joy.'"[6] Other alcoholic beverages were made from the dates of young palm trees[7], and the wine made from both red and white grapes.[8]

Evidently, the Medes and Persians knew the Babylonians would be celebrating this Jewish ten day fall festival between Rosh HaShanah and Yom Kippur. Moreover, because of their love of partying and revelry during festive occasions, they knew the Babylonians would be at their most vulnerable point when the Jewish festival ended at sundown on Yom Kippur.

Daniel records that Belshazzar, who had hosted a feast for a thousand of his nobles, ordered the golden vessels that were taken from the Temple by Nebuchadnezzar to be brought to the palace so that his princes, his wives, concubines, as well as Belshazzar himself, could drink from them and praise their gods. Daniel writes:

> 4 They drank wine, and praised the gods of gold, and of silver, of brass, of iron, of wood, and of stone.

5 In the same hour came forth fingers of a man's hand and wrote over against the candlestick upon the plaster of the wall of the king's palace: and the king saw the part of the hand that wrote.

. . . 26 This is the interpretation of the thing: MENE; God hath numbered thy kingdom, and finished it.

27 TEKEL; Thou art weighed in the balances, and art found wanting.

28 PERES; Thy kingdom is divided, and given to the Medes and Persians (Dan. 5:4-5, 26-28).

It is significant for us to understand that in Jewish thought, between the appointed festivals of Rosh HaShanah, which begins the civil New Year, and Holy Day of Yom Kippur ('Day of Atonement'), the Sages taught that Yahweh judges all of mankind, as well as nations, for all their deeds, whether good or bad.

According to the Sages, on Rosh HaShanah three books are opened: the book of the entirely righteous, the book of the entirely wicked, and the middle book, the book of the common. On Rosh HaShanah the righteous are inscribed in the book of the entirely righteous and sealed to live; the wicked are inscribed in the book of the entirely wicked and sealed to die; and the fate of those found in the middle book are held in the balance for the ten days of repentance between Rosh HaShanah and Yom Kippur. At the end of that ten day period, at sundown on Yom Kippur, if those found in the middle book have repented, they will live. If not, they are inscribed in the book of the wicked and sealed to die.

As a Torah observant rabbi, Daniel was well prepared to interpret the meaning of the writing on the wall of Belshazzar's palace. The words "Thou art weighed in the balances, and art found wanting" (v. 27), tells us precisely when the "Hand Writing Event" took place. It was after sundown on Yom Kippur, shortly after Belshazzar, his wives, concubines, and one thousand nobles drank from the golden vessels taken from the Temple to celebrate the end of the ten days of repentance, when God judges the nations of the earth.

Today, most people view those ten days of repentance between Rosh HaShanah and Yom Kippur as merely another festive Jewish season. Most certainly, Belshazzar and his drunken guests held this view *until* the fingers of "The Hand" appeared on the wall of the palace and began writing.

Daniel records that Belshazzar's "countenance changed, and his thoughts troubled him, and his loins were loosed, and his knees knocked against one another" (v. 6).

At that moment Belshazzar offered a third co-equal rulership of his kingdom to anyone who could tell him the meaning of what he had just witnessed (v. 7). Clearly this was a momentous event in the life of the king, as well as the Babylonian Empire. Belshazzar had just been confronted with the Divine significance of the appointed Holy Day of Yom Kippur; something he knew absolutely nothing about!

The real tragedy of Belshazzar's "Hand Writing Event" is that it did not have to happen. One of the greatest Jewish rabbis of all time was at his beckoning call—Rabbi Daniel, who would have been more than willing to instruct Belshazzar in the appointed festivals and righteous ways of the Lord. Instead, like his predecessors, Belshazzar put his trust in the council of the Chaldeans, the prognosticators, the astrologers, and Babylon's many soothsayers.

Unfortunately, when Belshazzar finally called upon Daniel it was too late. Too late for Belshazzar himself! Too late for his wives and children! Too late for his nobles! Too late for his generals! Too late for his thousands of valiant warriors! Too late for his great Babylonian Empire!

The Divine decree had been made at the close of the appointed Holy Day of Yom Kippur: written on the wall of the king's palace by "The Hand" of Yahweh Himself.

For Babylon's Jewish inhabitants, however, the Divine decree of Yom Kippur was a much different matter. Instead of a death sentence, it meant freedom. No longer would the Jewish exiles have to live in a land where they were daily being subjected to the idolatry, pagan customs, and false gods of Babylon. Their seventy years of captivity were over. They were now free to return to their beloved homeland in Israel. And most important, they could now begin to rebuild the sacred Temple.

The Fall of Latter Day "Babylon"

> 17 Alas, alas, that great city that was clothed in fine
> linen, and purple, And scarlet, and decked with gold, and
> precious stones, and pearls!
> 18 For in one hour so great riches is come to naught
> (Rev. 18:17–18).

Much like the fall of ancient Babylon, brought about by the
Medes and Persians, John tells his audience that the fall of this great
latter day nation code-named "Babylon" will also be sudden and
unexpected.

Although we are not told how "Babylon's" destruction will take
place, John gives his audience an important clue, saying:

> 8 Therefore shall her plagues come in one day, death,
> and mourning, and famine; and she shall be utterly
> burned with fire . . . .
> 9 And the kings of the earth . . . shall bewail her, and
> lament for her, when they shall see the smoke of her
> burning.
> 10. Standing afar off for her torment, saying, Alas, alas,
> that great city Babylon, that mighty city! for in one hour
> is thy judgment come.
> . . . 15 The merchants of these things shall stand afar
> off for the fear of her torment, weeping and wailing.
> . . . 17 . . . And every shipmaster, and all the company
> in ships, and sailors, and as many as trade by sea, stood afar
> off.
> 18 And cried when they saw the smoke of her
> burning, saying, What *city is* like unto this great city! (Rev.
> 18:8, 9, 10, 15, 17, 18).

Once again, John employs the figure *Hypotyposis,* or *Word-Picture*[9]
to give his audience a vivid *description* of the destruction of this great
latter day nation code-named "Babylon".

So here is the great question: Given the above vivid *description*
of the shipmasters and sailor's horror at seeing the "burning and

bellowing clouds of fire, smoke and dust" rising thousands of feet in the sky above this great latter day nation code-named "Babylon," what modern day example could it possibly represent? The answer is both obvious and ominous: there can be little doubt that the most potent modern day example of this ancient prediction is the U.S. atomic bombing of Hiroshima, on August 6, 1945.

On August 6, the people of Hiroshima awoke to a day just like any other. People dressed, went to work, and children went to school. Streets were crowded, shops were busy and, in spite of the war, the people of Hiroshima were getting on with their lives. Yet, history records that August 6, 1945, was a day unlike no other day in the history of Hiroshima, as well as for mankind.

Early that morning, three U.S. B-29s took off from North Field air base on Tinian (about six hours from Japan): the destination—the city of Hiroshima. One B-29, the *Enola Gay*, was loaded and armed with the world's first atomic bomb called "Little Boy".

At 9:15 A.M., it was "bombs away". At 9:16, Little Boy detonated 1,900 feet above the city of Hiroshima, resulting in a fireball that sent two shock waves in all directions at a velocity greater than the speed of sound, analogous to the sound of thunder generated by lightening.

Little Boy exploded with the force of 20 tons of TNT, 2,000 times the power of the largest bomb previously known to Man. The enormous blast was followed by a violent wind that destroyed everything in its path.

The first visible effect of the explosion was blinding light, accompanied by a radiant heat from the fireball. A large mushroom cloud rose above what once had been a city. Under the base of that huge cloud the entire city of Hiroshima was covered with boiling clouds of fire, smoke, and dust.

In four minutes the huge cloud had climbed 23,000 feet, turning different colors as it rose into the air. It is estimated that for a few seconds, at its core, the temperature reached 15 million degrees F.

The fireball was roughly two miles in diameter. At ground zero the temperature generated by the fireball was 9,000 degrees F., which was accompanied with an intense neutron and gamma radiation "fall out" known as **Black Rain** that was propelled into the atmosphere from the fireball.

The *Enola Gay* was 360 miles away from Hiroshima before the crew finally lost site of a massive mushroom cloud that was still boiling upwards.

It is believed that some 75,000 people were killed instantly. Many were vaporized. Sixty-three percent of Hiroshima's buildings were obliterated.

Most people close enough to receive lethal doses of direct radiation died in the firestorm. Some who initially survived died soon afterward due to acute radiation sickness. For others, the effects of radiation increased the incidence rates of cancer, leukemia, and other diseases.

Three days later, on August 9, the U.S. dropped the second atomic weapon "Fat Man," with a slightly bigger atomic payload, over the city of Nagasaki.

Atomic bomb mushroom clouds over Hiroshima (left) and Nagasaki (right).

As bad as the destructive power in the above photos, the weapons used in the atomic bombing of Hiroshima and Nagasaki were only a fraction of the destructive payload of today's nuclear weapons. For example, just one Russian R-36M (SS-18), a variant of the largest ICBM in history, the R-36 (SS-18 Satan), has the capacity to mount a payload of 10 warheads, each with a 550-750kt blast yield, as compared to the 16kt blast yield of Little Boy, and 21kt yield blast of Fat Man.

With today's advanced nuclear weapons, military experts have calculated that it would take only 23 minutes for Russian land-launched ICBMs to hit American targets. For submarine ICBMs launched off our coast the estimated time is only 6 minutes. As to the success of such an attack, weapon experts tell us that the explosion of one Electro Magnetic Pulse (EMP) bomb 200 miles above the earth's atmosphere could knock-out all systems of electronic communication, making the U. S. highly vulnerable to a massive ICBM first strike attack from an enemy nation(s).

Several military experts believe that an EMP attack on the U.S. is a very real possibility. The national security advisor and author Frank Gaffney, who held senior positions in the Ronald Reagan Defense Department, and is founder of the Washington, D.C.—based Center for Security Policy, says in his book entitled *War Footing:*

> The technological advances that make us an unequaled military and economic superpower are also the source of our gravest vulnerability.
>
> In a world wracked by terrorists and their state sponsors, America's strength has become a tempting target. And EMP technology may represent an irresistible opportunity.
>
> An EMP attack would target the very source of our technology achievements—the electronic circuit—as a way of bringing us to our knees. And it would do it by unleashing its own massive storm, in the form of a kind of rogue electromagnetic current. This tactic perhaps has a special appeal for the Islamofascists. Our enemies are undoubtedly also aware of these additional tactical considerations:

★ An EMP attack could severely degrade our ability to retaliate . . . .

★ Although U.S. forces deployed overseas might avoid damage in such an attack, the systems that transmit their orders and sustain their operations would almost certainly be disrupted.[10]

Simply stated: an EMP attack on the United States would disrupt all forms of communication, including military communications.

For those who understand the significance of an EMP attack on the United States there is little doubt that a single bomb exploding 200 miles above our atmosphere could be followed by a massive ICBM attack from an enemy nation(s) that could carpet-bomb the entire nation with ICBMs armed with multiple warheads, suddenly destroying the U.S.A. in "one hour".

Given this scenario, would not the knowledge of massive radiation fall-out from such an attack cause incoming merchant ships, their shipmasters and sailors, to stay far away from America's shores? Would not such a scenario cause these same merchants, shipmasters, and sailors to weep and mourn as they watched massive fireball clouds and smoke bellowing up into the sky from the explosive burning? Would not there be panic among the rulers and peoples of the world, especially in Europe, as they watched satellite images of "the smoke of her burning"? Would not that panic present the perfect opportunity for the "man of sin, the son of perdition" ('Antichrist') to step onto the stage of history and present a plan to the special appointed representatives of nations (ten in number) that would save their nations from a similar fate? And with the fate of those nations hanging in the balance, would not those ten representatives be compelled to immediately hand over their government's decision making authority to such a man?

Addressing this very scenario, John writes: "The ten horns which you saw are ten kings who have not yet received a kingdom, but they receive authority as kings with the beast for one hour. These have one purpose, and they give their power and authority to the beast" (Rev. 17:12-13; NASV).

For most theologians and Bible students, Revelation 17 & 18 is a mystery that can only be understood figuratively. The problem with this analysis is the failure to understand that in ancient times figures were understood as *literal*.

How are we to know when the words of Scripture are to be taken *literally*? As earlier noted, Dr. Bullinger informs us that the words of Scripture, written as figures, are to be understood as *literal*, except when a statement appears to be contrary to a known fact, or revealed truth.

Thus it is significant for us to understand that hundreds of years before the writing of Revelation 17 & 18 the Hebrew prophet Zechariah predicted the Divine judgment of the *Woman* known among the faithful followers of Yahweh as "Wickedness," whose image would be built, erected and set upon its own pedestal in a latter day country code-named "the land of Shinar" ('Babylonia') (Zech. 5:8-11).

Remarkably, some two thousand years ago the Hebrew prophet of the Apocalypse wrote about a historic *Woman,* the deified queen of Babylon, Semiramis, who he *personified* as a great latter day nation code-named "Babylon," saying:

> 2 Babylon the great is fallen, is fallen . . . . For in one hour so great riches is come to naught . . . for in one hour is she made desolate . . . . Thus with violence shall that great city Babylon be thrown down, and shall be found no more at all (Rev. 18:2, 17, 19, 21; AKJV).

The Great "Babylon" Debate

Today, in spite of the above evidence, many argue that both the *Woman,* "great whore," and "Babylon" of Revelation 17 & 18 is the Roman Catholic Church; that Papal worship, saint worship, and Mary worship are rooted in ancient Babylon worship; and that the "great whore," and "woman arrayed in purple and scarlet color" . . . that sits on seven hills (Rev. 17:4, 9), is proof that Rome is the ancient city of the apostate Church.

Others maintain that the *Woman,* "great whore," and "Babylon" of Revelation 17 & 18 is an evil worldwide system called *Ecclesiastical Babylon, Commercial Babylon,* and *Political Babylon,* which Christians are somehow "to come out of".

Then there are those who teach that the *Woman,* "great whore," and "Babylon" of Revelation 17 & 18 is a historic wicked city that will be rebuilt in the last days, such as when Saddam Hussein began to rebuild the ancient city of Babylon, in Iraq. For example, in 1971, when plans were announced by Iraq to rebuild Babylon according to its ancient architectural designs, and stating that funds were being provided by Iraq, many theologians and prophecy students believed they were witnessing the emergence of the great city of Babylon written about in Revelation 17 & 18.

Taking note of the renewed interest in the "Babylon" of Revelation 17 & 18, on October 11, 1990, the *New York Times* featured an article on the rebuilding of the former great empire of Babylon by Saddam Hussein, saying: "Under President Saddam Hussein, one of the world's most legendary cities has begun to rise again. More than an archeological venture, the new Babylon is dedicated to the idea that Nebuchadnezzar has a successor in Mr. Hussein, whose military prowess and vision will restore the Iraqis the glory their ancestors knew when all of what is now Iraq, Syria, Lebanon, Jordan, Kuwait, and Israel was under Babylonian control."

Bible teachers began preaching that the predicted "Babylon" of Revelation 17 & 18 had finally arrived. Dr. Charles Dyer, a professor of Bible exposition at Dallas Theological Seminary, wrote a book entitled *The Rise of Babylon: A Sign of the End Times.* On the book's back cover Dr. Dyer says: "Regardless of what happens to Saddam Hussein, the Bible makes it clear that Babylon will be rebuilt. The Middle East is the world's time bomb, and Babylon is the fuse that will ignite the events of the end times."[11]

Still, others maintain that both the *Woman,* "great whore," and "Babylon" of Revelation 17 & 18 is simply a mystery that cannot be understood. For example, the noted Bible teacher and author Noah Hutchings wrote a book at the beginning of the twenty-first century entitled *U. S. in Prophecy,* addressing the late Dr. Franklin Logsdon's book entitled *Is the U.S.A. in Prophecy?* (1968), which claims that America is indeed the latter day Babylon of Scripture. After well-over one hundred pages of debating the merits of Dr. Logsdon's claim, not only did Dr. Hutchings acknowledge his failure to understand the "Mystery" of "Babylon," he attributed the same lack of understanding to the late Dr. Franklin Logsdon, saying: "The Babylon of Revelation 17 & 18 is a mystery. Perhaps no one, including Dr. Logsdon and myself, has completely uncovered this mystery."[12]

Given all this confusion we should not be surprised that most Americans have absolutely no idea that America's exaltation of the Masonic Goddess statue *Liberty Enlightening the World/Statue of Liberty* is linked historically and biblically to the pagan cult worship of the Great Goddess of antiquity.

This, my friend, is the "Ancient Mystery" Bartholdi and the elite of Freemasonry have kept hidden from the people of America. But even more important, this is the "Ancient Mystery" Yahweh revealed to the Hebrew prophets over two thousand years ago.

Perhaps Dr. Logsdon put it best when he said the following:

> It seems strange that more consideration has not been accorded this subject. As I have spoken on the theme in cities across the country, there has been much interest evidenced, with the attendance swelled not infrequently to an overflow. People want to know, as never before, just what God has to say about our great nation. And—what does He have to say?
>
> The prevailing attitude in this connection seems to be, not that God has not spoken, but where and how has He spoken? How may one know?
>
> This is not an enigma. If God has spoken on any matter, He wants His people to know about it. Revelation is for information. Such information, with the assistance of God's guidance, is obtained by studying. Studying is searching. This we are commanded to do.[13]

Endnotes

Lady Liberty: The Ancient Goddess Of America
Preface
1. Albert G. Mackey, *Lexicon Of Freemasonry*, (China: Midas Printing International, Ltd., reprint 2004), p. 194.
2. Ibid.
3. Ibid., p. 195.
4. A. Ralph Epperson, *New World Order*, (Tucson, AZ: Publius Press, 1995), p. 152.
5. Albert Pike, *Morals and Dogma of the Ancient and Accepted Scottish Rite of Freemasonry*, (Richmond,VA: L. H. Jenkins, Inc., 1919), pp. 104-105.
6. Ibid., p. 819.

Part I Ancient Foundations Of The Great Goddess
Chapter 1 Ancient Land Of Shinar
1. Harry Thomas Frank, gen. ed., *The Atlas of the Bible*, "World of the Patriarchs," (Pleasantville, NY: Reader's Digest Association, 1981), pp. 50-54.
2. Ibid.
3. Ibid., p. 54.
4. *Jewish Encyclopedia. Com.*, "Babylon," http://www.jewishencyclopedia. com.htlm
5. Merrill F. Unger, *The New Unger's Bible Dictionary*, "Babel," (Chicago, IL: Moody Press, 1988), p. 133.
6. Ibid.
7. J. D. Douglas, gen. ed., *The Illustrated Bible Dictionary*, "Babel," (Wheaton, IL:Tyndale House Publishing, 1978),Vol. I, p. 155.

8. *Encyclopedia Judaica,* "Babel," (Israel: Keter Publishing House Jerusalem Ltd., 1978),Vol. IV, p. 24.

9. Cunningham Geikie, *Hours With The Bible,* (New York, NY: James Pott & Company, 1899),Vol. I, pp. 218-219.

10. *Encyclopedia Judaica,* Vol. IV, p. 25.

11. Ibid.

12. Frank, *Atlas of the Bible,* p. 10.

13. Ibid.

14. Ibid., pp. 10-11.

15. Jacob Bryant, *A New System; or, an Analysis of Ancient Mythology,* Vol. I, http://www.gutenberg.org/files/19153/19193-0.txt.htlm

16. Alexander Hislop, *The Two Babylons,* (England: A & C Black, 1916), pp. 26-27.

17. Ibid., p. 25.

18. *Jewish Encyclopedia. Com.,* "Nimrod".

19. Hislop, pp. 24-25.

20. Matthew Henry, "Genesis 10," http://www.studylight.org/ matthewhenry/commentaries/genesis.htlm

21. Geikie, p. 222.

22. Hislop, p. 51.

23. Ibid.

24. Pausanias, lib. ii.; *Corinthiaca,* cap. 15, p. 145; cited by Alexander Hislop, p. 51.

25. Gaius Hyginus, *Fab.* 143, p. 114; cited by Alexander Hislop, p. 51.

26. Lutatius Placidus, in *Stat. Theb.,* lib. iv. v. 589, *apud* Bryant, vol. iii. p. 65; cited by Alexander Hislop, p. 51.

27. Hislop, p. 51.

28. Ibid., p. 52.

29. Ibid.

30. Ibid., p. 55.

31. Ibid., p. 63.

32. Ibid.

33. Ibid., p. 64.

34. Ibid., pp. 66-67.

35. Ibid., p. 67.

36. Ibid.

37. John Gardner Wilkinson, *Manners And Customs Of The Ancient Egyptians,* (London: 1837),Vol.V, p. 326.

38. Eusebe Salverte, *Des Sciences Occultes,* chap. xxvi, p. 428; cited by Alexander Hislop, p. 9.

39. Hislop, p. 144.

40. Ibid.

41. Mustafa El-Amin, *Al-Islam, Christianity, and Freemasonry,* (Jersey City, NJ: New Mind Productions, 1985), p. 115.

42. Hislop, p. 57.

43. Ibid., p. 30.

44. Ovid, *Opera,* vol. iii.; *Fasti,* iv. 219-221; cited by Alexander Hislop, p. 30.

45. Austen Henry Layard, *Nineveh and Its Remains,* (New York, NY: George B. Putman, 1849),Vol. II, pp. 456, 457.

46. Bryant, Vol. I, http://www.gutenberg.org/files/19153/19153-0.txt. htlm

47. George Rawlinson, *Five Great Monarchies of the Ancient Eastern World,* (New York, NY: Dodd, Mead & Company, 1870),Vol. I, pp. 119-120.

48. Hislop, p. 75.

49. Ibid., p. 74.

50. Dionusiaca, lib. xli., in Bryant, Vol. III, p. 226; cited by Alexander Hislop, p. 75.

51. Hislop, p. 30

52. Ibid., pp. 85-86.

53. Ibid., pp. 5-6.

54. Ibid., p. 30.

55. Ibid., pp. 59, 78.

56. Ibid., p. 30.

57. Ibid., p. 52.

58. Bryant, Vol. I, http://www.gutenberg.org/files/19153/19153-0.txt. htlm

59. Unger, *Unger's Bible Dictionary,* p. 537.

60. *Smith's Bible Dictionary,* http://www.bible-history.com/assyria-archeology. htlm

61. Hislop, p. 77.

62. Ibid., p. 20.

63. Ibid., p. 77.

64. Ibid., p. 69.

65. Ibid.

Chapter 2 Great Goddess Of The Nations

1. Hislop, 20.
2. Ibid., pp. 20-21.
3. Ralph Edward Woodrow, *Babylon Mystery Religion,* (Riverside, CA: Ralph Woodrow Evangelistic Association, 1966), p. 7.
4. Ibid.
5. Marcus Bach, *Strange Sects and Curious Cults,* (New York, NY: Dodd & Mead Publishers, 1961), p. 12.
6. Ibid.
7. Rawlinson, Vol. I, p. 139.
8. Unger, *Unger's Bible Dictionary,* pp. 536-537.
9. Hislop, pp. 74-75.
10. Unger, *Unger's Bible Dictionary,* p. 484.
11. Hislop, p. 74.
12. Unger, *Unger's Bible Dictionary,* p. 484.
13. Ibid., pp. 484-485.
14. Ibid., p. 485.
15. Ibid.
16. Ibid.
17. Layard, *Nineveh and Its Remains,* Vol. II, p. 345-346.
18. Ibid., p. 346.
19. James Orr, gen. ed., *The International Standard Bible Encyclopedia,* (Grand Rapids, MI: William B. Eerdmans Publishing Company, 1939), Vol. II, p. 842.
20. Ibid.
21. Mircea Eliade, gen. ed., *The Encyclopedia of Religion,* "Diana," (New York, NY: Macmillan Publishing Company, 1987), Vol. IV, p. 349.
22. Ibid.
23. Ibid.
24. Ibid.
25. Ibid.
26. *Encyclopedia Americana,* "Libertas," (Danbury, CN: Grolier Inc., 1994), Vol. 17, p. 302.
27. Ibid.
28. Barry Moreno, *The Statue of Liberty Encyclopedia,* (New York, NY: Simon & Schuster, 2000), p. 142.
29. Salem Kirban, *Satan's Angels Exposed,* (Chattanooga, TN: AMG Publishers, 1980), p. 50.

Chapter 3 Great Goddess Of Two Continents

1. Frank, *Atlas of the Bible,* p. 152.
2. Merrill C. Tenney, *New Testament Times,* (Grand Rapids, MI: William B. Eerdmans Publishing Company, 1965), p. 117.
3. Cliff Hillegass, *Mythology,* (Lincoln, NB: Cliffs Notes, Inc., 1991), pp. 59-60.
4. Norman Davies, *Europe,* (New York, NY: HarperCollins Publishers, Inc., 1998), p. 89.
5. Ibid., p. xix.
6. Ibid., pp. 22, 98, 102-103.
7. Noah Webster, *The Original Webster's Unabridged Dictionary,* "Europe," (USA: The Dictionary Publishing Company, 1901), p. 413.
8. Hillegass, p. 25.
9. Davies, p. 103.
10. Ibid.
11. Winkie Pratney, *Devil Take The Youngest: The War on Childhood,* (Shreveport, LA: Huntington House, Inc., 1985), p. 30.
12. Manly P. Hall, *The Secret Teachings of All Ages,* (Los Angeles, CA: The Philosophical Research Society, 1977), p. 48.
13. Davies, p. 260.
14. Rawlinson, Vol. II, p. 119.
15. Hislop, p. 52.
16. Pratney, pp. 36-37.

Part II Modern Foundations Of The Great Goddess
Chapter 4 Freemasonry In Early America

1. Michael Baigent & Richard Leigh, *The Temple And The Lodge,* (New York, NY: Arcade Publishing, Inc., 1989), p. 201.
2. Ibid., p. 202.
3. Ibid., p. 203.
4. Ibid.
5. Ibid., p. 222.
6. Ibid.
7. Ibid.
8. Ibid.
9. Ibid.
10. Ibid.
11. Ibid., pp. 222-223.

12. Ibid., p. 211.
13. Vicomte Leon de Poncins, *Freemasonry And The Vatican,* (Hathorne, CA: Omni Book Club, 1968), pp. 50–51.
14. Manly P. Hall, *America's Assignment With Destiny,* (Los Angeles, CA: The Philosophical Research Society, Inc., 1951), pp. 49–50.
15. Manly P. Hall, *The Secret Destiny Of America,* (Los Angeles, CA: The Philosophical Research Society, Inc., 1944), pp. 133.
16. William Still, *New World Order,* (Lafayette, LA: Huntington House Publishers, 1990), p. 60.
17. Ibid., p. 59.
18. *Holy Bible, Masonic Edition,* (John A. Hertel Company, 1951), p. 49.
19. Still, p. 63.
20. Ibid.
21. Nesta Webster, *World Revolution: The Plot Against Civilization,* Anthony Gittens, edit., (Palmdale, CA: Omni Publications, 1921), p. 23.
22. Ibid., p. 87.
23. *Freeman Digest,* "Thomas Jefferson," (Salt Lake City, UT: The Freeman Institute, 1981), p. 83.
24. Kirban, p. 151; also see "United States Presidents and the Illuminati/ Masonic Power Structure," http://www.theforbiddenknowledge. com/roberthoward.htlm
25. Robert Howard, "United States Presidents and the Illuminati/ Masonic Power Structure," http://www.theforbiddenknowledge. com/roberthoward.htlm
26. Marie Bauer Hall, *Collections of Emblemes, Ancient and Moderne,* by George Wither, (Los Angeles, CA: Veritat Foundation, 1987), p. 10.
27. From an inscription in the entrance of the George Washington Masonic National Memorial in Alexandria, VA.
28. Baigent & Leigh, p. 261.
29. Henry C. Clausen, *Masons Who Helped Shape Our Nation,* (San Diego, CA: Neyenesch Printers, 1976), p. 12.
30. Ibid.
31. Ibid.
32. Ibid., p. 84.
33. Ibid.
34. Ibid.

35. Robert Howard, "United States Presidents and the Illuminati/ Masonic Power Structure," http://www.theforbiddenknowledge. com/roberthoward.htlm
36. Baigent & Leigh, pp. 261-262.
37. Ibid.
38. Ibid.
39. David Ovason, *The Secret Architecture Of Our Nation's Capital: The Masons And The Building Of Washington, D.C.,* (New York, NY: HarperCollins Publishers, 2000), p. 67.
40. Ibid.
41. Ibid.
42. Ibid., p. 72.
43. Clausen, p. 4.
44. Hall, *America's Assignment With Destiny,* p. 95.
45. Clausen, p. 9.
46. Baigent & Leigh, p. 219.
47. Clausen, p. 12.
48. Stephen Knight, *The Brotherhood,* (Briarcliff Manor, NY: Stein and Day Publishers, 1984), p. 34.
49. Joseph Ritner, *"Vindication of George Washington from the Stigma of Adherence to Secret Societies,"* (Anti-Masonic Phamplets, September 18, 1837), p. 26.
50. Ibid.
51. Epperson, *New World Order,* p. 164.
52. *Wikipedia. Com.,* "Phillis Wheately," http://www.wikipedia.com/ philliswheately.htlm
53. Marshall Cavendish, *Man, Magic and Myth: The Illustrated Encyclopedia of Mythology, Religion and the Unknown,* (New York, NY: Marshall Cavendish Corporation, 1995),Vol. 14, p. 2002.
54. *History Channel.Com.,* "The Founding Fathers," http://www. historychannel.com/foundingfathers.htlm
55. Hislop, pp. 5, 30.
56. Cavendish,Vol. 14, p. 2002.
57. Ovason, pp. 45-47.
58. Ibid., pp. 42-43.
59. *Encyclopedia Americana,* "Obelisk," (1972),Vol. 20, pp. 558-559.
60. Epperson, *New World Order,* p. 100.
61. Ovason, p. 351.

62. Ibid., pp. 488-493.
63. Ibid.
64. Ibid., pp. 28-29.
65. R. A. Coombs, *America, the Babylon: America's Destiny Foretold in Biblical Prophecy,* (Topeka, KS: Gilliland Printing, 1998), p. 209.
66. *History Channel. Com.,* "The Founding Fathers."
67. Ovason, p. 257.
68. Ibid.
69. Ibid.
70. Ibid., p. 253.
71. Mort Reed, *Cowles Complete Encyclopedia of U.S. Coins,* (New York, NY: Cowles Book Company, Inc., 1969), p. 3.
72. Ibid., p. 4.
73. Ibid.
74. Ibid., p. 5.
75. Ibid.
76. Ibid.
77. Ibid., p. 6.
78. Ibid.
79. Max Toth, *Pyramid Power,* (New York, NY: Warner Destiny Books, 1979), p. 24.
80. *History Channel.Com.,* "The Founding Fathers."
81. Reed, p. 7.
82. Epperson, *New World Order,* p. 145.
83. Texe Marrs, *Dark Majesty: The Secret Brotherhood and the Magic of a Thousand Points of Light,* (Austin, TX: Living Truth Publishers, 1992), p. 220.
84. F. Tupper Saussy, *Rulers of Evil,* (New York, NY: HarperCollins Publishers, Inc., 2001), p. 212.
85. Ibid., p. 213.
86. Ibid.
87. Hall, *Secret Teachings,* p. 140.
88. Epperson, *New World Order,* pp. 138-139, as quoted from *A Bridge To Light* by Rex Hutchens, published by the Supreme Council in 1988.
89. Ibid., p. 140.
90. Ibid., pp. 143-145.
91. Pike, *Morals and Dogma,* pp. 14-15.

92. C. William Smith, *New Age Magazine,* "God's Plan in America," Sept. 1950, p. 551.
93. Pike, *Morals and Dogma,* p. 321.
94. J. Edward Decker, Jr., *The Question of Freemasonry,* (Issaquah, WA: Free the Masons Ministries, nd), p. 6; also quoted by Cathy Burns, *Hidden Secrets of Masonry,* (Mt. Carmel, PA: Sharing Publishers, 1990), p. 27.
95. Reed, p. 25.
96. Ibid., p. 20.
97. Still, pp. 24-25.
98. Arthur Edward Waite, *A New Encyclopedia of Freemasonry and of Cognate Instituted Mysteries: Their Rites, Literature and History,* (New York, NY: Weathervaine Books, 1970), Vol. II, p. 110.

Chapter 5 Seeds Of World Revolution

1. *Wikipedia. Com.,* "Nesta Webster," http://www.wikipedia.com/nestawebster.htlm
2. Webster, *World Revolution,* p. 8.
3. Rousas Rushdoony, *The Nature of the American System,* (Fairfax, VA: Thoburn Press, 1965), p. 135.
4. A. Ralph Epperson, *The Unseen Hand: An Introduction Into The Conspiratorial View Of History,* (Tucson, AZ: Publius Press, 1985), p. 7.
5. Webster, *Original Webster's Unabridged Dictionary,* p. 254.
6. Epperson, *The Unseen Hand,* p. 7.
7. Antony C. Sutton, *America's Secret Establishment: An Introduction to The Order of Skull and Bones,* (Billings, MT: Liberty House Press, 1986), p. 3.
8. Hall, *Secret Destiny of America,* pp. 23-24.
9. Webster, *World Revolution,* p. 18.
10. *Wikipedia. Com.,* "Thomas More," http://www.wikipedia.com/thomasmore/utopia.htlm
11. *Encyclopedia Americana,* "Pathagoras," (1972) Vol. 23, pp. 45-46.
12. Mackey, p. 384.
13. Hall, *Secret Teachings of All Ages,* p. 40.
14. Webster, *World Revolution,* p. 34.
15. John W. Drane, gen. ed., *The Lion Encyclopedia of the Bible,* (London: Lion Publishing, 1978), pp. 294-295.
16. Waite, Vol. I, pp. 61-61.
17. Ibid., p. 175.

18. Nesta Webster, *Secret Societies and Subversive Movements,* (Palmdale, CA: Omni Publishers, 1924), pp. 31-32.
19. Ibid., p. 30.
20. Edith Starr Miller, *Occult Theocracy,* (Hawthorne, CA: The Christian Book Club of America, reprint 1980; orig. pub. 1933), p. 34.
21. Webster, *World Revolution,* p. 18.
22. Ibid., p. 23.
23. Webster, *Secret Societies,* pp. 197-198.
24. Webster, *World Revolution,* p. 26.
25. Ibid., p. 23-24.
26. Ibid., p. 24.
27. Ibid., p. 25.
28. Ibid., p. 34.
29. Ibid., p. 24.
30. John Robinson, *Proofs of a Conspiracy,* (Boston, MA: Western Islands edition, reprint 1967), p. 112.
31. Ibid., p. 92.
32. Ibid., p. 125.
33. Vicomte Leon de Poncins, *The Secret Powers Behind Revolution: A Struggle for Recognition,* Timothy Tindal-Robertson, trans., (Hawthorne, CA: Omni Christian Book Club, reprint 1968), p. 15.
34. Webster, *World Revolution,* p. 31.
35. Ibid.
36. Ibid., p. 36.
37. Ibid., p. 37.
38. Ibid.
39. Webster, *Secret Societies,* pp. 259-263.

Chapter 6 French Revolution 1789

1. Webster, *World Revolution,* p. 41.
2. Douglas Johnson, *The French Revolution,* (New York, NY: G. P. Putman's Sons, 1970), pp. 38-39.
3. Webster, *World Revolution,* p. 44.
4. Ibid.
5. Ibid., p. 46.
6. Ibid.
7. Johnson, p. 104.
8. Webster, *World Revolution,* p. 47.

9. Ibid., p. 22.
10. Ibid.
11. Robert H. Bork, *Slouching Towards Gomorrah: Modern Liberalism and American Decline,* (New York, NY: Regan Books, 2003), p. 276.
12. Webster, *World Revolution,* pp. 50-51.
13. Ibid., p. 51.
14. Ibid., p. 52.
15. Eugene Schroder, *Constitution: Fact or Fiction,* (Cleburne, TX: Buffalo Creek Press, 1995), pp. 36-37.
16. Ibid., p. 37.
17. Webster, *World Revolution,* p. 56.
18. Johnson, p. 90.
19. Michael Kennedy, *The Jacobin Clubs in the French Revolution (1793-1795),* (Berghahn Books, 2000), p. 176.
20. Henry Gouremetz, *Historical Epochs of the French Revolution,* (Hard Press, 2006); http://www.scribd.com/doc/2379520/historical-epochs-of-the-french-revolution.htlm
21. Ann Coulter, *Demonic: How The Liberal Mob Is Endangering America,* (New York, NY: Crown Forum, 2011), p. 119.
22. Ibid., p. 115.
23. Stanley K. Monteith, "The Population Control Agenda," http://www.radiolibrary.com.htlm
24. Ibid.
25. Ibid.
26. *Guttmacher Institute,* "Fact Sheet," http://www.guttmacher.org/pubs/fb-induced- abortion,htlm
27. Monteith, "The Population Control Agenda."
28. Webster, *World Revolution,* p. 209.
29. Ibid., p. 47.
30. Ibid., p. 208.
31. Ibid.
32. *McGuffey's Eclectic Readers,* (New York, NY: American Book Company, Revised Editions; orig. pub. 1879, 1896, 1907 and 1920).
33. *McGuffy's Eclectic Primer,* "Lesson LI," (New York, NY: Van Nostrand Reinhold, Revised Edition; orig. pub., 1881, 1896, 1909), pp. 58-59.
34. Stanley Monteith, *Brother of Darkness,* (Oklahoma City, OK: Hearthstone Publishing, 2000), pp. 73-74.

35. Paul Fisher, *Behind the Lodge Door,* (Rockford, IL: Tan Books and Publishers, Inc., nd), p. 244.
36. Jim Nelson Black, *America Adrift,* (Fort Lauderdale, FL: Coral Ridge Ministries, 2002), pp. 49-50.
37. *Jefferson's Letter to the Danbury Baptist Association*—Library of Congress Information Bullitin.
38. Fisher, p. 130.
39. Still, p. 90.
40. Bork, pp. 193-197.
41. Ibid., pp. 205-206.
42. Webster, *World Revolution,* p. 59.
43. *New York Times,* "French Pique," July 1, 2000.
44. Webster, *World Revolution,* p. 60.
45. Ibid.
46. Still, p. 116.
47. Johnson, p. 94.
48. Ibid.

Chapter 7 Revolution Comes To America
1. Still, p. 92.
2. Ibid.
3. Ibid.
4. Ibid., p. 87.
5. Ibid., pp. 87-88.
6. Ibid.
7. Ibid., p. 88.
8. Ibid., p. 90.
9. Kirbin, p. 150.
10. Ibid., p. 151.
11. Still, p. 93.
12. Des Griffin, *Descent Into Slavery,* (Pasadena, CA: Emissary Publications, 1980), p. 135.
13. Eugene Schroder, gen. ed., *War and Emergency Powers: A Special Report on the National Emergency in the United States of America,* (Dallas, TX: American Agriculture Movement, nd.), pp. 17-18.
14. Schroder, *Constitution: Fact or Fiction,* p. 66.
15. Still, p. 93.
16. Ibid.

17. Ibid., p. 94.
18. Ibid., p. 95.
19. Ibid.
20. Ibid., p. 97.
21. Epperson, *New World Order,* pp. 163-164.
22. Webster, *World Revolution,* pp. 85-86.
23. Ibid., p. 86.
24. Still, pp. 96-97.
25. Webster, *World Revolution,* pp. 86-87.
26. Ibid., p. 87.
27. Peter Kershaw, *Economic Solutions,* (Boulder, CO: Quality Press, 1994), p. 8.
28. Eustace Mullins, *The Secrets of the Federal Reserve,* (Staunton, VA: Banker Research Institute, 1991), p. 59.
29. James W. Wardner, *The Planned Destruction of America,* (DeBary, FL: Longwood Communications, 1994), p. 29.
30. Kershaw, p. 8.
31. Still, p. 147.
32. James Perloff, *The Shadows of Power: The Council on Foreign Relations and The American Decline,* (Appleton, WI: Western Islands, 1988), p. 21.
33. Dallas Plemmons, *The Illuminati,* (self-published tract, 1979), p. 4.

Chapter 8 The Federal Reserve
1. Griffin, *Descent Into Slavery,* p. 37.
2. Perloff, p. 22.
3. Ibid.
4. *Saturday Evening Post,* "Farm Boy to Financier," Frank Vanderlip, February 8, 1935.
5. Perloff, p. 22.
6. Mullins, p. 34.
7. Wardner, pp. 27-28.
8. William Guy Carr, *Pawns In The Game,* (Palmdale, CA: Omni Publications, nd.), p. 155.
9. Wardner, p. 28.
10. Davvy Kid, *Why A Bankrupt America?,* (Arvada, CO: Project Liberty, 1993), pp. 5-6.
11. Archibald E. Roberts, *The Most Secret Science,* (Ft. Collins, CO: Betsy Ross Press, 1984), p. 32.

12. Louis T. McFadden, *Collective Speeches as Compiled from the Congressional Record,* (Hawthorne, CA: Omni Publications, 1970), p. 239.
13. Ibid., p. 342.
14. Ibid., p. 298.
15. Kershaw, p. 8.
16. McFadden, *Collective Speeches,* p. 342.
17. Wardner, p. 24.
18. Kershaw, p. 15.
19. Wickliffe B.Vennard, *The Federal Reserve Hoax: The Age of Deception,* (Palmdale, CA: Omni Publications, nd.), p. 286.
20. Perloff, p. 57.
21. Ibid., p. 56.
22. Schroder, *War and Emergency Powers,* p. 15.
23. Ibid., p. 15, Exhibit 30 & 31.
24. Ibid., p. 16, Exhibit 31.
25. Ibid., p. 17, Exhibit 32.
26. Ibid., Exhibit 33.
27. Ibid., p. 415, Exhibit 19.
28. Ibid., p. 410, Exhibit 17.
29. Ibid., pp. 80–82, Exhibits 38 & 39.
30. Ibid.
31. Ibid.
32. Ibid.
33. Ibid., p. 5, Exhibit 9.
34. Ibid., p. 18, Exhibits 32 & 33.
35. Ibid., p. 7.
36. Ibid., p. 6, Exhibit 11.
37. Ibid., p. 22.
38. William Greider, *Secrets of the Temple,* (New York, NY: Simon & Schuster, 1987), p. 51.
39. Roberts, p. 31.
40. Kershaw, p. 6.
41. Epperson, *The Unseen Hand,* p. 174.
42. Kershaw, p. 3.
43. Greider, pp. 61–62.
44. Larry Bates, *The New Economic Disorder,* (Orlando, FL: Creation House, 1994), p. 140.

45. Martin Mayer, *The Fed,* (New York, NY: Penguin Group, 2002), p. 232.
46. Ibid., pp. 234-235.
47. Ibid., p. 239.
48. Ibid.
49. Ibid.
50. Ibid.
51. Greider, p. 48.
52. Hislop, pp. 30-31.
53. *Complete Word Study Old Testament, The,* (Iowa Falls, IA: World, 1994), Lexical Aids, #7562, p. 2368, #7564, p. 2367.

PART III American Foundations Of The Great Goddess
Chapter 9 'Let's Offer The Americans A Statue Of Liberty'

1. Christian Blanchet & Bertrand Dard, *Statue of Liberty: The First Hundred Years,* (New York, NY: American Heritage, 1985), p. 16.
2. Richard H. Schneider, *Freedom's Holy Light,* (Nashville, TN: Thomas Nelson, 1985), p. 21.
3. Blanchet & Dard, p. 44.
4. Barry Moreno, *The Statue of Liberty Encyclopedia,* (New York, NY: Simon & Schuster, 2000), p. 94.
5. Schneider, pp. 23-25.
6. Blanchet & Dard, p. 26.
7. Ibid., p. 24.
8. Marvin Trachtenberg, *Statue of Liberty,* (New York, NY: Penguin Books, 1974), pp. 54-55.
9. Ibid.
10. Blanchet & Dard, p. 17.
11. Trachtenberg, p. 43.
12. Ibid., p. 51.
13. Schneider, p. 31.
14. Ibid.
15. Ibid.
16. Unger, *Unger's Bible Dictionary,* p. 134.
17. Hislop, p. 52.
18. *Wikipedia. Com.,* "Feronia," http://www.wikipedia.com/feronia.htlm
19. Hislop, p. 52.
20. Ibid., p. 69.

21. Ibid., p. 75.
22. Moreno, p. 144.
23. Trachtenberg, p. 79.
24. Ibid., p. 71.
25. Ibid., p. 63.
26. Ibid., p. 22.
27. Ibid., p. 80.
28. Ibid.
29. Blanchet & Dard, p. 44.
30. Ibid.
31. Trachtenberg, p. 79.
32. Ibid.
33. Pike, *Morals and Dogma,* pp. 14-15.
34. Blanchet & Dard, p. 44.
35. Trachtenberg, p. 74.
36. Blanchet & Dard, p. 47.

Chapter 10 'To Build A Shrine For Her'

1. Oscar Handlin, *Statue of Liberty,* (New York, NY: Newsweek Book Division, 1971), p. 25.
2. Blanchet & Dard, p. 54.
3. Ibid., p. 71.
4. Ibid., p. 48.
5. Trachtenberg, pp. 59-60.
6. Blanchet & Dard, p. 62.
7. Ibid.
8. Ibid.
9. Ibid., p. 71.
10. Ibid.
11. Ibid., p. 73.
12. Ibid.
13. Schneider, p. 60.

Chapter 11 'A Stand Shall Be Erected For Her'

1. Blanchet & Dard, p. 77.
2. Trachtenberg, p. 182.
3. Schneider, p. 70.
4. Blanchet & Dard, p. 80.

5. Manly P. Hall, *The Lost Keys of Freemasonry,* (Richmond, VA: Macoy Publishing & Masonic Supply Company, Inc., 1923), pp. 53-56.
6. Ibid., p. 78.
7. Still, p. 31.
8. Foster Bailey, *The Spirit of Masonry,* (Kent, England: Lucis Press Limited, 1957), p. 23.
9. Blanchet & Dard, p. 80.
10. Schneider, p. 93.
11. Ibid., p. 95.
12. Blanchet & Dard, p. 85.
13. *New York Times,* "Cornerstone Ceremony," August 6, 1884; also see "Masons of Texas," http://www.masonsoftexas.com.htlm
14. Blanchet & Dard, p. 85.
15. Ibid.
16. Ibid.
17. *New York Times,* "Masonic Cornerstone Ceremony," August 17, 1884.
18. Trachtenberg, p. 163.
19. Hislop, p. 30.

Chapter 12 'Liberty Has Here Made Her Home'

1. *Augusta Chronicle,* "Liberty Dedication Ceremony," Augusta, GA: Augusta Public Library, Friday, October 29, 1886.
2. Ibid.
3. Ibid.
4. Ibid.
5. Ibid.
6. Ibid.
7. Ibid.
8. Ibid.
9. Ibid.
10. Ibid.
11. Ibid.
12. Ibid.
13. Ibid.
14. Ibid.
15. Ibid.
16. Ibid.
17. Ibid.

18. Ibid.

Chapter 13 'She Has Become Us'
1. Edward Robb Ellis, *The Epic of New York City,* (New York, NY: Kodansha America, Inc., 1966), p. 392.
2. Moreno, p. 231.
3. Blanchet & Dard, p. 132.
4. Ibid., p. 148.
5. Ibid., pp. 150-151.
6. Ibid., p. 153.
7. Moreno, pp. 145-146.
8. Ibid.
9. Blanchet & Dard, p. 153.
10. Schneider, p. 97.

PART IV Biblical Foundations Of The Great Goddess
Chapter 14 Figurative Language In The Bible
1. E. W. Bullinger, *Figures of Speech Used In The Bible,* (Grand Rapids, MI: Baker Book House, orig. pub. 1898, reprint 1968), p. v.
2. Ibid.
3. Ibid., pp. v-vi.
4. Ibid., p. v.
5. Ibid., p. xv.
6. Ibid., p. xvi.
7. Ibid., p. xi.

Chapter 15 'The Woman Is Wickedness'
1. Unger, *Unger's Bible Dictionary,* p. 1381.
2. *Jewish Encyclopedia. Com.,* "Zechariah," http://www.jewishencyclopedia.com/zechariah.htlm
3. John L. McKenzie, *Dictionary of the Bible,* (New York, NY: Macmillian Publishing Company, 1965), pp. 948-949.
4. Joseph Good, *Babylon is Fallen, Is Fallen,* (Port Arthur, TX: Hatikva Ministries, nd.), Audio Tape Series.
5. Bullinger, p. 444.
6. Ibid.
7. G. Campbell Morgan, *An Exposition of the Whole Bible,* (Old Tappan, NJ: Fleming H. Revell Company, 1959), pp. 399-400.

8. H. W. F. Gesenius, *Gesenius' Hebrew-Chaldee Lexicon to the Old Testament*, (Grand Rapids, MI: Baker Book House, 1979), #5375, p. 569.

9   James Strong, *Strong's Exhaustive Concordance of the Bible*, (Iowa Falls, IA: World Bible Publishers, 1989), Hebrew-Chaldee Dictionary of the O.T., #5777, p. 114, #6080, p. 90.

10. Unger, *Unger's Bible Dictionary*, pp. 864-865.

11. *Complete Word Study Old Testament*, Grammatical Notations, #57, p. 2278.

12. Gesenius, *Gesenius' Hebrew-Chaldee Lexicon to the O.T.*, #5375, p. 569.

13. Jerome; cited by Dave Baron, *Zechariah: A Commentary on His Visions and Prophecies*, p. 156.

14. Matthew Henry, *Matthew Henry Concise Commentary on the Whole Bible*, (Chicago, IL:Moody Press, 1983), pp. 661-662.

15. Ibid., p. 662.

16. Dave Baron, *Zechariah: A Commentary on His Visions and Prophecies*, (Grand Rapids, MI: Kregel Publications, 2001; first pub. in 1918), p. 160.

17. Michael Roaf, *Cultural Atlas of Mesopotamia and the Ancient Near East*, (Oxfordshire, England: Andromedia Oxford Limited, 1998), p. 110.

18. Ibid., pp. 83, 110.

19. Hislop, p. 59.

20. Ibid., p. 5.

21. Ibid., p. 157.

22. Bullinger, p. 861.

23. Morgan, pp. 399-400.

24. *Complete Word Study Old Testament*, Lexical Aids, #7562, p. 2367, #7563, p. 2367.

25. Bullinger, p. 861.

26. Gesenius, *Hebrew-Chaldee Lexicon to the O.T.*, #7307, pp. 760-761.

27. Strong, *Hebrew-Chaldee Dictionary of the O.T.*, #3671, p. 74.

28. Bullinger, p. 726.

29. Unger, *Unger's Bible Dictionary*, p. 78.

30. *World Book Encyclopedia, The*, "Stork," (Chicago, IL: World Book, Inc., 1975), Vol. 18, pp. 911-912.

31. Douglas, *Illustrated Bible Dictionary*, Vol. 1, p. 62.

32. *Jewish Encyclopedia. Com.* "Stork," http://www.jewishencyclopedia.com/stork.htlm

33. Gesenius, *Hebrew-Chaldee Lexicon to the O.T.*, #5375, p. 569.

34. Ibid., #1129, p. 127.
35. Ibid., #1004, p. 116.
36. Ibid., #776, p. 81.
37. Ibid., #8152, p. 841.
38. Unger, *Unger's Bible Dictionary*, p. 1185.
39. Gesenius, *Hebrew-Chaldee Lexicon to the O.T.*, #1004, pp. 115-117.
40. Ibid., #3559, p. 386.
41. Ibid., #776, p. 81.
42. Ibid., #5117, pp. 538-539.
43. Ibid., #4369, p. 471.

Chapter 16 'The Woman Is That Great City'
1. Morgan, p. 539.
2. H. D. M. Spence & Joseph S. Exell, gen. eds., *The Pulpit Commentary*, "The Revelation of St. John the Divine," A. Plummer, T. Randell, & A. T. Bott, expos., (Grand Rapids, MI: William B. Eerdmans Publishing Company, 1950),Vol. 22, p. 415.
3. W. Robertson Nicoll, gen. ed., *The Expositor's Greek New Testament*, "Revelation," James Moffatt, expos., (Grand Rapids, MI: William B. Eerdmans Publishing Company, 1967),Vol. 5, p. 451.
4. Bullinger, p. xvi.
5. Ibid., p. 861.
6. Ibid., pp. 867-868.
7. Ibid., p. 868.
8. Ibid., p. 861.
9. Unger, *Unger's Bible Dictionary*, p. 536.
10. Hislop, pp. 5-6.
11. Bullinger, p. 444.
12. Ibid.
13. William F. Arndt & F. Wilbur Gingrich, *A Greek-English Lexicon of the New Testament and Other Early Christian Literature*, (Chicago, IL: The University of Chicago Press, 1957), p. 467.
14. Ibid., p. 605.
15. Strong, Greek Dictionary of the N.T., #1484, p. 31.
16. Ibid., #1100, p. 24.
17. Bullinger, p. 446.
18. Hislop, p. 74.
19. Ibid., pp. 74-75.

20. Ibid., p. 5.
21. Ibid.
22. Bullinger, p. 445.
23. Unger, *Unger's Bible Dictionary*, p. 484.
24. Bork, p. 192.
25. John Leo, *U.S. News & World Report*, "The Leading Cultural Polluter," March 27, 1995, p. 16.
26. Hislop, pp. 4-5.
27. Spiros Zodhiates, gen. ed., *The Complete Word Study New Testament*, (Chattanooga, TN: AMB Publishers, 1992), Lexical Aids, #3466, p. 923.
28. Ibid.
29. *Holy Bible, Masonic Edition*, p. 49.
30. Ibid.
31. Mackey, p. 311.
32. Manly P. Hall, *What The Ancient Wisdom Expects From Its Disciples*, (Los Angeles, CA: The Philosophical Research Society, 1982), p. 23.
33. Alice Bailey, *The Externalism Of The Hierarchy*, (New York, NY: Lucis Publishing Company, nd), p. 514.
34. Bullinger, p. 868.
35. Unger, *Unger's Bible Dictionary*, p. 890.
36. Arndt & Gingrich, p. 700.
37. Webster, *The Original Webster's Unabridged Dictionary*, p. 535.
38. Hislop, p. 5.
39. Unger, *Unger's Bible Dictionary*, p. 484.
40. Joan Oates, *Babylon*, (New York, NY: Thames & Hudson, 1979), p. 24.
41. Spence & Exell, "The Revelation of St. John the Divine," Vol. 22. p. 418.
42. George Stephen Goodspeed, *A History of the Babylonians and Assyrians*, (New York, NY: Charles Scribner's Sons, 1904), pp. 263-264.
43. *Wikipedia. Com.*, "Economy of the United States," http://www.wikipedia.com/economy-of-the-u.s.htlm
44. *National Archives*, "Executive Orders Disposition Tables Index," Federal Register; http://www.archives.gov/federal-register/executive. htlm
45. Arndt & Gingrich, p. 699.
46. Ibid., p. 700.

47. David C. Korten, *When Corporations Rule The World,* (Bloomfield, CT: Kumarian Press, Inc., 2001), p. 155.

48. *Angelfire.Com.,* "Globalization of Popular Culture—MTV:The Global Grove," http://www.angelfire.com/i13/global/culture.htlm

49. Michael Medved, *Hollywood VS. America,* (New York, NY: Harper Perennial, 1992), pp. 96-99.

50. Ibid., p. 233.

51. *Variety. Com.,* "Entertainment News," http://www.variety.com/boxofficecharts.htlm

52. Hislop, p. 81.

53. Texe Marrs, *Mystery Mark of the New Age,* (Weschester, IL: Crossway Books, 1988), p. 119.

54. Arndt & Gingrich, p. 135.

55. Zodhiates, *Complete Word Study New Testament,* Lexical Aids, # 932, #935, p. 890.

56. Arndt & Gingrich, p. 256.

57. Patrick J. Buchanan, *The Great Betrayal,* (New York, NY: PJB Enterprises, Inc., 1998), p. 23.

58. Arndt & Gingrich, pp. 806-807.

59. George Liddell & Robert Scott, *Liddell and Scott's Greek-English Lexicon,* (Simon Wallenberg Press, 2007 edition; first published in 1909 by Clarendon Press, Oxford, in 1909), p. 798.

60. H. E. Dana & Julius R. Mantey, *A Manual Grammar of the Greek New Testament,* (New York, NY: The Macmillan Company, 1927), pp. 72-74.

61. Charles W. Calhoun, "Political Economy in the Gilded Age: The Republican Party's Industrial Policy," *Journal of Political History* 8, no. 3 (1996), p. 295.

62. Thomas A. Bailey, *A Diplomatic History of the American People,* (New York, NY: Meredith Publishing Company, 1964), p. 405.

63. Buchanan, p. 235.

64. Senate Joint Resolution No. 40, 61st Congress Session I, Vol. 36, Statues at Large p. 184.

65. Senate Joint Resolution 40,Vol. 36, Statues at Large, p. 184.

66. Arthur A. Ekirch, Jr., "The Sixteenth Amendment: The Historical Background," p. 175, "Cato Journal," Vol. 1, No. 1, Spring 1981, http://www.cato.org/pubs/journal/cj1n1/cj1n1-9.pdf.htlm

67. Arndt & Gingrich, pp. 498-499.

68. *Forbes. Com.,* "World's Business Leaders," http://www.forbes.com. htlm
69. Ibid., "The World's Biggest Public Companies," http://www.forbes. com/global2000/list.htlm
70. Ibid.
71. Ibid.
72. Ellis, pp. 593-594.
73. Arndt & Gingrich, p. 861; also *Complete Word Study N.T.,* Greek Dictionary of the N.T., #5331, #5332, p. 75.
74. Ibid., p. 672; *Complete Word Study N.T.,* #4105, p. 58.
75. Douglas, *Illustrated Bible Dictionary,* Vol. 2, pp. 931-933.
76. Unger, *Unger's Bible Dictionary,* p. 799.
77. Oates, p. 180.
78. Ibid.
79. Ibid.
80. John L. McKenzie, *Dictionary of the Bible,* (New York, NY: Macmillan Publishing Company, 1965), pp. 535-536.
81. Arabella Melville & Colin Johnson, *Cured To Death,* (New York, NY: Stein & Day Publishers, 1982), p. 3.
82. John Abramson, *Overdosed America,* (New York, NY: Harper Collins Publishers, 2004), p. 80.
83. Ibid.
84. Ibid., p. 85.
85. Ibid., p. 86.
86. Ibid., p. 90.
87. Melville & Johnson, p. 44.
88. Ibid., pp. 45-46.
89. Ibid.
90. Jay S. Cohen, *Overdose: The Case Against the Drug Companies,* (New York, NY: Penguin Putnam Inc., 2001), p. 70.
91. Ibid.
92. Arndt & Gingrich, p. 779.
93. Zodhiates, *Complete Word Study New Testament,* Grammatical Notations, #5, p. 862.
94. *U.S. Federal Budget,* "2010 United States Federal Budget," http:// en.wikipedia.org/wiki/2010 united_states_federal_budg.htlm
95. Spence & Exell, *Pulpit Commentary,* Vol. 22, p. 431.

96. Steve Wohlberg, *Exploding the Israel Deception,* (Roseville, CA: Amazing Facts, 2006), p. 101.
97. S. Franklin Logsdon, *Is The U.S.A. In Prophecy?,* (Grand Rapids, MI: Zondervan Publishing House, 1968), p. 21.
98. Arndt & Gingrich, p. 42.
99. Ibid., p. 17.
100. Ibid., p. 42.
101. Ibid., p. 17.
102. *Anti-Defamation League. Com.,* "Anti-Semitism on the Rise in America," http://www.adl.org/pasarele/asus.htlm
103. Ibid.
104. Ibid.
105. Ibid.
106. Ibid.
107. Reed, p. 4.

Chapter 17 'Babylon Is Fallen, Is Fallen'
1. Hislop, p. 30.
2. Ibid.
3. Unger, *Unger's Bible Dictionary,* p. 135.
4. Rawlinson,Vol. III, pp. 70-72.
5. Ibid., p. 71.
6. Oats, p. 194.
7. Ibid., p. 195.
8. Ibid., p. 197.
9. Bullinger, p. 444.
10. Frank J. Gaffney, *War Footing,* (Annapolis, MD: Naval Institute Press, 2006), pp. 107-108.
11. Charles H. Dyrer, *The Rise of Babylon: Sign of the End Times,* (Wheaton, IL:Tyndale House Publishers, 1991), back cover.
12. Noah Hutchings, *U.S. in Prophecy,* (Oklahoma City, OK: Hearthstone Publishing, 2000), p. 12.
13. Logsdon, p. 3.

Bibliography

Abrams, Richard I. & Bell, James B., *The Story of Liberty and Ellis Island*. New York, NY: Statue of Liberty—Ellis Island Centennial Commission, 1934.

Abramson, John, *Overdosed America*. New York, NY: HarperCollins Publishers, 2004.

Allen, Leslie, *Liberty: The Statue and the American Dream*. New York, NY: Statue of Liberty—Ellis Island Foundation, Inc., 1985.

Arndt, William F. & Gingrich, F. Wilbur, *A Greek-English Lexicon of the New Testament and Other Early Christian Literature*. Chicago, IL: The University of Chicago Press, 1957.

Augusta Chronicle. Augusta, Ga: Augusta Public Library, Friday, October 29, 1886.

Bach, Marcus, *Strange Sects and Curious Cults*. New York, NY: Dodd & Mead Publishers, 1961.

Baigent, Michael & Richard Leigh, *The Temple And The Lodge*. New York, NY: Arcade Publishing, 1989.

Bailey, Foster, *The Spirit of Masonry*. Kent, England: Lucis Press Limited, 1957.

Bates, Larry, *The New Economic Disorder*. Orlando, FL: Creation House, 1994.

Blanchet, Christian, & Dard, Bertrand, *Statue of Liberty: The First Hundred Years*. New York, NY: American Heritage, 1985.

Bork, Robert H., *Slouching Towards Gomorrah: Modern Liberalism And American Decline*. New York, NY: Regan Books, 1997.

Buchanan, Patrick J., *Where The Right Went Wrong*. New York, NY: Regan Books, 2003.

Buchanan, Patrick J., *The Great Betrayal*. New York, NY: PJB Enterprises, 1998.

Bullinger, E. W., *Figures of Speech Used In The Bible*. Grand Rpaids, MI: Baker Book House, orig. pub. 1898, reprint. 1968.

Burns, Cathy, *Hidden Secrets of Masonry*. Mt. Carmel, PA: Sharing Publishers, 1995.

Carr, William Guy, *Pawns In The Game*. Palmdale, CA: Omni Publications, nd.

Cavendish, Marshall, *Man, Magic and Myth: The Illustrated Encyclopedia of Mythology, Religion and the Unknown*. New York, NY: Marshall Cavendish Corporation, 1995.

Clausen, Henry C., *Masons Who Helped Shape Our Nation*. San Diego, CA: Neyenesch Printers, 1976.

Cohen, Jay S., *Overdosed America*. New York, NY: HarperCollins Publishers, 2004.

Coombs, R. A., *America, the Babylon: America's Destiny Foretold in Biblical Prophecy*. Topeka, KS: Gilliland Printing, 1998.

Coulter, Ann, *Demonic: How The Liberal Mob Is Endangering America*. New York, NY: Crown Forum, 2011.

Dall, Curtis B., *FDR: My Exploited Father-In-Law*. Washington, D.C.: Action Associates, 1970.

Davies, Norman, *Europe*. New York, NY: HarperCollins Publishers, 1998.

Decker, Edward, Jr., *The Question of Freemasonry*. Issaquah, WA: Free the Masons Ministries, nd.

Destruction Of A Constitutional Republic, The. Silverthorne, CO: Loyalist Press, nd.

Douglas, J. D., gen. ed., *The Illustrated Bible Dictionary*. Wheaton, IL: Tyndale House Publishers, 1978.

Dyer, Charles H., *The Rise of Babylon: Sign of the End Times*. Wheaton, IL: Tyndale Houston, 1991.

El-Amin, Mustafa, *Al-Islam, Christianity, and Freemasonry*. Jersey City, NJ: New Mind Productions, 1985.

Ellis, Edward Robb, *The Epic of New York City*. New York, NY: Kodansha America, Inc., 1966.

Encyclopedia of Religion. New York, NY: Macmillan Publishing Company, 1987.

Epperson, A. Ralph, *The New World Order.* Tucson, AZ: Publius Press, 1995.

Epperson, A. Ralph, *The Unseen Hand: An Introduction Into The Conspiratorial View Of History.* Tucson, AZ: Publius Press, 1985.

Finney, Charles, *The Character, Claims and Practical Workings of Freemasonry.* Hawthorne, CA: The Christian Book Club of America, nd.

Fisher, Paul A., *Behind The Lodge Door: Church, State and Freemasonry in America.* Bowie, MD: Shield Publishing, Inc., 1989.

Frank, Harry Thomas, *The Atlas of the Bible.* Pleasantville, NY: Readers Digest Association, 1981.

Gaffney, Frank J., *War Footing.* Annapolis, MD: Naval Institute Press, 2006.

Garrison, Elisha Ely, *Roosevelt, Wilson, and the Federal Reserve.* Boston, MA: Christopher Publications, 1931.

Geikie, Cunningham, *Hours With The Bible.* New York, NY: James Pott & Company, 1899.

Gesenius, H. W. F., *Hebrew-Chaldee Lexicon to the Old Testament.* Grand Rapids, MI: Baker Book House, 1979.

Good, Joseph, *Babylon Is Fallen, Is Fallen.* Port Arthur, TX: Hatikva Ministries, Tape Series, nd.

Good, Joseph, *Rosh HaShannah and The Messianic Kingdom To Come.* Nederland, TX: Hatikva Ministries, 1998.

Goodspeed, George Stephen, *A History of the Babylonians and Assyrians.* New York, NY: Charles Scribner's Sons, 1904.

Green Sr., J. P., gen. ed., *The Interlinear Hebrew-English Old Testament.* Lafayette, IN: Authors For Christ, Inc., 2005.

Greider, William, *Secrets of the Temple.* New York, NY: Simon & Schuster, 1987.

Griffin, Des, *Descent Into Slavery.* Pasadena, CA: Emissary Publications, 1980.

Griffin, Des, *The Fourth Reich of the Rich.* Pasadena, CA: Emissary Publications, 1978.

Hall, Manly P., *America's Assignment With Destiny.* Los Angeles, CA: The Philosophical Research Society, Inc., 1951.

Hall, Manly P., *The Lost Keys Of Freemasonry.* Richmond, VA: Macoy Publishing & Masonic Supply Company, Inc., 1923.

Hall, Manly P., *The Secret Destiny of America*. Los Angeles, CA: The Philosophical Research Society, Inc., 1944.

Hall, Manly P., *The Secret Teachings of All Ages*. Los Angeles, CA: The Philosophical Research Society, Inc., 1977.

Hall, Marie Bauer, *Collections of Emblems, Ancient and Moderne*. Los Angeles, CA: Veritat Foundation, 1987.

Hall, Verna, *Christian History of the Constitution of the United States of America: Christian Self-Government with Union*. San Francisco, CA: The Foundation for American Christian Education, 1979.

Handlin, Oscar, *Statue of Liberty*. New York, NY: Newsweek Book Division, 1971.

Henry, Matthew, *Matthew Henry Concise Commentary on the Whole Bible*. Chicago, IL: Moody Press, 1983.

Hillegass, Cliff, *Mythology*. Lincoln, NB: Cliffs Notes, Inc., 1991.

Hirsen, James L., *Government By Decree: From President To Dictator Through Executive Orders*. Lafayette, LA: Huntington House Publishers, 1999.

Hislop, Alexander, *The Two Babylons*. England: A & C Black, 1916.

Hutchinson, William, *The Spirit of Masonry*. New York, NY: Bell Publishing Company, 1982.

Johnson, Douglas, *The French Revolution*. New York, NY: G. P. Putnam's Sons, 1970.

Karsh, Efraim, *Arafat's War*. New York, NY: Grove Press, 2003.

Kershaw, Peter, *Economic Solutions*. Boulder, CO: Quality Press, nd.

Kid, Davvy, *Why A Bankrupt America?* Arvada, CO: Project Liberty, 1993.

Kirban, Salem, *Satan's Angels Exposed*. Chattanooga, TN: AMG Publishers, 1980.

Knight, Stephen, *The Brotherhood*. Briarcliff Manor, NY: Stein & Day Publishers, 1984.

Korten, David C., *When Corporations Rule The World*. Bloomfield, CT: Kumarian Press, Inc., 2001.

Liddell, George, & Scott, Robert, *Liddell & Scott's Greek-English Lexicon*. Simon Wallenberg Press, 2007; first published by Clarendon Press, Oxford, 1909.

Layard, Austen Henry, *Nineveh And Its Remains*. New York, NY: George P. Putnam, 1849.

Mackey, Albert G., *Lexicon of Freemasonry.* China: Midas Printing International, Ltd., 2004.

Marrs, Texe, *Dark Majesty: The Secret Brotherhood and the Magic of A Thousand Points of Light.* Austin, TX: Living Truth Publishers, 1992.

Marrs, Texe, *Mystery Mark of the New Age.* Westchester, IL: Crossway Books, 1988.

Mayer, Martin, *The Fed.* New York, NY: Penguin Group, 2002.

McFadden, Louis T., *Collective Speeches As Compiled From The Congressional Record.* Hawthorne, CA: Omni Publications, 1970.

McKenzie, John L., *Dictionary Of The Bible.* New York, NY: Macmillian Publishing Company, 1965.

Medved, Michael, *Hollywood VS. America.* New York, NY: Harper Perennial, 1992.

Melville, Arabella, & Johnson, Colin, *Cured To Death.* New York, NY: Stein & Day, 1982.

Miller, Edith Starr, *Occult Theocracy.* Hawthorne, CA: Christian Book Club of America, reprint 1980; orig. pub. 1933.

Moore, George Foote, *Judaism In The First Centuries Of The Christian Era.* Cambridge: Harvard University Press, 1944.

Moreno, Barry, *The Statue of Liberty Encyclopedia.* New York, NY: Simon & Schuster, 2000.

Morgan, G. Campbell, *An Exposition Of The Whole Bible.* Old Tappan, NJ: Fleming H. Revell Company, 1959.

Mullins, Eustace, *The Secrets Of The Federal Reserve.* Staunton, VA: Banker Research Institute, 1991.

New American Standard Bible. Grand Rapids, MI: Zondervan, 2002.

New York Times. New York, NY: August 6, 1884.

Nicoll, W. Robertson, *The Expositor's Greek New Testament.* Grand Rapids, MI: William B. Eerdmans Publishing Company, 1967.

Oats, Joan, *Babylon.* New York, NY: Regan Books, 2003.

Orr, James, gen. ed., *International Standard Bible Encyclopedia.* Grand Rapids, MI: William B. Eerdmans Publishing Company, 1939.

Ovason, David, *The Secret Architecture Of Our Nation's Capital: The Masons And The Building Of Washington, D.C.* New York, NY: HarperCollins Publishers, 2000.

Perloff, James, *The Shadows of Power: The Council on Foreign Relations and The American Decline.* Appleton, WI: Western Islands, 1988.

Pike, Albert, *Morals and Dogma of the Ancient and Accepted Scottish Rite of Freemasonry.* Richmond, VA: L. H. Jenkins, Inc., 1921.

Poncins, Vicomte Leon de, *The Secret Powers Behind Revolution.* Hawthorne, CA: Christian Book Club, reprint nd.

Poncins, Vicomte Leon de, *Freemasonry And The Vatican.* Hawthorne, CA: Omni Book Club, reprint 1968.

Pratney, Winkie, *Devil Take The Youngest: The War On Childhood.* Shreveport, LA: Huntington House, Inc., 1985.

Rawlinson, George, *Five Great Monarchies of the Ancient Eastern World.* New York, NY: Dodd, Mead & Company, 1870.

Reed, Mort, *Cowles Complete Encyclopedia of U.S. Coins.* New York, NY: Cowles Book Company, 1969.

Robinson, John, *Proofs Of A Conspiracy.* Boston, MA: Western Islands, reprint 1967.

Roaf, Michael, *Cultural Atlas of Mesopotamia and the Ancient Near East.* Oxfordshire, England: Andromedia Oxford Limited, 1998.

Rushdoony, Rousas, *The Nature Of The American System.* Fairfax, VA: Thoburn Press, 1965.

Saussy, F. Tupper, *Rulers of Evil.* New York, NY: HarperCollins Publishers, Inc., 2001.

Schroder, Eugene, gen. ed., *War and Emergency Powers: A Special Report on the National Emergency in the United States of America.* Dallas, TX: American Agriculture Movement, nd.

Spence, H. D. M. & Exell, Joseph S., gen. eds., *The Pulpit Commentary.* Grand Rapids, MI: William B. Eerdmans Publishing Company, 1950.

Still, William, *New World Order.* Lafayette, LA: Huntington House Publishers, 1990.

Strong, James, *Strong's Exhaustive Concordance of the Bible.* Iowa Falls, IA: World Bible Publishers, 1989.

Sutton, Antony C., *America's Secret Establishment: An Introduction to The Order of Skull and Bones.* Billings, MT: Liberty House Press, 1986.

Tompkins, Peter, *The Magic Of Obelisks.* New York, NY: Harper & Row Publishers, 1981.

Tanakh, The Holy Scriptures. Philadelphia, PN: The Jewish Publication Society, 1985.

Toth, Max, *Pyramid Power.* New York, NY: Destiny Books, 1979.

Trachtenberg, Marvin, *Statue of Liberty*. New York, NY: Penguin Books, 1976.

Unger, Merrill F., *The New Unger's Bible Dictionary*. Chicago, IL: Moody Press, 1988.

Vennard, Wickliffe B., *The Federal Reserve Hoax: The Age of Deception*. Palmdale, CA: Omni Publications, reprint nd.

Wardner, James, *The Planned Destruction of America*. DeBary, FL: Longwood Communications, 1994.

Webster, Nesta, *Secret Societies and Subversive Movements*. Hawthorne, CA: The Christian Book Club of America, reprint nd.

Webster, Nesta, *World Revolution: The Plot Against Civilization*. Palmdale, CA: Omni Publications, 1921.

Webster, Noah, *The Original Webster's Unabridged Dictionary*. U.S.A. Dictionary Publishing Company, 1901.

Whalen, William J., *Christianity and American Freemasonry*. Milwaukee, MI: Bruce Publishing Company, 1958.

Woodrow, Ralph Edward, *Babylon Mystery Religion*. Riverside, CA: Ralph Woodrow Evangelistic Association, 1966.

World Book Encyclopedia, The. Chicago, IL: World Book, Inc., 1975.

Wuest, Kenneth S., *Wuest's Word Studies From The Greek New Testament*. Grand Rapids, MI: William B. Eerdmans Publishing Company, 1961.

Zodhiates, Spiros, gen. ed., *The Complete Word Study New Testament*. Chattanooga, TN: AMB Publishers, 1992.

Index

V

Venus 19, 263
  occult pentagram symbol 53
Vicomte Leon de Poncins 43, 90
Victor Borie 163
Virgin of Prophecy 24, 253
Vladimir Putin 323
Voltaire 88

W

War Powers Act 140
Warren Harding 51
Washington Monument 56, 58, 62
Whiskey Rebellion 121
White House 62
W. Howard Taft 51
William Barton 67
William Cushing 47
William Evarts 195, 202, 208, 211,
    228
  made arrangements for
      cornerstone ceremony 213
William F. Albright 26
William Harding 65
William H. Ferkler 147
William Howard Taft 305
William McKinley 51
William Paterson 47
William P. G. Harding 132
William Tecumseh Sherman 57,
    200
Winston Churchill 79
Woodrow Wilson 77, 132, 155
World Trade Center 156
Wright Patman 145

Y

Yom Kippur 337

Z

Zbigniew Brzezinski 80
Zeus 33, 231
Zwack 91

Printed in the United States
By Bookmasters